The

AMERICAN

CRISIS

What Went Wrong.
How We Recover.

THE WRITERS OF *The Atlantic*

INTRODUCTION BY Jeffrey Goldberg

AFTERWORD BY Anne Applebaum

EDITED BY Cullen Murphy

Simon and Schuster

NEW YORK LONDON TORONTO
SYDNEY NEW DELHI

Simon & Schuster
1230 Avenue of the Americas
New York, NY 10020

First Simon & Schuster trade paperback edition September 2020

SIMON & SCHUSTER and colophon are registered trademarks
of Simon & Schuster, Inc.

For information about special discounts for bulk purchases,
please contact Simon & Schuster Special Sales at 1-866-506-1949
or business@simonandschuster.com.

The Simon & Schuster Speakers Bureau can bring authors to your
live event. For more information or to book an event, contact
the Simon & Schuster Speakers Bureau at 1-866-248-3049
or visit our website at www.simonspeakers.com.

Manufactured in the United States of America

1   3   5   7   9   10   8   6   4   2

Library of Congress Cataloging-in-Publication Data

ISBN 978-1-9821-5703-6
ISBN 978-1-9821-5704-3 (pbk)
ISBN 978-1-9821-5705-0 (ebook)

Contents

SECTION IV: BECOMING CITIZENS AGAIN

The

AMERICAN
CRISIS

Introduction

by Jeffrey Goldberg

WASHINGTON, D.C., JUNE 2020

On a bright May day in 2018, I walked from *The Atlantic*'s Washington, D.C., offices at the Watergate complex to the White House for lunch with Jared Kushner, President Donald Trump's son-in-law. I knew Kushner slightly; he was not fond of me, nor I of him, but he had something he needed to say, and journalism is journalism. Kushner's self-confidence is more impressive than his achievements, but unlike his father-in-law, who is pathologically bored by matters of policy, spherically ignorant, and unequipped for even simple intellectual challenges—all qualities that eventually brought America to the edge of the abyss—Kushner at least has the ability to assimilate new information. Well before Trump was inaugurated, Kushner had become one of the key officials tasked with devising administration policy—*someone* had to do it. During the 2016 campaign, Trump's oldest son, Don Jr., had tried to recruit John Kasich, then the governor of Ohio, to be his father's running mate. Kasich was promised control over foreign and domestic policy. This caused some confusion, there being no other policies to make. The question was asked, What would Trump be in charge of? Don Jr. answered: "Making America great again."

The ostensible subject of my lunch with Kushner that day was diplomacy. Trump had asked his son-in-law to make peace between the Israelis and the Palestinians, and Kushner had devised a plan, which he wanted to discuss with me. The particulars of the plan were declared off-the-record, but suffice it to say that, as of this writing, Kushner has not brought peace to the Middle East.

The memorable part of our conversation came a bit later. Like many Americans, I had been preoccupied by Trump's moral and intellectual defects since he emerged as a figure of political significance. It was these defects that had prompted *The Atlantic*, a year and a half before my White House meeting with Trump's son-in-law, to endorse his opponent, Hillary Clinton, for president. This had not been, for us, an obvious decision. *The Atlantic*'s founders, including among them such great figures of 19th-century letters as Ralph Waldo Emerson, James Russell Lowell, and Henry Wadsworth Longfellow, had promised readers that their magazine would be "of no party or clique." Political endorsements across our long history have been rare. The magazine supported Abraham Lincoln's candidacy in 1860 and Lyndon B. Johnson's candidacy in 1964. As we thought through our dilemma, we realized that had Jeb Bush or Marco Rubio (or, really, almost anyone else) been the Republican presidential nominee, we would not have considered making an endorsement of any sort. Our concern was not mainly over Trump's ideas, such as they were. His manifest character failings were what prompted us to declare for his opponent. We wrote, in an editorial published in October 2016, that Trump

> has no record of public service and no qualifications for public office. His affect is that of an infomercial huckster; he traffics in conspiracy theories and racist invective; he is appallingly sexist; he is erratic, secretive, and xenophobic; he expresses admiration for authoritarian rulers, and evinces authoritarian tendencies himself. He is easily goaded, a poor quality for someone seeking control of America's nuclear arsenal. He is an enemy of fact-based discourse; he is ignorant of, and indifferent to, the Constitution; he appears not to read.

By the spring of 2018, it had become clear that we had understated the case against Trump. As a reporter, I had covered his two predecessors. They were very different men with very different records; one came to office as a direct consequence of the other's mistakes. But George W. Bush and Barack Obama each took the presidency seriously; each man was changed by the office; each viewed himself to be president of all the people. One of Trump's true innovations as president is to feel no responsibility for Americans who didn't vote for him. Unlike previous presidents, he works not for reconciliation but for division. On his best days, Trump is numb to the fault lines that run under America—fault lines of region and religion, of class, ideology, and race. On his worst days, his presidency is an inversion of the motto of the United States. *E pluribus unum*—"Out of many, one"—has become, in our tormented era, "Out of one, many."

Another quality of Trump's, and one I would raise with Kushner, is his bottomless vulgarity. No president since Andrew Jackson—whose portrait now hangs in the Oval Office—has been so devoted to crudeness, both as a weapon and as an art. I mentioned to Kushner in plain terms my feelings about a recent burst of presidential boorishness and noted my view that his father-in-law was bringing discourse in America down to the coarsest level. Kushner, surprisingly, agreed. "No one can go as low as the president," Kushner told me. "You shouldn't even try." He said this with a satisfied smile. It took me a second to realize that Kushner was paying Trump a compliment. To Kushner, Trump's indecency was a virtue. The chasm between us felt, at that moment, unbridgeable. We were in the White House; Abraham Lincoln once lived here, the Lincoln who said, in his first inaugural address, "We are not enemies, but friends. We must not be enemies. Though passion may have strained, it must not break our bonds of affection." As I walked through the West Wing with Kushner, my thoughts concerned a White House defiled.

———

How did we get here? How did our politics become so appalling and dispiriting? How did a system meant to elevate the most qualified among us instead place a grifter in Lincoln's house? How did the gaps between rich and poor, men and women, black and white, immigrant and American-born, become so profound? How did the leader of the richest nation on Earth fail to protect his country from a deadly virus he was repeatedly told was coming? How could a leader be so thoroughly insensate to certain unforgiving realities of black life?

The story is larger than Donald Trump, and not simply because a grifter is actually powerless without an audience ready to be grifted. America has become unmoored from truths formerly self-evident— from the animating ideas of its creation, as articulated in our country's founding documents.

On the morning after Trump's election, I told the staff of *The Atlantic* that our magazine had a special responsibility in times like these— times of tension, and fracturing, and loss of national meaning. The magazine's 1857 manifesto, the one vowing that we will be of no party or clique, made another promise to our readers: that we would align ourselves with the forces of "Freedom, National Progress, and Honor, whether public or private."

Throughout *The Atlantic*'s long history, our writers and editors have tried to live up to this ideal by pursuing journalism that is true, meaningful, and consequential. Our best writing has explained America to itself, and to the world; has advanced the twin causes of knowledge and reason; and has been a proponent of science, literature, and art. It has had as a guiding principle the idea that America will always be imperfect but is designed with self-improvement in mind. One prerequisite for national betterment is a commitment to debating and illuminating America's meaning and purpose.

The Atlantic was, from its birth, a frank partisan of the abolitionist cause and of the general cause of justice. It published Julia Ward Howe's "Battle Hymn of the Republic," in order to raise the spirits of Union soldiers, and it published Frederick Douglass on Reconstruction and racial justice. Our magazine published Theodore Roosevelt on the need for clean government and John Muir on the case for national parks. It published Jacob Riis on poverty, Helen Keller on the cause of women's empowerment, Alfred Thayer Mahan on the importance of America's global reach, and Albert Einstein on the atomic bomb. In our pages—in 1945—Vannevar Bush predicted the coming of the internet. *The Atlantic* is also where Martin Luther King Jr. published what came to be known as "Letter From a Birmingham Jail," written by hand behind bars after his arrest in 1963.

The pace of *The Atlantic*'s contributions to the national conversation has only accelerated in recent years. That is why we have decided to publish an anthology of some of our best writing about this vexed era. When we first thought to create the book you are now reading, one of my chief worries concerned chaos. *The Atlantic* publishes thousands of articles, in print and online, each year, on a near-infinite range of subjects. Could we find coherence in the cacophony?

The answer is a definitive yes. Our editor at large, Cullen Murphy, expertly led the effort to organize the book along discernible lines. We open with articles about this period of intense, destabilizing social change. We move to the causes of political division, then look carefully at the man who personifies the dangers of the moment. Finally, we explore what recovery might look like, and the virtues that must be rediscovered if recovery is to happen.

I write this in June of 2020, in a Washington coming out (permanently, I hope) of pandemic lockdown, but also under police curfew. The mood in the country is grim, justifiably. But if a careful reading of *The Atlantic* through the years can teach us anything, it is that hope is as much a salient theme of American life as despair. Only by examining who we are, and by studying the consequences of our actions, do we have a chance of lighting a path out of our current crisis.

I. FALLING APART

There was a moment in American life, two centuries ago, that came to be known as the Era of Good Feelings. Whatever name is given to our own era, it won't be that. Stability, optimism, unity, pride, satisfaction, civility—yes, these qualities in a society can be overrated, and conceal deep flaws. Think of Edwardian Britain. Or America in the 1950s. But a broad retreat from those qualities, as we are seeing now, is no sign of health.

This first section of *The American Crisis* looks primarily not at national politics, the state of democracy, or the person in the Oval Office—nor primarily at the events of the past four years—but rather at underlying conditions of society as a whole that have been deteriorating for decades. The coronavirus pandemic may confirm that Americans still care for one another and still possess an ability to self-organize locally in the absence of leadership and honesty at the top. But income inequality continues to widen, as it has been doing since the '70s. Social mobility in America has not dropped to the levels of feudal Europe, but the best predictor of where you will end up in life is where you started out in life. Saying that there are gaps in the health-care system is like looking at a map and saying that there are gaps between the continents. The chipping away at the Affordable Care Act by politicians and judges—with no alternative in sight—has only made matters worse. Disparities along lines of race are entrenched, even as people in public life use race and ethnicity—maybe in coded language, maybe not—to rile up their followers. On the internet it's worse: White nationalists find one another in dark corners; conspiracy theories such as QAnon flourish everywhere, offering a "post-truth" alternative to reality-based perception. There is no post-truth version of a hurricane or wildfire, but denial of climate change remains more robust than our ability to prevent or pay for the consequences. This general unraveling was the context for a public-health crisis more serious than any humanity has faced in a century.

WHEN THE NEXT PLAGUE HITS

by Ed Yong

[JULY/AUGUST 2018]

Globalization, urbanization, migration, disease vector, climate change, wealth disparity—the terms are coldly clinical, but they capture a world in a state of dynamic crisis. *Atlantic* staff writer Ed Yong's prophetic 2018 article "When the Next Plague Hits" cited all these factors before issuing a warning. "Down through the centuries," Yong wrote, "diseases have always excelled at exploiting flux."

The coronavirus pandemic has thrown lives, societies, and the entire global economy into reverse. The one thing that should have been foreseeable was an outbreak of this scale. Yong portrays an American government that was negligent and unprepared, even as potential risks continued to multiply. He likens turnover in Donald Trump's public-health apparatus to Etch A Sketch drawings. He quotes Dr. Anthony Fauci, the director of the National Institute of Allergy and Infectious Diseases—now one of the key figures in the battle against the coronavirus—on the state of the public-health system: "It's like a chain—one weak link and the whole thing falls apart." One of the most important links during any epidemic, Yong wrote, is also one thing we do not have: a person in the Oval Office who can provide "reliable information and a unifying spirit."

Ed Yong is the author of *I Contain Multitudes: The Microbes Within Us and a Grander View of Life* (2016), about partnerships between animals and microbes, and the forth-coming *An Immense World*, about how animals see, hear, and perceive. His 2018 *Atlantic* article is excerpted here.

O ne hundred years ago, in 1918, a strain of H1N1 flu swept the world. It might have originated in Haskell County, Kansas, or in France or China—but soon it was everywhere. In two years, it killed as many as 100 million people—5 percent of the world's pop-ulation, and far more than the number who died in World War I. It killed not just the very young, old, and sick, but also the strong and fit, bringing them down through their own violent immune responses. It killed so quickly that hospitals ran out of beds, cities ran out of cof-fins, and coroners could not meet the demand for death certificates. It lowered Americans' life expectancy by more than a decade. "The flu resculpted human populations more radically than anything since the Black Death," Laura Spinney wrote in *Pale Rider*, her 2017 book about the pandemic. It was one of the deadliest natural disasters in history—a potent reminder of the threat posed by disease.

Humanity seems to need such reminders often. In 1948, shortly after the first flu vaccine was created and penicillin became the first mass-produced antibiotic, U.S. Secretary of State George Marshall re-portedly claimed that the conquest of infectious disease was imminent. In 1962, after the second polio vaccine was formulated, the Nobel Prize–winning virologist Sir Frank Macfarlane Burnet asserted, "To write about infectious diseases is almost to write of something that has passed into history."

Hindsight has not been kind to these proclamations. Despite ad-vances in antibiotics and vaccines, and the successful eradication of smallpox, *Homo sapiens* is still locked in the same epic battle with vi-ruses and other pathogens that we've been fighting since the beginning of our history. When cities first arose, diseases laid them low, a process repeated over and over for millennia. When Europeans colonized the Americas, smallpox followed. When soldiers fought in the first global war, influenza hitched a ride, and found new opportunities in the un-precedented scale of the conflict. Down through the centuries, diseases have always excelled at exploiting flux.

Humanity is now in the midst of its fastest-ever period of change. There were almost 2 billion people alive in 1918; there are now 7.6 billion, and they have migrated rapidly into cities, which since 2008 have been home to more than half of all human beings. In these dense throngs, pathogens can more easily spread and more quickly evolve resistance to drugs. Not coincidentally, the total number of outbreaks per decade has more than tripled since the 1980s.

Globalization compounds the risk: Airplanes now carry almost 10 times as many passengers around the world as they did four decades ago. In the '80s, HIV showed how potent new diseases can be, by launching a slow-moving pandemic that has since claimed about 35 million lives. In 2003, another newly discovered virus, SARS, spread decidedly more quickly. A Chinese seafood seller hospitalized in Guangzhou passed it to dozens of doctors and nurses, one of whom traveled to Hong Kong for a wedding. In a single night, he infected at least 16 others, who then carried the virus to Canada, Singapore, and Vietnam. Within six months, SARS had reached 29 countries and infected more than 8,000 people. This is a new epoch of disease, when geographic barriers disappear and threats that once would have been local go global.

Last year, with the centennial of the 1918 flu looming, I started looking into whether America is prepared for the next pandemic. I fully expected that the answer would be no. What I found, after talking with dozens of experts, was more complicated—reassuring in some ways, but even more worrying than I'd imagined in others. Certainly, medicine has advanced considerably during the past century. The United States has nationwide vaccination programs, advanced hospitals, the latest diagnostic tests. In the National Institutes of Health, it has the world's largest biomedical research establishment, and in the CDC, arguably the world's strongest public-health agency. America is as ready to face down new diseases as any country in the world.

Yet even the U.S. is disturbingly vulnerable—and in some respects is becoming quickly more so. It depends on a just-in-time medical economy, in which stockpiles are limited and even key items are made to order. Most of the intravenous bags used in the country are manufactured in Puerto Rico, so when Hurricane Maria devastated the island last September, the bags fell in short supply. Some hospitals were forced to inject saline with syringes—and so syringe supplies started running low, too. The most common lifesaving drugs all depend on long supply chains that include India and China—chains that would likely break in a severe pandemic. "Each year, the system gets leaner and leaner," says Michael Osterholm, the director of the Center for Infectious Disease Research and Policy at the University of Minnesota. "It doesn't take much of a hiccup anymore to challenge it."

Perhaps most important, the U.S. is prone to the same forgetfulness and shortsightedness that befall all nations, rich and poor—and the myopia has worsened considerably in recent years. Public-health programs are low on money; hospitals are stretched perilously thin; crucial funding is being slashed. And while we tend to think of science when we think of pandemic response, the worse the situation, the more the defense depends on political leadership.

When Ebola flared in 2014, the science-minded President Barack Obama calmly and quickly took the reins. The White House is now home to a president who is neither calm nor science-minded. We should not underestimate what that may mean if risk becomes reality.

Bill Gates, whose foundation has studied pandemic risks closely, is not a man given to alarmism. But when I spoke with him, he described simulations showing that a severe flu pandemic, for instance, could kill more than 33 million people worldwide in just 250 days. That possibility, and the world's continued inability to adequately prepare for it, is one of the few things that shake Gates's trademark optimism and challenge his narrative of global progress. "This is a rare case of me being the bearer of bad news," he told me. "Boy, do we not have our act together."

Preparing for a pandemic ultimately boils down to real people and tangible things: A busy doctor who raises an eyebrow when a patient presents with an unfamiliar fever. A nurse who takes a travel history. A hospital wing in which patients can be isolated. A warehouse where protective masks are stockpiled. A factory that churns out vaccines. A line on a budget. A vote in Congress. "It's like a chain—one weak link and the whole thing falls apart," says Anthony Fauci, the director of the National Institute of Allergy and Infectious Diseases. "You need no weak links."

———

Among all known pandemic threats, influenza is widely regarded as the most dangerous. Its various strains are constantly changing, sometimes through subtle mutations in their genes, and sometimes through dramatic reshuffles. Even in non-pandemic years, when new viruses aren't sweeping the world, the more familiar strains kill up to 500,000 people around the globe. Their ever-changing nature explains why the flu vaccine needs to be updated annually. It's why a disease that is sometimes little worse than a bad cold can transform into a mass-murdering monster. And it's why flu is the disease the U.S. has invested the most in tracking. An expansive surveillance network constantly scans for new flu viruses, collating alerts raised by doctors and results from lab tests, and channeling it all to the CDC, the spider at the center of a thrumming worldwide web.

Yet just 10 years ago, the virus that the world is most prepared for caught almost everyone off guard. In the early 2000s, the CDC was focused mostly on Asia, where H5N1—the type of flu deemed most likely to cause the next pandemic—was running wild among poultry and waterfowl. But while experts fretted about H5N1 in birds in the East, new strains of H1N1 were evolving within pigs in the West. One of those swine strains jumped into humans in Mexico, launching outbreaks there and in the U.S. in early 2009. The surveillance web picked it up only in mid-April of that year, when the CDC tested samples from two California children who had recently fallen ill.

One of the most sophisticated disease-detecting networks in the world had been blindsided by a virus that had sprung up in its backyard, circulated for months, and snuck into the country unnoticed. "We joked that the influenza virus is listening in on our conference calls," says Daniel Jernigan, who directs the CDC's Influenza Division. "It tends to do whatever we're least expecting."

The pandemic caused problems for vaccine manufacturers, too. Most flu vaccines are made by growing viruses in chicken eggs—the same archaic method that's been used for 70 years. Every strain grows differently, so manufacturers must constantly adjust to each new peculiarity. Creating flu vaccines is an artisanal affair, more like cultivating a crop than making a pharmaceutical. The process works reasonably well for seasonal flu, which arrives on a predictable schedule. It fails miserably for pandemic strains, which do not.

In 2009, the vaccine for the new pandemic strain of H1N1 flu arrived slowly. (Then–CDC director Tom Frieden told the press, "Even if you yell at the eggs, it won't grow any faster.") Once the pandemic was officially declared, it took four months before the doses even *began* to roll out in earnest. By then the disaster was already near its peak. Those doses prevented no more than 500 deaths—the fewest of any flu season in the surrounding 10-year period. Some 12,500 Americans died.

The egg-based system depends on chickens, which are themselves vulnerable to flu. And since viruses can mutate within the eggs, the resulting vaccines don't always match the strains that are circulating. But vaccine makers have few incentives to use anything else. Switching to a different process would cost billions, and why bother? Flu vaccines are low-margin products, which only about 45 percent of Americans get in a normal year. So when demand soars during a pandemic, the supply is not set to cope.

American hospitals, which often operate unnervingly close to full capacity, likewise struggled with the surge of patients. Pediatric units were hit especially hard by H1N1, and staff became exhausted from continuously caring for sick children. Hospitals almost ran out of the life-support units that sustain people whose lungs and hearts start to fail. The health-care system didn't break, but it came too close for comfort—especially for what turned out to be a training-wheels pandemic. The 2009 H1N1 strain killed merely 0.03 percent of those it infected; by contrast, the 1918 strain had killed 1 to 3 percent, and the H7N9 strain currently circulating in China has a fatality rate of 40 percent.

"A lot of people said that we dodged a bullet in 2009, but nature just shot us with a BB gun," says Richard Hatchett, the CEO of the

Coalition for Epidemic Preparedness Innovations. Tom Inglesby, a biosecurity expert at the Johns Hopkins Bloomberg School of Public Health, told me that if a 1918-style pandemic hit, his hospital "would need in the realm of seven times as many critical-care beds and four times as many ventilators as we have on hand."

That the U.S. could be so ill-prepared for flu, of all things, should be deeply concerning. The country has a dedicated surveillance web, antiviral drugs, and an infrastructure for making and deploying flu vaccines. None of that exists for the majority of other emerging infectious diseases.

Anthony Fauci's office walls are plastered with certificates, magazine articles, and other mementos from his 34-year career as NIAID director, including photos of him with various presidents. In one picture, he stands in the Oval Office with Bill Clinton and Al Gore, pointing to a photo of HIV latching onto a white blood cell. In another, George W. Bush fastens the Presidential Medal of Freedom around his neck. Fauci has counseled every president from Ronald Reagan through Barack Obama about the problem of epidemics, because each of them has needed that counsel. "This transcends administrations," he tells me.

Reagan and the elder Bush had to face the emergence and proliferation of HIV. Clinton had to deal with the arrival of West Nile virus. Bush the younger had to contend with anthrax and SARS. Barack Obama saw a flu pandemic in his third month in office, MERS and Ebola at the start of his second term, and Zika at the dusk of his presidency. The responses of the presidents varied, Fauci told me: Clinton went on autopilot; the younger Bush made public health part of his legacy, funding an astonishingly successful anti-HIV program; Obama had the keenest intellectual interest in the subject.

And Donald Trump? "I haven't had any interaction with him yet," Fauci says. "But in fairness, there hasn't been a situation."

There surely will be, though. At some point, a new virus will emerge to test Trump's mettle. What happens then? He has no background in science or health, and has surrounded himself with little such expertise.

The President's Council of Advisers on Science and Technology, a group of leading scientists who consult on policy matters, is dormant. The Office of Science and Technology Policy, which has advised presidents on everything from epidemics to nuclear disasters since 1976, is diminished. The head of that office typically acts as the president's chief scientific consigliere, but to date no one has been appointed.

Organizing a federal response to an emerging pandemic is harder than one might think. The largely successful U.S. response to Ebola in 2014 benefited from the special appointment of an "Ebola czar"—Ron Klain—to help coordinate the many agencies that face unclear responsibilities. How will Trump manage such a situation? Back in 2014, he called Obama a "psycho" for not banning flights from Ebola-afflicted countries, even though no direct flights existed, and even though health experts noted that travel restrictions hadn't helped control SARS or H1N1. Counterintuitively, flight bans increase the odds that outbreaks will spread by driving fearful patients underground, forcing them to seek alternative and even illegal transport routes. They also discourage health workers from helping to contain foreign outbreaks, for fear that they'll be denied reentry into their home country. Trump clearly felt that such Americans *should* be denied re-entry. "KEEP THEM OUT OF HERE!" he tweeted, before questioning the evidence that Ebola is not as contagious as is commonly believed.

Trump called Obama "dumb" for deploying the military to countries suffering from the Ebola outbreak, and he now commands that same military. His dislike of outsiders and disdain for diplomacy could lead him to spurn the cooperative, outward-facing strategies that work best to contain emergent pandemics.

Perhaps the two most important things a leader can personally provide in the midst of an epidemic are reliable information and a unifying spirit. In the absence of strong countermeasures, severe outbreaks tear communities apart, forcing people to fear their neighbors; the longest-lasting damage can be psycho-social. Trump's tendency to tweet rashly, delegitimize legitimate sources of information, and readily buy into conspiracy theories could be disastrous.

THE BIRTH OF A NEW AMERICAN ARISTOCRACY

by Matthew Stewart

[JUNE 2018]

The pandemic that Ed Yong foreshadowed—the global coronavirus outbreak—did not affect everyone in the U.S. equally, a subject that *The Atlantic* explored from many angles. Just look at employment: Many workers could continue their jobs remotely, without interruption; those whose employment was bound to the physical world were hit hard, and immediately. Essential workers—in hospitals, convenience stores, delivery trucks—were likely to be low-paid and unprotected. The pandemic threw class divisions and inequities into sharp relief.

Social mobility has long served both as a social glue and as a moral justification for the system we have. Is America a place where the ordinary person gets a fair shake and a pretty good chance to move up the ladder? Or is it more often the case that people born with advantages of wealth and privilege pass those advantages to their descendants? The first idea is embodied in rags-to-riches stories from the 19th century and in self-help books from our own time. The second is summed up by a familiar saying about being born on third base and thinking you've hit a triple. There has always been a tension—some would say a contradiction—between these views of American life. The notion of "meritocracy" lies at the center of the argument. One side says: Anyone can succeed who can jump through the hoops. The other side counters: Generation after generation, a small group gets help.

The philosopher Matthew Stewart called this small group "the 9.9 percent" in a 2018 *Atlantic* cover story, "The Birth of a New American Aristocracy," abridged here. Stewart, the author of *Nature's God: The Heretical Origins of the American Republic* (2014) and *The Management Myth: Why Experts Keep Getting It Wrong* (2019), focused intently on this central fact: Social mobility is at a low point and economic inequality at a high—and mountains of data from many countries underscore the relationship between the two phenomena. In particular, Stewart summarized the findings of the economist Alan Krueger: "Rising immobility and rising inequality aren't like two pieces of driftwood that happen to have shown up on the beach at the same time . . . They wash up together on every shore." The class divide in America, Stewart warned, is fast becoming unbridgeable.

Let's talk first about money—even if money is only one part of what makes the new aristocrats special. There is a familiar story about rising inequality in the United States, and its stock characters are well known. The villains are the fossil-fueled plutocrat, the Wall Street fat cat, the callow tech bro, and the rest of the so-called top 1 percent. The good guys are the 99 percent, otherwise known as "the people" or "the middle class." The arc of the narrative is simple: Once we were equal, but now we are divided. The story has a grain of truth to it. But it gets the characters and the plot wrong in basic ways.

It is in fact the top 0.1 percent who have been the big winners in the growing concentration of wealth over the past half century. According to the UC Berkeley economists Emmanuel Saez and Gabriel Zucman, the 160,000 or so households in that group held 22 percent of America's wealth in 2012, up from 10 percent in 1963. If you're looking for the kind of money that can buy elections, you'll find it inside the top 0.1 percent alone.

Every piece of the pie picked up by the 0.1 percent, in relative terms, had to come from the people below. But not everyone in the 99.9 percent gave up a slice. Only those in the bottom 90 percent did. At their peak, in the mid-1980s, people in this group held 35 percent of the nation's wealth. Three decades later that had fallen 12 points—exactly as much as the wealth of the 0.1 percent rose.

In between the top 0.1 percent and the bottom 90 percent is a group that has been doing just fine. It has held on to its share of a growing pie decade after decade. And as a group, it owns substantially more wealth than do the other two combined. This is the new aristocracy. We are the 9.9 percent.

So what kind of characters are we, the 9.9 percent? We are mostly not like those flamboyant political manipulators from the 0.1 percent. We're a well-behaved, flannel-suited crowd of lawyers, doctors, dentists, mid-level investment bankers, M.B.A.s with opaque job titles, and assorted other professionals—the kind of people you might invite to dinner. In fact, we're so self-effacing, we deny our own existence. We keep insisting that we're "middle class."

As of 2016, it took $1.2 million in net worth to make it into the 9.9 percent; $2.4 million to reach the group's median; and $10 million to get into the top 0.9 percent. (And if you're not there yet, relax: Our club is open to people who are on the right track and have the right attitude.) "We are the 99 percent" sounds righteous, but it's a slogan, not an analysis. The families at our end of the spectrum wouldn't know what to do with a pitchfork.

We are also mostly, but not entirely, white. According to a Pew Research Center analysis, African Americans represent 1.9 percent of the top 10th of households in wealth; Hispanics, 2.4 percent; and all other minorities, including Asian and multiracial individuals, 8.8 percent—even though those groups together account for 35 percent of the total population.

One of the hazards of life in the 9.9 percent is that our necks get stuck in the upward position. We gaze upon the 0.1 percent with a mixture of awe, envy, and eagerness to obey. As a consequence, we are missing the other big story of our time. We have left the 90 percent in the dust—and we've been quietly tossing down roadblocks behind us to make sure that they never catch up.

Let's suppose that you start off right in the middle of the American wealth distribution. How high would you have to jump to make it into the 9.9 percent? In financial terms, the measurement is easy and the trend is unmistakable. In 1963, you would have needed to multiply your wealth six times. By 2016, you would have needed to leap twice as high—increasing your wealth 12-fold—to scrape into our group. If you boldly aspired to reach the middle of our group rather than its lower edge, you'd have needed to multiply your wealth by a factor of 25. On this measure, the 2010s look much like the 1920s.

If you are starting at the median for people of color, you'll want to practice your financial pole-vaulting. The Institute for Policy Studies calculated that, setting aside money invested in "durable goods" such as furniture and a family car, the median black family had net wealth of $1,700 in 2013, and the median Latino family had $2,000, compared with $116,800 for the median white family. A 2015 study in Boston found that the wealth of the median white family there was $247,500, while the wealth of the median African American family was $8. That is not a typo. That's two grande cappuccinos. That and another 300,000 cups of coffee will get you into the 9.9 percent.

———————

None of this matters, you will often hear, because in the United States everyone has an opportunity to make the leap: Mobility justifies inequality. As a matter of principle, this isn't true. In the United States, it also turns out not to be true as a factual matter. Contrary to popular myth, economic mobility in the land of opportunity is not high, and it's going down.

Imagine yourself on the socioeconomic ladder with one end of a rubber band around your ankle and the other around your parents' rung. The strength of the rubber determines how hard it is for you to escape the rung on which you were born. If your parents are high on the ladder, the band will pull you up should you fall; if they are low, it will drag you down when you start to rise. Economists represent this concept with a number they call "intergenerational earnings elasticity," or IGE, which measures how much of a child's deviation from average income can be accounted for by the parents' income. An IGE of zero means that there's no relationship at all between parents' income and that of their offspring. An IGE of one says that the destiny of a child is to end up right where she came into the world.

According to Miles Corak, an economics professor at the City University of New York, half a century ago IGE in America was less than 0.3. Today, it is about 0.5. In America, the game is half over once you've selected your parents. IGE is now higher here than in almost every other developed economy. On this measure of economic mobility, the United States is more like Chile or Argentina than Japan or Germany.

The story becomes even more disconcerting when you see just where on the ladder the tightest rubber bands are located. Canada, for example, has an IGE of about half that of the U.S. Yet from the middle rungs of the two countries' income ladders, offspring move up or down through the nearby deciles at the same respectable pace. The difference is in what happens at the extremes. In the United States, it's the children of the bottom decile and, above all, the top decile—the 9.9 percent—who settle down nearest to their starting point. Here in the land of opportunity, the taller the tree, the closer the apple falls.

All of this analysis of wealth percentiles, to be clear, provides only a rough start in understanding America's evolving class system. People move in and out of wealth categories all the time without necessarily changing social class, and they may belong to a different class in their own eyes than they do in others'. Yet even if the trends in the monetary statistics are imperfect illustrations of a deeper process, they are nonetheless registering something of the extraordinary transformation that's taking place in our society.

A few years ago, Alan Krueger, an economist and a former chairman of the Obama administration's Council of Economic Advisers, was reviewing the international mobility data when he caught a glimpse of the fundamental process underlying our present moment. Rising immobility and rising inequality aren't like two pieces of driftwood that happen to have shown up on the beach at the same time, he noted. They wash up together on every shore. Across countries, the higher the inequality, the higher the IGE. It's as if human societies have a natural tendency to separate, and then, once the classes are far enough apart, to crystallize.

Economists are prudent creatures, and they'll look up from an analysis like Krueger's and remind you that it shows only correlation, not causation. That's a convenient hedge for those of us at the top because it keeps alive one of the founding myths of America's meritocracy: that *our* success has nothing to do with *other people's* failure. It's a pleasant idea. But around the world and throughout history, the wealthy have advanced the crystallization process in a straightforward way. They have taken their money out of productive activities and put it into walls. Throughout history, moreover, one social group above all others has assumed responsibility for maintaining and defending these walls. Its members used to be called aristocrats. Now we're the 9.9 percent. The main difference is that we have figured out how to use the pretense of being part of the middle as one of our strategies for remaining on top.

Krueger gave his findings about immobility and inequality a name: the Great Gatsby Curve.

———

Money can't buy you class, or so my grandmother used to say. But it can buy a private detective. Grandmother was a Kentucky debutante and sometime fashion model (kind of like Daisy Buchanan in *The Great Gatsby*, weirdly enough), so she knew what to do when her eldest son announced his intention to marry a woman from Spain. A gumshoe promptly reported back that the prospective bride's family made a living selling newspapers on the streets of Barcelona. Grandmother instituted an immediate and total communications embargo. In fact, my mother's family owned and operated a large paper-goods factory. When children came, Grandmother at last relented. Determined to do the right thing, she arranged for the new family, then on military assignment in Hawaii, to be inscribed in the New York *Social Register*.

Sociologists would say, in their dry language, that my grandmother was a zealous manager of the family's social capital—and she wasn't about to let some Spanish street urchin run away with it. She did have a point, even if her facts were wrong. Money may be the measure of wealth, but it is far from the only form of it. Family, friends, social networks, personal health, culture, education, and even location are all ways of being rich, too. These nonfinancial forms of wealth, as it turns out, aren't simply perks of membership in our aristocracy. They define us.

We are the people of good family, good health, good schools, good neighborhoods, and good jobs. We may want to call ourselves the "5Gs" rather than the 9.9 percent. We are so far from the not-so-good people on all of these dimensions, we are beginning to resemble a new species. And, just as in Grandmother's day, the process of speciation begins with a love story—or, if you prefer, sexual selection.

The polite term for the process is *assortative mating*. The phrase is sometimes used to suggest that this is another of the wonders of the internet age, where popcorn at last meets butter and Yankees fan finds Yankees fan. In fact, the frenzy of assortative mating today results from a truth that would have been generally acknowledged by the heroines of any Jane Austen novel: Rising inequality decreases the number of suitably wealthy mates even as it increases the reward for finding one and the penalty for failing to do so. According to one study, the last time marriage partners sorted themselves by educational status as much as they do now was in the 1920s.

For most of us, the process is happily invisible. You meet someone under a tree on an exclusive campus or during orientation at a high-powered professional firm, and before you know it, you're twice as rich. But sometimes—Grandmother understood this well—extra measures are called for. That's where our new technology puts bumbling society detectives to shame. Ivy Leaguers looking to mate with their equals can apply to join a dating service called the League. It's selective, naturally: Only 20 to 30 percent of New York applicants get in. It's sometimes called "Tinder for the elites."

It is misleading to think that assortative mating is symmetrical, as in city mouse marries city mouse and country mouse marries country mouse. A better summary of the data would be: Rich mouse finds love, and poor mouse gets screwed. It turns out—who knew?—that people who are struggling to keep it all together have a harder time hanging on to their partner. According to the Harvard political scientist Robert Putnam, 60 years ago just 20 percent of children born to parents with a high-school education or less lived in a single-parent household; now that figure is nearly 70 percent. Among college-educated households, by contrast, the single-parent rate remains less than 10 percent. Since the 1970s, the divorce rate has declined significantly among college-educated couples, while it has risen dramatically among couples with only a high-school education—even as marriage itself has become less common. The rate of single parenting is in turn the single most significant predictor of social immobility across counties, according to a study led by the Stanford economist Raj Chetty.

None of which is to suggest that individuals are wrong to seek a suitable partner and make a beautiful family. People should—and presumably always will—pursue happiness in this way. It's one of the delusions of our meritocratic class, however, to assume that if our actions are individually blameless, then the sum of our actions will be good for society. We may have studied Shakespeare on the way to law school, but we have little sense for the tragic possibilities of life. The fact of the matter is that we have silently and collectively opted for inequality, and this is what inequality does. It turns marriage into a luxury good, and a stable family life into a privilege that the moneyed elite can pass along to their children. How do we think that's going to work out?

The skin colors of the nation's elite student bodies are more varied now, as are their genders, but their financial bones have calcified over the past 30 years. In 1985, 54 percent of students at the 250 most selective colleges came from families in the bottom three quartiles of the income distribution. A similar review of the class of 2010 put that figure at just 33 percent. According to a 2017 study, 38 elite colleges—among them five of the Ivies—had more students from the top 1 percent than from the bottom 60 percent. In his 2014 book, *Excellent Sheep*, William Deresiewicz, a former English professor at Yale, summed up the situation nicely: "Our new multiracial, gender-neutral meritocracy has figured out a way to make itself hereditary."

The wealthy can also draw on a variety of affirmative-action programs designed just for them. As Daniel Golden points out in *The Price of Admission*, legacy-admissions policies reward those applicants with the foresight to choose parents who attended the university in question. Athletic recruiting, on balance and contrary to the popular wisdom, also favors the wealthy, whose children pursue lacrosse, squash, fencing, and the other cost-intensive sports at which private schools and elite public schools excel. And, at least among members of the 0.1 percent, the old-school method of simply handing over some of Daddy's cash has been making a comeback. (Witness Jared Kushner, Harvard graduate.)

The mother lode of all affirmative-action programs for the wealthy, of course, remains the private school. Only 2.2 percent of the nation's students graduate from nonsectarian private high schools, and yet these graduates account for 26 percent of students at Harvard and 28 percent of students at Princeton. The *other* affirmative-action programs, the kind aimed at diversifying the look of the student body, are no doubt well intended. But they are to some degree merely an extension of this system of wealth preservation. Their function, at least in part, is to indulge rich people in the belief that their college is open to all on the basis of merit.

The plummeting admission rates of the very top schools nonetheless leave many of the children of the 9.9 percent facing long odds. But not to worry, junior 9.9 percenters! We've created a new range of elite colleges just for you. Thanks to ambitious university administrators and the ever-expanding rankings machine at *U.S. News & World Report*, 50 colleges are now as selective as Princeton was in 1980, when I applied. The colleges seem to think that piling up rejections makes them special. In fact, it just means that they have collectively opted to deploy their massive, tax-subsidized endowments to replicate privilege rather than fulfill their duty to produce an educated public.

The only thing going up as fast as the rejection rates at selective colleges is the astounding price of tuition. Measured relative to the national median salary, tuition and fees at top colleges more than tripled from 1963 to 2013. Throw in the counselors, the whisperers, the violin lessons, the private schools, and the cost of arranging for Junior to save a village in Micronesia, and it adds up. To be fair, financial aid closes the gap for many families and keeps the average cost of college from growing as fast as the sticker price. But that still leaves a question: Why are the wealthy so keen to buy their way in?

The short answer, of course, is that it's worth it.

In the United States, the premium that college graduates earn over their non-college-educated peers in young adulthood exceeds 70 percent. The return on education is 50 percent higher than what it was in 1950, and is significantly higher than the rate in every other developed country. In Norway and Denmark, the college premium is less than 20 percent; in Japan, it is less than 30 percent; in France and Germany, it's about 40 percent.

All of this comes before considering the all-consuming difference between "good" schools and the rest. Ten years after starting college, according to data from the Department of Education, the top decile of earners from all schools had a median salary of $68,000. But the top decile from the 10 highest-earning colleges raked in $220,000—make that $250,000 for No. 1, Harvard—and the top decile at the next 30 colleges took home $157,000. (Not surprisingly, the top 10 had an average acceptance rate of 9 percent, and the next 30 were at 19 percent.)

It is entirely possible to get a good education at the many schools that don't count as "good" in our brand-obsessed system. But the "bad" ones really are bad for you. For those who made the mistake of being born to the wrong parents, our society offers a kind of virtual education system. It has places that look like colleges—but aren't really. It has debt—and that, unfortunately, is real. The people who enter into this class hologram do not collect a college premium; they wind up in something more like indentured servitude.

So what is the real source of this premium for a "good education" that we all seem to crave?

One of the stories we tell ourselves is that the premium is the reward for the knowledge and skills the education provides us. Another, usually unfurled after a round of drinks, is that the premium is a reward for the superior cranial endowments we possessed before setting foot on campus. We are, as some sociologists have delicately put it, a "cognitive elite."

Behind both of these stories lies one of the founding myths of our meritocracy. One way or the other, we tell ourselves, the rising education premium is a direct function of the rising value of meritorious people in a modern economy. That is, not only do the meritorious get ahead, but the rewards we receive are in direct proportion to our merit.

But the fact is that degree holders earn so much more than the rest not primarily because they are better at their job, but because they mostly take different categories of jobs. Well over half of Ivy League graduates, for instance, typically go straight into one of four career tracks that are generally reserved for the well educated: finance, management consulting, medicine, or law. To keep it simple, let's just say that there are two types of occupations in the world: those whose members have collective influence in setting their own pay, and those whose members must face the music on their own. It's better to be a member of the first group. Not surprisingly, that is where you will find the college crowd.

————

From my Brookline home, it's a pleasant, 10-minute walk to get a haircut. Along the way, you pass immense elm trees and brochure-ready homes beaming in their reclaimed Victorian glory. Apart from a landscaper or two, you are unlikely to spot a human being in this wilderness of oversize closets, wood-paneled living rooms, and Sub-Zero refrigerators. If you do run into a neighbor, you might have a conversation like this: "Our kitchen remodel went way over budget. We had to fight just to get the tile guy to show up!" "I know! We ate Thai takeout for a month because the gas guy's car kept breaking down!" You arrive at the Supercuts fresh from your stroll, but the nice lady who cuts your hair is looking stressed. You'll discover that she commutes an hour through jammed highways to work. The gas guy does, too, and the tile guy comes in from another state. None of them can afford to live around here. The rent is too damn high.

From 1980 to 2016, home values in Boston multiplied 7.6 times. When you take account of inflation, they generated a return of 157 percent to their owners. San Francisco returned 162 percent in real terms over the same period; New York, 115 percent; and Los Angeles, 114 percent. If you happen to live in a neighborhood like mine, you are surrounded by people who consider themselves to be real-estate geniuses. (That's one reason we can afford to make so many mistakes in the home-renovation department.) If you live in St. Louis (3 percent) or Detroit (minus 16 percent), on the other hand, you weren't so smart. In 1980, a house in St. Louis would trade for a decent studio apartment in Manhattan. Today that house will buy an 80-square-foot bathroom in the Big Apple.

The returns on (the right kind of) real estate have been so extraordinary that, according to some economists, real estate alone may account for essentially all of the increase in wealth concentration over the past half century. It's not surprising that the values are up in the major cities: These are the gold mines of our new economy. Yet there is a paradox. The rent is so high that people—notably people in the middle class—are leaving town rather than working the mines. From 2000 to 2009, the San Francisco Bay Area had some of the highest salaries in the nation, and yet it lost 350,000 residents to lower-paying regions. Across the United States, the journalist and economist Ryan Avent writes in *The Gated City*, "the best opportunities are found in one place, and for some reason most Americans are opting to live in another." According to estimates from the economists Enrico Moretti and Chang-Tai Hsieh, the migration away from the productive centers of New York, San Francisco, and San Jose alone lopped 9.7 percent off total U.S. growth from 1964 to 2009.

It is well known by now that the immediate cause of the insanity is the unimaginable pettiness of backyard politics. Local zoning regulation imposes excessive restrictions on housing development and drives up prices. What is less well understood is how central the process of depopulating the economic core of the nation is to the intertwined stories of rising inequality and falling social mobility.

Real-estate inflation has brought with it a commensurate increase in economic segregation. Every hill and dale in the land now has an imaginary gate, and it tells you up front exactly how much money you need to stay there overnight. Educational segregation has accelerated even more. In my suburb of Boston, 53 percent of adults have a graduate degree. In the suburb just south, that figure is 9 percent.

This economic and educational sorting of neighborhoods is often represented as a matter of personal preference, as in red people like to hang with red, and blue with blue. In reality, it's about the consolidation of wealth in all its forms, starting, of course, with money. Gilded zip codes are located next to giant cash machines: a too-big-to-fail bank, a friendly tech monopoly, and so on. Local governments, which collected a record $523 billion in property taxes in 2016, make sure that much of the money stays close to home.

But proximity to economic power isn't just a means of hoarding the pennies; it's a force of natural selection. Gilded zip codes deliver higher life expectancy, more-useful social networks, and lower crime rates. Lengthy commutes, by contrast, cause obesity, neck pain, stress, insomnia, loneliness, and divorce, as Annie Lowrey reported in *Slate*. One study found that a commute of 45 minutes or longer by one spouse increased the chance of divorce by 40 percent.

Nowhere are the mechanics of the growing geographic divide more evident than in the system of primary and secondary education. Public schools were born amid hopes of opportunity for all; the best of them have now been effectively reprivatized to better serve the upper classes. According to a widely used school-ranking service, out of more than 5,000 public elementary schools in California, the top 11 are located in Palo Alto. They're free and open to the public. All you have to do is move into a town where the median home value is $3,211,100. Scarsdale, New York, looks like a steal in comparison: The public high schools in that area funnel dozens of graduates to Ivy League colleges every year, and yet the median home value is a mere $1,403,600.

Racial segregation has declined with the rise of economic segregation. We in the 9.9 percent are proud of that. What better proof that
we care only about merit? But we don't really want too much proof.
Beyond a certain threshold—5 percent minority or 20 percent, it var-
ies according to the mood of the region—neighborhoods suddenly go
completely black or brown. It is disturbing, but perhaps not surprising,
to find that social mobility is lower in regions with high levels of racial
segregation. The fascinating revelation in the data, however, is that the
damage isn't limited to the obvious victims. According to Raj Chetty's
research team, "There is evidence that higher racial segregation is associated with lower social mobility for white people." The relationship
doesn't hold in every zone of the country, to be sure, and is undoubt-
edly the statistical reflection of a more complex set of social mechanisms. But it points to a truth that America's 19th-century slaveholders
understood very well: Dividing by color remains an effective way to
keep all colors of the 90 percent in their place.

With localized wealth comes localized political power, and not
just of the kind that shows up in voting booths. Which brings us
back to the depopulation paradox. Given the social and cultural capital that flows through wealthy neighborhoods, is it any wonder that
we can defend our turf in the zoning wars? We have lots of ways to
make that sound public-spirited. It's all about saving the local environment, preserving the historic character of the neighborhood,
and avoiding overcrowding. In reality, it's about hoarding power and
opportunity inside the walls of our own castles. This is what aristoc-
racies do.

Zip code is who we are. It defines our style, announces our values,
establishes our status, preserves our wealth, and allows us to pass it
along to our children. It's also slowly strangling our economy and killing our democracy. It is the brick-and-mortar version of the Gatsby
Curve. The traditional story of economic growth in America has been
one of arriving, building, inviting friends, and building some more.
The story we're writing looks more like one of slamming doors shut
behind us and slowly suffocating under a mass of commercial-grade
kitchen appliances.

The political theology of the meritocracy has no room for resentment. We are taught to run the competition of life with our eyes on the clock and not on one another, as if we were each alone. If someone scores a powerboat on the Long Island waterways, so much the better for her. The losers will just smile and try harder next time.

In the real world, we humans are always looking from side to side. We are intensely conscious of what other people are thinking and doing, and conscious to the point of preoccupation with what they think about us. Our status is visible only through its reflection in the eyes of others.

Perhaps the best evidence for the power of an aristocracy is to be found in the degree of resentment it provokes. By that measure, the 9.9 percent are doing pretty well indeed. The surest sign of an increase in resentment is a rise in political division and instability. We're positively acing that test. You can read all about it in the headlines of the past two years.

The 2016 presidential election marked a decisive moment in the history of resentment in the United States. In the person of Donald Trump, resentment entered the White House. It rode in on the back of an alliance between a tiny subset of super-wealthy 0.1 percenters (not all of them necessarily American) and a large number of 90 percenters who stand for pretty much everything the 9.9 percent are not.

According to exit polls by CNN and Pew, Trump won white voters by about 20 percent. But these weren't just any old whites (though they were old, too). The first thing to know about the substantial majority of them is that they weren't the winners in the new economy. To be sure, for the most part they weren't poor, either. But they did have reason to feel judged by the market—and found wanting. The counties that supported Hillary Clinton represented an astonishing 64 percent of the GDP, while Trump counties accounted for a mere 36 percent. Aaron Terrazas, a senior economist at Zillow, found that the median home value in Clinton counties was $250,000, while the median in Trump counties was $154,000. When you adjust for inflation, Clinton counties enjoyed real-estate price appreciation of 27 percent from January 2000 to October 2016; Trump counties got only a 6 percent bump.

The residents of Trump country were also the losers in the war on human health. According to Shannon Monnat, an associate professor of sociology at Syracuse, the Rust Belt counties that put the anti-government-health-care candidate over the top were those that lost the most people in recent years to deaths of despair—those due to alcohol, drugs, and suicide.

To make all of America as great as Trump country, you would have to torch about a quarter of total GDP, wipe a similar proportion of the nation's housing stock into the sea, and lose a few years in life expectancy. There's a reason why one of Trump's favorite words is *unfair*. That's the only word resentment wants to hear.

Even so, the distinguishing feature of Trump's (white) voters wasn't their income but their education, or lack thereof. Pew's latest analysis indicates that Trump lost college-educated white voters by a humiliating 17 percent margin. But he got revenge with non-college-educated whites, whom he captured by a stomping 36 percent margin. According to an analysis by Nate Silver, the 50 most educated counties in the nation surged to Clinton: In 2012, Obama had won them by a mere 17 percentage points; Clinton took them by 26 points. The 50 least educated counties moved in the opposite direction; whereas Obama had lost them by 19 points, Clinton lost them by 31. Majority-minority counties split the same way: The more educated moved toward Clinton, and the less educated toward Trump.

The historian Richard Hofstadter drew attention to *Anti-intellectualism in American Life* in 1963; Susan Jacoby warned in 2008 about *The Age of American Unreason*; and Tom Nichols announced *The Death of Expertise* in 2017. In Trump, the age of unreason has at last found its hero. The "self-made man" is always the idol of those who aren't quite making it. He is the sacred embodiment of the American dream, the guy who answers to nobody, the poor man's idea of a rich man. It's the educated phonies this group can't stand. With his utter lack of policy knowledge and belligerent commitment to maintaining his ignorance, Trump is the perfect representative for a population whose idea of good governance is just to scramble the eggheads. When reason becomes the enemy of the common man, the common man becomes the enemy of reason.

Did I mention that the common man is white? That brings us to the other side of American-style resentment. You kick down, and then you close ranks around an imaginary tribe. The problem, you say, is the moochers, the snakes, the handout queens; the solution is the flag and the religion of your (white) ancestors. According to a survey by the political scientist Brian Schaffner, Trump crushed it among voters who "strongly disagree" that "white people have advantages because of the color of their skin," as well as among those who "strongly agree" that "women seek to gain power over men." It's worth adding that these responses measure not racism or sexism directly, but rather resentment. They're good for picking out the kind of people who will vehemently insist that they are the least racist or sexist person you have ever met, even as they vote for a flagrant racist and an accused sexual predator.

No one is born resentful. As mass phenomena, racism, xenophobia, anti-intellectualism, narcissism, irrationalism, and all other variants of resentment are as expensive to produce as they are deadly to democratic politics. Only long hours of television programming, intelligently manipulated social-media feeds, and expensively sustained information bubbles can actualize the unhappy dispositions of humanity to the point where they may be fruitfully manipulated for political gain. Racism in particular is not just a legacy of the past, as many Americans would like to believe; it also must be constantly reinvented for the present. Mass incarceration, fearmongering, and segregation are not just the results of prejudice, but also the means of reproducing it.

The raging polarization of American political life is not the consequence of bad manners or a lack of mutual understanding. It is just the loud aftermath of escalating inequality. It could not have happened without the 0.1 percent (or, rather, an aggressive subset of its members). Wealth always preserves itself by dividing the opposition. The Gatsby Curve does not merely cause barriers to be built on the ground; it mandates the construction of walls that run through other people's minds.

But that is not to let the 9.9 percent off the hook. We may not be the ones funding the race-baiting, but we are the ones hoarding the opportunities of daily life. We are the staff that runs the machine that funnels resources from the 90 percent to the 0.1 percent. We've been happy to take our cut of the spoils. We've looked on with smug disdain as our labors have brought forth a population prone to resentment and ripe for manipulation. We should be prepared to embrace the consequences.

The first important thing to know about these consequences is the most obvious: Resentment is a solution to nothing. It isn't a program of reform. It isn't "populism." It is an affliction of democracy, not an instance of it. The politics of resentment is a means of increasing inequality, not reducing it. Every policy change that has waded out of the Trump administration's baffling morass of incompetence makes this clear. The new tax law; the executive actions on the environment and telecommunications, and on financial-services regulation; the judicial appointments of conservative ideologues—all will have the effect of keeping the 90 percent toiling in the foothills of merit for many years to come.

The second thing to know is that we are next in line for the chopping block. As the population of the resentful expands, the circle of joy near the top gets smaller. The people riding popular rage to glory eventually realize that we are less useful to them as servants of the economic machine than we are as model enemies of the people. The anti-blue-state provisions of the recent tax law have miffed some members of the 9.9 percent, but they're just a taste of the bad things that happen to people like us as the politics of resentment unfolds.

The past year provides ample confirmation of the third and most important consequence of the process: instability. Unreasonable people also tend to be ungovernable. I won't belabor the point. Just try doing a frequency search on the phrase *constitutional crisis* over the past five years. That's the thing about the Gatsby Curve. You think it's locking all of your gains in place. But the crystallization process actually has the effect of making the whole system more brittle. If you look again at history, you can get a sense of how the process usually ends.

LEFT BEHIND

by Tara Westover and Jeffrey Goldberg

[DECEMBER 2019]

The diversity of America—within the 9.9 percent, among the 90.1 percent—is extensive. How much do we truly have in common? Do we mean the same thing when we use a phrase like *the American dream*? Do all of us even use that phrase? Decades ago, *Atlantic* editor William Whitworth fought a be-hind-the-scenes battle to discourage writers from using the term *the average American*, on the grounds that there was no such thing. He was from Arkansas, transplanted to the East Coast. He understood how wide the gulf between groups can be and how easily that fact can be overlooked or forgotten. It is also easily ignored: Everyone's default setting is "people like me," and social media encourages us to stay permanently in that mode. One result is what the author Tara Westover has called "a breaking of charity."

Westover was raised by survivalist parents in the mountains of rural Idaho, and did not go to school. "Dad said public school was a ploy by the Government to lead children away from God," she wrote in her best-selling 2018 memoir, *Educated*. Still, she taught herself enough to attend college at Brigham Young University, and later earned a doctorate from Cambridge University. Today, she lives in New York City. For a 2019 special issue of *The Atlantic*, "How to Stop a Civil War," Westover spoke with editor in chief Jeffrey Goldberg about cultural separation and mutual misunderstanding in America.

Jeffrey Goldberg: You told me once that there is an "experience gap" in our national life—that we no longer share some underlying common experience as Americans.

Tara Westover: Yes, and the experience gap is fast becoming an empathy gap.

Goldberg: Do people in Idaho and people in New York City have more in common than they think? Or are we really becoming two countries?

Westover: We have a shared history and shared interests as Americans, that's true, but it's also true that Democrats and Republicans increasingly live and work in different places. We have different experiences. As a general rule, I think we focus far too much on Donald Trump. We act like he's the problem, but he's not. He's just a symptom—a sign of poor political hygiene.

Goldberg: Poor political hygiene?

Westover: Social media has flooded our consciousness with caricatures of each other. Human beings are reduced to data, and data nearly always under-represent reality. The result is this great flattening of human life and human complexity. We think that because we know someone is pro-choice or pro-life, or that they drive a truck or a Prius, we know everything we need to know about them. Human detail gets lost in the algorithm. Thus humanity gives way to ideology.

Goldberg: So good political hygiene includes a respect for human complexity?

Westover: Our political system requires us to have a basic level of respect for each other, of empathy for each other. That loss of empathy is what I call a breaking of charity.

Goldberg: What does that mean?

Westover: It's a term that's associated with the Salem witch trials, and it refers to the moment when two members of a tribe disfellowship each other, and become two tribes. That, I think, is the biggest threat to our country, more than any single issue or politician. It's the fact that the left and the right, the elite and the non-elite, the urban and the rural—however you want to slice it up—they no longer see themselves reflected in the other person. They no longer interpret each other as having charitable intent.

Goldberg: What caused this?

Westover: The fact that Democrats and Republicans now have a different experience of life in this country. Broadly speaking, the modern economy works well for cities and badly for the countryside. In recent years, growth has been hyper-concentrated in our cities, which are hubs of technology and finance. Meanwhile, the hinterlands, which rely on agriculture and manufacturing—what you might call the "old economy"—have sunk into a deep decline. There are places in the United States where the recession never ended. For them, it has been 2009 for 10 years. That does something to people, psychologically.

Goldberg: And that's what is causing the current political divide?

Westover: That's what I think. And everyone used to think that. When Trump first won the nomination, it was generally thought that his populism was fueled by economic disparities, but for some reason, after he was elected, that view went out of fashion. I don't know why, because it is quite obviously the case—although to see it you need to think in terms of ecosystems, rather than individual incomes. Democratic strongholds are thriving. There's this abundance of tech and professional jobs, and an educated population to fill them. Many Republican districts are experiencing negative growth, left behind by a changing economy. There is no place for them in this future we are making.

You can see this even at the state level. Take the 20 poorest states, by median household income, and you'll see that 18 of them went for Trump. If you take the 10 richest states, nine went for Hillary Clinton. Our economic divide now tracks almost perfectly with our political divide. The 2016 election was about geospatial inequality. It was about the parts of the country that are suffering under technological change and globalization.

Goldberg: How do you factor in the xenophobia and racism and tribalism that we're seeing, particularly in those parts of the United States?

Westover: I can't answer that question to my own satisfaction. Some of the rhetoric coming out of the right is completely unacceptable. There is no way to justify it. There is no way to rationalize it. The best I can do is try to understand what is behind it.

Prejudice is not new in this country. What is new is that, at the moment when we thought we had at last banished it to the fringe, here it is again, displayed openly in our public spaces. My own view is that economic distress activates prejudice. It makes it lethal. Of course, our country struggled with prejudice before Trump, but I don't think that prejudice had been weaponized to the extent that it is now. Immigration and affirmative action were not the top issues on people's minds. They probably weren't even in the top three.

But in a climate of desperation and economic realignment, of uncertainty about the future, people become tribal. They become vulnerable to narratives that demonize those who are not like them. Most rural Americans don't understand the vast technological and geopolitical shifts that are destroying their way of life. How could they? I don't understand those shifts, and I've been trying pretty hard. It's very easy for someone to come along and tell them that the problem is immigration. That's what happened in 2016. Trump told a more convincing story about what was happening in America than the left did.

Goldberg: So who does the Democratic Party represent?

Westover: It represents the most disadvantaged and disenfranchised people in our country—those held down by the overwhelming forces of structural prejudice. But it is difficult to defend the idea that, in general, it is the voice of the economically disenfranchised. Recently, the Brookings Institution and *The Wall Street Journal* found that in the United States, districts represented by Democrats are responsible for two-thirds of our national GDP. Just think about that. It's uncomfortable, but it might be time for us to admit that as a country we are engaged in a struggle between the haves and the have-nots, and there is a meaningful sense in which many of us on the left are the haves.

Goldberg: And those Democratic districts look very different from where you're from?

Westover: Where I'm from is dying. It's an entire ecosystem in decline. I was with my cousin recently, driving through the county seat where I grew up—a little town of about 5,000 people called Preston, Idaho. We were passing down the main street, and I saw that every single shop we'd gone to as kids was boarded up. But there was a brand-new funeral parlor, bringing the town's total funeral parlors to two. That means the town now has one grocery store and two funeral parlors. My cousin turned to me and said, "You know what? It's getting so the only thing there is to do around here is die."

Goldberg: Do you think of where you grew up as parochial?

Westover: I used to think of Idaho as parochial, and I used to think of cities as sophisticated. And in many ways, I was right. You can get a better education in a city; you can learn more technical skills, and more about certain types of culture. But as I've grown older, I've come to believe that there are many ways a person can be parochial. Now I define parochial as only knowing people who are just like you—who have the same education that you have, the same political views, the same income. And by that definition, New York City is just about the most parochial place I've ever lived. I have become more parochial since I came here.

It's astonishingly difficult in this city to be truly close to someone who is not in your same socioeconomic group. For me, it's the single most striking fact about living here. Meaningful interactions are difficult to engineer. The divide is deep. And it is largely between those who sit in the front of the Uber and those who sit in the back of it.

Goldberg: Do people in Idaho assume that now that you live in New York, you've really left Idaho in some important way?

Westover: They do assume that, and they are right. At some point, you have to acknowledge that you can't embody your origins forever. At some point, you have to surrender your card. I'm more urbanite now than hayseed. I can't change that, but I certainly feel some grief over it.

Goldberg: So you have not broken charity with your home state?

Westover: I try not to. And a lot of people on the left haven't either. But from time to time you hear a strong tone of condescension emanating from our urban centers. You hear it in the way people talk about obesity rates in the rural United States, or about the lower number of college graduates from rural areas. These are serious problems that are hitting rural America specifically because of devastating shifts in our economic system, because of underinvestment in education, because people in these areas don't have access to decent health care or sometimes to any health care at all. You look at where the holes are in Obamacare—they're in rural areas. You look at where the opioid epidemic hit hard—it's in rural areas. You look at educational outcomes for rural kids—they're troubling, every report. These facts should be the foundation of our empathy, not of our contempt.

RED STATE, BLUE CITY

by David A. Graham

[MARCH 2017]

As a nation, Tara Westover observed, "we are engaged in a struggle between the haves and the have-nots"—a struggle mirrored in the different condition of urban America and rural America. City versus country has long been one of the central divisions in the American life. It is reflected in the U.S. Constitution, which gave the same number of senators to smaller and less populous states as it did to those with large and growing cities. That division is also reflected in most state legislatures, where politicians from nonurban areas have historically fought above their weight. It is a line of demarcation that runs through American literature.

That line has not always tracked neatly with ideology and partisanship. As late as the 1960s and '70s, conservative rural Democrats and liberal urban Republicans, both now virtually extinct, were a force in American politics. A combination of factors—the civil-rights movement; the migration of African Americans to urban areas; and Republican Richard Nixon's "southern strategy," which exploited racial fears to win the votes of white Democrats—brought geography and politics into closer alignment. As David A. Graham, an *Atlantic* staff writer, noted in a 2017 article, the United States is coming to resemble two countries: one rural and one urban, one conservative and one liberal. Reporting from North Carolina, with its urban blue pockets surrounded by a sea of rural red, Graham asked: What happens when city and state go to war?

Thehe United States now has its most metropolitan president in recent memory: a Queens-bred, skyscraper-building, apartment-
dwelling Manhattanite. Yet it was rural America that carried
Donald Trump to victory; the president got trounced in cities. Republican reliance on suburbs and the countryside isn't new, of course, but
in the presidential election, the gulf between urban and nonurban voters was wider than it had been in nearly a century. Hillary Clinton won
88 of the country's 100 biggest counties, but still went down to defeat.

American cities seem to be cleaving from the rest of the country,
and the temptation for liberals is to try to embrace that trend. With
Republicans controlling the presidency, both houses of Congress, and
most statehouses, Democrats are turning to local ordinances as their
best hope on issues ranging from gun control to the minimum wage to
transgender rights. Even before Inauguration Day, big-city mayors laid
plans to nudge the new administration leftward, especially on immigration—and, should that fail, to join together in resisting its policies.

But if liberal advocates are clinging to the hope that federalism
will allow them to create progressive havens, they're overlooking a big
problem: Power may be decentralized in the American system, but it
devolves to the state, not the city. Recent events in red states where
cities are pockets of liberalism are instructive, and cautionary. Over the
past few years, city governments and state legislatures have fought each
other in a series of battles involving preemption—the principle that
state law trumps local regulation, just as federal law supersedes state
law. It hasn't gone well for the city dwellers.

Close observers of these clashes expect them to proliferate in the
years to come, with similar results. "We are about to see a shitstorm
of state and federal preemption orders, of a magnitude greater than
anything in history," says Mark Pertschuk of Grassroots Change, which
tracks such laws through an initiative called Preemption Watch. By the
group's count, at least 36 states introduced laws preempting cities in
2016.

State legislatures have put their oar in on issues ranging from the
expansive to the eccentric. Common examples involve blocking local
minimum-wage and sick-leave ordinances, which are opposed by

business groups, and bans on plastic grocery bags, which arouse retailers' ire. Some states have prohibited cities from enacting firearm regulations, frustrating leaders who say cities have different gun problems than do rural areas. Alabama and Arizona both passed bills targeting "sanctuary cities"—those that do not cooperate with the enforcement of federal immigration laws. Even though courts threw out much of that legislation, other states have considered their own versions.

Arizona also made sure cities couldn't ban the gifts in Happy Meals (cities elsewhere had talked about outlawing them, on the theory that they lure kids to McDonald's), and when some of its cities cracked down on puppy mills, it barred local regulation of pet breeders, too. Cities in Oklahoma can't regulate e-cigarettes. Mississippi decreed that towns can't ban sugary drinks, and the beverage industry is expected to press other states to follow suit.

Most of these laws enforce conservative policy preferences. That's partly because Republicans enjoy unprecedented control in state capitals—they hold 33 governorships and majorities in 32 state legislatures. The trend also reflects a broader shift: Americans are in the midst of what's been called "the Big Sort," as they flock together with people who share similar socioeconomic profiles and politics. In general, that means rural areas are becoming more conservative, and cities more liberal. Even the reddest states contain liberal cities: Half of the U.S. metro areas with the biggest recent population gains are in the South, and they are Democratic. Texas alone is home to four such cities; Clinton carried each of them. Increasingly, the most important political and cultural divisions are not between red and blue states but between red states and the blue cities within.

Nowhere has this tension been more dramatic than in North Carolina. The state made headlines last March when its GOP-dominated general assembly abruptly overturned a Charlotte ordinance banning discrimination against LGBT people (and stating, among other things, that transgender people could use the bathroom of their choice). Legislators didn't just reverse Charlotte's ordinance, though; the state law, HB2, also barred every city in the state from passing nondiscrimination regulations, and banned local minimum-wage laws, too.

North Carolina's legislature wasn't new to preemption—previously, it had banned sanctuary cities, prohibited towns from destroying guns confiscated by the police, and blocked local fracking regulations. It had restructured the Greensboro city council so as to dilute Democratic clout. In Wake County, home to Raleigh, it had redrawn the districts for both the school board and county commission, shifting power from urban to suburban voters. The state had seized Asheville's airport and tried to seize its water system too. Lawmakers had also passed a bill wresting control of Charlotte's airport from the city and handing it to a new commission.

HB2 was different, though—it set off a fierce nationwide backlash, including a U.S. Department of Justice lawsuit and boycotts by businesses, sports leagues, and musicians. Since corporate expansions, conventions, and concerts tend to take place in cities, North Carolina's cities have suffered the most. Within two months of HB2's passage, Charlotte's Chamber of Commerce estimated that the city had lost nearly $285 million and 1,300 jobs—and that was before the NBA yanked its 2017 All-Star Game from the city. Asheville, a bohemian tourist magnet in the Blue Ridge Mountains, lost millions from canceled conferences alone.

For Asheville residents, the series of preemption bills felt like bullying. "People are furious. They're confused," Esther Manheimer, Asheville's mayor, told me as her city battled to retain control of its water system. "We're a very desirable city to live in. We're on all the top-ten lists. How would anyone have an issue with the way Asheville is running its city, or the things that the people of Asheville value?"

National mythology cherishes the New England town-hall meeting as the foundation of American democracy, and once upon a time, it was. But the Constitution doesn't mention cities at all, and since the late 19th century, courts have accepted that cities are creatures of the state.

Some states delegate certain powers to cities, but states remain the higher authority, even if city dwellers don't realize it. "Most people think, *We have an election here, we elect a mayor and our city council, we organize our democracy—we should have a right to control our own city in our own way,"* says Gerald Frug, a Harvard Law professor and an expert on local government. "You go to any place in America and ask, 'Do you think this city can control its own destiny?' 'Of course it can!' The popular conception of what cities do runs in direct conflict with the legal reality."

The path to the doctrine of state supremacy was rocky. In 1857, when New York State snatched some of New York City's powers— including its police force—riots followed. But after the Civil War, the tide of public and legal opinion turned against local government. Following rapid urban growth, fueled in part by immigration, cities came to be seen as dens of licentiousness and subversive politics. Moreover, many municipalities brought trouble on themselves, spending profligately to lure railroads through town. Unable to make good on their debts, some towns and cities dissolved, leaving states holding the bag and inspiring laws that barred cities from independently issuing bonds. In an 1868 decision, the jurist John Forrest Dillon declared that cities were entirely beholden to their state legislature: "It breathes into them the breath of life, without which they cannot exist. As it creates, so may it destroy. If it may destroy, it may abridge and control."

Today's clampdowns on cities echo 19th-century anxieties about urban progressivism, demographics, and insolvency. Many of the southern cities that have been targeted for preemption are seen as magnets for out-of-state interlopers. Republican officeholders have blasted non-discrimination ordinances like Charlotte's as contravening nature and Christian morality. They've argued that a patchwork of wage and sick-leave laws will drive away businesses, and that fracking bans will stifle the economy.

Yet the economic reality that underpinned rural-urban distrust in the 19th century is now inverted: In most states, agriculture is no longer king. Rural areas are struggling, while densely packed areas with highly educated workforces and socially liberal lifestyles flourish. In turn, rural voters harbor growing resentment toward those in cities, from Austin to Atlanta, from Birmingham to Chicago.

In this context of increasing rural-urban division, people on both sides of the political aisle have warmed to positions typically associated with their adversaries. The GOP has long viewed itself as the party of decentralization, criticizing Democrats for trying to dictate to local communities from Capitol Hill, but now Republicans are the ones preempting local government. Meanwhile, after years of seeing Democratic reforms overturned by preemption, the party of big government finds itself championing decentralized power.

Both sides may find their new positions unexpectedly difficult. As North Carolina's experience shows, preemption-happy state governments have a tendency to overreach: The state supreme court ruled the attempted takeover of Asheville's water system unconstitutional. Federal courts struck down the redistricting efforts in Greensboro and Wake County. The takeover of Charlotte's airport foundered when the FAA pointed out that the state didn't have the authority to transfer the airport's certification. In November, voters ousted Governor Pat McCrory, in part because of HB2's deep unpopularity.

In a particularly odd twist, last summer Republicans in the North Carolina statehouse joined Democrats in rejecting a bill, offered by a powerful outgoing Republican senator, to redistrict Asheville's city council. In a heated debate, Representative Michael Speciale, a Republican, mocked his colleagues for suddenly acting as if they knew better than the people of Asheville. "We may not agree ideologically with the citizens of Asheville or the city council of Asheville," he said. "I'm sorry, but we don't need to agree with them, because we don't live there."

By and large, though, cities hold the weaker hand. It makes sense that these areas, finding themselves economically vital, increasingly progressive, and politically disempowered, would want to use local ordinances as a bulwark against conservative state and federal policies. But this gambit is likely to backfire. Insofar as states have sometimes granted cities leeway to enact policy in the past, that forbearance has been the result of political norms, not legal structures. Once those norms crumble, and state legislatures decide to assert their authority, cities will have very little recourse.

An important lesson of last year's presidential election is that American political norms are much weaker than they had appeared, allowing a scandal-plagued, unpopular candidate to triumph—in part because voters outside of cities objected to the pace of cultural change. Another lesson is that the United States is coming to resemble two separate countries, one rural and one urban.

Only one of them, at present, appears entitled to self-determination.

CARRY ME BACK

by Drew Gilpin Faust

[AUGUST 2019]

Issues involving race are inseparable from American politics, whether they manifest openly or lurk deep below the surface. Like North Carolina's cities, the urban and urbanizing areas in Virginia—Richmond, Norfolk, Charlottesville, the suburbs adjacent to Washington, D.C.—are majority Democrat. The state as a whole, also like North Carolina, now fluctuates uneasily between Democrat and Republican. In 2017, white supremacists and neo-Nazis demonstrated in the streets of Charlottesville—a show of force that led to the murder of an innocent young woman and injuries to many others when one of the white supremacists drove his car into a crowd. In 2019, the state's governor, Ralph Northam, a Democrat, professed surprise to learn that his yearbook page from medical school displayed a racist photograph—a white student in blackface along with another student dressed as a member of the Ku Klux Klan; he eventually acknowledged that he was the student in blackface.

Those events, still fresh, provided the public backdrop for a personal essay by the historian Drew Gilpin Faust on race and memory in Virginia. Faust, a contributing writer at *The Atlantic* and a former president of Harvard University, was raised in Virginia's Shenandoah Valley, where her family had been prominent for generations. In her essay, excerpted here, she reflected on Virginia's "long history of endeavoring to cover its racial inequities with a surface gentility" and also with a mythic story about "the supposed benevolence of paternalism."

As Faust emphasized, Virginia's history may possess a particular character, but the core of that history is not Virginia's alone. And it is not merely history.

Faust is the author of *Mothers of Invention: Women of the Slaveholding South in the American Civil War* (1996), which won the Francis Parkman Prize, and *This Republic of Suffering: Death and the American Civil War* (2008), which won the Bancroft Prize.

We stopped first at the cemetery. My brother had picked me up at the Philadelphia airport, and we had driven south and west from there—to Baltimore and Frederick, then down through the hills of the Blue Ridge, past the confluence of the Shenandoah and Potomac Rivers at Harpers Ferry and into the Valley of Virginia. Civil War country. The route of the Antietam and Gettysburg campaigns. The site of John Brown's incendiary attempt to foment a slave uprising. The place where we grew up.

Apart from one brief drive-through, I hadn't been back in nearly two decades—not since a visit the year after my father died. Now we could see next to his grave the dirt already unearthed to make a place for my stepmother's ashes the next day. We had come for her funeral and in my father's memory.

I had attended many burials here. The family plot houses uncles, aunts, grandparents, and great-grandparents, but no graves nearly as old as those dug soon after the nearby chapel was built in the 1790s. Edmund Randolph, the U.S. secretary of state and the nation's first attorney general, a Virginia governor and a member of the Constitutional Convention, is a few yards away, surrounded by a crowd of Randolphs, Pages, Burwells, and Carters—members of the First Families of Virginia who had migrated to this northern end of the Shenandoah Valley when the children of the 18th-century Tidewater gentry began to seek new lands and new opportunities. Nestled behind what has come to be known as the Old Chapel, in the quiet of an isolated crossroad, the beautiful little cemetery is so small that no one is much more than a stone's throw from everyone else.

My brother and I, the only visitors, wandered, reading epitaphs that called up Virginia's storied past or reminded us of figures from our childhood: the leader of my Girl Scout troop; a teacher from our elementary school; a classmate's mother, who was an extraordinary horsewoman; and my father's drinking buddy and his long-suffering wife.

But I wanted to be sure my brother saw one plaque in particular. I remembered its words dimly and had perhaps even tried to forget them altogether. But now here I was again, and I needed to remind myself. I knew it was at the back of the oldest part of the cemetery, and there I found it, partially hidden by leaves and vines, and covered with lichen that nearly obscured its inscription. But I could still read:

TO THE GLORY OF GOD
AND IN REMEMBRANCE OF THE MANY PERSONAL
SERVANTS BURIED HERE BEFORE 1865.
FAITHFUL AND DEVOTED IN LIFE, THEIR FRIENDS
AND MASTERS LAID THEM NEAR THEM IN DEATH
WITH AFFECTION AND GRATITUDE.
THEIR MEMORY REMAINS, THOUGH THEIR WOODEN MARKERS,
LIKE THE WAY OF LIFE OF THAT DAY,
ARE GONE FOREVER.
I.T.G. 1957

I.T.G. was my grandmother. In 1957, I was 10 years old. We both lived here.

There is a monument to the Confederate dead in this cemetery; there are markers for unknown Confederates killed in skirmishes nearby. That is complicated enough. But what is to be made of this invocation of slavery offered during my own lifetime? Of this tangible link between who we are now and who we were more than a century and a half ago? Between attitudes and practices that were taught to me as a child and the person I could or would become? Between the Virginia of 1957 or 1857 and the one that—on the very day in February

2019 when I stood in the Old Chapel cemetery—was confronting the crisis of a governor whose medical-school yearbook page had just been discovered to have included a repugnant, racist photograph of a man in blackface and another in Klan robes?

What had my grandmother been thinking? The language and tone are right out of what is sometimes called the "moonlight and magnolias" version of the pre–Civil War South—the romanticization of plantation culture, the erasure of slavery and its brutalities. Here on the plaque we have not slaves but "servants," "faithful and devoted" rather than subjugated against their will. The words describe affectionate and appreciative masters—a benign domination, not the cruel system of physical brutality, lives stolen, and human beings bought and sold that we know slavery to have been. The marker declares a nostalgia for an era, a "way of life" that is "gone forever." Gone, we might say, with the wind. Margaret Mitchell's book, published in 1936, and the movie that followed in 1939 were still exerting their influence in 1957, as they have well into our own time. And I think, too, of the "Mammy" memorial approved by the U.S. Senate in 1923, and the numerous "Mammy" monuments proposed at that time across the South.

But this wasn't 1923 or even 1936. It was 1957. Why did my grandmother go to the trouble—and expense—of erecting the plaque at this particular time? It was more than just an expression of views that had persisted since the ideology of the Lost Cause and the idealization of the Old South had solidified among white people in the years after Appomattox, views that she had been indoctrinated to embrace from the time of her birth in Tennessee in 1894.

The year 1957 was a crucial time in Virginia and in the South generally. Three years earlier, the Supreme Court had struck down school segregation in *Brown v. Board of Education*, and the implications of that decision were beginning to become clear. In September 1957, nine African American students entering the previously all-white Central High School, in Little Rock, Arkansas, were greeted by a segregationist mob supported, per the order of the governor, by the state's National Guard. President Dwight Eisenhower was compelled to mobilize the 101st Airborne Division to enforce integration and uphold the law. Closer to home, Senator Harry Byrd—who lived just a few miles from the Old Chapel graveyard—had called for "massive resistance" to the Supreme Court's ruling. Engineering a plan to close rather than desegregate schools, Byrd and his aroused followers were transforming the 1957 Virginia governor's election into a referendum on race and, in a broader sense, on the morality and legitimacy of the white South's discriminatory assumptions and practices. In the face of such controversy and opprobrium, the plaque invoked a redemptive narrative of the southern past, one designed to reassure a society under siege that it was not just right but righteous. It proclaimed a virtuousness fashioned out of a fantastical history, a virtuousness to be reinforced by the generous act of noticing and remembering that the plaque was meant to be.

But why did my grandmother choose this graveyard and this statement to subdue her unease about the challenges to her taken-for-granted world—her unease, I imagine (and hope), about that very world itself? Why a plaque? It wasn't filling a gaping need. In both its language and its very existence, it protests too much.

Local circumstances had generated an additional motivation. The far end of the cemetery—the land beyond the plaque—had housed graves of enslaved people, though their locations and markers had all but disappeared. As a child, I remember hearing discussions among the adults in my family about how growing demand for graveyard plots had led to a consideration of extending the white cemetery into the area the slave cemetery occupied. This was not understood as sharing—and certainly not as integrating—the space. Instead, the older graves would essentially be erased from the landscape and from the minds and memories of the white church and its members.

But not from my grandmother's. The puzzling plaque represented her discomfort with (though not, significantly, any overt objection to) a plan to so callously disrespect the dead. She meant to remember and memorialize them with a permanent stone marker that would not rot and disappear. But as a white southern woman imbued with a conventional understanding of the past and its racial practices, she was memorializing a world that had never been. And she was perpetuating a narrative about race that has continued to poison Virginia and the nation more than a century and a half after slavery's end.

—————

Virginia has a long history to confront. Our nation's experience with slavery began there, when some 20 captive Africans arrived on a warship in Jamestown in 1619. Black bondage existed in Virginia for close to a century longer than black freedom has. Slavery made colonial Virginia prosperous, creating a plantation society founded on tobacco production, social and economic stratification, and unfree labor. It also produced a class of white owners whose daily witness to the degradations of bondage instilled in them a fierce devotion to their own freedom. They were determined to be the masters not just of their households, their estates, and their laborers, but also of their society, their polity, and their destiny. George Washington, Thomas Jefferson, James Madison, James Monroe, George Mason—slaveholders all. That so many of the Founding Fathers, including the leaders of the Revolution and the authors of the Declaration of Independence, the Constitution, and the Bill of Rights, were slaveholders is both an irony and a paradox. As Samuel Johnson remarked with scorn for the revolutionaries across the Atlantic: "How is it that we hear the loudest yelps for liberty among the drivers of negroes?"

But in another sense, as the historian Edmund Morgan argued so powerfully nearly half a century ago, slavery and freedom were not at odds, but integrally intertwined, even mutually constitutive. It was the unfreedom of 40 percent of Virginia's population that made the liberty of the rest imaginable as well as materially possible. The economic viability of both the colony and the new nation depended on slave labor. And so did the viability of the Revolution's political experiment and the Founders' republican vision. The Virginia gentry could countenance the extension of freedom to some men because it was withheld from others; the exclusion of a portion of the population from the polity, their subjugation and control, made possible the advocacy of equality for the rest. The nation conceived in liberty was also the nation conceived in slavery. The state of Virginia and the country it did so much to create were born out of a set of conflicting commitments that have destabilized the republic ever since. Yet the presence of this paradox at the heart of the Founders' vision is perhaps the good news, for freedom has had its own driving logic, has claimed its own agenda, has propelled us over time toward better angels.

In the earliest years of colonial Virginia, the nature and extent of bondage remained undefined. While most Africans were unfree laborers, some exercised liberties that later would be unthinkable. Distinctions between white indentured servants and bound black laborers became firm and rigid only over time. As the system of slavery was established during the 17th century, perpetual inherited unfreedom gradually became the exclusive fate of Africans and their descendants.

A century separated the legal codification of slavery in Virginia and the beginnings of the revolutionary movement. The Founders had no memory of a society without bondage and no experience of a world where blackness and degradation had not been conjoined— where white supremacy and black inferiority had not been enshrined in both law and culture. The racial definition of American slavery placed yet another contradiction at the new nation's heart, one that transcended the political difficulties of reconciling slavery and freedom. What did it mean to be human? This question posed a fundamental challenge to the execution of the laws: Was a slave a person or property? Could slaves be seen as having free will and thus legal accountability for their actions? Antebellum southern judges struggled with these inconsistencies. "A slave is not in the condition of a horse," a Tennessee judge insisted. "The laws [cannot] . . . deprive him of his many rights which are inherent in man." But a North Carolina judge disagreed, baldly underscoring the ultimate logic of slavery: "The power of the master must be absolute, to render the submission of the slave perfect . . . Such obedience is the consequence only of uncontrolled authority over the body." Commitment to a republican form of government was incompatible with the absolute power that defined the system of slavery.

This dilemma was more than a problem of law or government. It was about human identities, emotions, and values. A rallying cry of the

19th-century abolitionist movement would capture it well, with the words of a slave imploring: "Am I not a man and a brother?" The racial definitions of slavery required white southerners to resist that entreaty every day. Yet denial was not always possible. The force of common humanity could at times reach across the chains of the color line to generate compassion, guilt, doubt, and of course desire. Racism muted these human instincts, even as laws banning interracial sex, prohibiting manumission, and outlawing criticism of slavery acknowledged their existence. Thomas Jefferson's attraction to Sally Hemings, with whom he fathered five children, embodied the tragedy present at the very creation of American freedom.

White Virginians struggled with the idea of slavery even as they exercised its required cruelties and reaped its benefits. Jefferson observed that the existence of the institution was like having a "wolf by the ears." The threat it posed not just to the ideals of white Virginian society but to its very security and survival became vividly real in August 1831 when Nat Turner, an enslaved preacher from Southampton County, asserted his claim to freedom. The uprising he led resulted in the deaths of 55 white people as well as uncounted—some estimates indicate more than 100—black people attacked by both mobs and the militia called up to quell the revolt. More than a dozen captured rebels, including Turner himself, were executed.

The revolt provoked near hysteria among white people not just in Virginia but across the South. Could there be a Nat Turner in every household? Could black people, subjugated and assumed to be inferior, share their masters' longing for freedom and possess the fearlessness to try to attain it? When the Virginia legislature convened just weeks after Turner's execution, the lawmakers took up the future of slavery in unprecedented debates that reflected the tensions at its core. In the words of one delegate advocating slavery's elimination, "It is ruinous to whites—retards improvement—roots out an industrious population." Another added that it threatened to bring about more such "melancholy occurrences" as "the tragical massacre at Southampton." But nearly all agreed that emancipation would somehow have to be linked to deportation and African colonization, because living with a population of freed black people was unthinkable. The debates were never about black justice, but about white safety and prosperity.

Slavery did not end in Virginia in 1832. It would take three more decades and hundreds of thousands of lives lost to bondage, and later to war. Indeed, the debates in the legislature yielded new laws intended to strengthen slavery's hold. Yet these discussions demonstrated that white Virginians felt profoundly and persistently uneasy about a way of life the state had known for two centuries.

In the aftermath of the Virginia debates and the doubts and divisions they exposed, voices in the state and beyond began to defend slavery more vigorously. A proliferation of "positive good" arguments insisted that the institution was not just acceptable and justifiable but the best possible arrangement economically, politically, and even morally. Virginia could no longer afford the kind of ambivalence Jefferson had exhibited, proclaiming slavery an evil yet living on its fruits. As the historian Eugene Genovese put it: "One generation might be able to oppose slavery and favor everything it made possible, but the next had to choose sides." Nat Turner had made that choice seem more urgent. By the 1830s, slavery was in many ways weakening in Virginia, with the decline of the tobacco economy and the sale and forced migration of thousands of enslaved people from Virginia to the cotton economy of the Deep South. Yet Virginians played prominent roles in slavery's emerging ideological defense.

And it would not be long before Virginians would be asked to choose sides again. As secession fever mounted across the South in the wake of Abraham Lincoln's election in November 1860, Virginia remained cautious. South Carolina rushed headlong into separation from the union, voting to secede before year's end, but the Virginia convention called to consider the issue resisted strenuous appeals from its neighbors to join a pro-slavery Confederacy. Virginia's decision was all-important, for without the Old Dominion and its human, industrial, and agricultural resources, the new nation had little chance of success. Virginia's white population of 1.1 million was the largest of any southern state, and it ended up supplying the most soldiers to the Confederacy. But some advocates for secession both within and beyond the state saw another element at stake in Virginia's position: They worried that if Virginia did not emphatically embrace the slave republic, it was likely to abandon slavery altogether in the decades to come. These observers noted the emergence of mixed agriculture in northern Virginia, an economic system increasingly like that of the Middle States rather than the Deep South. And they noted as well the decreasing proportion of slaves in the population as Virginia masters sold their unprofitable bondsmen south to supply labor for the cotton plantations of Alabama, Mississippi, Louisiana, and Texas.

Yet after initially voting against secession in the early spring of 1861, Virginia responded to the firing on Fort Sumter and Lincoln's call for an army of 75,000 men to march against the South by declaring itself all in for the Confederate cause. And Virginia did not just join the Confederacy; it became the capital and the chief battleground. The decision would come at enormous cost. The war would destroy lands, lives, and the world white Virginians intended to preserve.

————————

The Civil War destroyed the legal foundations of slavery, but the racism that had reinforced it for so long persisted. Emancipation meant black Virginians were no longer property, but white people pushed back forcefully against change, bringing an end to Reconstruction and retaining control over social, economic, and political arrangements in the state. The North's commitment to overturning the old order of the South waned in the face of white intransigence, and a new system of subjugation and injustice emerged to take slavery's place.

White Virginians of the late 19th and early 20th centuries congratulated themselves on the harmony of race relations within the state. Political and business leaders disavowed the race-baiting that emerged farther south and endeavored to maintain a system of paternalistic control in order to ensure the perpetuation of racial supremacy. Force could be held in reserve if black people accepted their assigned roles within an enduring racial hierarchy. Yet in its essence, this was a system that rested on spoken and unspoken threats of coercion and violence. Between the end of Reconstruction and 1950, 84 lynchings occurred in Virginia—significantly fewer than in any other southern state, but more than sufficient to transmit the message of racial terror.

Extralegal violence was one guarantor of order, or at least the order the white South deemed necessary. But Virginia's white elite preferred to uphold its control with the seemingly more legitimate and defensible instruments of the law. In Virginia, as across the South, newly devised Black Codes regulated postwar social arrangements, and vagrancy laws preserved white power to coerce labor. The public whipping post—used overwhelmingly for black offenders—marked disturbing continuities with slavery's practices. Tellingly, it provoked not just strong black opposition across the state, but debate among white people who worried that its highly visible brutality undermined the idealized narrative of racial tranquility. In 1898, the Virginia legislature at last voted to abolish the whipping post.

Yet just as one instrument of violence and coercion was abandoned, others took its place. A modernized form of unfreedom, the penitentiary imprisoned black people at rates dramatically higher than the rates for white people. In 1893, one in every 5,000 white Virginians was incarcerated; the figure for black Virginians was 7.5 out of every 5,000. And African Americans were almost exclusively the victims of the emerging convict-leasing system, which rented prisoners to owners of Virginia's quarries, mines, canals, and railroads. It has been called slavery by another name.

For a time during Reconstruction and the years that followed, freedmen in Virginia voted and even served in the legislature, but by the turn of the century, a variety of measures, including literacy tests and poll taxes, worked to exclude African Americans from the ballot box. A system of racial separation that came to be known as Jim Crow was set firmly in place, segregating schools, transportation, and public entertainment, and forbidding interracial marriage. In 1896, the Supreme Court in *Plessy v. Ferguson* proclaimed its approval. Yet this new "separate but equal" doctrine as the supposed logic and justification for segregation represented just another in a long line of distortions and deceptions the white South embraced. "Separate" was—and was designed to be—unequal. That was the point.

But elite white Virginians created a narrative of an invented past and a distorted portrait of their own time to reassure themselves of the justice of their social order and of their own benevolence. The cult of the Lost Cause embraced an apocryphal history suffused with nostalgia for a world of valorous Confederates, kindly masters, and contented slaves. And it mischaracterized the present, extolling the "Virginia Way," a distinctive form of Jim Crow in which blacks and whites lived peaceably together in lives of "separation by consent," in the words of Douglas Southall Freeman, a Richmond newspaper editor and renowned Robert E. Lee biographer. Freeman acknowledged that this was a social order designed to perpetuate "the continued and unchallengeable dominance of Southern whites," who, he told his readers, would work to provide assurance of safety and security to black Virginians in return for their acquiescence in the status quo. "Southern Negroes," he explained, "have far more to gain by conforming than by rebellion . . . by deserving rather than demanding more." Elite white Virginians had inherited a legacy of gentility accompanied by the imperatives of noblesse oblige; Virginia's black people, in turn, were "inherently of a higher type than those of any other state." Nowhere else, Freeman insisted, "are the Negroes more encouraged through the influence of friendship for and confidence in them, on the part of whites, to be law abiding and industrious." But never to claim equality.

———————

I grew up in that Virginia, on a 500-acre farm a mile and a half from the town of Millwood, home in the 1950s to about 200 people, most of them black. My childhood friends—all white—lived on surrounding farms like ours. Almost all the properties had names, and although our house dated from the early 19th century, many had stood since the time of the American Revolution. Saratoga had been built by Daniel Morgan in the 1780s to commemorate the 1777 battlefield victory. Carter Hall, Pagebrook, and Long Branch were all erected after the

Revolution by scions of the Tidewater gentry. In Millwood itself, most African Americans lived in dwellings that lacked running water.

This was a world in which silences distorted lives, and falsehoods perpetuated structures of power rooted in centuries of injustice. This was still the Virginia of the poll tax and of segregated schools. Every adult black person I knew worked for white people as either a laborer or a domestic. Nevertheless, this was not the Deep South. The myth of "consent" required that white people be able to claim—and convince themselves—that black people happily accepted their assigned places. Daily life did not include colored and white signs on water fountains or in waiting rooms. In my small rural community, people just knew. Or learned. Even my own house was segregated. The African Americans who cooked and cleaned ate in the kitchen. We ate in the dining room, except for Sunday supper, when the workers had the evening off and my mother, who could scarcely cook at all, contrived to produce a meal, while we all longed for Monday and the cook's return. Behind the kitchen was a separate servants' bathroom. When I used it once, my mother reprimanded me for invading their privacy.

I never witnessed physical cruelty toward black people in my community; I never heard the N-word. Prejudice was hidden beneath a surface of politeness and civility that scarcely masked the assumption of superiority, of greater intelligence, of entitlement. Amused condescension, mockery cast as patronizing affection, often inflected white attitudes toward "the colored people." Yet as I think back, there was a nervousness about the laughter, a need for mutual reassurance as the adults around me recounted tales of people so close at hand yet so mysteiously and frighteningly different from themselves.

Racial custom was carefully yet obliquely taught. It encompassed all the contradictions that had confronted white Virginians for centuries. We grew up in the constant company of human beings who were central to our lives, yet we somehow came to understand that an unspoken hierarchy required our distance—both physical and emotional—from them. An African American man who worked for my family for decades did everything from shining shoes to mowing the lawn to driving us around the county—to school, to piano lessons, to scout meetings. He was as present in my childhood as my brothers and my parents. He quizzed us on state capitals and the order of the presidents, made sure we remembered our lunch boxes and homework, and told us jokes and riddles. He always spoke not of "driving" us here or there, but of "carrying" us, a usage that to my child's ears communicated a kind of concerned protectiveness. But I scarcely knew anything about his own life. He had a daughter not far from my age, but I rarely saw her, because she of course went to the segregated black school. I never even knew where it was.

We had—and were taught we deserved—better houses, better education, a better future. Yet at the very same time, we were learning in school that our nation was founded on the belief that all men are created equal; we were hearing in our all-white church that we were all the same before God. "Join hands, disciples of the faith," the hymn commanded, "what'er your race may be. / All children of the living God are surely kin to me."

For many white southerners of my generation, a life-defining question has been how long it took us to notice. When did the contradictions become troubling? When did they become unbearable? What was the moment of epiphany, the circumstance that made the inconsistencies undeniable? When did it become imperative to confront the legacies of slavery and segregation, to be honest with ourselves and one another and purge the untruths that, like malignancies, had permeated our society and our lives? "It's that obliviousness, the unexamined assumption, that so pains me now," the photographer Sally Mann has written about her 1950s Virginia childhood. "How could I not have wondered, not have asked." For her, going north to school and encountering the writings of William Faulkner

> threw wide the door of my ignorant childhood, and the future, the heartbroken future filled with hitherto unasked questions, strolled easefully in. It wounded me, then and there, with the great sadness and tragedy of our American life, with the truth of all that I had not seen, had not known, and had not asked.

For many, the civil-rights movement and the racist pushback to it served as a wake-up call, forcing an end to silences, exposing the violence on which Jim Crow rested, and removing the veneer of timeless inevitability that whites had strived to create. And a growing assertiveness by black Virginians made it ever more difficult to maintain the fiction of separation and subjugation "by consent."

I was 9 years old when the news reports about "massive resistance" and battles over segregation made me suddenly realize that it was not a matter of accident that my school was all-white. I wrote an outraged letter to President Eisenhower—outraged because this wasn't just, but also outraged that I only now understood, that I had been somehow implicated in this without my awareness. I have wondered whether I was motivated in part by my growing recognition of my own disadvantage as a girl whose mother insisted I learn to accept that I lived in a "man's world." I resented that my three brothers were not expected to wear itchy organdy dresses and white gloves, or learn to curtsy, or sit decorously, or accept innumerable other constraints on their freedom. I was becoming acutely attuned to what was and wasn't *fair*. And because my parents seemed to take for granted that this was both a white world and a man's world, I took it upon myself to appeal—without telling them—to a higher power: "Please Mr. Eisenhower please try and have schools and other things accept colored people," I wrote. "Colored people aren't given a chance . . . So what if their skin is black. They still have feelings but most of all are God's people." And I acknowledged the accident of my own privilege: "If I painted my face black I wouldn't be let in any public schools etc." I seem to have figured out "etc." before I recognized the realities of the racial arrangements that surrounded me. And, curiously, I framed what I had recognized as the contingency of race and the arbitrariness of my own entitlement by invoking blackface.

Many moments in the years between *Brown* and the Civil Rights Act of 1964 and the Voting Rights Act of 1965 imposed new truth on white Americans. It was a fundamental strategy of the civil-rights movement to create such occasions. As Martin Luther King Jr. explained, peaceful demonstrators would force the poison out and make it visible. The beating of the Freedom Riders in 1961, the jailing of child protesters in Birmingham in 1963, the clubbing and gassing of John Lewis and other marchers on the bridge in Selma in 1965—all were vividly displayed to the American public in a manner TV had made newly possible. These horrors challenged complacency and compelled many Americans to ask themselves, "Which Side Are You On?"

———————

But we know now, half a century later, that none of this was even close to enough to overturn centuries of racial injustice. By the time of King's murder, in April 1968, little sense of consoling moral clarity remained. King himself had embraced controversial new positions—taking his protests into the North, insisting on confronting economic inequality, and speaking out against the Vietnam War. Many African American activists had broken with King, advocating Black Power rather than racial reconciliation, abandoning nonviolence, and denouncing King as an accommodationist. The nation has forgotten that a poll taken in 1966 revealed that nearly two-thirds of Americans had an unfavorable opinion of the civil-rights leader.

His death muted voices of criticism and opposition and punctuated the end of an era: Montgomery to Memphis. Like King himself, those years were transformed into a myth of national redemption—and, dangerously, of work complete. Now that the era seemed safely over, no longer a threat to the status quo, we could celebrate it. The story of the civil-rights movement became, as Julian Bond commented with no little bitterness: "Rosa sat down, Martin stood up, then the white folks saw the light and saved the day."

Bond was right that the movement compelled many white people to begin to see the light. He was also correct that there remained a great deal we had scarcely begun to see, much less do something about. But the emergence of the oversimplified and consoling narrative of the civil-rights movement gave many white Americans permission to not look further. The nation retreated into a kind of post-'60s fatigue, as Richard Nixon and Ronald Reagan ascended to office with the support of a not-so-silent majority that believed black people had progressed quite far enough. Many white Virginians were comforted to return to the traditional narrative of racial harmony, now imbued with far greater legitimacy after the drama—and the accomplishments—of the civil-rights movement.

BEING BLACK IN AMERICA CAN BE HAZARDOUS TO YOUR HEALTH

by Olga Khazan

[JULY/AUGUST 2018]

"Permission to not look further"—Drew Gilpin Faust's phrase applies to what Americans deliberately choose not to see, but also to what we see and acknowledge only in the abstract. The pervasiveness of racial inequality is not news. It saturates the educational system, the health-care system, the criminal-justice system. It affects the availability and location of housing. The list is long. All of this is revealed—but, in a way, also hidden— by a scrim of statistics.

To put a human face on the statistics, *Atlantic* staff writer Olga Khazan drew an intimate portrait of Kiarra Boulware, a 27-year-old African American woman with a binge-eating disorder. The article, presented here in abridged form, traces a young life that intersects with racial inequality at every turn. The central focus is medical. Across the United States, African Americans have a lower life expectancy than whites. In Baltimore, where Boulware lives, and in other segregated cities, this gap is as much as 20 years. Boulware's struggle to get better shows why.

One morning this past September, Kiarra Boulware boarded the 26 bus to Baltimore's Bon Secours Hospital, where she would seek help for the most urgent problem in her life: the 200-some excess pounds she carried on her 5-foot-2-inch frame.

To Kiarra, the weight sometimes felt like a great burden, and at other times like just another fact of life. She had survived a childhood marred by death, drugs, and violence. She had recently gained control over her addiction to alcohol, which, last summer, had brought her to a residential recovery center in the city's Sandtown neighborhood, made famous by the Freddie Gray protests in 2015. But she still struggled with binge eating—so much so that she would eat entire plates of quesadillas or mozzarella sticks in minutes.

As the bus rattled past rowhouses and corner stores, Kiarra told me she hadn't yet received the CPAP breathing machine she needed for her sleep apnea. The extra fat seemed to constrict her airways while she slept, and a sleep study had shown that she stopped breathing 40 times an hour. She remembered one doctor saying, "I'm scared you're going to die in your sleep." In the haze of alcoholism, she'd never followed up on the test. Now doctors at Bon Secours were trying to order the machine for her, but insurance hurdles had gotten in the way.

Kiarra's weight brought an assortment of old-person problems to her 27-year-old life: sleep apnea, diabetes, and menstrual dysregulation, which made her worry she would never have children. For a while, she'd ignored these issues. Day to day, her size mostly made it hard to shop for clothes. But the severity of her situation sank in when a diabetic friend had to have a toe amputated. Kiarra visited the woman in the hospital. She saw her tears and her red, bandaged foot, and resolved not to become an amputee herself.

Kiarra arrived at the hospital early and waited in the cafeteria. Bon Secours is one of several world-class hospitals in Baltimore. Another, Johns Hopkins Hospital, is in some respects the birthplace of modern American medicine, having invented everything from the medical residency to the surgical glove. But of course not even the best hospitals in America can keep you from getting sick in the first place.

It was lunchtime, but Kiarra didn't have any cash—her job, working the front desk at the recovery center where she lived, paid a stipend of just $150 a week. When she did have money, she often sought comfort in fast food. But when her cash and food stamps ran out, she sometimes had what she called "hungry nights," when she went to bed without having eaten anything all day.

When I'd first met Kiarra, a few months earlier, I'd been struck by how upbeat she seemed. Her recovery center—called Maryland Community Health Initiatives, but known in the neighborhood as Penn North—sits on a grimy street crowded with men selling drugs. Some of the center's clients, fresh off their habits, seemed withdrawn, or even morose. Kiarra, though, had the bubbly demeanor of a student-council president.

She described the rough neighborhoods where she'd grown up as fun and "familylike." She said that although neither of her parents had been very involved when she was a kid, her grandparents had provided a loving home. Regarding her diabetes, she told me she was "grateful that it's reversible." After finishing her addiction treatment, she planned to reenroll in college and move into a dorm.

Now, though, a much more anxious Kiarra sat before her doctor, a young white man named Tyler Gray, who began by advising Kiarra to get a Pap smear.

"Do we have to do it today?" she asked.

"Is there something you're concerned about or nervous about?" Gray asked.

Kiarra was nervous about a lot of things. She "deals by not dealing," as she puts it, but lately she'd had to deal with so much. "Ever since the diabetes thing, I hate hearing I have something else," she said softly, beginning to cry. "I've been fat for what seems like so long, and now I get all the fat problems."

"I don't want to be fat," she added, "but I don't know how to not be fat."

Kiarra's struggles with her weight are imbued with this sense, that getting thin is a mystery she might never solve, that diet secrets are literally secret. On a Sunday, she might diligently make a meal plan for the week, only to find herself reaching for Popeyes fried chicken by Wednesday. She blames herself for her poor health—as do many of the people I met in her community, where obesity, diabetes, and heart disease are ubiquitous. They said they'd made bad choices. They used food, and sometimes drugs, to soothe their pain. But these individual failings are only part of the picture.

In Baltimore, a 20-year gap in life expectancy exists between the city's poor, largely African American neighborhoods and its wealthier, whiter areas. A baby born in Cheswolde, in Baltimore's far-northwest corner, can expect to live until age 87. Nine miles away in Clifton-Berea, near where *The Wire* was filmed, the life expectancy is 67, roughly the same as that of Rwanda, and 12 years shorter than the American average. Similar disparities exist in other segregated cities, such as Philadelphia and Chicago.

These cities are among the most extreme examples of a national phenomenon: Across the United States, black people suffer disproportionately from some of the most devastating health problems, from cancer deaths and diabetes to maternal mortality and preterm births. Although the racial disparity in early death has narrowed in recent decades, black people have the life expectancy, nationwide, that white people had in the 1980s—about three years shorter than the current white life expectancy. African Americans face a greater risk of death at practically every stage of life.

Except in the case of a few specific ailments, such as non-diabetic kidney disease, scientists have largely failed to identify genetic differences that might explain racial health disparities. The major underlying causes, many scientists now believe, are social and environmental forces that affect African Americans more than most other groups.

To better understand how these forces work, I spent nearly a year reporting in Sandtown and other parts of Baltimore. What I found in Kiarra's struggle was the story of how one person's efforts to get better—imperfect as they may have been—were made vastly more difficult by a daunting series of obstacles. But it is also a bigger story, of how African Americans became stuck in profoundly unhealthy neighborhoods, and of how the legacy of racism can literally take years off their lives. Far from being a relic of the past, America's racist and segregationist history continues to harm black people in the most intimate of ways—seeping into their lungs, their blood, even their DNA.

When Kiarra was a little girl, Baltimore was, as it is today, mired in violence, drugs, and poverty. In 1996, the city had the highest rate of drug-related emergency-room visits in the nation and one of the country's highest homicide rates.

With her father in and out of jail for robbery and drug dealing, Kiarra and her mother, three siblings, and three cousins piled into her grandmother's home. It was a joyous but chaotic household. Kiarra describes her grandmother as "God's assistant"—a deeply religious woman who, despite a house bursting with hungry mouths, would still make an extra dinner for the addicts on the block. Kiarra's mother, meanwhile, was "the hood princess," a woman who would do her hair just to go to the grocery store. She was a teen mom, like her own mother had been.

Many facets of Kiarra's youth—the fact that her parents weren't together, her father's incarceration, the guns on the corners—are what researchers consider "adverse childhood experiences," or ACEs, stressful events early in life that can cause health problems in adulthood. An abnormally large proportion of the children in Baltimore—nearly a third—have two or more ACEs. People with four or more ACEs are seven times as likely to be alcoholics as people with no ACEs, and twice as likely to have heart disease. One study found that six or more ACEs can cut life expectancy by as much as 20 years. Kiarra had at least six.

She and others I interviewed recall the inner-city Baltimore of their youth fondly. Everyone lived crammed together with siblings and cousins, but people looked out for one another; neighbors hosted back-to-school cookouts every year, and people took pride in their homes. Kiarra ran around with the other kids on the block until her grandma called her in each night at 8 o'clock. She made the honor roll in fifth grade and got to speak in front of the whole class. She read novels by Sister Souljah and wrote short stories in longhand.

Yet Kiarra also describes some jarring incidents. When she was 8, she heard a loud *bop bop bop* outside and ran out to find her stepbrother lying in the street, dead. One friend died of asthma in middle school; another went to jail, then hanged himself. (Other people I spoke with around Penn North and other recovery facilities had similarly traumatic experiences. It seemed like every second person I met told me they had been molested as a child, and even more said their family members had struggled with addiction.)

Kiarra told me she got pregnant by a friend when she was 12, and gave birth to a boy when she was 13. Within a year, the baby died unexpectedly, and Kiarra was so traumatized that she ended up spending more than a month in a psychiatric hospital. When she came home, her boyfriend physically and sexually abused her. He "slapped me so hard, I was seeing stars," she said.

She took solace in eating, a common refuge for victims of abuse. One 2013 study of thousands of women found that those who had been severely physically or sexually abused as children had nearly double the risk of food addiction. Kiarra ate "everything, anything," she said, "mostly bad foods, junk food, pizza," along with chicken boxes—the fried-chicken-and-fries combos slung by Baltimore's carryout joints.

At first, she thought the extra weight looked good on her. Then she started feeling fat. Eventually, she said, "it was like, *Fuck it. I'm fat.*" As her high-school graduation approached, she tried on the white gown she'd bought just weeks earlier and realized that it was already too tight.

Kiarra didn't know many college-educated people, but she wanted to go to Spelman, a historically black college in Georgia, and join a sorority. Her family talked her out of applying, she said. Instead, she enrolled in one local college after another, but she kept dropping out, sometimes to help her siblings with their children and other times because she simply lost interest. After accumulating $30,000 in student loans, she had only a year's worth of credits.

So Kiarra put college on hold and worked at Kmart and as a home health aide—solid jobs but, as she likes to say, "not my ceiling." She longed for a purpose. Sometimes, she had an inkling that she was meant to be an important person; she would picture herself giving a speech to an auditorium full of people. But she remained depressed, stuck, and, increasingly, obese.

She began doing ecstasy, and, later, downing a pint of vodka a day. She remembers coming to her home-health-aide job drunk one time and leaving a patient on the toilet. "Did you forget me?" the woman asked, half an hour later. Kiarra broke down crying.

Soon after, she checked into Penn North for her first try at recovery. This past year's attempt was her third.

Sandtown is 97 percent black, and half of its families live in poverty. Its homicide rate is more than double that of the rest of the city, and last year about 8 percent of the deaths there were due to drug and alcohol overdose. Still, its top killers are heart disease and cancer, which African Americans nationwide are more likely to die from than other groups are.

The way African Americans became trapped in Baltimore's poorest— and least healthy—neighborhoods mirrors their history in the ghettos of other major cities. It began with outright bans on their presence in certain neighborhoods in the early 1900s and continued through the 2000s, when policy makers, lenders, and fellow citizens employed subtler forms of discrimination.

In the early 1900s, blacks in Baltimore disproportionately suffered from tuberculosis, so much so that one area not far from Penn North was known as the "lung block." In 1907, an investigator hired by local charities described what she saw in Meyer Court, a poor area in Baltimore. The contents of an outdoor toilet "were found streaming down the center of this narrow court to the street beyond," she wrote. The smell within one house was "'sickening' . . . No provision of any kind is made for supplying the occupants of this court with water." Yet one cause, the housing investigator concluded, was the residents' "low standards and absence of ideals."

When blacks tried to flee to better areas, some had their windows smashed and their steps smeared with tar. In 1910, a Yale-educated black lawyer named George McMechen moved into a house in a white

neighborhood, and Baltimore reacted by adopting a segregation ordinance that *The New York Times* called "the most pronounced 'Jim Crow'
measure on record." Later, neighborhood associations urged homeowners to sign covenants promising never to sell to African Americans.

For much of the 20th century, the Federal Housing Administration
declined to insure mortgages for blacks, who instead had to buy homes
by signing contracts with speculators who demanded payments that,
in many cases, amounted to most of the buyer's income. (As a result,
many black families never reaped the gains of homeownership—a key
source of Americans' wealth.) Housing discrimination persisted well
beyond the Jim Crow years, as neighborhood associations rejected proposals to build low-income housing in affluent suburbs. In the 1990s,
house flippers would buy up homes in Baltimore's predominantly black
neighborhoods and resell them to unsuspecting first-time home buyers
at inflated prices by using falsified documents. The subsequent foreclo-
sures are a major reason so many properties in the city sit vacant today.

Some of Baltimore's rowhouses are so long-forsaken, they have trees
growing through the windows. These dilapidated homes are in themselves harmful to people's health. Neighborhoods with poorly maintained houses or a large number of abandoned properties, for instance,
face a high risk of mouse infestation. Every year, more than 5,000 Baltimore children go to the emergency room for an asthma attack—and
according to research from Johns Hopkins, mouse allergen is the biggest environmental factor in those attacks.

The allergen, found in mouse urine, travels through the air on dust,
and Johns Hopkins researchers have found high levels of it on most of
the beds of poor Baltimore kids they have tested. When kids inhale the
allergen, it can spark inflammation and mucus buildup in their lungs,
making them cough and wheeze. These attacks can cause long-term
harm: Children with asthma are more likely to be obese and in overall
poorer health as adults. Getting rid of the mice requires sealing up
cracks and holes in the house—a process that can cost thousands of
dollars, given the state of many Baltimore homes.

The mice, of course, are just one symptom of the widespread neglect
that can set in once neighborhoods become as segregated as Baltimore's

are. One study estimated that, in the year 2000, racial segregation caused 176,000 deaths—about as many as were caused by strokes.

———

Kiarra has trouble concentrating sometimes, and she thinks the reason might be that she and her brother were exposed to lead from old paint. When Kiarra was 6, her grandmother heard that a girl living in another property owned by the same landlord had been hospitalized. She took Kiarra to get tested. The results showed that the concentration of lead in her blood was more than six times the level the Centers for Disease Control and Prevention considers elevated—an amount that can irreversibly lower IQ and reduce attention span. Kiarra, too, was hospitalized, for a month.

Scientists and industry experts knew in the 19th century that lead paint was dangerous. "Lead is a merciless poison," an executive with a Michigan lead-paint company admitted in a book in 1892. It "gradually affects the nerves and organs of circulation to such a degree that it is next to impossible to restore them to their normal condition." But as late as the 1940s and '50s, trade groups representing companies that made lead products, including the Lead Industries Association, promoted the use of lead paint in homes and successfully lobbied for the repeal of restrictions on that use. Lead-paint companies published coloring books and advised their salesmen to "not forget the children— some day they may be customers." According to *The Baltimore Sun*, a study in 1956 found that lead-poisoned children in the slums of Baltimore had six times as much lead in their systems as severely exposed workers who handled lead for a living.

In speeches and publications, Lead Industries Association officials cast childhood lead poisoning as vanishingly rare. When they did acknowledge the problem, they blamed "slum" children for chewing on wood surfaces—"gnaw-ledge," as Manfred Bowditch, the group's health-and-safety director, called it—and their "ignorant parents" for allowing them to do so. In a letter to the Baltimore health department, Bowditch called the lead-poisoned toddlers "little human rodents."

Even after stricter regulations came along, landlords in segregated neighborhoods—as well as the city's own public-housing agency—neglected properties, allowing old paint to chip and leaded dust to accumulate. Some landlords, seeking to avoid the expense of renovating homes and the risk of tenant lawsuits, refused to rent to families with children, since they would face the greatest risk from lead exposure. Poor families feared that if they complained about lead, they might be evicted.

Partly because of Maryland's more rigorous screening, the state's lead-poisoning rate for children was 15 times the national average in the '90s; the majority of the poisoned children lived in the poor areas of Baltimore. In some neighborhoods, 70 percent of children had been exposed to lead. The city's under-resourced agencies failed to address the problem. Clogged by landlords who hid behind shell companies, Baltimore's lead-paint enforcement system had ground to a halt by the time Kiarra was poisoned. According to *Tapping Into* The Wire, a book co-authored by Peter L. Beilenson, the city's former health commissioner, Baltimore didn't bring a single lead-paint enforcement action against landlords in the '90s. (A subsequent crackdown on landlords has lowered lead-poisoning rates dramatically.)

When Kiarra was 14, her family sued their landlord for damages, but their lawyer dropped the case because the landlord claimed he had no money and no insurance with which to compensate them. Kiarra remembers her grandmother not wanting to give up, demanding of the lawyer, "What do you mean there's nothing you can do?"—only to get lost in a tangle of legal rules she didn't fully understand.

Fried food has long been Kiarra's legal high—cheap, easily acquired, something to brighten the gloomiest day. It is also one of the few luxuries around.

Predominantly black neighborhoods tend to become what researchers call "food swamps," or areas where fast-food joints outnumber healthier options. (Food deserts, by contrast, simply lack grocery stores.) One study in New York found that as the number of African Americans who lived in a given area increased, so did the distance to the nearest clothing store, pharmacy, electronics store, office-supply store. Meanwhile, one type of establishment drew nearer: fast-food restaurants.

That's not a coincidence. After the riots of the 1960s, the federal government began promoting the growth of small businesses in minority neighborhoods as a way to ease racial tensions. "What we need is to get private enterprise into the ghetto, and put the people of the ghetto into private enterprises," President Richard Nixon said around the time he created the Office of Minority Business Enterprise, in 1969. As Chin Jou, a senior lecturer at the University of Sydney, describes in her book, *Supersizing Urban America*, fast-food companies were some of the most eager entrants into this "ghetto" market.

Fast-food restaurants spent the next few decades "rushing into urban markets," as one *Detroit News* report put it, seeking out these areas' "untapped labor force" and "concentrated audience." In the 1990s, the federal government gave fast-food restaurants financial incentives to open locations in inner cities, including in Baltimore. The urban expansion made business sense. "The ethnic population is better for us than the general market," Sidney Feltenstein, Burger King's executive vice president of brand strategy, explained to the *Miami Herald* in 1992. "They tend to have larger families, and that means larger checks." (Supermarket chains didn't share this enthusiasm; in part because the widespread use of food stamps causes an uneven flow of customers throughout the month, they have largely avoided expanding in poor areas.)

Fast-food executives looked for ways to entice black customers. Burger King made ads featuring Shaft. KFC redecorated locations in cities like Baltimore to cater to stereotypically black tastes, and piped "rap, rhythm and blues, and soul music" into the restaurants, Jou writes. "Employees were given new Afro-centric uniforms consisting of kente cloth dashikis." A study from 2005 found that TV programs aimed at African Americans feature more fast-food advertisements than other shows do, as well as more commercials for soda and candy. Black children today see twice as many soda and candy ads as white children do.

Before the rise of fast food and processed foods, many low-income black families grew their own food and ate lots of grains and beans. In

1965, one study found, poor and middle-income blacks ate health-ier—though often more meager—diets than rich whites did. But over the next few decades, the price of meat, junk food, and simple carbo-hydrates plummeted, while the price of vegetables rose. By the mid-'90s, 28 percent of African Americans were considered by the U.S. Department of Agriculture to have a "poor" diet, compared with just 16 percent of whites.

The diets of low-income people have changed dramatically. The marketing and franchising onslaught worked.

THE UNDOCUMENTED AGENT

by Jeremy Raff

[FEBRUARY 2020]

The human cost of certain social arrangements—how we treat our sick, run our schools, police our borders—is impossible to encompass. Numbers are bloodless, and flesh-and-blood stories are by definition anecdotal. Multiply an anecdote—the story of Kiarra Boulware, say—by a thousand or a million, and you are back in the kingdom of data. What stories do possess is an ability to lodge in the seams and cracks of consciousness. They also possess an ability to expose the seams and cracks—and gaping holes—in the way we conduct the nation's business.

The experience of Raul Rodriguez, one of the more than 50,000 officers who patrol the border and the interior of the United States, provides such a story. After spending nearly two decades facilitating deportations as a Customs and Border Protection officer, Rodriguez discovered that he was not a U.S. citizen. He had been born across the southern border, in Mexico, to parents who told him that he had in fact been born in the United States. Rodriguez had lived in the U.S. with relatives since early childhood. He went to high school in Texas, served for five years in the Navy, and then joined the Immigration and Naturalization Service. In 2007, he had received a national award for integrity in the line of duty. Now, suddenly, documentation had surfaced that revealed his true background— putting Rodriguez himself at risk of deportation. His plight was described by Jeremy Raff, at the time a documentary-video producer at *The Atlantic*. Raff was raised in the border town of McAllen, Texas.

One afternoon in April 2018, Raul Rodriguez was working on his computer at the U.S. Customs and Border Protection office in Los Indios, Texas, when two managers entered the building. *Somebody must be in trouble*, he thought. The managers usually arrived in pairs when they needed a witness.

For nearly two decades, Rodriguez had searched for people and drugs hidden in cargo waiting to get into the United States. He was proud of his work as a Customs and Border Protection officer; it gave him stability and a sense of purpose. Even in the spring of 2018, when public scrutiny of CBP began to intensify—the agency had officially started separating children from their parents—Rodriguez remained committed to his job. Though he wasn't separating any families at the border, he'd canceled the visas and initiated the deportations of thousands of people in his years of service.

"Hey, Raulito," one of the managers said, calling him over. Rodriguez walked past agents who were trying to look busy on their computers. Just two years from being eligible to retire, Rodriguez says he had an unblemished record. He couldn't imagine what the managers wanted.

Rodriguez had been crossing bridges at the border since his parents, who were Mexican, had sent him to live with relatives in Texas when he was 5 years old. He'd wanted to stay in Mexico, but his mother insisted that he go: He was a United States citizen. She'd given birth to him just across the border in hopes that he would have a better life, and it was time for him to seize that opportunity. He started first grade at a public school in Mission, Texas. From then on, he saw his parents only on school breaks.

As a child, he'd admired immigration agents' crisp uniforms and air of authority. When he grew into a teenager, though, agents began to question him more aggressively, doubting his citizenship despite his Texas-issued birth certificate. He chalked it up to simple prejudice, no different from the white students at Sharyland High who provoked him to fistfights by calling him "wetback." He decided he'd defy their stereotypes by one day becoming an agent himself. He would enforce the law, but without demeaning people as he did it.

Rodriguez joined the Navy in 1992. As a recruit, he cleaned floors and toilets, cooked, and drove a bus. Visiting his parents in Mexico, he wore his uniform. They didn't say they were proud, but the looks on their faces made him feel as though growing up in Texas really had been worthwhile. And whenever he headed back across the border in uniform, he approached the agents on the bridge and thought: *Now they're going to have to accept me as an American.*

But on that day in Los Indios in 2018, one of Rodriguez's managers slid an envelope across the desk. Rodriguez remembers reading: "You are no longer a law-enforcement officer, pending further investigation." His gun and badge were confiscated without explanation. He left the building in a stupor.

Days later, he sat down with investigators at a federal building in nearby McAllen, Texas. They told him his career in immigration and his military service before that—his identity as a veteran, an agent, and an American—were based on a lie. His United States citizenship was fraudulent. He was an undocumented immigrant himself.

———

Rodriguez joined the Immigration and Naturalization Service, a CBP predecessor agency, in 2000, after five years in the Navy. Soon after he graduated from training, Rodriguez's parents hosted a cookout at their home, in the rural outskirts of Matamoros, Mexico. His wife chatted with his mom and sisters, while their two young children, Daira and Raul Jr., played with their cousins. *Corridos* played on the stereo and fajitas sizzled on the barbecue in front of the adobe house. Hurricanes had flattened similar structures nearby, but his family's home still stood, because Rodriguez had refinished the walls with mud and grass every other year during school breaks.

His father, Margarito, had tutored Rodriguez in a strict vision of right and wrong. A farmer who wore a sweat-stained cowboy hat and a polyester shirt, Margarito kept big bags of cash at home earmarked for his agricultural co-op members' hospital bills and funeral costs. He made sure Rodriguez understood that he never skimmed off the communal funds, though he could have gotten away with it. While other members bought new cars with stolen money, Margarito walked around town on foot asking for rides. "Always do the right thing, no matter what," he told Rodriguez. Now Margarito advised him that, as an immigration agent, he must enforce the law no matter what—no exceptions, not even for family.

"You're *migra* now," one of Rodriguez's cousins said during the barbecue. *Immigration.* As boys, he and Rodriguez had spent countless hours hunting rabbits and quail in the brush, gossiping like brothers about goings-on at the ranch. But the cousin had begun trafficking drugs and carrying a gun. "We're on opposite ends," Rodriguez recalled telling him. He cut ties with the cousin, and with close relatives who were living in the United States illegally.

Rodriguez began putting in long hours and overnight shifts, exacerbating tensions in his already-rocky marriage. He and his wife eventually separated. His son, Raul Jr., who was 10 or 11 at the time, told me his father became an intermittent presence in his life as Rodriguez threw himself into his work.

———

By then, Rodriguez had already met his current wife, Anita, at the training academy they attended in Glynco, Georgia. During training, they'd found that they had a lot in common. Anita had grown up in Southern California, where immigration enforcement was a part of everyday life. As a kid, she would prank her undocumented cousins by yelling "*La migra!*" just to watch them run. Later, when Anita was 17, she became homeless and lived for a time in a car outside Yuma, Arizona, with an older sister and her sister's five kids. Unauthorized immigrants making their way into the States ran over a footbridge near where they slept. Border Patrol officers noticed the homeless family and began bringing them food, water, and even Christmas presents. "Nobody was taking care of us except those Border Patrol agents," Anita told me. "I wanted to be like them." Her own father had moved to the United States from Mexico, and she wanted to help facilitate immigration. "The name of your company is Immigration and Naturalization *Service*," she remembered an instructor at the academy saying. "I took that to heart."

She moved from Arizona to South Texas, where Rodriguez was already stationed. After he separated from his wife, he and Anita married and had two kids of their own.

He was assigned to work one of the same bridges he'd crossed as a teen, and an agent who had given him a hard time back then became his colleague. His co-workers told him he looked like an undocumented immigrant, and they nicknamed him "*la nutria*," after an invasive aquatic rodent that swims the Rio Grande—but now he was in on the joke. After long shifts, Rodriguez and his buddies would hang out together, drinking beer late into the night in the bridge parking lot.

Sometimes, he recognized employees of a Texas furniture factory, where he'd been a security guard, as they reentered the United States. One guy was so proud of Rodriguez for becoming an agent that he sought out his inspection lane just to see him in uniform. Rodriguez knew the man worked at the factory, in violation of the tourist visa he held. "Why did you have to come through my lane?" Rodriguez asked, before canceling his visa. He revoked about 10 workers' papers this way.

Several years into his tenure with CBP, Rodriguez was buying cigarettes at a gas station near the bridge when a woman approached to ask if he would help her smuggle a child through his inspection lane. She wrote her phone number on a scrap of paper and pressed it into his hand. The proposition was brazen, but not uncommon—corruption was rampant within CBP. In the years after 9/11, officials had lowered hiring standards so that they could quickly bring in thousands of agents. Drug traffickers tried to infiltrate their ranks, Department of Homeland Security officials have said, and rogue agents seemed to flout the rules almost as often as they enforced them, accepting millions of dollars in bribes to allow drugs and undocumented immigrants to move into the U.S. undetected. (CBP did not respond to requests for comment. A spokesperson confirmed to the *Los Angeles Times* that Rodriguez had been employed by the agency but declined any further comment.)

Rodriguez called the woman's phone number and set up a meeting. He agreed to accept a bribe of $300. The woman and child entered the United States through his inspection lane and were arrested immediately—Rodriguez had worn a wire and taped the encounter.

For his role in the operation, CBP flew Rodriguez to Washington in 2007 to accept the agency's national award for integrity. "Nothing is more critical to CBP's mission," then-Commissioner W. Ralph Basham said at the ceremony. In a flat-brimmed hat and white gloves, Rodriguez walked across the stage to shake Basham's hand.

———————

Anita told me that when people of Mexican heritage become agents, their family members tend to be ambivalent. "On one hand they're very proud of us, because to work for the government—that's a lofty thing in Mexico," Anita said. "But then on the other hand, *traicionero*—you're a traitor, because you're deporting your own people." Rodriguez says he never let that stop him: Too much empathy could lead an agent to bend the rules. But some cases did haunt him.

In his early years as an officer, an English-speaking teenager walked up to him on the bridge from the Mexican side. Quiet and alert, the kid was not unlike Rodriguez had been at that age, except for his lack of papers. He admitted that he'd been living illegally in the U.S. most of his life; he needed to return to continue high school. Rodriguez asked why he had risked a trip to Mexico if he knew he wouldn't be allowed back into the U.S. The boy explained that his grandmother had died and he'd gone to pay his respects before she was buried. "I wanted to see her one last time," he said. Rodriguez told him his best hope for returning was to one day marry a U.S. citizen. But for now, Rodriguez had little doubt about the rules. He sent the teen back to Mexico.

That night, the boy attempted to swim across the Rio Grande. Agents found his body floating beneath the bridge the next morning.

In the twilight of the Obama administration, Central American children and families began arriving at the border in droves, seeking protection from poverty and gang violence, and reunion with family in the U.S. Rodriguez, by then a veteran CBP officer, believed that many asylum seekers had been coached to tell the same sad stories so that they would be released into the United States to await their day in court. The then–presidential candidate Donald Trump promised to lock these people up. Rodriguez voted for Trump. The Rio Grande Valley soon became the epicenter of CBP's effort to deter migrant families by removing thousands of children from their parents.

Any parent could see the separations were inhumane, Rodriguez told me. Someone in Washington had taken the crackdown too far. But what could he do, as a nobody on the bridge? He told trainee officers, "Leave your heart at home." He focused on his sense of duty and followed orders.

———

As the uproar over family separations engulfed the Trump administration, Rodriguez sat before a pair of investigators in a dim room with a one-way mirror, facing a crisis of his own. They showed him a document filled out in longhand with his and his parents' names. The header read ACTA DE NACIMIENTO—a certificate of birth, issued in the Mexican state of Tamaulipas. It was evidence, they said, that Rodriguez had been born in Mexico, not the United States. "Do you recognize this?"

Rodriguez was incredulous. He wrote in a handwritten statement that morning, "I have always believed I was a United States Citizen and still believe I'm a United States Citizen." His mother had died in 2013, so his father was the one living witness who could clear things up. Rodriguez offered to arrange for investigators to meet with Margarito later that day. He called a nephew and told him to get his father from Mexico to the meeting spot—a Starbucks near the border—even if he had to drag him there. A few hours later, Margarito arrived to speak with Rodriguez and the investigators.

Margarito was evasive when officials first showed him the *acta*. "I need to know the truth," Rodriguez told him. "Tell me the truth."

Margarito looked down at the table. Rodriguez had been born at the adobe house outside Matamoros. He explained that about two months later, one of his sisters had arranged for a midwife to register a false birth certificate.

The fraudulent document had come to light because Rodriguez had petitioned for one of his brothers in Mexico to get a green card. An officer with U.S. Citizenship and Immigration Services, the agency that issues green cards, flagged the petition because Rodriguez's Texas-issued birth certificate had been registered by a midwife who was later convicted of fraud. (According to *The Washington Post*, government officials have said that cases against midwives during the 1990s uncovered roughly 15,000 falsely registered babies born in Mexico.) Rodriguez now had no legal status in the country, and was fired from Customs and Border Protection for failing to meet a basic condition of employment: U.S. citizenship.

———

In July 2018, a month after he was fired, Rodriguez got a large CBP badge tattooed on his left shoulder. A Mexican flag splits the badge into two halves.

He applied to become a lawful permanent resident as the spouse of a U.S. citizen, and was forthright in his interview. Yes, he told the official, he had made a false claim to U.S. citizenship, but only because he hadn't known the truth. Yes, he had voted in a federal election as an undocumented immigrant. He expected no special treatment, just the pension, health benefits, and safety from deportation he felt he'd earned through his nearly two decades at CBP. With some patience, he was confident that he could get his status sorted out. By last fall, he had been waiting for a response for almost a year and a half.

Rodriguez says he can now see the impacts of immigration enforcement that he once preferred to leave unexamined. "I can relate to people who I turned back, people that I deported," he said. "They call it karma."

Still, he doesn't regret his service, and distinguishes himself from other unauthorized immigrants. "There are a lot of people trying to do it the easier way," he told me. "I just found out, and I'm trying to do it correctly."

If deported, he would live on family property in Tamaulipas. The State Department's "Do not travel" warning to U.S. citizens says of the area: "Murder, armed robbery, carjacking, kidnapping, extortion, and sexual assault [are] common along the northern border." As an agent, Rodriguez had put traffickers in jail, and his face is widely recognizable from his years on the bridge. "I don't know how long I can survive," he told me.

Despite those risks, Rodriguez dismissed the idea that he should apply for asylum—a legal pathway to U.S. residence that the Trump administration has sought to eradicate, claiming it is rife with fraud. "I'm not going to do it that way. I'd rather get deported," Rodriguez said. "I'm going to practice what I preach."

Once passionate about her work, Anita told me she has "lost faith in the system." But without a college education, she sees no other option. Her job in immigration, she said, "is what's feeding my family." Rodriguez "lives by the rules . . . and even now he says that if the government chooses to deport him, he's going to go," Anita said, her voice catching. He would turn himself in before he would hide from ICE. "I can't let that happen. What am I going to do? What are my kids going to do? What is he going to do over there? He's a federal officer." Anita researches Rodriguez's case most nights and keeps a close watch on other military veterans in the news facing deportation.

In October, Rodriguez received a letter from Citizenship and Immigration Services. His green-card application had been denied because he had falsely claimed to be an American citizen and illegally voted. The letter argued that Rodriguez did not qualify for leniency, even if he did not know about his status at the time. (USCIS declined to comment on specific cases.)

In our interviews, Rodriguez said he understood that the government had to apply the rules to him the way it did to everyone else— his undocumented relatives, his former co-workers, and the boy who drowned under the bridge. But he drew a distinction between how he'd carried out his duties and how officials were handling his case. "I wasn't being strict; I was just abiding by what the law says," he told me. "And these people are not doing what the law says." He believed that he still qualified for an exemption provided by the law for those who make a false claim to U.S. citizenship unwittingly. But in its denial letter, USCIS said it could not make an exception for Rodriguez even if he was unaware of his status at the time, citing recent precedent. Still, Rodriguez held out hope that he could convince the agency to reverse its decision. Immigration lawyers told me, however, that federal officials are granting fewer exceptions across the board. "Apply the right laws, and apply the right rules," Rodriguez told me. He believed the agency was singling him out unfairly. "Treat me the same—that's all I want." His problem might be that it already is.

BROTHERHOOD
OF LOSERS

by Angela Nagle

[DECEMBER 2017]

Nativism is the term for xenophobic nationalism, with its populist affirmation of the virtues of the native born (if the native born are white) and its suspicion and even hatred of immigrants and other "outsiders." It has a long history in America, and new chapters are being written now. Family separations at the border, roundups by U.S. agents at courthouses, federal funds diverted toward the cost of building a wall to keep out undocumented immigrants coming through Mexico—all of these efforts share nativist DNA.

Down the years, nativism has shown a protean capacity to combine with other toxic attitudes—racism, white supremacy, misogyny, anti-Semitism, conspiracy theorizing. Combine all of them at once and feed them into the autoclave of social media, and you have something that resembles the "alt-right" at its most extreme. As Angela Nagle—the author of *Kill All Normies: Online Culture Wars From 4chan and Tumblr to Trump and the Alt-Right*—explained in her 2017 *Atlantic* article "Brotherhood of Losers," the alt-right is not so much a traditional movement as it is "a fractious, fluid coalition comprising bloggers and vloggers, gamers, social-media personalities, and charismatic ringleaders" like the Nazi-saluting Richard Spencer, one of the instigators of the white-nationalist Charlottesville demonstrations. In its milder, "alt-lite" forms, the alt-right offered angry, unmoored men a sense of belonging.

Charlottesville revealed its true ugliness, leaving many adherents horrified, and once again adrift. Where they land next could define American politics for a generation.

The sudden emergence of the so-called alt-right from the dark recesses of the internet into the American mainstream was at first more baffling than shocking. The young people sharing strange, coded frog memes and declaring their commitment to white identity politics on obscure websites remained in the realm of the unserious—or at least the unknowable and weird.

Then, last November, *The Atlantic* published footage of a prominent alt-right provocateur, Richard Spencer, raising a glass to Donald Trump's election at a conference in Washington, D.C. "Hail Trump!" he shouted, and in response, audience members saluted in unmistakably Nazi style. The incident made waves—here were young men behaving, in public, like fascists. But Spencer laughed it off, claiming that the gestures were "ironic." The methods and meaning of the alt-right were as yet elusive.

It wasn't until the events in Charlottesville, Virginia, in August that the alt-right took on a form that most Americans could finally grasp as a real, and unambiguous, political movement. A disciplined, torchlit procession snaked through a college town, with white men shouting explicitly white-nationalist slogans in chorus. A true believer drove his Dodge Challenger into a crowd of counterprotesters and was charged with killing a woman named Heather Heyer. Could it be that these "ironic" young men had meant what they were saying all along?

To answer this question—and to comprehend the powerful and unexpected effect Charlottesville is having on the alt-right itself—we need to understand what the movement is, and what it is not. Unlike old-fashioned, monolithic political movements, the alt-right is a fractious, fluid coalition comprising bloggers and vloggers, gamers, social-media personalities, and charismatic ringleaders like Spencer, who share an anti-establishment, anti-left politics and an enthusiasm for the political career of Donald Trump. Older theorists who predate the 2016 election—men such as Jared Taylor of the "white advocacy" organization American Renaissance and the neoreactionary Curtis Yarvin, who writes under the name Mencius Moldbug—exert influence. But what is new, and unusual, about today's far right is the large number of young people, most of them men, who have been drawn into its orbit—or, as they would put it, "red-pilled." The metaphor comes from *The Matrix*, the dystopian science-fiction movie in which the protagonist, Neo, is offered a red pill that allows him to see through society's illusions and view the world in its true, ugly reality.

For eight years, I have been closely observing an array of rightist forums as they have followed a strange and marked evolution. Initially, at least, taking the red pill was more closely associated with antifeminist and men's-rights forums like Reddit's /r/TheRedPill, which launched in 2012, than with the nativist or racist corners of the online right. TheRedPill was infamous for its mix of virulent misogyny and retrograde dating advice. The young men who frequented it obsessed over the male pecking order, evolutionary sexual psychology, and the decline of Western men, who had become too meek to stand up to their women. It also played a significant role in popularizing terms now associated with the racial politics of the alt-right, including *cuck*, a derivative of *cuckold* first used to describe an emasculated man and later adapted to brand conservatives who were seen as weak on immigration, or just weak.

Over time, this online "manosphere" would embrace an increasingly hard-line antifeminism, one that began to shade into broader critiques of a fraying social order. Daryush Valizadeh, known as "Roosh V," launched his writing career with the *Bang* series of books, many of them essentially travel guides for pickup artists. His site, Return of Kings, was at first dedicated to crude misogyny and pickup advice. But by 2015, he was ranging further afield in his search for the source of male woe, writing pieces like "The Damaging Effects of Jewish Intellectualism and Activism on Western Culture," a positive review of an anti-Semitic conspiracy text popular among the alt-right. The Proud

Boys, a group founded by the former *Vice* impresario Gavin McInnes to fight the forces of emasculation (in part through a renunciation of masturbation), also blended sexism and creeping nativism. While some adherents were attracted by the campaign against self-abuse, or the fraternity-like initiation rituals, membership also entailed support for closed borders and what McInnes called, in a clever stroke of euphemism, "western chauvinism."

The anonymous forum 4chan provided another portal into the nascent movement. Some of the young geeks who populated the site were interested in transgression for transgression's sake—the fun of trolling what they saw as an increasingly politically correct culture. One running joke, captured by the phrase *the current year*, mocked Baby Boomer liberalism for constantly undermining those who refused to keep pace with its progressive pieties, its cries of "You can't still think that—it's 2017!"

Posters in these online forums became adept at using offbeat humor and new media to wrong-foot the establishment. Anyone caught fretting about the right's online youth movement was met with the contention that the entire thing was a joke—and anyone taking it at face value was a clueless outsider. Last winter, for instance, an elaborate hoax originated on 4chan. "Operation O-KKK" called for pranksters to flood social media with claims that the "okay" hand gesture was a symbol of white supremacy. "Leftists have dug so deep down into their lunacy," wrote the original poster of the hoax plan. "We must force [them] to dig more, until the rest of society ain't going anywhere near that shit." In April, when the pro-Trump writers Mike Cernovich and Cassandra Fairbanks were photographed in the White House press-briefing room making "okay" signs, Emma Roller, a reporter at Fusion, wrote on Twitter that the writers were "doing a white power hand gesture." Fairbanks sued Roller for defamation.

At a moment in history when the right seemed to have died of terminal uncoolness, this strategy of making the left seem puritanical and humorless represented no small cultural revolution. Ever since the 1960s, the right, holding fast to stuffy tradition, had struggled to compete with the youthful vibrancy of the left. But the earnestness and fervor of contemporary progressives, particularly on college campuses, opened the left up to mockery.

One of the most successful propaganda weapons the alt-right produced was its caricature of the Social-Justice Warrior. Rightists flooded YouTube with "cringe compilations" depicting liberal vloggers, protesters, and college students—mostly young women—screaming at opponents, calling out their racism, sexism, and hate speech. In an interview, Richard Spencer described these figures as a gift from the left to the alt-right. "I love Social-Justice Warriors," he said. "I might donate money to them or something. I want them to become even more, just, ridiculous." Andrew Anglin, who runs the alt-right site The Daily Stormer, wrote, "Right now, a divide is happening. And there are only going to be two sides. Either you are with the SJWs or you are with the Fascists."

Watching YouTube videos of college-age liberals decrying microaggressions and demanding safe spaces, the young men of the alt-right may have cheered Anglin as he threw down this gauntlet. Then Charlottesville happened, and it became clear what, exactly, it meant to be "with the Fascists." The useful idiots of the less extreme "alt-lite" tier of the new right had successfully deployed irony to confound the alt-right's critics. But they had also given cover to its most radical elements. The rally brought into the open the movement's racist core—not the winking shit-posters and fuzzy faced geeks wearing obscure-internet-joke T-shirts, but a small army of unapologetic white nationalists. Anyone who flirted with the alt-right now understood what they were pledging allegiance to.

Charlottesville splintered the alt-right, though along fault lines that had appeared well before the violence there. The rally had been dubbed Unite the Right, but it proved to be the culmination of a vicious period of internecine squabbling. In June, the alt-right and the alt-lite had held rival free-speech rallies in Washington, D.C., with Spencer whipping up the hard-liners at the Lincoln Memorial while Cernovich hosted a tamer group outside the White House. Spencer accused the alt-lite of being "cucks." Cernovich said the alt-right's "big tent" had folded after "Hail-gate." After Charlottesville, he disparagingly called its members "Nazi boys."

Gavin McInnes also took pains to distance himself from the movement. "Charlottesville changed everything," he said to Boston Herald Radio. "I don't advocate the alt-right. I don't advocate their politics." Even Steve Bannon, who, as the head of *Breitbart News*, had done more than anyone else to disseminate alt-right ideas into mainstream American politics, and had once proudly called his site a platform for the alt-right, now described its adherents as "losers" and a "collection of clowns."

For those, like Spencer, who wanted the movement to pursue its most radical goals, the Charlottesville rally looks like a fatal mistake. It happened too soon, before enough young recruits had had time to steep in toxic ideology and see their ironic pranking curdle into something more like real conviction. (A common path to the worst sorts of extremism begins with a search for camaraderie and tribe; the adoption and hardening of truly extreme ideological views come later.)

Arriving when it did, Unite the Right was devastating for the movement. The euphoria of the first, tiki-torch-lit night was followed by arrests and humiliation. The names of rally attendees were exposed, which in several cases resulted in the loss of jobs. Online-infrastructure companies booted the alt-right websites they'd hosted and supported, including Anglin's The Daily Stormer.

Even so, the young men who found brotherhood and a sense of purpose in the movement have not disappeared. In the immediate aftermath of Charlottesville, forums like 4chan's politics board were full of discussions about the need to shift tactics and do damage control. But I've seen nothing to suggest that those who were convinced that civilization is in decline—and that feminism, liberalism, and demographic change are to blame—have been unconvinced of those things. "This was fucking ignorant and now it was all for nothing," one 4chan poster lamented. "Liberal media will blast this for years and scare younger generations from our cause." By definition, those who have been red-pilled feel that they have seen the world as it really is and can never go back. So where will they go now?

It is often said that the left won the culture war and the right won the economic war. From the point of view of angry young white men, however, neither side has scored any victories. A generation ago, Ronald Reagan and Margaret Thatcher championed the individual and the market, while liberals abandoned institutions like religion, national pride, even the nuclear family in favor of individual freedom. Together, right and left created a world in which a young person could invent his own identity and curate his own personal brand online, but also had dimmed hopes for enjoying what used to be considered the most basic elements of a decent life—marriage, a job, a house, a community. (Liberalism claimed that a village could raise a child, but never got around to building the village.)

Amid this desert of meaning into which Millennials were born, the new far right expertly pinpointed the existential questions, particularly for those who couldn't be permitted a collective identity, namely straight white men: Who are we? What is our story? What is our future? The alt-right overplayed its hand, fracturing before it coalesced and consolidated its gains. But the forces behind the movement, not least the rapid demographic transformation of the Western world, are not going away.

THE MOST EXPENSIVE WEATHER YEAR EVER

by Annie Lowrey

[DECEMBER 2017]

Daniel Patrick Moynihan, who was a professor before becoming a New York senator, came up with a phrase that has no end of application: *defining deviancy down*. The idea is that as certain social conditions and forms of behavior, once seen as unwelcome outliers, become more prevalent, the tendency is to reset the concept of "normal" to make room for them. Moynihan was thinking about social dynamics. But he could just as well have been talking about the way many people react to extreme weather and changing climate—the way catastrophe has become business as usual.

At the end of 2017, Annie Lowrey, an *Atlantic* staff writer, looked back at the weather events of that year: the droughts, the hurricanes, the forest fires, the destructive tides. This was the year when Puerto Rico was slammed by Hurricane Maria, a tragedy from which the island has never fully recovered. Every day seemed to bring weather-related headlines. In terms of the sheer economic damage caused by wind and rain and sun, 2017 was the costliest year in American history, a record not likely to hold for very long. That was also the year in which President Trump took the first steps to withdraw the United States from the Paris Agreement on climate change, saying, "I was elected to represent the citizens of Pittsburgh, not Paris." (For his part, the mayor of Pittsburgh announced his intention to adhere to the agreement's guidelines.)

There were the hurricanes that rained down biblical floods on Texas and Florida and devastated Puerto Rico and the Virgin Islands. There were the fires that smoked wine country and coated Montana and Oregon in ash, and the fires that are burning down houses in Santa Barbara, California. There were the king tides that flooded Miami, the heat waves that seared the Southwest, the tornadoes that scarred the Southeast, and the rains that never came in the Cascades. No wonder the National Oceanic and Atmospheric Administration has deemed this the second most extreme year, weather-wise, in the past century.

That extreme weather has taken a devastating and unknowable human toll, on families from San Juan to San Francisco. And it has taken an economic one as well. This year will almost certainly be the most expensive in American history in terms of natural disasters—and a preview of the trillions of dollars of costs related to climate change yet to come.

The effect is perhaps clearest in terms of property damage, in the United States' territories as well as in the states, as governments, insurers, and individuals count up the losses from torn-apart homes, flooded cars, downed bridges, destroyed electrical grids, and shuttered hospitals. Early in the fall, Hurricane Maria devastated the island of Puerto Rico, which had already suffered a decade-long recession. The government there has asked for $95 billion to rebuild the electric grid, infrastructure, and homes, and the storm caused an estimated $85 billion in insured losses. The credit-rating agency Moody's puts the estimate of the storm's damage at $40 billion in lost economic output and $55 billion in property damage, in a region with a GDP of about $100 billion a year. The numbers are similarly devastating in the Virgin Islands, which were hit by Hurricane Irma.

———

Though the storms did less catastrophic damage on the mainland, that damage was more costly because of the value of the homes, businesses, and public infrastructure there. "We're going to have to rebuild everything," Bonnie Stephenson, the mayor of the tiny town of Rose

City, Texas, told me when I visited. Six weeks after Harvey, mold was growing up the sides of homes, and heaps of mucked-out garbage lined the streets. The whole town would have to be gutted, reframed, and rebuilt, as would much of southwest Texas and western Florida. The government estimates the damages from the storms and floods at $131 billion.

Wildfires also lit up a number of dry western states this year, and some of them continue to rage today. Fires in California alone have caused at least $9.4 billion in damage. "These numbers not only represent staggering losses to tens of thousands of Californians," Dave Jones, the state's insurance commissioner, said in a statement. "The October wildfires that devastated whole communities and tragically cost 44 people their lives have now proven to be the most destructive and deadliest in our state's history." That number is likely to prove a fractional estimate, not taking into account the damages from the uncontained fires still alight in Southern California and not accounting for uninsured losses.

All told, the U.S. experienced at least 15 weather events costing at least $1 billion each in 2017, the second most since 1980, the government estimates. To be fair, weather gets costlier over time because the value of America's homes and businesses and the economy itself gets bigger over time, as noted by Roger Pielke Jr., a political scientist at the University of Colorado at Boulder. Still, when the damages are tallied up, the winds, floods, and fires are likely to end up wiping away 0.2 or 0.3 percent of the nation's wealth—causing as much of a hit in percentage terms, in other words, as the Great Chicago Fire of 1871 or the Great Mississippi Flood of 1927. This year really was different.

Another, related way of looking at the toll is in terms of the costs to the government to fight fires, move families, save stranded individuals, and rebuild. There are the significant direct costs for disaster relief, for one. Congress has provided more than $50 billion in emergency spending related to storms and floods, including emergency nutrition assistance for Puerto Rico, debt relief for the federal flood-insurance program, and new funds for the Federal Emergency Management

Agency. The Forest Service has also spent $3 billion on firefighting, and state and local governments have committed similar sums.

But that does not fully capture the way that storms, fires, and droughts act as a drain on public resources. There is also the cost of cuts to other agencies to free up money for disasters, and the burden of increased spending on social insurance and safety-net programs, such as food stamps. Consider this analysis of the California fires, just one catastrophic event among many this year: "The cost to contain and fight the fire and deal with the aftermath will be in the billions," wrote Joel N. Myers, the chairman of the forecasting firm AccuWeather. "The loss in tax revenue from businesses no longer around, including the vineyards; the workers who have lost their jobs and can no longer pay taxes as well as other impacts will be quite costly. This will create a hole in the California budget, which may necessitate an increase in taxes. If California has to borrow more this might negatively impact its bond ratings and it will have to pay higher interest rates on all borrowings." He estimates the impact at $70 billion to $100 billion.

———————

Despite the prevalence and devastation of storms like Katrina and Sandy and Maria, as well as fires and tornadoes and earthquakes, the U.S. government does not have a full accounting of the budget effect of extreme weather—nor a sense of how more-frequent and more-intense storms might tax public coffers in the years to come. "Little is known about the fiscal costs of natural disasters, especially regarding social safety nets," writes Tatyana Deryugina, an economist at the University of Illinois. She notes "substantial" increases in unemployment insurance and medical costs for a full decade after a hurricane, with the government spending $780 to $1,150 more per capita on social insurance for every $155 to $160 it spent per person on disaster aid. "This implies, among other things, that the fiscal costs of natural disasters have been significantly underestimated," she concludes.

Then, there is the cost to growth and jobs—those headline economic figures—which tends to see something of a yo-yo effect: A storm hits, or a fire strikes. Businesses close and stay closed. Families flee, and damage from water, wind, ash, and debris keeps them away for some time. Jobs and economic activity disappear. But soon after, the rebuilding starts. In Houston, for instance, the surge of activity caused by Hurricane Harvey was obvious when I visited. Volunteer crews were pulling down and replacing rotten siding. Families were restocking their cabinets and closets. Car dealerships were advertising deals. People were scavenging for metals and repairable goods in the debris. Lowe's and Walmart were crowded with people who had lost something, or everything, and needed it replaced. "It has been crazy in here, crazy all the time," a shift manager at a Home Depot in Beaumont, a coastal town west of Houston, told me. "Shop-Vacs, drywall, electrical, appliances."

This surge in activity is financed, in part, with money pouring into a disaster area from insurers, volunteer groups, and the federal government. "FEMA has already filled hundreds of temporary positions to help rebuild communities impacted in Texas, Florida, Puerto Rico and the U.S. Virgin Islands," wrote Rebecca Henderson, of the human-resources company Randstad Sourceright, in a research note. "Job openings for contingent talent have also spiked in the construction and hospitality sectors," she continued, "and we expect to see similar demand from the engineering and environmental sectors."

As such, the medium-term overall effect on GDP is often negligible, with a local economy slowing down to a halt and then speeding up again; the national numbers rarely change much. "Hurricanes Harvey, Irma, and Maria have devastated many communities, inflicting severe hardship," the Federal Reserve said in a September statement. "Storm-related disruptions and rebuilding will affect economic activity in the near term, but past experience suggests that the storms are unlikely to materially alter the course of the national economy."

But economists stress that GDP and jobs numbers are not necessarily a good way to capture the effect of extreme weather events—not this year or any year, not for families and not for the government and not for the nation as a whole. "You've destroyed a bunch of housing stock and public buildings and disrupted for a short period of time people getting to work and dealing with tragedy, and then the rebuilding will start," says Chris Varvares of the research firm Macroeconomic Advisers. "What you don't measure is the welfare loss of what happened to people's lives, their businesses, their pets, their photo albums. Part of the story is that GDP is perhaps not the best measure of the near-term impact of these storms, or the widening of the weather cycles."

Natural disasters tend to have a disparate impact on the rich and the poor, for one. Not all families are equally vulnerable to the terrible events, and not all families are equally capable of rebuilding. Studies have found that the rich and the poor are more likely than the middle class to live in flood zones, and are thus the most likely to be faced with property destruction and a mandate to try to rebuild. "Higher-income households often live in high-risk areas because of the aesthetic attributes of living next to water," one study of flooding and income concluded. "Low-income households live in higher-risk areas than middle-income households in order to find affordable housing." But the rich have greater capacity to flee a storm and to rebuild after it, given their likelihood of having insurance and their wealth. The poor, on the other hand, often get hit hard and struggle to recover. That seems true this year. Harvey has caused a spike in homelessness, and has hit the lowest-income communities the hardest. The Santa Rosa fires have been particularly devastating for people living in trailer parks and for migrant workers.

There is also the way in which natural disasters change the economic geography of a place, leading some families to flee and leaving others stuck. Higher-income residents of a given region tend to leave when devastation strikes, for instance. That might lead to higher earnings for them, but less economic vitality for the towns and cities that they left behind—something that seems a certainty in the case of Puerto Rico: Tens of thousands of its residents are expected to relocate to Florida, New York, and elsewhere. "It is generally accepted among environmental geographers that there is no such thing as a natural disaster," argues Neil Smith, an anthropologist and geographer at the City University of New York. "In every phase and aspect of a disaster—causes, vulnerability, preparedness, results and response, and reconstruction—the contours of disaster and the difference between who lives and who dies is to a greater or lesser extent a social calculus." Who is exposed to storms, who is sheltered from tornadoes, who recovers from fires—all of these things are a matter of choice and public policy, in other words.

————————

More broadly, catastrophic weather events change individuals' and businesses' economic decision making—with a profound longer-term effect on the economy that is not always apparent in a jobs report or a GDP number. A family that lost its house might not be able to pay for a child to go to college. An entrepreneur might decide to retire early, rather than rebuild. An insurer might decide to charge more for building in a given region. Extreme weather, in some ways, acts as a tax on long-term economic vitality. "It affects people's behavior and their investment decisions for many, many years, and that in turn affects economic growth," says Solomon Hsiang, an economist at UC Berkeley. "For the 10 years after a storm, there's lower economic growth, in proportion to the intensity of the storm. It doesn't show up as a huge spike; it's much more like a gentle drift." Part of the reason, he says, is that "people tend to shift their behavior away from things that look like investment, like education and health care, and tend to spend a larger fraction of their earnings on things like consumption, things like food. Those are things they need in the short term, but don't produce extra benefits in the long term."

As hard as it might be to suss out the impact of extreme weather in 2017, yet harder is sussing out the impact of the changing climate, now and in the future—due to the difficulty of tying individual weather events to epochal changes like global warming, the inability of headline economic figures to capture the messy fullness of human life, and the inadequacy of the available data to measure changes in the natural and the economic world. "If people are giving you straight answers about this, they're probably making it up," Elizabeth Stanton, an economist at the Global Development and Environment Institute at Tufts University, told me when I asked her how much climate change had cost the U.S. in 2017. "I don't think we can measure it, not at all. We're missing vital information, and it's impairing our ability to make decisions, decisions that are very important and very time-sensitive. It's dangerous."

But scientists have found a clear link between anthropogenic climate change and certain extreme weather events. Independent analyses have found that climate change intensified Harvey's rainfall and has made similar storms wetter and more likely to occur, for instance. Hsiang and his co-authors have estimated that every degree Celsius the Earth warms will cost the U.S. more than a percentage point of GDP, worsening income inequality as well. If emissions are not contained, the climate effect would rival that of the Great Recession. Even those numbers are speculative and do not account for all the ways that a hotter planet might change human lives, researchers warn.

The country is pitching toward a more violent future, then, without a full sense of what storms, floods, and fires are costing it now and without a full sense of what is to come.

THE PROPHECIES
OF Q

by Adrienne LaFrance

[JUNE 2020]

Pestilence, earthquakes, famine, war—the signs of the approaching End of Days are well known. To this list, the conspiracy theorists of QAnon would add the continued power of Hillary Clinton, the "deep state," and other elite malefactors. While QAnon is easy to dismiss as just another fringe movement, its online presence is extensive and its memes are picked up and recycled on Fox News and even by the White House. The rhetoric and commentary of QAnon believers sometimes verge on incitement to violence—which is why the group has been banned from Reddit and cited by the FBI as a potential domestic terrorism threat.

Adrienne LaFrance, the executive editor of *The Atlantic*, has reported on conspiracy theories and theorists for many years. In key ways, as LaFrance explains in "The Prophecies of Q," excerpted here, the QAnon phenomenon is different. Like other conspiracy theories, QAnon promotes a slippery belief system that has proved impervious to frontal attack. Like others, it is bound up in politics and current events. And like others, it stands as an example of what happens when basic notions of evidence and objectivity are widely devalued. But QAnon also cultivates a quasi-religious character. Many of its followers are evangelical Christians. Guided by a figure known only as "Q," they look forward to a coming battle between

good and evil—perhaps precipitated by the coronavirus—and
the advent of a Great Awakening.

The origins of QAnon are recent, but even so, separating myth
from reality can be hard. One place to begin is with Edgar Madison Welch, a deeply religious father of two, who until Sunday,
December 4, 2016, had lived an unremarkable life in the small town of
Salisbury, North Carolina. That morning, Welch grabbed his cellphone,
a box of shotgun shells, and three loaded guns—a 9-mm AR-15 rifle,
a six-shot .38-caliber Colt revolver, and a shotgun—and hopped into
his Toyota Prius. He drove 360 miles to a well-to-do neighborhood
in Northwest Washington, D.C.; parked his car; put the revolver in
a holster at his hip; held the AR-15 rifle across his chest; and walked
through the front door of a pizzeria called Comet Ping Pong.

Comet happens to be the place where, on a Sunday afternoon two
years earlier, my then-baby daughter tried her first-ever sip of water.
Kids gather there with their parents and teammates after soccer games
on Saturdays, and local bands perform on the weekends. In the back,
children challenge their grandparents to Ping-Pong matches as they
wait for their pizzas to come out of the big clay oven in the middle of
the restaurant. Comet Ping Pong is a beloved spot in Washington.

That day, people noticed Welch right away. An AR-15 rifle makes
for a conspicuous sash in most social settings, but especially at a place
like Comet. As parents, children, and employees rushed outside, many
still chewing, Welch began to move through the restaurant, at one
point attempting to use a butter knife to pry open a locked door, before
giving up and firing several rounds from his rifle into the lock. Behind
the door was a small computer-storage closet. This was not what he
was expecting.

Welch had traveled to Washington because of a conspiracy theory
known, now famously, as Pizzagate, which claimed that Hillary Clinton was running a child sex ring out of Comet Ping Pong. The idea
originated in October 2016, when WikiLeaks made public a trove of

emails stolen from the account of John Podesta, a former White House chief of staff and then the chair of Clinton's presidential campaign; Comet was mentioned repeatedly in exchanges Podesta had with the restaurant's owner, James Alefantis, and others. The emails were mainly about fundraising events, but high-profile pro–Donald Trump figures such as Mike Cernovich and Alex Jones began advancing the claim—which originated in trollish corners of the internet (such as 4chan) and then spread to more accessible precincts (Twitter, YouTube)—that the emails were proof of ritualistic child abuse. Some conspiracy theorists asserted that it was taking place in the basement at Comet, where there is no basement. References in the emails to "pizza" and "pasta" were interpreted as code words for "girls" and "little boys."

Shortly after Trump's election, as Pizzagate roared across the internet, Welch started binge-watching conspiracy-theory videos on YouTube. He tried to recruit help from at least two people to carry out a vigilante raid, texting them about his desire to sacrifice "the lives of a few for the lives of many" and to fight "a corrupt system that kidnaps, tortures and rapes babies and children in our own backyard." When Welch finally found himself inside the restaurant and understood that Comet Ping Pong was just a pizza shop, he set down his firearms, walked out the door, and surrendered to police, who had by then secured the perimeter. "The intel on this wasn't 100 percent," Welch told *The New York Times* after his arrest.

Welch seems to have sincerely believed that children were being held at Comet Ping Pong. His family and friends wrote letters to the judge on his behalf, describing him as a dedicated father, a devout Christian, and a man who went out of his way to care for others. Welch had trained as a volunteer firefighter. He had gone on an earthquake-response mission to Haiti with the local Baptist Men's Association. A friend from his church wrote, "He exhibits the actions of a person who strives to learn biblical truth and apply it." Welch himself expressed what seemed like genuine remorse, saying in a handwritten note submitted to the judge by his lawyers: "It was never my intention to harm or frighten innocent lives, but I realize now just how foolish and reckless my decision was." He was sentenced to four years in prison.

Pizzagate seemed to fade. Some of its most visible proponents, such as Jack Posobiec, a conspiracy theorist who is now a correspondent for the pro-Trump cable-news channel One America News Network, backed away. Facing the specter of legal action by Alefantis, Alex Jones, who runs the conspiracy-theory website Infowars and hosts an affiliated radio show, apologized for promoting Pizzagate.

While Welch may have expressed regret, he gave no indication that he had stopped believing the underlying Pizzagate message: that a cabal of powerful elites was abusing children and getting away with it. Judging from a surge of activity on the internet, many others had found ways to move beyond the Comet Ping Pong episode and remain focused on what they saw as the larger truth. If you paid attention to the right voices on the right websites, you could see in real time how the core premises of Pizzagate were being recycled, revised, and reinterpreted. The millions of people paying attention to sites like 4chan and Reddit could continue to learn about that secretive and untouchable cabal; about its malign actions and intentions; about its ties to the left wing and specifically to Democrats and especially to Clinton; about its bloodlust and its moral degeneracy. You could also—and this would prove essential—read about a small but swelling band of underground American patriots fighting back.

All of this, taken together, defined a worldview that would soon have a name: QAnon, derived from a mysterious figure, "Q," posting anonymously on 4chan. QAnon does not possess a physical location, but it has an infrastructure, a literature, a growing body of adherents, and a great deal of merchandising. It also displays other key qualities that Pizzagate lacked. In the face of inconvenient facts, it has the ambiguity and adaptability to sustain a movement of this kind over time. For QAnon, every contradiction can be explained away; no form of argument can prevail against it.

Conspiracy theories are a constant in American history, and it is tempting to dismiss them as inconsequential. But as the 21st century has progressed, such a dismissal has begun to require willful blindness. I was a city-hall reporter for a local investigative-news site called *Hono-lulu Civil Beat* in 2011 when Donald Trump was laying the ground-work for a presidential run by publicly questioning whether Barack Obama had been born in Hawaii, as all facts and documents showed. Trump maintained that Obama had really been born in Africa, and therefore wasn't a natural-born American—making him ineligible for the highest office. I remember the debate in our Honolulu newsroom: Should we even cover this "birther" madness? As it turned out, the allegations, based entirely on lies, captivated enough people to give Trump a launching pad.

Nine years later, as reports of a fearsome new virus suddenly emerged, and with Trump now president, a series of ideas began bur-bling in the QAnon community: that the coronavirus might not be real; that if it was, it had been created by the "deep state," the star chamber of government officials and other elite figures who secretly run the world; that the hysteria surrounding the pandemic was part of a plot to hurt Trump's reelection chances; and that media elites were cheering the death toll. Some of these ideas would make their way onto Fox News and into the president's public utterances. As of late last year, according to *The New York Times*, Trump had retweeted accounts often focused on conspiracy theories, including those of QAnon, on at least 145 occasions.

The power of the internet was understood early on, but the full nature of that power—its ability to shatter any semblance of shared reality, undermining civil society and democratic governance in the process—was not. The internet also enabled unknown individuals to reach masses of people, at a scale Marshall McLuhan never dreamed of. The warping of shared reality leads a man with an AR-15 rifle to invade a pizza shop. It brings online forums into being where people color-fully imagine the assassination of a former secretary of state. It offers the promise of a Great Awakening, in which the elites will be routed and the truth will be revealed. It causes chat sites to come alive with commentary speculating that the coronavirus pandemic may be the moment QAnon has been waiting for. None of this could have been imagined as recently as the turn of the century.

QAnon is emblematic of modern America's susceptibility to conspiracy theories, and its enthusiasm for them. But it is also already much more than a loose collection of conspiracy-minded chat-room inhabitants. It is a movement united in mass rejection of reason, objectivity, and other Enlightenment values. And we are likely closer to the beginning of its story than the end. The group harnesses paranoia to fervent hope and a deep sense of belonging. The way it breathes life into an ancient preoccupation with end-times is also radically new. To look at QAnon is to see not just a conspiracy theory but the birth of a new religion.

Many people were reluctant to speak with me about QAnon as I reported this story. The movement's adherents have sometimes proved willing to take matters into their own hands. Last year, the FBI classified QAnon as a domestic-terror threat in an internal memo. The memo took note of a California man arrested in 2018 with bomb-making materials. According to the FBI, he had planned to attack the Illinois capitol to "make Americans aware of 'Pizzagate' and the New World Order (NWO) who were dismantling society." The memo also took note of a QAnon follower in Nevada who was arrested in 2018 after blocking traffic on the Hoover Dam in an armored truck. The man, heavily armed, was demanding the release of the inspector general's report on Hillary Clinton's emails. The FBI memo warned that conspiracy theories stoke the threat of extremist violence, especially when individuals "claiming to act as 'researchers' or 'investigators' single out people, businesses, or groups which they falsely accuse of being involved in the imagined scheme."

QAnon adherents are feared for ferociously attacking skeptics online and for inciting physical violence. On a now-defunct Reddit board dedicated to QAnon, commenters took delight in describing Clinton's potential fate. One person wrote: "I'm surprised no one has assassinated her yet honestly." Another: "The buzzards rip her rotting corpse to shreds." A third: "I want to see her blood pouring down the gutters!"

When I spoke with Clinton recently about QAnon, she said, "I just get under their skin unlike *anybody else* . . . If I didn't have Secret Service protection going through my mail, finding weird stuff, tracking

the threats against me—which are still very high—I would be worried."
She has come to realize that the invented reality in which conspiracy
theorists place her is not some bizarre parallel universe but actually one
that shapes our own. Referring to internet trolling operations, Clinton
said, "I don't think until relatively recently most people understood
how well organized they were, and how many different components of
their strategy they have put in place."

On October 28, 2017, the anonymous user now widely referred to as
"Q" appeared for the first time on 4chan, a so-called image board that
is known for its grotesque memes, sickening photographs, and brutal
teardown culture. Q predicted the imminent arrest of Hillary Clinton
and a violent uprising nationwide, posting this:

> HRC extradition already in motion effective yesterday with sev-
> eral countries in case of cross border run. Passport approved to
> be flagged effective 10/30 @ 12:01am. Expect massive riots or-
> ganized in defiance and others fleeing the US to occur. US M's
> will conduct the operation while NG activated. Proof check:
> Locate a NG member and ask if activated for duty 10/30 across
> most major cities.

And then this:

> Mockingbird HRC detained, not arrested (yet). Where is Huma?
> Follow Huma. This has nothing to do w/ Russia (yet). Why
> does Potus surround himself w/ generals? What is military in-
> telligence? Why go around the 3 letter agencies? What Supreme
> Court case allows for the use of MI v Congressional assembled
> and approved agencies? Who has ultimate authority over our
> branches of military w/o approval conditions unless 90+ in war-
> time conditions? What is the military code? Where is AW being
> held? Why? POTUS will not go on tv to address nation. POTUS
> must isolate himself to prevent negative optics. POTUS knew

removing criminal rogue elements as a first step was essential to free and pass legislation. Who has access to everything classified? Do you believe HRC, Soros, Obama etc have more power than Trump? Fantasy. Whoever controls the office of the Presidency controls this great land. They never believed for a moment they (Democrats and Republicans) would lose control. This is not a R v D battle. Why did Soros donate all his money recently? Why would he place all his funds in a RC? Mockingbird 10.30.17 God bless fellow Patriots.

Clinton was not arrested on October 30, but that didn't deter Q, who continued posting ominous predictions and cryptic riddles—with prompts like "Find the reflection inside the castle"—often written in the form of tantalizing fragments and rhetorical questions. Q made it clear that he wanted people to believe he was an intelligence officer or military official with Q clearance, a level of access to classified information that includes nuclear-weapons design and other highly sensitive material. (I'm using *he* because many Q followers do, though Q remains anonymous—hence "QAnon.") Q's tone is conspiratorial to the point of cliché: "I've said too much," and "Follow the money," and "Some things must remain classified to the very end."

What might have languished as a lonely screed on a single image board instead incited fervor. Its profile was enhanced, according to Brandy Zadrozny and Ben Collins of NBC News, by several conspiracy theorists whose promotion of Q in turn helped build up their own online profiles. By now, nearly three years since Q's original messages appeared, there have been thousands of what his followers call "Q drops"—messages posted to image boards by Q. He uses a password-protected "tripcode," a series of letters and numbers visible to other image-board users to signal the continuity of his identity over time. (Q's tripcode has changed on occasion, prompting flurries of speculation.) As Q has moved from one image board to the next—from 4chan to 8chan to 8kun, seeking a safe harbor—QAnon adherents have only become more devoted. If the internet is one big rabbit hole containing infinitely recursive rabbit holes, QAnon has somehow found its way down all of them, gulping up lesser conspiracy theories as it goes.

In its broadest contours, the QAnon belief system looks something like this: Q is an intelligence or military insider with proof that corrupt world leaders are secretly torturing children all over the world; the malefactors are embedded in the deep state; Donald Trump is working tirelessly to thwart them. ("These people need to ALL be ELIMINATED," Q wrote in one post.) The eventual destruction of the global cabal is imminent, Q prophesies, but can be accomplished only with the support of patriots who search for meaning in Q's clues. To believe Q requires rejecting mainstream institutions, ignoring government officials, battling apostates, and despising the press. One of Q's favorite rallying cries is "You are the news now." Another is "Enjoy the show," a phrase that his disciples regard as a reference to a coming apocalypse: When the world as we know it comes to an end, everyone's a spectator.

People who have taken Q to heart like to say they've been paying attention from the very beginning, the way someone might brag about having listened to Radiohead before *The Bends*. A promise of foreknowledge is part of Q's appeal, as is the feeling of being part of a secret community, which is reinforced through the use of acronyms and ritual phrases such as "Nothing can stop what is coming" and "Trust the plan."

One phrase that serves as a special touchstone among QAnon adherents is "the calm before the storm." Q first used it a few days after his initial post, and it arrived with a specific history. On the evening of October 5, 2017—not long before Q first made himself known on 4chan—President Trump stood beside the first lady in a loose semicircle with 20 or so senior military leaders and their spouses for a photo in the State Dining Room at the White House. Reporters had been invited to watch as Trump's guests posed and smiled. Trump couldn't seem to stop talking. "You guys know what this represents?" he asked at one point, tracing an incomplete circle in the air with his right index finger. "Tell us, sir," one onlooker replied. The president's response was self-satisfied, bordering on a drawl: "Maybe it's the calm before the storm."

"What's the storm?" one of the journalists asked.

"Could be the calm—the calm before the storm," Trump said again. His repetition seemed to be for dramatic effect. The whir of camera shutters grew louder.

The reporters became insistent: "What storm, Mr. President?"

A curt response from Trump: "You'll find out."

Those 37 seconds of presidential ambiguity made headlines right away—relations with Iran had been tense in recent days—but they would also become foundational lore for eventual followers of Q. The president's circular hand gesture is of particular interest to them. You may think he was motioning to the semicircle gathered around him, they say, but he was really drawing the letter *Q* in the air. Was Trump playing the role of John the Baptist, proclaiming what was to come? Was he himself the anointed one?

It's impossible to know the number of QAnon adherents with any precision, but the ranks are growing. At least 35 current or former congressional candidates have embraced Q, according to an online tally by the progressive nonprofit Media Matters for America. Those candidates have either directly praised QAnon in public or approvingly referenced QAnon slogans. (One Republican candidate for Congress, Matthew Lusk of Florida, includes QAnon under the "issues" section of his campaign website, posing the question: "Who is Q?") QAnon has by now made its way onto every major social and commercial platform and any number of fringe sites. Tracy Diaz, a QAnon evangelist, known online by the name TracyBeanz, has 185,000 followers on Twitter and more than 100,000 YouTube subscribers. She helped lift QAnon from obscurity, facilitating its transition to mainstream social media. (A publicist described Diaz as "really private" and declined requests for an interview.) On TikTok, videos with the hashtag #QAnon have garnered millions of views. There are too many QAnon Facebook groups, plenty of them ghost towns, to do a proper count, but the most active ones publish thousands of items each day. (In 2018, Reddit banned QAnon groups from its platform for inciting violence.)

Adherents are ever looking out for signs from on high, plumbing for portents when guidance from Q himself is absent. The coronavirus, for instance—what does it signify? In several of the big Facebook groups, people erupted in a frenzy of speculation, circulating a theory that Trump's decision to wear a yellow tie to a White House briefing about the virus was a sign that the outbreak wasn't real: "He is telling us there is no virus threat because it is the exact same color as the maritime flag that represents the vessel has no infected people on board," someone wrote in a post that was widely shared and remixed across social media. Three days before the World Health Organization officially declared the coronavirus a pandemic, Trump was retweeting a QAnon-themed meme. "Who knows what this means, but it sounds good to me!" the president wrote on March 8, sharing a Photoshopped image of himself playing a violin overlaid with the words "Nothing can stop what is coming."

On March 9, Q himself issued a triptych of ominous posts that seemed definitive: The coronavirus is real, but welcome, and followers should not be afraid. The first post shared Trump's tweet from the night before and repeated, "Nothing Can Stop What Is Coming." The second said: "The Great Awakening is Worldwide." The third was simple: "GOD WINS."

A month later, on April 8, Q went on a posting spree, dropping nine posts over the span of six hours and touching on several of his favorite topics—God, Pizzagate, and the wickedness of the elites. "They will stop at nothing to regain power," he wrote in one scathing post that alleged a coordinated propaganda effort by Democrats, Hollywood, and the media. Another accused Democrats of promoting "mass hysteria" about the coronavirus for political gain: "What is the primary benefit to keep public in mass-hysteria re: COVID-19? Think voting. Are you awake yet? Q." And he shared these verses from Ephesians: "Finally, be strong in the Lord and in the strength of His might. Put on the full armor of God so that you will be able to stand firm against the schemes of the devil."

Anthony Fauci, the longtime director of the National Institute of Allergy and Infectious Diseases, has become an object of scorn among QAnon supporters who don't like the bad news he delivers or the way he has contradicted Trump publicly. In one March press conference,

Trump referred to the State Department as the "Deep State Department," and Fauci could be seen over the president's shoulder, suppressing a laugh and covering his face. By then, QAnon had already declared Fauci irredeemably compromised, because WikiLeaks had unearthed a pair of emails he sent praising Hillary Clinton in 2012 and 2013. Sentiment about Fauci among QAnon supporters on social-media platforms ranges from "Fauci is a Deep State puppet" to "FAUCI is a BLACK-HAT!!!"—the term QAnon uses for people who support the evil cabal that Q warns about. One person, using the hashtags #DeepStateCabal and #Qanon, tweeted this: "Watch Fauci's hand signals and body language at the press conferences. What is he communicating?" Another shared an image of Fauci standing in a lab with Barack Obama, with the caption "Obama and 'Dr.' Fauci in the lab creating coronovirus [sic]. #DeepstateDoctor." The Justice Department recently approved heightened security measures for Fauci because of the mounting volume of threats against him.

In the final days before Congress passed a $2 trillion economic-relief package in late March, Democrats insisted on provisions that would make it easier for people to vote by mail, prompting Q himself to weigh in with dismay: "These people are sick! Nothing can stop what is coming. Nothing."

———

On a bone-cold Thursday in early January, a crowd was swelling in downtown Toledo, Ohio. By lunchtime, seven hours before the start of Trump's first campaign rally of the new year, the line to get into the Huntington Center had already snaked around two city blocks. The air was electric with possibility, and the whole scene possessed a Jimmy Buffett–meets–Michigan Militia atmosphere: lots of white people, a good deal of vaping, red-white-and-blue everything. Down the street, someone had affixed a two-story banner across the top of a burned-out brick building. It read: PRESIDENT TRUMP, WELCOME TO TOLEDO, OHIO: WHO IS Q . . . MILITARY INTELLIGENCE? Q+? ("Q+" is QAnon shorthand for Trump himself.) Vendors at the event were selling Q buttons and T-shirts. QAnon merchandise comes in a great variety; online, you can buy Great Awakening coffee ($14.99) and QAnon bracelets with tiny silver pizza charms ($20.17).

I worked my way toward the back of the line, making small talk and asking who, if anyone, knew anything about QAnon. One woman's eyes lit up, and in a single fluid motion she unzipped and removed her jacket, then did a little jump so that her back was to me. I could see a *Q* made out of duct tape, which she'd pressed onto her red T-shirt. Her name was Lorrie Shock, and the first thing she wanted me to know was this: "We're not a domestic-terror group."

Shock was born in Ohio and never left, "a lifer," as she put it. She had worked at a Bridgestone factory, making car parts, for most of her adult life. "Real hot and dirty work, but good money," she told me. "I got three kids through school." Today, in what she calls her preretirement job, she cares for adults with special needs, spending her days in a tender routine of playing games with them and helping them in and out of a swimming pool. Shock came to the Trump rally with her friend Pat Harger, who had retired after 32 years at Whirlpool. Harger's wife runs a catering business, which is what had kept her from attending the rally that day. Harger and Shock are old friends. "Since the fourth grade," Harger told me, "and we're 57 years old."

Now that Shock's girls are grown and she's not working a factory job, she has more time for herself. That used to mean reading novels in the evening—she doesn't own a television—but now it means researching Q, who first came to her notice when someone she knew mentioned him on Facebook in 2017: "What caught my attention was 'research.' *Do your own research. Don't take anything for granted.* I don't care who says it, even President Trump. Do your own research, make up your own mind."

The QAnon universe is sprawling and deep, with layer upon layer of context, acronyms, characters, and shorthand to learn. The "castle" is the White House. "Crumbs" are clues. CBTS stands for "calm before the storm," and WWG1WGA stands for "Where we go one, we go all," which has become an expression of solidarity among Q followers. (Both of these phrases, oddly, are used in the trailer for the 1996 Ridley Scott film *White Squall*—watch it on YouTube, and you'll see that the comments section is flooded with pro-Q sentiment.) There is also a "Q clock," which refers to a calendar some factions of Q supporters use to try to decode supposed clues based on time stamps of Q drops and Trump tweets.

At the height of her devotion, Shock was spending four to six hours a day reading and rereading Q drops, scouring documents online, taking notes. Now, she says, she spends closer to an hour or two a day. "When I first started, everybody thought I was crazy," Shock said. That included her daughters, who are "very liberal Hillary and Bernie supporters," Shock said. "I still love them. They think I'm crazy, but that's all right."

Harger, too, once thought Shock had lost it. "I was doubting her," he told me. "I would send her texts saying, *Lorrie.*"

"He was like, 'What the hell?'" Shock said, laughing. "So my comment to him would be 'Do your own research.'"

"And I did," Harger said. "And it's like, *Wow.*"

Taking a page from Trump's playbook, Q frequently rails against legitimate sources of information as fake. Shock and Harger rely on information they encounter on Facebook rather than news outlets run by journalists. They don't read the local paper or watch any of the major television networks. "You can't watch the news," Shock said. "Your news channel ain't gonna tell us shit." Harger says he likes One America News Network. Not so long ago, he used to watch CNN, and couldn't get enough of Wolf Blitzer. "We were glued to that; we always have been," he said. "Until this man, Trump, really opened our eyes to what's happening. And Q. Q is telling us beforehand the stuff that's going to happen." I asked Harger and Shock for examples of predictions that had come true. They could not provide specifics and instead encouraged me to do the research myself. When I asked them how they explained the events Q had predicted that never happened, such as Clinton's arrest, they said that deception is part of Q's plan. Shock added, "I think there were more things that were predicted that *did* happen." Her tone was gentle rather than indignant.

Harger wanted me to know that he'd voted for Obama the first time around. He grew up in a family of Democrats. His dad was a union guy. But that was before Trump appeared and convinced Harger that he shouldn't trust the institutions he always thought he could. Shock nodded alongside him. "The reason I feel like I can trust Trump more is, he's not part of the establishment," she said. At one point, Harger told me I should look into what happened to John F. Kennedy Jr.— who died in 1999, when his airplane crashed into the Atlantic Ocean off Martha's Vineyard—suggesting that Hillary Clinton had had him assassinated. (Alternatively, a contingent of QAnon believers say that JFK Jr. faked his death and that he's a behind-the-scenes Trump supporter, and possibly even Q himself. Some anticipate his dramatic public return so that he can serve as Trump's running mate in 2020.) When I asked Harger whether there's any evidence to support the assassination claim, he flipped my question around: "Is there any evidence not to?"

Reading Shock's Facebook page is an exercise in contradictions, a toggling between banality and hostility. There she is in a yellow kayak in her profile photo, bright-red hair spilling out of a ski hat, a giant smile on her face. There are the photos of her daughters, and of a granddaughter with Shirley Temple curls. Yet Q is never far away. On Christmas Eve, Shock shared one post that seemed to come straight out of the QAnon universe but also pulled in an older, classic conspiracy: "X marks the spot over Roswell NM. X17 Fifth Force Particle. X + Q Coincidence?" That same day, she shared a separate post suggesting that Michelle Obama is secretly a man. Someone responded with skepticism: "I am still not convinced. She shows and acts evil, but a man?" Shock's reply: "Research it." There was a post claiming that Representative Adam Schiff had raped the body of a dead boy at the Chateau Marmont, in Los Angeles—Harger shows up here, with a "huh??" in the comments—and a warning that George Soros was going after Christian evangelicals. In other posts, Shock playfully taunted "libs" and her "Trump-hating friends," and also shared a video of her daughter singing Christmas carols.

In Toledo, I asked Shock if she had any theories about Q's identity. She answered immediately: "I think it's Trump." I asked if she thinks Trump even knows how to use 4chan. The message board is notoriously confusing for the uninitiated, nothing like Facebook and other social platforms designed to make it easy to publish quickly and often. "I think he knows way more than what we think," she said. But she also wanted me to know that her obsession with Q wasn't about Trump. This had been something she was reluctant to speak about at first. Now, she said, "I feel God led me to Q. I really feel like God pushed me in this direction. I feel like if it was deceitful, in my spirit, God would be telling me, 'Enough's enough.' But I don't feel that. I pray about it. I've said, 'Father, should I be wasting my time on this?' . . . And I don't feel that feeling of *I should stop.*"

Watchkeepers for the End of Days can easily find signs of impending doom—in comets and earthquakes, in wars and pandemics. It has always been this way. In 1831, a Baptist preacher in rural New York named William Miller began to publicly share his prediction that the Second Coming of Jesus was imminent. Eventually he settled on a date: October 22, 1844. When the sun came up on October 23, his followers, known as the Millerites, were crushed. The episode would come to be known as the Great Disappointment. But they did not give up. The Millerites became the Adventists, who in turn became the Seventh-day Adventists, who now have a worldwide membership of more than 20 million. "These people in the QAnon community—I feel like they are as deeply delusional, as deeply invested in their beliefs, as the Millerites were," Travis View, one of the hosts of a podcast called *QAnon Anonymous*, which subjects QAnon to acerbic analysis, told me. "That makes me pretty confident that this is not something that is going to go away with the end of the Trump presidency."

QAnon carries on a tradition of apocalyptic thinking that has spanned thousands of years. It offers a polemic to empower those who feel adrift. In his classic 1957 book, *The Pursuit of the Millennium*, the historian Norman Cohn examined the emergence of apocalyptic thinking over many centuries. He found one common condition: This way of thinking consistently emerged in regions where rapid social and economic change was taking place—and at periods of time when displays of spectacular wealth were highly visible but unavailable to most people. This was true in Europe during the Crusades in the 11th century, and during the Black Death in the 14th century, and in the Rhine Valley in the 16th century, and in William Miller's New York in the 19th century. It is true in America in the 21st century.

The Seventh-day Adventists and the Church of Jesus Christ of Latter-day Saints are thriving religious movements indigenous to America. Do not be surprised if QAnon becomes another. It already has more adherents by far than either of those two denominations had in the first decades of their existence. People are expressing their faith through devoted study of Q drops as installments of a foundational text, through the development of Q-worshipping groups, and through sweeping expressions of gratitude for what Q has brought to their lives. Does it matter that we do not know who Q is? The divine is always a mystery. Does it matter that basic aspects of Q's teachings cannot be confirmed? The basic tenets of Christianity cannot be confirmed. Among the people of QAnon, faith remains absolute. True believers describe a feeling of rebirth, an irreversible arousal to existential knowledge. They are certain that a Great Awakening is coming. They'll wait as long as they must for deliverance.

Trust the plan. Enjoy the show. Nothing can stop what is coming.

THEY HAD IT COMING

by Caitlin Flanagan

[APRIL 2019]

QAnon is an extreme case, but suspicion and hostility are engines of attention on social media. Anger has become a lingua franca of political discourse. Often it is directed at people with wealth and power by people who have neither. Less understandably, a segment of society's most advantaged stratum is angry, too, seeing itself both as a persecuted minority and as an elect to whom ordinary rules should not apply.

In 2019, as the result of an FBI investigation called Operation Varsity Blues, the Justice Department swooped in with indictments of wealthy parents on the East and West Coasts who had employed a variety of illegal methods to gain admission for their children to top colleges and universities. For Caitlin Flanagan—a staff writer at *The Atlantic* and the author of *To Hell With All That: Loving and Loathing Our Inner Housewife* (2006) and *Girl Land* (2012)—the indictments rekindled memories of her experience as a young guidance counselor at an elite prep school in Los Angeles. In her 2019 article "They Had It Coming," Flanagan wrote: "I just about got an ulcer sitting in that office listening to rich people complaining bitterly about an 'unfair' or a 'rigged' system. Sometimes they would say things so outlandish that I would just stare at them, trying to beam into their mind the question, *Can you* hear *yourself?*"

S weet Christ, vindication!

How long has it been? Years? No, decades. If hope is the thing with feathers, I was a plucked bird. Long ago, I surrendered myself to the fact that the horrible, horrible private-school parents of Los Angeles would get away with their nastiness forever. But even before the molting, never in my wildest imaginings had I dared to dream that the arc of the moral universe could describe a 90-degree angle and smite down mine enemies with such a hammer fist of fire and fury that even I have had a moment of thinking, *Could this be a bit too much?*

Let's back up.

Thirty years ago, having tapped out of a Ph.D. program, I moved to Los Angeles (long story) and got hired at the top boys' school in the city, which would soon become co-educational. For the first four years, I taught English. Best job I've ever had. For the next three, I was a college counselor. Worst job I've ever had.

When I was a teacher, my job was a source of self-respect; I had joined a great tradition. I was a young woman from a certain kind of good but not moneyed family who could exchange her only salable talents—an abiding love of books and a fondness for teenagers—for a job. Poor, obscure, plain, and little, I would drive through the exotic air of early-morning Los Angeles to the school, which was on a street with a beautiful name, Coldwater Canyon, in a part of the city originally designated the Central Motion Picture District. It sat on a plot of land that in the 1920s composed part of the Hollywood Hills Country Club, an institution that has a Narnia-like aspect, in that not even the California historian Kevin Starr knew whether it ever really existed, or whether it was merely a fiction promoted by real-estate developers trying to entice new homeowners to the Edenic San Fernando Valley. Across from a round tower connecting the upper and lower campuses was Saint Saviour's, a chapel that the founders of the school built in 1914 as an exact replica of the one built in 1567 for the Rugby School in England, with pews facing the center aisle in the Tudor style. This combination of the possibly imaginary country club and the assumption behind the building of the chapel—get the set right, and you can make the whole production work—seemed to me like something from an Evelyn Waugh novel. But it also meant that—unlike Exeter or Choate—this school was a place where I could belong. There were no traditions, no expectation of familiarity with the Book of Common Prayer. All you needed to have was a piercing love of your subject and a willingness to enter into an apprenticeship with great teachers. I had those things.

This was before cellphones and laptops, and in the chalk-dusted eternity of a 42-minute class period, there was such a thrumming, adolescent need for stimulation that when I opened whatever book we were reading—all of them great, all of them chosen by teachers far more thoughtful and experienced than I—and began reading aloud, the stream of words was the only thing going, and many of the students couldn't help themselves from slipping into that stream and letting it carry them along.

> *I met a traveller from an antique land,*
> *Who said—"Two vast and trunkless legs of stone*
> *Stand in the desert . . . Near them, on the sand,*
> *Half sunk a shattered visage lies*

I did not come from a religious family, but we had a god, and the god was art, specifically literature. Taking a job teaching "Ozymandias" to a new generation was, for me, the equivalent of taking religious orders.

And so when a job opened in the college-counseling office, I should not have taken it. My god was art, not the SAT. In my excitement at this apparent promotion, I did not pause to consider that my beliefs about the new work at hand made me, at best, a heretic. I honestly believed—still believe—that hundreds of very good colleges in the country have reasonable admissions requirements; that if you've put in your best effort, a B is a good grade; and that expecting adolescents to do five hours of homework on top of meeting time-consuming athletic demands is, in all but exceptional cases, child abuse. Most of all, I believed that if you had money for college and a good high-school education under your belt, you were on third base headed for home plate with the ball soaring high over the bleachers.

I did not know—even after four years at the institution—that the school's impressive matriculation list was not the simple by-product of excellent teaching, but was in fact the end result of parental campaigns undertaken with the same level of whimsy with which the Japanese Navy bombed Pearl Harbor.

Every parent assumed that whatever alchemy of good genes and good credit had gotten his child a spot at the prep school was the same one that would land him a spot at a hyper-selective college. It was true that a quarter of the class went to the Ivy League, and another quarter to places such as Stanford, MIT, and Amherst. But that still left half the class, and I was the one who had to tell their parents that they were going to have to be flexible. Before each meeting, I prepared a list of good colleges that the kid had a strong chance of getting into, but these parents didn't want colleges their kids had a strong chance of getting into; they wanted colleges their kids didn't have a chance in hell of getting into. A successful first meeting often consisted of walking them back from the crack pipe of Harvard to the Adderall crash of Middlebury and then scheduling a follow-up meeting to douse them with the bong water of Denison.

The new job meant that I had signed myself up to be locked in a small office, appointment after appointment, with hugely powerful parents and their mortified children as I delivered news so grimly received that I began to think of myself less as an administrator than as an oncologist. Along the way they said such crass things, such rude things, such greedy things, and such borderline-racist things that I began to hate them. They, in turn, began to hate me. A college counselor at an elite prep school is supposed to be a combination of cheerleader, concierge, and talent agent, radically on the side of each case and applying steady pressure on the dream college to make it happen. At the very least, the counselor is not supposed to be an adversary.

I just about got an ulcer sitting in that office listening to rich people complaining bitterly about an "unfair" or a "rigged" system. Sometimes they would say things so outlandish that I would just stare at them, trying to beam into their mind the question, *Can you* hear *yourself?* That so many of them were (literal) limousine liberals lent the meetings an element of radical chic. They were down for the revolution, but there was no way *their* kid was going to settle for Lehigh.

Some of the parents—especially, in those days, the fathers—were such powerful professionals, and I (as you recall) was so poor, obscure, plain, and little that it was as if they were cracking open a cream puff with a panzer. This was before crying in the office was a thing, so I had to just sit there and take it. Then the admissions letters arrived from the colleges. If the kid got in, it was because he was a genius; if he didn't, it was because I screwed up. When a venture capitalist and his ageless wife storm into your boss's office to get you fired because you failed to get their daughter (conscientious, but no atom splitter) into the prestigious school they wanted, you can really start to question whether it's worth the 36K.

Sometimes, in anger and frustration, the parents would blame me for the poor return on investment they were getting on their years of tuition payments. At that point, I was living in a rent-controlled apartment and paying $198 a month on a Civic with manual windows. I was in no position to evaluate their financial strategies. Worst of all, the helpless kid would be sitting right there, shrinking into the couch cushions as his parents all but said that his entire secondary education had been a giant waste of money. The parents would simmer down a bit, and the four of us would stew in misery. Nobody wanted to hear me read "Ozymandias."

I will now add as a very truthful disclaimer that the horrible parents constituted at most 25 percent of the total, that the rest weren't just unobjectionable, but many—perhaps most—were lovely people who were so wise about parenting that when I had children of my own, I often remembered things they had told me. But that 25 percent was a lesson that a lifetime of reading novels hadn't yet taught me. In the classroom I was Jane Eyre, strong and tranquil in the truth of my gifts; in the college-counseling office, I was the nameless heroine of *Rebecca*, running up and down the servant stairs at the Hôtel d'Azur as Mrs. Van Hopper barked at me.

During those three years before the mast, I saw no evidence of any of the criminal activity that the current scandal has delivered. But I absolutely saw the raw materials that William Rick Singer would use to create his scam. The system, even 25 years ago, was full of holes.

The first was sports. Legacy admissions have often been called affirmative action for white people, but the rich-kid sports—water polo, tennis, swimming, gymnastics, volleyball, and even (God help us all) sailing and actual polo—are the true affirmative action for the rich. I first became acquainted with this fact when I was preparing for a meeting with the parents of a girl who was a strong but not dazzling student; the list her parents had submitted, however, consisted almost exclusively of Ivy League colleges. I brought her file in to my boss for guidance. She looked it over and then, noticing something in the section on extracurricular activities and tapping it decisively with her pen, said, "Oh, she'll get in—volleyball."

Volleyball? Yale was going to let her in—above half a dozen much more academically qualified and many much more interesting kids on my roster—because she played *volleyball*? I soon learned that the coaches of all these sports were allowed a certain number of recruits each year, and that so long as a kid met basic academic qualifications—which our kids easily did—the coaches got their way. I never heard an admissions person question a coach; "She's on the soccer list," the admissions person would say, and we'd move on to the next kid.

The second flaw in the system was an important change to the way testing is reported to the colleges. When I began the job, the SAT and the ACT offered extended-time testing to students with learning disabilities, provided that they had been diagnosed by a professional. However, an asterisk appeared next to extended-time scores, alerting the college that the student had taken the test without the usual time limit. But during my time at the school, this asterisk was found to violate the Americans With Disabilities Act, and the testing companies dropped it. Suddenly it was possible for everyone with enough money to get a diagnosis that would grant their kid two full days—instead of four hours—to take the SAT, and the colleges would never know. By 2006, according to *Slate*, "in places like Greenwich, Conn., and certain zip codes of New York City and Los Angeles, the percentage of untimed test-taking is said to be close to 50 percent." Taking a test under normal time limits in one of these neighborhoods is a sucker's game—you've voluntarily handicapped yourself.

And, finally, there were large parts of the process over which no one entity had complete oversight. The kids were encouraged, but not required, to bring us their essays. Ditto the lists of extracurricular activities they were required to submit to the colleges. The holy trinity of documents—transcript, test scores, and teacher recommendations—never touches the kids' hands. But the veracity of everything else depends on a tremendous leap of good faith on the part of the admissions offices.

And it was through these broken saloon doors—the great power conferred on coaches, extended-time testing, and the ease with which an application can be crammed with false information—that Singer pushed unqualified students into colleges they wanted to attend. He told the parents to get their kids diagnosed with learning disabilities, and then arranged for them to take the test alone in a room with a fake proctor—someone who was so skilled at taking these tests that he could (either by correcting the student's test before submitting it or by simply taking the thing himself) arrive at whatever score the client requested. ("I own two schools," Singer told a client about the testing sites, one in West Hollywood and the other in Houston, where his fake proctors could do their work.) He allowed coaches to monetize any extra spots on their recruitment lists by selling them to his clients. And he offered a service that he called "cleaning up" the transcript, which involved, at the very least, having his employees take online courses in the kids' name and then adding those A's to their record.

All this malfeasance has led to the creation of a 200-page affidavit, and a bevy of other court documents, that can best be described as a kind of posthumous Tom Wolfe novella, one with a wide cast of very rich people behaving in such despicable ways that it makes *The Bonfire of the Vanities* look like *The Pilgrim's Progress*. If you have not read the affidavit, and if you're in the mood for a novel of manners of the kind not attempted since the passing of the master, I recommend that you and your book club put it on the list for immediate consumption.

The one compliment the FBI paid the indicted parents is that it took college admissions as seriously as they did. The investigation included wiretaps, stakeouts, reviews of bank statements, travel records, cell-site data, emails, and interviews with cooperating witnesses—chief among them Singer, who seems not simply to have thrown his clients under a bus, but rather to have taken them to Port Authority and thrown them under an entire fleet.

How did his scam come to light? Let the reader be introduced to Morrie Tobin, upon whose character and doings much will depend. A 55-year-old stockbroker and father of six who lives in the elegant Los Angeles neighborhood of Hancock Park, he got pinched last spring for an SEC violation that allegedly defrauded clients of millions of dollars. Desperate to lighten his punishment, the *Los Angeles Times* reported, he offered an unrelated claim: There was a Yale soccer coach, Rudy Meredith, who accepted bribes to let kids into the university. Of all the things Tobin could have given up, this seems an especially cruel one—he had two daughters enrolled at Yale, one had graduated from the university, and a fourth had recently been accepted. At the very least, this revelation put their admissions in an unflattering light. The FBI had Tobin wear a wire to a private meeting with the coach, during which Singer's name came up, and from there the full investigation— Varsity Blues—began.

Most of the families involved in the scandal lived in the California dreamscapes of a Nancy Meyers movie: Newport Beach, Hillsborough, Laguna Beach, San Francisco, Del Mar, Ross. The out-of-staters are no slouches, either. One family divides its time between Aspen and New York; another lives in Greenwich. Let's start there, in Greenwich, where not getting your kid into the right college is cause for seppuku. We are in the home of Gordon Caplan and his wife, Amy. Gordon was—until placed on "leave" post-indictment—the co-chairman of a New York– based global law firm, where he was a partner in the private-equity group. Amy is the heiress daughter of the late telecommunications magnate Richard Treibick. He also lived in Greenwich, summering in the Hamptons on a 32-acre spread in Sagaponack that included a seven-bedroom house on the dunes with a pool overlooking the ocean, which his family sold shortly after his death in 2014 for a reported $35 million. (As of this writing, Caplan had not commented publicly on the allegations contained in the filings, or entered a plea; a court appearance was scheduled.)

Gordon graduated from Cornell, but ended up pursuing his law degree at sweaty-browed Fordham, suggesting the combination of privilege and hustle that can really get a certain kind of guy ahead. He was the board chairman of the world's most quixotic nonprofit organization, Publicolor, which seeks to "improve education in youth by promoting an imaginative use of color in school buildings." In 2018—the year he was negotiating with Singer about his daughter's future—*The American Lawyer* magazine named him Dealmaker of the Year.

He seems to have had Cornell on his mind for his daughter, having dramatically upped his annual giving to the low six figures during her sophomore and junior years of high school. But her grades and scores were apparently too low for the traditional approach, and he and Singer began talking about a scheme. "What is the, what is the, the number?" he asks Singer. "At Cornell for instance."

"Hold on a second," Singer says, carefully bleeding his client one pint at a time. "The number on the testing is $75,000." (Singer seems to have operated on a sliding scale. He charged Caplan $75,000 for the testing scam, yet he charged Felicity Huffman only $15,000. Perhaps *The American Lawyer* needs to cast a wider net when selecting its Dealmakers of the Year.)

"I can do anything and everything, if you guys are amenable to doing it," he tells Caplan, explaining the elaborate system he employed to falsify test scores: "I can guarantee her a score."

Caplan takes a few hours to digest this idea, and then has a second phone call with Singer. "This notion of effectively going in, flying out to L.A., sitting with your proctor, and taking the exam is pretty interesting."

"It's the home run of home runs," Singer tells him.

"So, how do I get this done with you?" Caplan asks. "What do I need to do?"

Singer gives an interesting answer: "I'm gonna talk to our psychologist, and we may have to send her to you, or you to her." Sure enough, per the criminal complaint, "On or about July 21, 2018, CAPLAN and his daughter flew to Los Angeles to meet with a psychologist in an effort to obtain the medical documentation required to receive extended time on the ACT exam."

This is the only section of the complaint that mentions the character of "our psychologist." There are more educational psychologists in Greenwich, Connecticut, than there are Labrador retrievers. Hotfoot it over to New Haven or Manhattan, and you have to beat them off with a stick. Why was Singer so certain that this particular psychologist would produce the documentation the student needed? The government is clearly continuing its investigation—student records have been subpoenaed from several private schools in Los Angeles, and it's not hard to imagine that more indictments, perhaps many more, are coming. "Our psychologist" might play a role in these investigations.

The problem with getting newly diagnosed with a learning disability in 11th or 12th grade is that the companies that own the tests know they're probably being manipulated, and will often deny the application for extended-time testing. Sure enough, the ACT denied the Caplan daughter's first request, and also her appeal. But then, a surprising bit of good news. "You were right," Caplan tells Singer; "it was like third time was the charm . . . Everybody was telling us there's no way, and then all of a sudden it comes in." But one of the delights of this novel is that the reader is often in possession of information the main characters lack. While Caplan crows, we smirk: "The ACT ultimately granted CAPLAN'S daughter extended time on the exam at the request of law enforcement."

The only obstacle Caplan has in executing his plan (other than the FBI, but that outfit is still months away from making itself known to him) is the old ball and chain. In the obdurate way of heiresses who grew up in the cleansing sea air of Sagaponack summers and not amid the hard-roll-with-butter realities of Fordham Law, she has her niceties. In July, when both Amy and Gordon get on speakerphone with Singer, the con man suggests having one of his operatives take an online class for their daughter as a means of bringing up her GPA. But "CAPLAN's spouse replied that she had a 'problem with that.'"

Caplan grabs the phone off the cradle, effectively taking Miss Scruples off the call.

"It's just you and me," he tells Singer. "Is that kosher?"

No, it's not kosher. Obviously.

"Absolutely," Singer says. "I do it all the time, man."

By November, the Gordon/Amy situation had reached one of those marital impasses in which Partner A is going ahead with something Partner B thinks is messed up, but isn't willing to outright squash, because who knows? Maybe it will work. It's a high-risk/high-reward prospect for Partner A. "I'm taking [Amy] off of this," Caplan tells Singer at one point; [Amy] is very nervous about all this."

But the Dealmaker of the Year spent considerable time kicking the tires on this one. "Keep in mind I am a lawyer," Caplan said at one point, according to the affidavit. "So I'm sort of rules oriented." And, later, "I'm not worried about the moral issue here. I'm worried about the, if she's caught doing that, you know, she's finished."

Much of the discussion of this scandal has centered on the corruption in the college-admissions process. But think about the kinds of jobs that the indicted parents held. Four of them worked in private equity, a fifth in the field of "investments," others in real-estate development and the most senior management of huge corporations. Together, they have handled billions of dollars' worth of assets within heavily regulated fields—yet look how easily and how eagerly they allegedly embrace a crooked scheme, as quoted in the court documents.

Here is Bill McGlashan, then a senior executive at a global private-equity fund, reacting to Singer's plan to get his son (who does not play football) admitted to USC via the football team: "That's just totally hilarious."

Here is Robert Zangrillo, the founder and CEO of a private-investment firm, talking with one of Singer's employees who is planning to bring up his daughter's grades by taking online classes in her name: "Just makes [*sic*] sure it gets done as quickly as possible."

Here is John B. Wilson, the founder and CEO of a private-equity and real-estate-development firm, on getting his son into USC using a fake record of playing water polo: "Thanks again for making this happen!" And, "What are the options for the payment? Can we make it for consulting or whatever . . . so that I can pay it from the corporate account?" He can. "Awesome!"

Here is Douglas Hodge, the former CEO of a large investment-management company, learning from Singer that his son will be admitted to USC via a bribery scheme, and that it's time to send a check: "Fanstatic [*sic*]!! Will do."

The word *entitlement*—even in its full, splendid range of meanings—doesn't begin to cover the attitudes on display. Devin Sloane is the CEO of a Los Angeles company that deals in wastewater management. Through Singer, he allegedly bribed USC to get his son admitted as a water-polo player. But a guidance counselor at his school learned of the scheme and contacted USC—the boy did not play the sport; something was clearly awry. Singer smoothed it over, but the whole incident enraged Sloane: "The more I think about this, it is outrageous! They have no business or legal right considering all the students privacy issues to be calling and challenging/question [my son's] application," he wrote to Singer.

There are several instances of college counselors gumming up the works with their small-timers' insistence on ethical behavior. That someone as lowly, as contemptibly puny, as a guidance counselor should interfere with a rich person's desires is the cause of electric rage. For this reason, after having read the 200-page affidavit many times and trying to be as objective as possible, I had to conclude that the uncontested winners of Worst People (So Far) to Be Indicted are Lori Loughlin, an actress, and her husband, Mossimo Giannulli, a designer. When a college counselor at their daughter's high school realized something was suspicious about her admission to USC and asked the girl about it, the parents roared onto campus in such a rage that they almost blew up the whole scam.

The couple paid $500,000 to get both of their daughters into USC on the preposterous claim that they rowed crew. Their daughter Olivia has become a particularly ridiculed character in the saga, because there are pre-indictment videos in which she describes both her lack of desire to attend college and how rarely she attended high school during her senior year. But I have sympathy for her. She knew higher education wasn't where she belonged, but her parents insisted that she go. Up until the scandal, the girl had a thriving cosmetics line, was a popular YouTuber, and was clearly making the best of what Hillary Clinton would call her God-given potential. Now she's a punch line, and Sephora has pulled her products off the shelves.

The court filings don't state when the parents began working with Singer, but they appear to have felt a sense of urgency on April 22, 2016, when they took part in a standard component of prep-school college counseling: the family meeting with a college counselor during spring of junior year. "We just met with [Olivia's] college counselor this am," Giannulli wrote in an email to Singer. "I'd like to maybe sit with you after your session with the girls as I have some concerns and want to fully understand the game plan . . . as it relates to [her] and getting her into a school other than ASU!"

Mentioning Arizona State University to the private-school parents of a freshman is the equivalent of throwing a flash-bang grenade; it won't kill anyone, but it will sure as hell get their attention. But mention it to the parents of a second-semester junior, and you're no longer issuing warnings. ASU is the unconditional surrender.

"If you want [U]SC," Singer replies, "I have the game plan ready to go into motion."

But the college counselor at the girls' high school had always doubted that the first girl rowed crew; when the second one got into the same school for the same reason, she realized that something suspicious was going on. She confronted the girl.

The counselor was acting honorably. Loughlin and Giannulli—if the affidavit is to be believed—were in the midst of a criminal operation. Yet instead of hanging his head in shame, Giannulli apparently roared onto the high-school campus apoplectic. Singer got a panicked email from his USC contact: "I just want to make sure that, you know, I don't want the . . . parents getting angry and creating any type of disturbance at the school . . . I just don't want anybody going into . . . [the daughter's high school], you know, yelling at counselors. That'll shut everything—that'll shut everything down."

It's hell on Earth for college counselors when people like this show up angry that their kid didn't get an acceptance from Williams. But to endure it because you've gotten in the way of a giant scam? Hideous.

One way or another, the counselor was impelled—I would imagine by some freaked-out higher-up—to send the parents an email:

> I wanted to provide you with an update on the status of [your younger daughter's] admission offer to USC. First and foremost, they have no intention of rescinding [her] admission and were surprised to hear that was even a concern for you and your family. You can verify that with [the USC senior assistant director of admissions] . . . if you would like. I also shared with [the USC senior assistant director of admissions] that you had visited this morning and affirmed for me that [your younger daughter] is truly a coxswain.

As Jerry Maguire said about being a sports agent, being a prep-school college counselor is an "up-at-dawn, pride-swallowing siege." But no work of fiction could prepare these employees for the fact that there are now L.A. private-school parents who are intent on maligning the guidance counselors who they have decided must have been in on the scheme. The president of one school sent this email to parents: "I want to emphasize that I have absolute confidence in the honesty of our deans, the accuracy of the information they provide to colleges and their focus on personal character in the guidance they provide our students." Honesty of the deans? It's the dishonesty of the parents that's the problem.

————

Ever since the scandal became public, two opinions have been widely expressed. The first is that the schemes it revealed are not much different from the long-standing admissions preference for big donors, and the second is that these admissions gained on fraudulent grounds have harmed underprivileged students. These aren't quite right. As off-putting as most of us find the role that big-ticket fundraising plays in elite-college admissions, those monies go toward programs and facilities that will benefit a wide number of students—new dormitories, new libraries, enriched financial-aid funds are often the result of rich parents being tapped for gifts at admissions time. But the Singer scheme benefits no one at all except the individual students, and the people their parents paid off.

The argument that the scheme hurt disadvantaged applicants—or even just non-rich applicants who needed financial aid to attend these stratospherically expensive colleges—isn't right, either. Elite colleges pay deep attention to the issue of enrollment management; the more elite the institution, the more likely it is to be racially and socioeconomically diverse. This is in part because attaining this kind of diversity has become a foundational goal of most admissions offices, and also because the elite colleges have the money to make it happen. In 2017, Harvard announced with great fanfare that it had enrolled its first class in which white students were in the minority.

When I was a prep-school college counselor 25 years ago, I thought that whatever madness was whirring through the minds of the parents was a blip of group insanity that would soon abate. It has only gotten more and more extreme. Anyone can understand a parent's disappointment if he had thought for 17 years that his child would go to Yale one day, only to learn that it's not in the cards. But what accounted for the intensity of emotion these parents expressed, their sense of a profound loss, of rage at being robbed of what they believed was rightfully theirs? They were experiencing the same response to a changing America that ultimately brought Donald Trump to office: white displacement and a revised social contract. The collapse of manufacturing jobs has been to poor whites what the elite college-admissions crunch has been to wealthy ones: a smaller and smaller slice of pie for people who were used to having the fattest piece of all.

In the recent past—the past in which this generation of parents grew up—a white student from a professional-class or wealthy family who attended either a private high school or a public one in a prosperous school district was all but assured admission at a "good" college. It wasn't necessarily going to be Harvard or Yale, but it certainly might be Bowdoin or Northwestern. That was the way the system worked. But today, there's a squeeze on those kids. The very strong but not spectacular white student from a good high school is now trying to gain access to an ever-shrinking pool of available spots at the top places. He's not the inherently attractive prospect he once was.

These parents—many of them avowed Trump haters—are furious that what once belonged to them has been taken away, and they are driven mad with the need to reclaim it for their children. The changed admissions landscape at the elite colleges is the aspect of American life that doesn't feel right to them; it's the lost thing, the arcadia that disappeared so slowly they didn't even realize it was happening until it was gone. They can't believe it—they truly can't believe it—when they realize that even the colleges they had assumed would be their child's backup, emergency plan probably won't accept them. They pay thousands and thousands of dollars for extended-time testing and private counselors; they scour lists of board members at colleges, looking for any possible connections; they pay for enhancing summer programs that only underscore their children's privilege. And—as poor whites did in the years leading up to 2016—they complain about it endlessly. At every parent coffee, silent auction, dinner party, Clippers game, book club, and wine tasting, someone is bitching about admissions. And some of these parents, it turns out, haven't just been bitching; some of them decided to go MAGA.

And so it was that at 5:59 on the morning of March 12 in the sacramentally beautiful section of the Hollywood Hills called Outpost Estates, all was quiet, save for the sounds of the natural world. In the mid-century modern house of a beloved actress—a champion of progressive values, as is her husband—and two lovely daughters, everyone slept. But at the strike of 6:00, there was the kind of unholy pounding at the door that must have sounded more like an earthquake than a visitor: FBI agents, guns drawn, there to apprehend . . . *Felicity Huffman*? Felicity "Congress is attempting to eviscerate women's health care. Like many women across America, I am outraged" Huffman? For the crime of . . . paying to get her daughter an extra 400 points on the SAT?

Down, down, down she went in the FBI car, in her handcuffs and athleisure, down below Outpost, down below Lake Hollywood, down below the Dolby Theatre where she had been so many times—in a beautiful gown, with her famous husband, William H. Macy, beside her—to watch the Academy Awards, once as a nominee. All the way down to—*my God!*—the downest place of all: Spring Street. *The federal courthouse!* This was where Donald Trump was supposed to go, not Felicity Huffman. Cool your heels, defender of the downtrodden: There is no rushing through all this—the mug shot, the phone call, the hearing. And this can't even be grist for the mill of a new devotion to the plight of American mass incarceration. You're now Exhibit A of law enforcement finally treating rich, white Americans as unsparingly as it treats poor, black ones.

All she wanted was an even playing field for her rich, white daughter! All she wanted was a few hundred SAT points so the girl didn't get lost in the madness that has made college admissions so stressful, so insane, so broken, so unfair. "We're talking about Georgetown," Macy informed Singer about their hopes for their younger daughter. Fortunately for them, and for the younger daughter—and possibly for Georgetown itself—they had not employed him to work on this goal before the indictments were handed down. Fortunately for Macy (who seems to have taken a modified Parent B position), only Huffman has been indicted in the scheme.

Huffman, like all of the other indicted parents, was expressing an attitude I first encountered not in the great books, but in the Charlie Brown Christmas special, when Sally dictates her endless list of toys to Charlie. "All I want is what I have coming to me," she tells him; "all I want is my fair share."

A WARNING
FROM EUROPE

by Anne Applebaum

[OCTOBER 2018]

Who owes what to whom? What do we mean by fairness? When does "I want mine!" cross a line? Is loyalty a principled social concept or a narrow transactional one? All of these questions speak to the idea of a social contract. In America, a social contract—the obligations of citizens to government, government to citizens, and people to one another—has rarely been more than implied. Today, it seems barely to exist. The political scientist Danielle Allen has used the term "informal constitution" to refer to popular understandings woven through any society. Depending on what they are, they can either give force to political arrangements or tear them apart.

"Given the right conditions, any society can turn against democracy," wrote Anne Applebaum in a 2018 *Atlantic* essay. "Indeed, if history is anything to go by, all societies eventually will." As Applebaum explained in "A Warning From Europe," presented here in abridged form, recent events in the United States follow a pattern that Europeans know all too well, and that has by no means run its course. Polarization. Conspiracy theories. Attacks on the free press. An obsession with allegiance to one's subgroup. The erosion of democratic norms. The spread of nationalist rhetoric.

Applebaum is an *Atlantic* staff writer and a Pulitzer Prize–winning historian. Her books *Gulag: A History* (2003), *Iron Curtain: The Crushing of Eastern Europe, 1944–1956* (2012), and *Red Famine: Stalin's War on Ukraine* (2017) have appeared in more than two dozen translations. The essay here forms part of Applebaum's most recent book, *Twilight of Democracy: The Seductive Lure of Authoritarianism*, published this summer.

O n December 31, 1999, we threw a party. It was the end of one millennium and the start of a new one; people very much wanted to celebrate, preferably somewhere exotic. Our party fulfilled that criterion. We held it at Chobielin, the manor house in northwest Poland that my husband and his parents had purchased a decade earlier, when it was a mildewed ruin. We had restored the house, very slowly. It was not exactly finished in 1999, but it did have a new roof. It also had a large, freshly painted, and completely unfurnished salon—perfect for a party.

The guests were various: journalist friends from London and Berlin, a few diplomats based in Warsaw, two friends who flew in from New York. But most of them were Poles, friends of ours and colleagues of my husband, who was then a deputy foreign minister in the Polish government. A handful of youngish Polish journalists came, too—none then particularly famous—along with a few civil servants and one or two members of the government.

You could have lumped the majority of them, roughly, in the general category of what Poles call the right—the conservatives, the anti-Communists. But at that moment in history, you might also have called most of my guests liberals—free-market liberals, or classical liberals—or maybe Thatcherites. Even those who might have been less definite about economics certainly believed in democracy, in the rule of law, and in a Poland that was a member of NATO and on its way to joining the European Union—an integrated part of modern Europe. In the 1990s, that was what being "on the right" meant.

As parties go, it was a little scrappy. There was no such thing as catering in rural Poland in the 1990s, so my mother-in-law and I made vats of beef stew and roasted beets. There were no hotels, either, so our 100-odd guests stayed in local farmhouses or with friends in the nearby town. I kept a list of who was staying where, but nevertheless, a couple of people wound up sleeping on a sofa in our basement. The music—mixtapes, made in an era before Spotify—created the only serious cultural divide of the evening: The songs that my American friends remembered from college were not the same as the songs that the Poles remembered from college, so it was hard to get everybody to dance at the same time. At one point I went upstairs, learned that Boris Yeltsin had resigned, wrote a brief column for a British newspaper, then went back downstairs and had another glass of wine. At about three in the morning, one of the wackier Polish guests pulled a small pistol out of her handbag and shot blanks into the air out of sheer exuberance.

It was that kind of party. It lasted all night, continued into "brunch" the following afternoon, and was infused with the optimism I remember from that time. We had rebuilt our house. Our friends were rebuilding the country. I have a particularly clear memory of a walk in the snow—maybe it was the day before the party, maybe the day after—with a bilingual group, everybody chattering at once, English and Polish mingling and echoing through the birch forest. At that moment, when Poland was on the cusp of joining the West, it felt as if we were all on the same team. We agreed about democracy, about the road to prosperity, about the way things were going.

That moment has passed. Nearly two decades later, I would now cross the street to avoid some of the people who were at my New Year's Eve party. They, in turn, would not only refuse to enter my house, they would be embarrassed to admit they had ever been there. In fact, about half the people who were at that party would no longer speak to the other half. The estrangements are political, not personal. Poland is now one of the most polarized societies in Europe, and we have found ourselves on opposite sides of a profound divide, one that runs through not only what used to be the Polish right but also the old Hungarian right, the Italian right, and, with some differences, the British right and the American right, too.

Some of my New Year's Eve guests continued, as my husband and I did, to support the pro-European, pro-rule-of-law, pro-market center-right—remaining in political parties that aligned, more or less, with European Christian Democrats, with the liberal parties of Germany and the Netherlands, and with the Republican Party of John McCain. Some now consider themselves center-left. But others wound up in a different place, supporting a nativist party called Law and Justice—a party that has moved dramatically away from the positions it held when it first briefly ran the government, from 2005 to 2007, and when it occupied the presidency (not the same thing in Poland), from 2005 to 2010.

Since then, Law and Justice has embraced a new set of ideas, not just xenophobic and deeply suspicious of the rest of Europe but also openly authoritarian. After the party won a slim parliamentary majority in 2015, its leaders violated the constitution by appointing new judges to the constitutional court. Later, it used a similarly unconstitutional playbook to attempt to pack the Polish Supreme Court. It took over the state public broadcaster, Telewizja Polska; fired popular presenters; and began running unabashed propaganda, sprinkled with easily disprovable lies, at taxpayers' expense. The government earned international notoriety when it adopted a law curtailing public debate about the Holocaust. Although the law was eventually changed under American pressure, it enjoyed broad support by Law and Justice's ideological base—the journalists, writers, and thinkers, including some of my party guests, who believe anti-Polish forces seek to blame Poland for Auschwitz.

These kinds of views make it difficult for me and some of my New Year's guests to speak about anything at all. I have not, for example, had a single conversation with a woman who was once one of my closest friends, the godmother of one of my children—let's call her Marta—since a hysterical phone call in April 2010, a couple of days after a plane carrying the then-president crashed near Smolensk, in Russia. In the intervening years, Marta has grown close to Jarosław Kaczyński, the leader of Law and Justice and the late president's twin brother. She regularly hosts lunches for him at her apartment and discusses whom he should appoint to his cabinet. I tried to see her recently in Warsaw, but she refused. "What would we talk about?" she texted me, and then went silent.

Another of my guests—the one who shot the pistol in the air—eventually separated from her British husband. She now appears to spend her days as a full-time internet troll, fanatically promoting a whole range of conspiracy theories, many of them virulently anti-Semitic. She tweets about Jewish responsibility for the Holocaust; she once posted an image of an English medieval painting depicting a boy supposedly crucified by Jews, with the commentary "And they were surprised that they were expelled." She follows and amplifies the leading lights of the American "alt-right," whose language she repeats.

I happen to know that both of these women are estranged from their children because of their political views. But that, too, is typical—this line of division runs through families as well as groups of friends. We have a neighbor near Chobielin whose parents listen to a progovernment, Catholic-conspiratorial radio station called Radio Maryja. They repeat its mantras, make its enemies their enemies. "I've lost my mother," my neighbor told me. "She lives in another world."

To be clear about my interests and biases here, I should explain that some of this conspiratorial thinking is focused on me. My husband was the Polish defense minister for a year and a half, in a coalition government led by Law and Justice during its first, brief experience of power; later, he broke with that party and was for seven years the foreign minister in another coalition government, this one led by the center-right party Civic Platform; in 2015 he didn't run for office. As a journalist and his American-born wife, I have always attracted some press interest. But after Law and Justice won that year, I was featured on the covers of two pro-regime magazines, *wSieci* and *Do Rzeczy*—former friends of ours work at both—as the clandestine Jewish coordinator of the international press and the secret director of its negative coverage of Poland. Similar stories have appeared on Telewizja Polska's evening news.

Eventually, they stopped writing about me: Negative international press coverage of Poland has grown much too widespread for a single person, even a single Jewish person, to coordinate all by herself. Though naturally the theme recurs on social media from time to time.

In a famous journal he kept from 1935 to 1944, the Romanian writer Mihail Sebastian chronicled an even more extreme shift in his own country. Like me, Sebastian was Jewish; like me, most of his friends were on the political right. In his journal, he described how, one by one, they were drawn to fascist ideology, like a flock of moths to an inescapable flame. He recounted the arrogance and confidence they acquired as they moved away from identifying themselves as Europeans—admirers of Proust, travelers to Paris—and instead began to call themselves blood-and-soil Romanians. He listened as they veered into conspiratorial thinking or became casually cruel. People he had known for years insulted him to his face and then acted as if nothing had happened. "Is friendship possible," he wondered in 1937, "with people who have in common a whole series of alien ideas and feelings—so alien that I have only to walk in the door and they suddenly fall silent in shame and embarrassment?"

This is not 1937. Nevertheless, a parallel transformation is taking place in my own time, in the Europe that I inhabit and in Poland, a country whose citizenship I have acquired. And it is taking place without the excuse of an economic crisis of the kind Europe suffered in the 1930s. Poland's economy has been the most consistently successful in Europe over the past quarter century. Even after the global financial collapse in 2008, the country saw no recession. What's more, the refugee wave that has hit other European countries has not been felt here at all. There are no migrant camps, and there is no Islamist terrorism, or terrorism of any kind.

More important, though the people I am writing about here, the nativist ideologues, are perhaps not all as successful as they would like to be (about which more in a minute), they are not poor and rural, they are not in any sense victims of the political transition, and they are not an impoverished underclass. On the contrary, they are educated, they speak foreign languages, and they travel abroad—just like Sebastian's friends in the 1930s.

What has caused this transformation? Were some of our friends always closet authoritarians? Or have the people with whom we clinked glasses in the first minutes of the new millennium somehow changed over the subsequent two decades? My answer is a complicated one, because I think the explanation is universal. Given the right conditions, any society can turn against democracy. Indeed, if history is anything to go by, all societies eventually will.

———————

Monarchy, tyranny, oligarchy, democracy—these were all familiar to Aristotle more than 2,000 years ago. But the illiberal one-party state, now found all over the world—think of China, Venezuela, Zimbabwe—was first developed by Lenin, in Russia, starting in 1917. In the political-science textbooks of the future, the Soviet Union's founder will surely be remembered not for his Marxist beliefs, but as the inventor of this enduring form of political organization. It is the model that many of the world's budding autocrats use today.

Unlike Marxism, the Leninist one-party state is not a philosophy. It is a mechanism for holding power. It works because it clearly defines who gets to be the elite—the political elite, the cultural elite, the financial elite. In monarchies such as pre-revolutionary France and Russia, the right to rule was granted to the aristocracy, which defined itself by rigid codes of breeding and etiquette. In modern Western democracies, the right to rule is granted, at least in theory, by different forms of competition: campaigning and voting, meritocratic tests that determine access to higher education and the civil service, free markets. Old-fashioned social hierarchies are usually part of the mix, but in modern Britain, America, Germany, France, and until recently Poland, we have assumed that competition is the most just and efficient way to distribute power. The best-run businesses should make the most money. The most appealing and competent politicians should rule. The contests between them should take place on an even playing field, to ensure a fair outcome.

Lenin's one-party state was based on different values. It overthrew the aristocratic order. But it did not put a competitive model in place. The Bolshevik one-party state was not merely undemocratic; it was also anticompetitive and antimeritocratic. Places in universities, civil-service jobs, and roles in government and industry did not go to the most industrious or the most capable. Instead, they went to the most loyal. People advanced because they were willing to conform to the rules of party membership. Though those rules were different at different times, they were consistent in certain ways. They usually excluded the former ruling elite and their children, as well as suspicious ethnic groups. They favored the children of the working class. Above all, they favored people who loudly professed belief in the creed, who attended party meetings, who participated in public displays of enthusiasm. Unlike an ordinary oligarchy, the one-party state allows for upward mobility: True believers can advance. As Hannah Arendt wrote back in the 1940s, the worst kind of one-party state "invariably replaces all first-rate talents, regardless of their sympathies, with those crackpots and fools whose lack of intelligence and creativity is still the best guarantee of their loyalty."

Lenin's one-party system also reflected his disdain for the idea of a neutral state, of apolitical civil servants and an objective media. He wrote that freedom of the press "is a deception." He mocked freedom of assembly as a "hollow phrase." As for parliamentary democracy itself, that was no more than "a machine for the suppression of the working class." In the Bolshevik imagination, the press could be free, and public institutions could be fair, only once they were controlled by the working class—via the party.

This mockery of the competitive institutions of "bourgeois democracy" and capitalism has long had a right-wing version, too. Hitler's Germany is the example usually given. But there are many others. Apartheid South Africa was a de facto one-party state that corrupted its press and its judiciary to eliminate blacks from political life and promote the interests of Afrikaners, white South Africans descended mainly from Dutch settlers, who were not succeeding in the capitalist economy created by the British empire.

In Europe, two such illiberal parties are now in power: Law and Justice, in Poland, and Viktor Orbán's Fidesz party, in Hungary. Others, in Austria and Italy, are part of government coalitions or enjoy wide support. These parties tolerate the existence of political opponents. But they use every means possible, legal and illegal, to reduce their opponents' ability to function and to curtail competition in politics and economics. They dislike foreign investment and criticize privatization, unless it is designed to benefit their supporters. They undermine meritocracy. Like Donald Trump, they mock the notions of neutrality and professionalism, whether in journalists or civil servants. They discourage businesses from advertising in "opposition"—by which they mean illegitimate—media.

Notably, one of the Law and Justice government's first acts, in early 2016, was to change the civil-service law, making it easier to fire professionals and hire party hacks. The Polish foreign service also dropped its requirement that diplomats know two foreign languages, a bar that was too high for favored candidates to meet. The government fired heads of Polish state companies. Previously, the people in these roles had had at least some government or business experience. Now these jobs are largely filled by Law and Justice Party members, as well as their friends and relatives. Typical is Janina Goss, an old friend of Kaczyński's from whom the former prime minister once borrowed a large sum of money, apparently to pay for a medical treatment for his mother. Goss, an avid maker of jams and preserves, is now on the board of directors of Polska Grupa Energetyczna, the largest power company in Poland, an employer of 40,000 people.

You can call this sort of thing by many names: nepotism, state capture. But if you so choose, you can also describe it in positive terms: It represents the end of the hateful notions of meritocracy and competition, principles that, by definition, never benefited the less successful. A rigged and uncompetitive system sounds bad if you want to live in a society run by the talented. But if that isn't your primary interest, then what's wrong with it?

If you believe, as my old friends now believe, that Poland will be better off if it is ruled by people who deserve to rule—because they loudly proclaim a certain kind of patriotism, because they are loyal to the party leader, or because they are, echoing the words of Kaczyński himself, a "better sort of Pole"—then a one-party state is actually *more* fair than a competitive democracy. Why should different parties be allowed to compete on an even playing field if only one of them has the moral right to form the government? Why should businesses be allowed to compete in a free market if only some of them are loyal to the party and therefore deserving of wealth?

This impulse is reinforced, in Poland as well as in Hungary and many other formerly Communist countries, by the widespread feeling that the rules of competition are flawed because the reforms of the 1990s were unfair. Specifically, they allowed too many former Communists to recycle their political power into economic power.

But this argument, which felt so important a quarter century ago, seems thin and superficial now. Since at least 2005, Poland has been led solely by presidents and prime ministers whose political biographies began in the anti-Communist Solidarity movement. And there is no powerful ex-Communist business monopoly in Poland, either—at least not at the national level, where plenty of people have made money without special political connections. Poignantly, the most prominent former Communist in Polish politics right now is Stanisław Piotrowicz, a Law and Justice member of parliament who is, perhaps unsurprisingly, a great enemy of judicial independence.

Nevertheless, this argument about the continuing influence of Communism retains an appeal for the right-wing political intellectuals of my generation. For some of them, it seems to explain their personal failures, or just their bad luck. Not everybody who was a dissident in the 1970s got to become the prime minister, or a best-selling writer, or a respected public intellectual, after 1989. And for many this is a source of burning resentment. If you are someone who believes that you deserve to rule, then your motivation to attack the elite, pack the courts, and warp the press to achieve your ambitions is strong. Resentment, envy, and above all the belief that the "system" is unfair—these are important sentiments among the intellectuals of the Polish right.

This is not to say that the illiberal state lacks a genuine appeal. But it is also good for some of its proponents personally—so much so that picking apart personal and political motives is extremely difficult. That's what I learned from the story of Jacek Kurski, the director of Polish state television and the chief ideologist of the Polish illiberal state. He started out in the same place, at the same time, as his brother, Jarosław Kurski, who edits the largest and most influential liberal Polish newspaper. They are two sides of the same coin.

————

To understand the Kurski brothers, it's important to understand where they came from: the port city of Gdańsk, on the Baltic Sea, where shipyard cranes loom like giant storks over Hanseatic street facades. The Kurskis came of age there in the early 1980s, when Gdańsk was both the hub of anti-Communist activity in Poland and a shabby backwater, a place where intrigue and boredom were measured out in equal doses.

At that particular moment, in that particular place, the Kurski brothers stood out. Senator Bogdan Borusewicz, one of the most important underground trade-union activists from the time, told me that their school was widely known to be "*zrewoltowane*"—in revolt against the Communist system. Jarosław represented his class in the school parliament and was part of a group that read conservative history and literature. Jacek, slightly younger, was less interested in the intellectual battle against Communism, and thought of himself as an activist and a radical. In the immediate wake of martial law, both brothers went to marches, shouted slogans, waved banners. Both worked first on the illegal school newspaper and then on *Solidarność*, the illegal opposition newspaper of Solidarity, the trade union in Gdańsk.

In October 1989, Jarosław went to work as the press secretary to Lech Wałęsa, the leader of Solidarity, who, after the election of Poland's first non–Communist government, felt out of sorts and ignored; in the chaos created by revolutionary economic reforms and rapid political change, there was no obvious role for him. Eventually, in late 1990, Wałęsa ran for president and won, by galvanizing people who already resented the compromises that had accompanied the negotiated collapse of Communism in Poland (the decision not to jail or punish former Communists, for example). The experience made Jarosław realize that he didn't like politics, especially not the politics of resentment: "I saw what doing politics was really about . . . awful intrigues, searching for dirt, smear campaigns." That was also his first encounter with Kaczyński, "a master of that. In his political thinking, there is no such thing as an accident . . . If something happened, it was the machination of an outsider. *Conspiracy* is his favorite word." (Unlike Jarosław, Jacek would not speak with me. A mutual friend gave me his private cellphone number; I texted, and then called a couple of times and left messages. I called again and someone cackled when I stated my name, repeated it loudly, and said, "Of course, of course"—naturally the chairman of Polish television would return my call. But he never did.)

Eventually Jarosław quit and joined *Gazeta Wyborcza*, the newspaper founded at the time of Poland's first partially free elections, in 1989. In the new Poland, he could help build something, create a free press, he told me, and that was enough for him. Jacek went in precisely the opposite direction. "You are an idiot," he told his brother when he learned he had quit working for Wałęsa. Although he was still in high school, Jacek was already interested in a political career himself, and even suggested that he take over his brother's job, on the grounds that no one would notice. He was—in his brother's description—always "fascinated" by the Kaczyński brothers, by the plots, the schemes, the conspiracies. Although he was on the right, he was not particularly interested in the trappings of Polish conservatism, in the books or the debates that had captivated his brother. A friend of both brothers told me she didn't think Jacek had any real political philosophy at all. "Is he a conservative? I don't think so, at least not in the strict definition of conservatism. He's a person who wants to be on top." And from the late 1980s onward, that was where he aimed to be.

The complete story of what Jacek did next would require more than a single magazine article to describe. He eventually turned against Wałęsa, perhaps because Wałęsa didn't give him the job he thought he deserved. He married and divorced; he sued his brother's newspaper several times, and the newspaper sued him back. He co-authored a fiery book and made a conspiratorial film about the secret forces lined up against the Polish right. He was a member, at different times, of different parties or factions, sometimes quite marginal and sometimes more centrist. He became a member of the European Parliament. He came to specialize in so-called black PR. Famously, he helped torpedo the presidential campaign of Donald Tusk (who eventually became prime minister), in part by spreading the rumor that Tusk had a grandfather who had voluntarily joined the Wehrmacht, the Nazi army. Asked about this invention, Jacek reportedly told a small group of journalists that of course it wasn't true, but *"Ciemny lud to kupi"*—which, roughly translated, means "The ignorant peasants will buy it." Borusewicz describes him as "without scruples."

Jacek did not win the popular acclaim he thought a teenage Solidarity activist was entitled to. And this was a huge disappointment. Jarosław says of his brother: "All of his life, he believed that he is owed a great career . . . that he will be prime minister, that he is predestined to do something great. Yet fate dictated that he failed over and over again . . . He concluded that this was a great injustice." And of course, Jarosław was successful, a member of the establishment.

In 2015, Kaczyński plucked Jacek out of the relative obscurity of fringe politics and made him the director of state television. Since his arrival at Telewizja Polska, the younger Kurski has changed the station beyond recognition, firing the best-known journalists and radically reorienting its politics. Although the station is funded by taxpayers, the news broadcasts no longer make any pretense of objectivity or neutrality. In April of this year, for example, the station made an advertisement for itself. It showed a clip from a press conference; the leader of the opposition party, Grzegorz Schetyna, is asked what his party achieved during its eight years in government, from 2007 to 2015. Schetyna pauses and frowns; the video slows down and then ends. It's as if he had nothing to say.

In reality, Schetyna spoke for several minutes and listed a number of achievements, from the mass construction of roads to rural investments to advances in foreign policy. But this manipulated clip was deemed such a success that for several days, it remained pinned to the top of Telewizja Polska's Twitter feed. Under Law and Justice, state television doesn't just produce regime propaganda; it celebrates the fact that it is doing so. It doesn't just twist and contort information; it glories in deceit.

Jacek—deprived of respect for so many years—is finally having his revenge. He is right where he thinks he should be: at the center of attention, the radical throwing figurative Molotov cocktails into the crowd. The illiberal one-party state suits him perfectly. And if Communism isn't really available anymore as a genuine enemy for him and his colleagues to fight, then new enemies will have to be found.

From Orwell to Koestler, the European writers of the 20th century were obsessed with the idea of the Big Lie. The vast ideological constructs that were Communism and fascism, the posters demanding fealty to the Party or the Leader, the Brownshirts and Blackshirts marching in formation, the torchlit parades, the terror police—these Big Lies were so absurd and inhuman, they required prolonged violence to impose and the threat of violence to maintain. They required forced education, total control of all culture, the politicization of journalism, sports, literature, and the arts.

By contrast, the polarizing political movements of 21st-century Europe demand much less of their adherents. They don't require belief in a full-blown ideology, and thus they don't require violence or terror police. They don't force people to believe that black is white, war is peace, and state farms have achieved 1,000 percent of their planned production. Most of them don't deploy propaganda that conflicts with everyday reality. And yet all of them depend, if not on a Big Lie, then on what the historian Timothy Snyder once told me should be called the Medium-Size Lie, or perhaps a clutch of Medium-Size Lies. To put it differently, all of them encourage their followers to engage, at least part of the time, with an alternative reality. Sometimes that alternative reality has developed organically; more often, it's been carefully formulated, with the help of modern marketing techniques, audience segmentation, and social-media campaigns.

Americans are of course familiar with the ways a lie can increase polarization and inflame xenophobia: Donald Trump entered American politics on the back of birtherism, the false premise that President Barack Obama was not born in America—a conspiracy theory whose power was seriously underestimated at the time, and that paved the way for other lies, from "Mexican rapists" to "Pizzagate." But in Poland, and in Hungary, too, we now have examples of what happens when a Medium-Size Lie—a conspiracy theory—is propagated first by a political party as the central plank of its election campaign, and then by a ruling party, with the full force of a modern, centralized state apparatus behind it.

In Hungary, the lie is unoriginal: It is the belief, shared by the Russian government and the American alt-right, in the super-human powers of George Soros, the Hungarian Jewish billionaire who is supposedly plotting to bring down the nation through the deliberate importation of migrants, even though no such migrants exist in Hungary.

In Poland, at least the lie is sui generis. It is the Smolensk conspiracy theory: the belief that a nefarious plot brought down the president's plane in April 2010. The story has special force in Poland because the crash had eerie historical echoes. The president who died, Lech Kaczyński, was on his way to an event commemorating the massacre in Katyn, the place where Stalin murdered more than 21,000 Poles—a big chunk of the country's elite—in 1940. Dozens of senior military figures and politicians were also on board, many of them friends of mine. My husband reckons that he knew everybody on the plane, including the flight attendants.

A huge wave of emotion followed the accident. A kind of hysteria, something like the madness that took hold in the United States after 9/11, engulfed the nation. Television announcers wore black mourning ties; friends gathered at our Warsaw apartment to talk about history repeating itself in that dark, damp Russian forest. At first the tragedy seemed to unify the country. After all, politicians from every major party had been on the plane, and huge funerals were held in many cities. Even Vladimir Putin, then the Russian prime minister, seemed moved. He went to Smolensk to meet Tusk, then the Polish prime minister, on the evening of the crash. The next day, one of Russia's most-watched television channels broadcast *Katyn*, an emotional and very anti-Soviet Polish film, directed by Andrzej Wajda, the country's greatest director. Nothing like it has ever been shown so widely in Russia, before or since.

But the crash did not bring people together. Nor did the investigation into its cause.

Teams of Polish experts were on the ground that same day. They did their best to identify bodies, many of which were nothing but ash. They examined the wreckage. Once the black box was found, they began to transcribe the cockpit tape. The truth, as it began to emerge, was not comforting to the Law and Justice Party or to its leader, the dead president's twin brother. The plane had taken off late; the president was likely in a hurry to land, because he wanted to use the trip to launch his reelection campaign. There was thick fog in Smolensk, which did not have a real airport, just a landing strip in the forest; the pilots considered diverting the plane, which would have meant a drive of several hours to the ceremony. After the president had a brief phone call with his brother, his advisers apparently pressed the pilots to land. Some of them, against protocol, walked in and out of the cockpit during the flight. Also against protocol, the chief of the air force came and sat beside the pilots. *"Zmieścisz się śmiało"*—"You'll make it, be bold," he said. Seconds later, the plane collided with the tops of some birch trees, rolled over, and hit the ground.

Initially, Jarosław Kaczyński seems to have believed that the crash was an accident. "It's your fault and the fault of the tabloids," he told my husband, then the foreign minister, who informed him of the crash. By that, he meant that it was the government's fault because, intimidated by populist journalism, it had refused to buy new airplanes. But as the investigation unfolded, its findings were not to his liking. There was nothing wrong with the plane.

Perhaps, like so many people who rely on conspiracy theories to make sense of random tragedies, Kaczyński simply couldn't accept that his beloved brother had died pointlessly; perhaps he could not accept the even more difficult fact that the evidence suggested Lech and his team had pressured the pilots to land, thus causing the crash. Or perhaps, like Donald Trump, he saw how a conspiracy theory could help him attain power.

Much as Trump used birtherism and the fabricated threat of immigrant crime to motivate his core supporters, Kaczyński has used the Smolensk tragedy to galvanize his followers, and convince them not to trust the government or the media. Sometimes he has implied that the Russian government downed the plane. At other times, he has blamed the former ruling party, now the largest opposition party, for his brother's death: "You destroyed him, you murdered him, you are scum!" he once shouted in parliament.

None of his accusations can be proved, however. Perhaps to distance himself somewhat from the lies that needed to be told, he gave the job of promoting the conspiracy theory to one of his oldest and strangest comrades. Antoni Macierewicz is a member of Kaczyński's generation, a longtime anti-Communist, though one with some weird friends and habits. His odd stare and his obsessions—he has said that he finds *The Protocols of the Elders of Zion* to be a plausible document—even led the Law and Justice Party to make an election promise in 2015: Macierewicz would definitely not be the defense minister.

But as soon as the party won, Kaczyński broke that promise and appointed Macierewicz. Immediately, Macierewicz began to institutionalize the Smolensk lie. He created a new investigation commission composed of cranks, among them an ethnomusicologist, a retired pilot, a psychologist, a Russian economist, and other people with no knowledge of air crashes. The previous official report was removed from a government website. Police entered the homes of the aviation experts who had testified during the original investigation, interrogated them, and confiscated their computers. When Macierewicz went to Washington, D.C., to meet his American counterparts at the Pentagon, the first thing he did was ask whether U.S. intelligence had any secret information on Smolensk. I'm told that the reaction was widespread concern about the minister's mental state.

When, some weeks after the election, European institutions and human-rights groups began responding to the actions of the Law and Justice government, they focused on the undermining of the courts and public media. They didn't focus on the institutionalization of the Smolensk conspiracy theory, which was, frankly, just too weird for outsiders to understand. And yet the decision to put a fantasy at the heart of government policy really was the source of the authoritarian actions that followed.

Although the Macierewicz commission has never produced a credible alternate explanation for the crash, the Smolensk lie laid the moral groundwork for other lies. Those who could accept this elaborate theory, with no evidence whatsoever, could accept anything. They could accept, for example, the broken promise not to put Macierewicz in the government. They could accept—even though Law and Justice is supposedly a "patriotic" and anti-Russian party—Macierewicz's decisions to fire many of the country's highest military commanders, to cancel weapons contracts, to promote people with odd Russian links, to raid a NATO facility in Warsaw in the middle of the night. The lie also gave the foot soldiers of the far right an ideological basis for tolerating other offenses. Whatever mistakes the party might make, whatever laws it might break, at least the "truth" about Smolensk would finally be told.

The Smolensk conspiracy theory, like the Hungarian migration conspiracy theory, served another purpose: For a younger generation that no longer remembered Communism, and a society where former Communists had largely disappeared from politics, it offered a new reason to distrust the politicians, businesspeople, and intellectuals who had emerged from the struggles of the 1990s and now led the country. More to the point, it offered a means of defining a new and better elite. There was no need for competition, or for exams, or for a résumé bristling with achievements. Anyone who professes belief in the Smolensk lie is by definition a true patriot—and, incidentally, might well qualify for a government job.

————

The emotional appeal of a conspiracy theory is in its simplicity. It explains away complex phenomena, accounts for chance and accidents, offers the believer the satisfying sense of having special, privileged access to the truth. But—once again—separating the appeal of conspiracy from the ways it affects the careers of those who promote it is very difficult. For those who become the one-party state's gatekeepers, for those who repeat and promote the official conspiracy theories, acceptance of these simple explanations also brings another reward: power.

Mária Schmidt wasn't at my New Year's Eve party, but I've known her for a long time. She invited me to the opening of the Terror Háza—the House of Terror museum—in Budapest in 2002, and I've been more or less in communication with her ever since. The museum, which she directs, explores the history of totalitarianism in Hungary and, when it opened, was one of the most innovative new museums in the eastern half of Europe.

From its opening day, it has also had harsh critics. Many visitors didn't like the first room, which has a panel of televisions on one wall broadcasting Nazi propaganda, and a panel of televisions on the opposite wall broadcasting Communist propaganda. In 2002, it was still a shock to see the two regimes compared, though perhaps it is less so now. Others felt that the museum gave insufficient weight and space to the crimes of fascism, though Communists ran Hungary for far longer than the fascists did, so there is more to show. I liked the fact that the museum showed ordinary Hungarians collaborating with both regimes, which I thought might help Hungary understand its responsibility for its own politics, and avoid the narrow nationalist trap of blaming problems on outsiders.

Yet this is precisely the narrow nationalist trap into which Hungary has now fallen. Hungary's belated reckoning with its Communist past—putting up museums, holding memorial services, naming perpetrators—did not, as I thought it would, help cement respect for the rule of law, for restraints on the state, for pluralism. On the contrary, 16 years after the Terror Háza's opening, Hungary's ruling party respects no restraints of any kind. It has gone much further than Law and Justice in politicizing the state media and destroying the private media, achieving the latter by issuing threats and blocking access to advertising. It has created a new business elite that is loyal to Orbán. One Hungarian businessman who preferred not to be named told me that soon after Orbán first took over the government, regime cronies demanded that the businessman sell them his company at a low price; when he refused, they arranged for "tax inspections" and other forms of harassment, as well as a campaign of intimidation that forced him to hire bodyguards. Eventually he sold his Hungarian property and left the country.

Like the Polish government, the Hungarian state promotes a Medium-Size Lie: It pumps out propaganda blaming Hungary's problems on nonexistent Muslim migrants, the European Union, and, as noted, George Soros. Schmidt—a historian, scholar, and museum curator—is one of the primary authors of that lie. She periodically publishes long, angry blog posts fulminating against Soros; against Budapest's Central European University, originally founded with his money; and against "left intellectuals," by which she seems to mostly mean liberal democrats, from the center-left to the center-right.

Ironies and paradoxes in her life story are plentiful. Schmidt is a prime beneficiary of Hungary's supposedly tainted transition; her late husband made a fortune in the post-Communist real-estate market, thanks to which she lives in a spectacular house in the Buda hills. Although she has led a publicity campaign designed to undermine Central European University, her son is a graduate. And although she knows very well what happened in her country in the 1940s, she followed, step-by-step, the Communist Party playbook when she took over *Figyelő*, a respected Hungarian magazine: She pushed out the independent reporters and replaced them with reliably progovernment writers.

Figyelő remains "private property." But it's not hard to see who supports the magazine. An issue that featured an attack on Hungarian NGOs—the cover visually equated them with the Islamic State—also included a dozen pages of government-paid advertisements, for the Hungarian National Bank, the treasury, the state anti-Soros campaign. This is a modern reinvention of the progovernment, one-party-state press, complete with the same sneering, cynical tone that the Communist publications once used.

Schmidt agreed to speak with me—after calling me "arrogant and ignorant"—only if I would listen to her objections to an article I'd just written for *The Washington Post*. With this invitation, I flew to Budapest. Unsurprisingly, what I'd hoped for—an interesting conversation—proved impossible. Schmidt speaks excellent English, but she told me that she wanted to use a translator. She produced a rather terrified young man who, judging by the transcripts, left out chunks of what she said. And though she has known me for nearly two decades, she plunked a tape recorder on the table, in what I took to be a sign of distrust.

She then proceeded to repeat the same arguments that had appeared in her blog posts. As her main bit of evidence that George Soros "owns" the Democratic Party in the United States, she cited an episode of *Saturday Night Live*. As proof that the U.S. is "a hard-core ideologically based colonizing power," she cited a speech Barack Obama gave in which he mentioned that a Hungarian foundation had proposed building a statue to honor Bálint Hóman, the man who wrote Hungary's anti-Jewish laws in the '30s and '40s. She repeated her claim that immigration poses a dire threat to Hungary, and became annoyed when I asked, several times, where all the immigrants were. "They're in Germany," she finally snapped, asserting that the Germans will eventually force Hungary to take "these people back."

Schmidt embodies what the Bulgarian writer Ivan Krastev recently described as the desire of many eastern and central Europeans to "shake off the colonial dependency implicit in the very project of Westernization," to rid themselves of the humiliation of having been imitators, followers of the West rather than founders. Schmidt told me that the Western media, presumably myself included, "talk down from above to those below like it used to be with colonies." Western talk of Hungarian anti-Semitism, corruption, and authoritarianism is "colonialism." Yet despite being dedicated to the uniqueness of Hungary and the promotion of "Hungarianness," she has borrowed much of her ideology wholesale from *Breitbart News*, right down to the caricatured description of American universities and the sneering jokes about "transsexual bathrooms." She has even invited Steve Bannon and Milo Yiannopoulos to Budapest.

Listening to her, I became convinced that there was never a moment when Schmidt's views "changed." She never turned against liberal democracy, because she never believed in it, or at least she never thought it was all that important. For her, the antidote to Communism is not democracy but national sovereignty. And if national sovereignty takes the form of a state whose elite is defined not according to its talent but according to its "patriotism"—meaning, in practice, its willingness to toe Orbán's line—then she's fine with that.

Her cynicism is profound. Soros's support for Syrian refugees cannot be philanthropy; it must come from a deep desire to destroy Hungary. Angela Merkel's refugee policy could not derive from a desire to help people, either. "I think it is just bullshit," Schmidt said. "I would say she wanted to prove that Germans, this time, are the good people. And they can lecture everybody on humanism and morality. It doesn't matter for the Germans what they can lecture the rest of the world on; they just have to lecture someone."

It's clear that the Medium-Size Lie is working for Orbán—just as it has for Donald Trump—if only because it focuses the world's attention on his rhetoric rather than his actions. Schmidt and I spent most of our unpleasant two-hour conversation arguing about nonsensical questions: Does George Soros own the Democratic Party? Are nonexistent immigrants, who don't want to live in Hungary anyway, a threat to the nation? We spent no time at all discussing Russia's influence in Hungary, which is now very strong. We did not talk about corruption, or the myriad ways (documented by the *Financial Times* and others) that Orbán's friends have benefited from European subsidies and legislative sleight of hand. (A ruling party that has politicized its courts and suppressed the media is a party that finds it much easier to steal.)

Nor, in the end, did I learn much about Schmidt herself. Others in Budapest believe she is motivated by her own drive for wealth and power. Zsuzsanna Szelényi, a member of parliament who used to belong to Fidesz, Orbán's party, but is now an independent, was one of several people who told me that "nobody can be rich in Hungary without having some relation to the prime minister." Thanks to Orbán, Schmidt oversees the museum and a couple of historical institutes, giving her a unique ability to shape how Hungarians remember their history, which she relishes. Maybe she really believes that Hungary is facing a dire, existential threat in the form of George Soros and some invisible Syrians. Or maybe she's just as cynical about her own side as she is about her opponents, and it's all an elaborate game.

What happened after I interviewed her provides a clue: Without my permission, Schmidt published on her blog a heavily edited transcript, which was confusingly presented as her interview of me. The transcript also appeared on the Hungarian government's official website, in English. (Try to imagine the White House publishing the transcript of a conversation between, say, the head of the Smithsonian Institution and a foreign critic of Trump and you'll understand how strange this is.) But, of course, the interview was not conducted for my benefit. It was a performance, designed to prove to other Hungarians that Schmidt is loyal to the regime and willing to defend it. Which she is.

Not long ago, at a fish restaurant in an ugly square on a beautiful night in Athens, I described my 1999 New Year's Eve party to a Greek political scientist. Quietly, he laughed at me. Or rather, he laughed with me; he didn't mean to be rude. But this thing I was calling polarization was nothing new. "The post-1989 liberal moment—this was the exception," Stathis Kalyvas told me. Polarization is normal. More to the point, I would add, skepticism about liberal democracy is also normal. And the appeal of authoritarianism is eternal.

Kalyvas is, among other things, the author of several well-known books about civil wars, including Greece's civil war, in the 1940s, one of many moments in European history when radically divergent political groups took up arms and started to kill one another. But *civil war* and *civil peace* are relative terms in Greece at the best of times. We were speaking just as some Greek intellectuals were having a centrist moment. It was suddenly fashionable to be "liberal," lots of people in Athens told me, by which they meant neither Communist nor authoritarian, neither far-left, like the Syriza ruling party, nor far-right, like its nationalist coalition partner, the Independent Greeks. Cutting-edge young people were calling themselves "neoliberal," adopting a term that had been anathema only a few years earlier.

But even the most optimistic centrists were not convinced that this change would last. "We survived the left-wing populists," several people told me gloomily, "and now we are bracing for the right-wing populists." A nasty argument had long been brewing about the name and status of Macedonia, the ex–Yugoslav republic neighboring Greece; soon after I left, the Greek government expelled some Russian diplomats for trying to foment anti-Macedonia hysteria in the northern part of the country. Whatever equilibrium your nation reaches, there is always someone, at home or abroad, who has reasons to upset it.

It's a useful reminder. Americans, with our powerful founding story, our unusual reverence for our Constitution, our relative geographic isolation, and our two centuries of economic success, have long been convinced that liberal democracy, once achieved, cannot be altered. American history is told as a tale of progress, always forward and upward, with the Civil War as a kind of blip in the middle, an obstacle that was overcome. In Greece, history feels not linear but circular. There is liberal democracy and then there is oligarchy. Then there is liberal democracy again. Then there is foreign subversion, then there is an attempted Communist coup, then there is civil war, and then there is dictatorship. And so on, since the time of the Athenian republic.

History feels circular in other parts of Europe, too. The divide that has shattered Poland is strikingly similar to the divide that split France in the wake of the Dreyfus affair. The language used by the European radical right—the demand for "revolution" against "elites," the dreams of "cleansing" violence and an apocalyptic cultural clash—is eerily similar to the language once used by the European radical left. The presence of dissatisfied, discontented intellectuals—people who feel that the rules aren't fair and that the wrong people have influence—isn't even uniquely European. Moisés Naím, the Venezuelan writer, visited Warsaw a few months after the Law and Justice Party came to power. He asked me to describe the new Polish leaders: What were they like, as people? I gave him some adjectives—*angry, vengeful, resentful.* "They sound just like Chavistas," he told me.

In truth, the argument about who gets to rule is never over, particularly in an era when people have rejected aristocracy, and no longer believe that leadership is inherited at birth or that the ruling class is endorsed by God. Some of us, in Europe and North America, have settled on the idea that various forms of democratic and economic competition are the fairest alternative to inherited or ordained power.

But we should not have been surprised—*I* should not have been surprised—when the principles of meritocracy and competition were challenged. Democracy and free markets can produce unsatisfying outcomes, after all, especially when badly regulated, or when nobody trusts the regulators, or when people are entering the contest from very different starting points. Sooner or later, the losers of the competition were always going to challenge the value of the competition itself.

More to the point, the principles of competition, even when they encourage talent and create upward mobility, don't necessarily answer deeper questions about national identity, or satisfy the human desire to belong to a moral community. The authoritarian state, or even the semi-authoritarian state—the one-party state, the illiberal state— offers that promise: that the nation will be ruled by the best people, the deserving people, the members of the party, the believers in the Medium-Size Lie. It may be that democracy has to be bent or business corrupted or court systems wrecked in order to achieve that state. But if you believe that you are one of those deserving people, you will do it.

II. THE FAILURE
OF POLITICS

America has been sharply divided at many key moments in recent history—during the civil-rights era, the Vietnam War, and the Watergate scandal, to name three examples—and yet Washington still got things done. Disagreements were also sharp during the 1980s, but the only names Ronald Reagan and Thomas P. O'Neill called each other were "Mr. President" and "Tip." Today's dysfunction is undeniable, especially at the national level. Why now?

When looking at history, there's an age-old battle over the weight to accord individuals and the weight to accord larger forces. In this section, we explore both. From an individual perspective, both former House Speaker Newt Gingrich (who turned Republican representatives into partisan warriors) and the political consultant Paul Manafort (an amoral grifter and enabler of same) exemplify contemporary Washington—and, in their different ways, helped make the capital what it has become. Individual evangelical leaders, too, now wield great influence in a kingdom that is very much of this Earth. Intransigence, corruption, zealotry—together they make for a corrosive combination.

As for larger forces, racism infects attitudes and institutions. The country is undergoing demographic change of unprecedented scope; one reaction comes in the form of voter suppression and gerrymandering. Meanwhile, decades of "reform"—the proliferation of primaries and ballot initiatives, for instance—have reduced the stabilizing power of political parties and party leaders. Information technology may be inherently undemocratic, and its advances are likely unstoppable. The advent of social media has already eroded concepts such as "fact" and "truth" while normalizing fever dreams and hate.

NEWT GINGRICH SAYS YOU'RE WELCOME

by McKay Coppins

[NOVEMBER 2018]

No single factor—no person, event, or structural condition—deserves all the blame for the breakdown of ordinary politics during the past quarter century. But *Atlantic* staff writer McKay Coppins set out to give Newt Gingrich the recognition he deserves as an architect of this new reality. Gingrich's current presence as a panel-filling pontificator on cable news betrays little hint of his brutal effectiveness in the 1990s in weaponizing the Republican rank and file in the House of Representatives to a point where he himself was no longer in control. "Gingrich's career," Coppins observed in his 2018 profile of the politician, excerpted here, "can perhaps be best understood as a grand exercise in devolution—an effort to strip American politics of the civilizing traits it had developed over time and return it to its most primal essence." Responding to the article in a letter to the magazine, one reader wrote: "Gingrich seems to believe that, to paraphrase Clausewitz, politics is the continuation of war by other means."

Before coming to *The Atlantic*, Coppins was a reporter for BuzzFeed News, where he covered two presidential campaigns. He is the author of *The Wilderness: Deep Inside the Republican Party's Combative, Contentious, Chaotic Quest to Take Back the White House* (2015).

There's something about Newt Gingrich that seems to capture the spirit of America circa 2018. With his immense head and white mop of hair; his cold, boyish grin; and his high, raspy voice, he has the air of a late-empire Roman senator—a walking bundle of appetites and excesses and hubris and wit. In conversation, he toggles unnervingly between grandiose pronouncements about "Western civilization" and partisan cheap shots that seem tailored for cable news. It's a combination of self-righteousness and smallness, of pomposity and pettiness, that personifies the decadence of this era.

In the clamorous story of Donald Trump's Washington, it would be easy to mistake Gingrich for a minor character. A loyal Trump ally in 2016, Gingrich forwent a high-powered post in the administration and has instead spent the years since the election cashing in on his access—churning out books (three Trump hagiographies, one spy thriller), working the speaking circuit (where he commands as much as $75,000 per talk for his insights on the president), and popping up on Fox News as a paid contributor. He spends much of his time in Rome, where his wife, Callista, serves as Trump's ambassador to the Vatican and where, he likes to boast, "We have yet to find a bad restaurant."

But few figures in modern history have done more than Gingrich to lay the groundwork for Trump's rise. During his two decades in Congress, he pioneered a style of partisan combat—replete with name-calling, conspiracy theories, and strategic obstructionism—that poisoned America's political culture and plunged Washington into permanent dysfunction. Gingrich's career can perhaps be best understood as a grand exercise in devolution—an effort to strip American politics of the civilizing traits it had developed over time and return it to its most primal essence.

When I ask him how he views his legacy, Gingrich takes me on a tour of a Western world gripped by crisis. In Washington, chaos reigns as institutional authority crumbles. Throughout America, right-wing Trumpites and left-wing resisters are treating midterm races like calamitous fronts in a civil war that must be won at all costs. And in Europe, populist revolts are wreaking havoc in capitals across the Continent.

Twenty-five years after engineering the Republican Revolution,

Gingrich can draw a direct line from his work in Congress to the upheaval now taking place around the globe. But as he surveys the wreckage of the modern political landscape, he is not regretful. He's gleeful.

"The old order is dying," he tells me. "Almost everywhere you have freedom, you have a very deep discontent that the system isn't working."

And that's a good thing? I ask.

"It's essential," he says, "if you want Western civilization to survive."

On June 24, 1978, Gingrich stood to address a gathering of College Republicans at a Holiday Inn near the Atlanta airport. It was a natural audience for him. At 35, he was more youthful-looking than the average congressional candidate, with fashionably robust sideburns and a cool-professor charisma that had made him one of the more popular faculty members at West Georgia College.

But Gingrich had not come to deliver an academic lecture to the young activists before him—he had come to foment revolution.

"One of the great problems we have in the Republican Party is that we don't encourage you to be nasty," he told the group. "We encourage you to be neat, obedient, and loyal, and faithful, and all those Boy Scout words, which would be great around the campfire but are lousy in politics."

For their party to succeed, Gingrich went on, the next generation of Republicans would have to learn to "raise hell," to stop being so "nice," to realize that politics was, above all, a cutthroat "war for power"—and to start acting like it.

The speech received little attention at the time. Gingrich was, after all, an obscure, untenured professor whose political experience consisted of two failed congressional bids. But when, a few months later, he was finally elected to the House of Representatives on his third try, he went to Washington a man obsessed with becoming the kind of leader he had described that day in Atlanta.

The GOP was then at its lowest point in modern history. Scores of Republican lawmakers had been wiped out in the aftermath of

Watergate, and those who'd survived seemed, to Gingrich, sadly resigned to a "permanent minority" mindset. "It was like death," he
recalls of the mood in the caucus. "They were morally and psychologically shattered."

But Gingrich had a plan. The way he saw it, Republicans would
never be able to take back the House as long as they kept compro-
mising with the Democrats out of some high-minded civic desire to
keep congressional business humming along. His strategy was to blow
up the bipartisan coalitions that were essential to legislating, and then
seize on the resulting dysfunction to wage a populist crusade against
the institution of Congress itself. "His idea," says Norm Ornstein, a
political scientist who knew Gingrich at the time, "was to build toward
a national election where people were so disgusted by Washington and
the way it was operating that they would throw the ins out and bring
the outs in."

Gingrich recruited a cadre of young bomb throwers—a group of
12 congressmen he christened the Conservative Opportunity Society—and together they stalked the halls of Capitol Hill, searching for
trouble and TV cameras. Their emergence was not, at first, greeted
with enthusiasm by the more moderate Republican leadership. They
were too noisy, too brash, too hostile to the old guard's cherished sense
of decorum. They even *looked* different—sporting blow-dried pompa-
dours while their more camera-shy elders smeared Brylcreem on their
comb-overs.

Gingrich and his cohort showed little interest in legislating, a task
that had heretofore been seen as the primary responsibility of elected
legislators. Bob Livingston, a Louisiana Republican who had been
elected to Congress a year before Gingrich, marveled at the way the
hard-charging Georgian rose to prominence by ignoring the traditional
path taken by new lawmakers. "My idea was to work within the committee structure, take care of my district, and just pay attention to
the legislative process," Livingston told me. "But Newt came in as a
revolutionary."

For revolutionary purposes, the House of Representatives was less
a governing body than an arena for conflict and drama. And Gingrich

found ways to put on a show. He recognized an opportunity in the newly installed C-SPAN cameras, and began delivering tirades against Democrats to an empty chamber, knowing that his remarks would be beamed to viewers across the country.

As his profile grew, Gingrich took aim at the moderates in his own party—calling Bob Dole the "tax collector for the welfare state"— and baited Democratic leaders with all manner of epithet and insult: *pro-communist, un-American, tyrannical.* In 1984, one of his floor speeches prompted a red-faced eruption from Speaker Tip O'Neill, who said of Gingrich's attacks, "It's the lowest thing that I've ever seen in my thirty-two years in Congress!" The episode landed them both on the nightly news, and Gingrich, knowing the score, declared victory. "I am now a famous person," he gloated to *The Washington Post.*

It's hard to overstate just how radical these actions were at the time. Although Congress had been a volatile place during periods of American history—with fistfights and canings and representatives bellowing violent threats at one another—by the middle of the 20th century, lawmakers had largely coalesced around a stabilizing set of norms and traditions. Entrenched committee chairs may have dabbled in petty corruption, and Democratic leaders may have pushed around the Republican minority when they were in a pinch, but as a rule, comity reigned. "Most members still believed in the idea that the Framers had in mind," says Thomas Mann, a scholar who studies Congress. "They believed in genuine deliberation and compromise . . . and they had institutional loyalty."

This ethos was perhaps best embodied by Republican Minority Leader Bob Michel, an amiable World War II veteran known around Washington for his aversion to swearing—*doggone it* and *by Jiminy* were fixtures of his vocabulary—as well as his penchant for carpooling and golfing with Democratic colleagues. Michel was no liberal, but he believed that the best way to serve conservatism, and his country, was by working honestly with Democratic leaders—pulling legislation inch by inch to the right when he could, and protecting the good faith that made aisle-crossing possible.

Gingrich was unimpressed by Michel's conciliatory approach. "He

represented a culture which had been defeated consistently," he recalls. More important, Gingrich intuited that the old dynamics that
had produced public servants like Michel were crumbling. Tectonic
shifts in American politics—particularly around issues of race and civil
rights—had triggered an ideological sorting between the two parties.
Liberal Republicans and conservative Democrats (two groups that had
been well represented in Congress) were beginning to vanish, and with
them, the cross-party partnerships that had fostered cooperation.

This polarization didn't originate with Gingrich, but he took advantage of it, as he set out to circumvent the old power structures and
build his own. Rather than letting the party bosses in Washington decide which candidates deserved institutional support, he took control
of a group called GOPAC and used it to recruit and train an army of
mini-Newts to run for office.

Gingrich hustled to keep his cause—and himself—in the press. "If
you're not in *The Washington Post* every day, you might as well not
exist," he told one reporter. His secret to capturing headlines was simple, he explained to supporters: "The No. 1 fact about the news media
is they love fights . . . When you give them confrontations, you get
attention; when you get attention, you can educate."

Effective as these tactics were in the short term, they had a corrosive
effect on the way Congress operated. "Gradually, it went from legislating, to the weaponization of legislating, to the permanent campaign, to
the permanent war," Mann says. "It's like he took a wrecking ball to the
most powerful and influential legislature in the world."

But Gingrich looks back with pride on the transformations he set
in motion. "Noise became a proxy for status," he tells me. And no one
was noisier than Newt.

———————

By 1988, Gingrich's plan to conquer Congress via sabotage was well
under way. As his national profile had risen, so, too, had his influence
within the Republican caucus—his original quorum of 12 disciples
having expanded to dozens of sharp-elbowed House conservatives who
looked to him for guidance.

Gingrich encouraged them to go after their enemies with catchy, alliterative nicknames—"Daffy Dukakis," "the loony left"—and schooled them in the art of partisan blood sport. Through GOPAC, he sent out cassette tapes and memos to Republican candidates across the country who wanted to "speak like Newt," providing them with carefully honed attack lines and creating, quite literally, a new vocabulary for a generation of conservatives. One memo, titled "Language: A Key Mechanism of Control," included a list of recommended words to use in describing Democrats: *sick, pathetic, lie, anti-flag, traitors, radical, corrupt.*

The goal was to reframe the boring policy debates in Washington as a national battle between good and evil, white hats versus black—a fight for the very soul of America. Through this prism, any news story could be turned into a wedge. Woody Allen had an affair with his partner's adoptive daughter? "It fits the Democratic Party platform perfectly," Gingrich declared. A deranged South Carolina woman murdered her two children? A symptom of a "sick" society, Gingrich intoned—and "the only way you can get change is to vote Republican."

Gingrich was not above mining the darkest reaches of the right-wing fever swamps for material. When Vince Foster, a staffer in the Clinton White House, committed suicide, Gingrich publicly flirted with fringe conspiracy theories that suggested he had been assassinated. "He took these things that were confined to the margins of the conservative movement and mainstreamed them," says David Brock, who worked as a conservative journalist at the time, covering the various Clinton scandals, before later becoming a Democratic operative. "What I think he saw was the potential for using them to throw sand in the gears of Clinton's ability to govern."

Despite his growing grassroots following, Gingrich remained unpopular among a certain contingent of congressional Republicans, who were scandalized by his tactics. But that started to change when Democrats elected Texas Congressman Jim Wright as speaker. Whereas Tip O'Neill had been known for working across party lines, Wright came off as gruff and power-hungry—and his efforts to sideline the Republican minority enraged even many of the GOP's mild-mannered moderates. "People started asking, 'Who's the meanest, nastiest son of a bitch we can get to fight back?'" recalls Mickey Edwards, a Republican who was then representing Oklahoma in the House. "And, of course, that was Newt Gingrich."

Gingrich unleashed a smear campaign aimed at taking Wright down. He reportedly circulated unsupported rumors about a scandal involving a teenage congressional page, and tried to tie Wright to shady foreign-lobbying practices. Finally, one allegation gained traction—that Wright had used $60,000 in book royalties to evade limits on outside income. Watergate, this was not. But it was enough to force Wright's resignation, and hand Gingrich the scalp he so craved.

The episode cemented Gingrich's status as the de facto leader of the GOP in Washington. Heading into the 1994 midterms, he rallied Republicans around the idea of turning Election Day into a national referendum. On September 27, more than 300 candidates gathered outside the Capitol to sign the "Contract With America," a document of Gingrich's creation that outlined 10 bills Republicans promised to pass if they took control of the House.

"Today, on these steps, we offer this contract as a first step towards renewing American civilization," Gingrich proclaimed.

While candidates fanned out across the country to campaign on the contract, Gingrich and his fellow Republican leaders in Congress held fast to their strategy of gridlock. As Election Day approached, they maneuvered to block every piece of legislation they could—even those that might ordinarily have received bipartisan support, like a lobbying-reform bill—on the theory that voters would blame Democrats for the paralysis.

Pundits, aghast at the brazenness of the strategy, predicted backlash from voters—but few seemed to notice. Even some Republicans were surprised by what they were getting away with. Bill Kristol, then a GOP strategist, marveled at the success of his party's "principled obstructionism." An up-and-coming senator named Mitch McConnell was quoted crowing that opposing the Democrats' agenda "gives gridlock a good name." When the 103rd Congress adjourned in October, *The Washington Post* declared it "perhaps the worst Congress" in 50 years.

Yet Gingrich's plan worked. By the time voters went to the polls, exit surveys revealed widespread frustration with Congress and a deep appetite for change. Republicans achieved one of the most sweeping electoral victories in modern American history. They picked up 54 seats in the House and seized state legislatures and governorships across the country; for the first time in 40 years, the GOP took control of both houses of Congress.

On election night, Republicans packed into a ballroom in the Atlanta suburbs, waving placards that read LIBERALS, YOUR TIME IS UP! and sporting RUSH LIMBAUGH FOR PRESIDENT T-shirts. The band played "Happy Days Are Here Again" and Gingrich—the next speaker of the House, the new philosopher-king of the Republican Party—took the stage to raucous cheers.

With victory in hand, Gingrich did his best to play the statesman, saying he would "reach out to every Democrat who wants to work with us" and promising to be "speaker of the House, not speaker of the Republican Party."

But the true spirit of the Republican Revolution was best captured by the event's emcee, a local talk-radio host in Atlanta who had hitched his star to the Newt wagon early on. Grinning out at the audience, he announced that a package had just arrived at the White House with some Tylenol in it.

President Clinton, joked Sean Hannity, was about to "feel the pain."

The freshman Republicans who entered Congress in January 1995 were lawmakers created in the image of Newt: young, confrontational, and determined to inflict radical change on Washington.

Gingrich encouraged this revolutionary zeal, quoting Thomas Paine— "We have it in our power to begin the world over again"—and working to instill a conviction among his followers that they were political gate-crashers, come to leave their dent on American history. What Gingrich didn't tell them—or perhaps refused to believe himself—was that in Congress, history is seldom made without consensus-building and horse-trading. From the creation of interstate highways to the passage of civil-rights legislation, the most significant, lasting acts of Congress have been achieved by lawmakers who deftly maneuver through the legislative process and work with members of both parties.

On January 4, Speaker Gingrich gaveled Congress into session, and promptly got to work transforming America. Over the next 100 days, he and his fellow Republicans worked feverishly to pass bills with names that sounded like they'd come from Republican Mad Libs—the American Dream Restoration Act, the Taking Back Our Streets Act, the Fiscal Responsibility Act. But when the dust settled, America didn't look all that different. Almost all of the House's big-ticket bills got snuffed out in the Senate, or died by way of presidential veto.

Instead, the most enduring aspects of Gingrich's speakership would be his tactical innovations. Determined to keep Republicans in power, Gingrich reoriented the congressional schedule around filling campaign war chests, shortening the official workweek to three days so that members had time to dial for dollars. From 1994 to 1998, Republicans raised an unprecedented $1 billion, and ushered in a new era of money in politics.

Gingrich's famous budget battles with Bill Clinton in 1995 gave way to another great partisan invention: the weaponized government shutdown. There had been federal funding lapses before, but they tended to be minor affairs that lasted only a day or two. Gingrich's shutdown, by contrast, furloughed hundreds of thousands of government workers for several weeks at Christmastime, so Republicans could use their paychecks as a bartering chip in negotiations with the White House. The gambit was a bust—voters blamed the GOP for the crisis, and Gingrich was castigated in the press—but it ensured that the shutdown threat would loom over every congressional standoff from that point on.

There were real accomplishments during Gingrich's speakership, too—a tax cut, a bipartisan health-care deal, even a balanced federal budget—and for a time, truly historic triumphs seemed within reach. Over the course of several secret meetings at the White House in the fall of 1997, Gingrich told me, he and Clinton sketched out plans for a center-right coalition that would undertake big, challenging projects such as a wholesale reform of Social Security.

But by then, the poisonous politics Gingrich had injected into Washington's bloodstream had escaped his control. So when the stories started coming out in early 1998—the ones about the president and the intern, the cigar and the blue dress—and the party faithful were clamoring for Clinton's head on a pike, and Gingrich's acolytes in the House were stomping their feet and crying for blood . . . well, he knew what he had to do.

This is "the most systematic, deliberate obstruction-of-justice cover-up and effort to avoid the truth we have ever seen in American history!" Gingrich declared of the Monica Lewinsky scandal, pledging that he would keep banging the drum until Clinton was impeached. "I will never again, as long as I am speaker, make a speech without commenting on this topic."

Never mind that Republicans had no real chance of getting the impeachment through the Senate. Removing the president wasn't the point; this was an opportunity to humiliate the Democrats. Politics was a "war for power," just as Gingrich had prophesied all those years ago—and he wasn't about to give up the fight.

The rest is immortalized in the history books that line Gingrich's library. The GOP's impeachment crusade backfired with voters, Republicans lost seats in the House—and Gingrich was driven out of his job by the same bloodthirsty brigade he'd helped elect. "I'm willing to lead," he sniffed on his way out the door, "but I'm not willing to preside over people who are cannibals."

———

The great irony of Gingrich's rise and reign is that, in the end, he did fundamentally transform America—just not in the ways he'd hoped. He thought he was enshrining a new era of conservative government. In fact, he was enshrining an attitude—angry, combative, tribal—that would infect politics for decades to come.

In the years since he left the House, Gingrich has only doubled down. When GOP leaders huddled at a Capitol Hill steak house on the night of President Barack Obama's inauguration, Gingrich was there to advocate a strategy of complete obstruction. And when Senator Ted

Cruz led a mob of Tea Party torchbearers in shutting down the government over Obamacare, Gingrich was there to argue that shutdowns are "a normal part of the constitutional process."

Mickey Edwards, the Oklahoma Republican, who served in the House for 16 years, told me he believes Gingrich is responsible for turning Congress into a place where partisan allegiance is prized above all else. He noted that during Watergate, President Richard Nixon was forced to resign only because leaders of his own party broke ranks to hold him accountable—a dynamic Edwards views as impossible in the post-Gingrich era. "He created a situation where you now stand with your party at all costs and at all times, no matter what," Edwards said. "Our whole system in America is based on the Madisonian idea of power checking power. Newt has been a big part of eroding that."

But when I ask Gingrich what he thinks of the notion that he played a part in toxifying Washington, he bristles. "I took everything the Democrats had done brilliantly to dominate and taught Republicans how to do it," he tells me. "Which made me a bad person because when Republicans dominate, it *must* be bad." He adopts a singsong whine to imitate his critics in the political establishment: "'Oh, the mean, nasty Republicans actually got to win, and we hate it, because we're a Democratic city, our real estate's based on big government, and the value of my house will go down if they balance the budget.' That's the heart of this."

These days, Gingrich seems to be revising his legacy in real time—shifting the story away from the ideological sea change that his populist disruption was supposed to enable, and toward the act of populist disruption itself. He places his own rise to power and Trump's in the same grand American narrative. There have been four great political "waves" in the past half century, he tells me: "Goldwater, Reagan, Gingrich, then Trump." But when I press him to explain what connects those four "waves" philosophically, the best he can do is say they were all "anti-liberal."

Political scientists who study our era of extreme polarization will tell you that the driving force behind American politics today is not actually partisanship, but negative partisanship—that is, hatred of the other team more than loyalty to one's own. Gingrich's speakership was both a symptom and an accelerant of that phenomenon.

On December 19, 1998, Gingrich cast his final vote as a congressman—a vote to impeach Bill Clinton for lying under oath about an affair. By the time it was revealed that the ex-speaker had been secretly carrying on an illicit relationship with a 23-year-old congressional aide named Callista throughout his impeachment crusade, almost no one was surprised. This was, after all, the same man who had famously been accused by his first wife (whom he'd met as a teenager, when she was his geometry teacher) of trying to discuss divorce terms when she was in the hospital recovering from tumor-removal surgery, the same man who had for a time reportedly restricted his extramarital dalliances to oral sex so that he could claim he'd never slept with another woman. (Gingrich declined to comment on these allegations.)

Detractors could call it hypocrisy if they wanted; Gingrich might not even argue. ("It doesn't matter what I do," he once rationalized, according to one of his ex-wives. "People need to hear what I have to say.") But if he had taught America one lesson, it was that any sin could be absolved, any trespass forgiven, as long as you picked the right targets and swung at them hard enough.

When Gingrich's personal life became an issue during his short-lived presidential campaign in 2012, he knew just who to swing at. Asked during a primary debate about an allegation that he'd requested an open marriage with his second wife, Gingrich took a deep breath, gathered all the righteous indignation he could muster, and let loose one of the most remarkable—and effective—non sequiturs in the history of campaign rhetoric: "I think the destructive, vicious, negative nature of much of the news media makes it harder to govern this country, harder to attract decent people to run for public office—and I am *appalled* that you would begin a presidential debate on a topic like that."

The CNN moderator grew flustered, the audience erupted in a standing ovation, and a few days later, the voters of South Carolina delivered Gingrich a decisive victory in the Republican primary.

WHAT'S AILING
AMERICAN POLITICS?

by Jonathan Rauch

[JULY/AUGUST 2016]

Shortly before Donald Trump officially became the Republican presidential nominee, *The Atlantic* published Jonathan
Rauch's cover story "What's Ailing American Politics?" Rauch,
a senior fellow at the Brookings Institution and a longtime
Atlantic contributing writer, trained his focus on essential political structures that have been weakened or dismantled over a
period of half a century. In particular, he lamented the erosion
of the power of mediating institutions and brokers—political
parties, career politicians, congressional leaders. *Smoke-filled
rooms* is shorthand for the way politics was conducted in the
past, and there is much not to miss about the old days. But what
we have now—"chaos syndrome," to use Rauch's term—is not
an improvement: As the role of intermediaries fades, "politicians, activists, and voters all become more individualistic and
unaccountable. The system atomizes. Chaos becomes the new
normal—both in campaigns and in the government itself."

As is often the case, a prime culprit turns out to be good intentions. Rauch offered this epitaph: "Our intricate, informal
system of political intermediation, which took many decades
to build, did not commit suicide or die of old age; we reformed
it to death."

Rauch's books include *Demosclerosis: The Silent Killer of
American Government* (1994) and *Political Realism: How*

*Hacks, Machines, Big Money, and Back-Room Deals Can
Strengthen American Democracy* (2015).

The Founders knew all too well about chaos. It was the condition that brought them together in 1787 under the Articles of Confederation. The central government had too few powers and powers of the wrong kinds, so they gave it more powers, and also multiple power centers. The core idea of the Constitution was to restrain ambition and excess by forcing competing powers and factions to bargain and compromise.

The Framers worried about demagogic excess and populist caprice, so they created buffers and gatekeepers between voters and the government. Only one chamber, the House of Representatives, would be directly elected. A radical who wanted to get into the Senate would need to get past the state legislature, which selected senators; a usurper who wanted to seize the presidency would need to get past the Electoral College, a convocation of elders who chose the president; and so on.

They were visionaries, those men in Philadelphia, but they could not foresee everything, and they made a serious omission. Unlike the British parliamentary system, the Constitution makes no provision for holding politicians accountable to one another. A rogue member of Congress can't be "fired" by his party leaders, as a member of Parliament can; a renegade president cannot be evicted in a vote of no confidence, as a British prime minister can. By and large, American politicians are independent operators, and they became even more independent when later reforms, in the 19th and early 20th centuries, neutered the Electoral College and established direct election to the Senate.

The Constitution makes no mention of many of the essential political structures that we take for granted, such as political parties and congressional committees. If the Constitution were all we had, politicians would be incapable of getting organized to accomplish even routine tasks. Every day, for every bill or compromise, they would have to start from scratch, rounding up hundreds of individual politicians and answering to thousands of squabbling constituencies and millions of voters. By itself, the Constitution is a recipe for chaos.

So Americans developed a second, unwritten constitution. Beginning in the 1790s, politicians sorted themselves into parties. In the 1830s, under Andrew Jackson and Martin Van Buren, the parties established patronage machines and grassroots bases. The machines and parties used rewards and the occasional punishment to encourage politicians to work together. Meanwhile, Congress developed its seniority and committee systems, rewarding reliability and establishing cooperative routines. Parties, leaders, machines, and congressional hierarchies built densely woven incentive structures that bound politicians into coherent teams. Personal alliances, financial contributions, promotions and prestige, political perks, pork-barrel spending, endorsements, and sometimes a trip to the woodshed or the wilderness: All of those incentives and others, including some of dubious respectability, came into play. If the Constitution was the system's DNA, the parties and machines and political brokers were its RNA, translating the Founders' bare-bones framework into dynamic organizations and thus converting conflict into action.

The informal constitution's intermediaries have many names and faces: state and national party committees, county party chairs, congressional subcommittees, leadership PACs, convention delegates, bundlers, and countless more. For purposes of this essay, I'll call them all *middlemen*, because all of them mediated between disorganized swarms of politicians and disorganized swarms of voters, thereby performing the indispensable task that the great political scientist James Q. Wilson called "assembling power in the formal government."

The middlemen could be undemocratic, high-handed, devious, secretive. But they had one great virtue: They brought order from chaos. They encouraged coordination, interdependency, and mutual accountability. They discouraged solipsistic and antisocial political behavior. A loyal, time-serving member of Congress could expect easy renomination, financial help, promotion through the ranks of committees and leadership jobs, and a new airport or research center for his district. A

turncoat or troublemaker, by contrast, could expect to encounter os-
tracism, marginalization, and difficulties with fundraising. The system
was hierarchical, but it was not authoritarian. Even the lowliest pre-
cinct walker or officeholder had a role and a voice and could expect a
reward for loyalty; even the highest party boss had to cater to multiple
constituencies and fend off periodic challengers.

Parties, machines, and hacks may not have been pretty, but at their
best they did their job so well that the country forgot why it needed
them. Politics seemed almost to organize itself, but only because the
middlemen recruited and nurtured political talent, vetted candidates
for competence and loyalty, gathered and dispensed money, built bases
of donors and supporters, forged coalitions, bought off antagonists,
mediated disputes, brokered compromises, and greased the skids to
turn those compromises into law. Though sometimes arrogant, middlemen were not generally elitist. They excelled at organizing and representing unsophisticated voters, as Tammany Hall famously did for
the working-class Irish of New York, to the horror of many Progressives
who viewed the Irish working class as unfit to govern or even to vote.

The old machines were inclusive only by the standards of their day,
of course. They were bad on race—but then, so were Progressives such
as Woodrow Wilson. The more intrinsic hazard with middlemen and
machines is the ever-present potential for corruption, which is a real
problem. On the other hand, overreacting to the threat of corruption
by stamping out influence-peddling (as distinct from bribery and extortion) is just as harmful. Political contributions, for example, look
unseemly, but they play a vital role as political bonding agents. When
a party raised a soft-money donation from a millionaire and used it to
support a candidate's campaign (a common practice until the 2002
McCain-Feingold law banned it in federal elections), the exchange of
favors tied a knot of mutual accountability that linked candidate, party,
and donor together and forced each to think about the interests of the
others. Such transactions may not have comported with the Platonic
ideal of democracy, but in the real world they did much to stabilize the
system and discourage selfish behavior.

Middlemen have a characteristic that is essential in politics: They stick around. Because careerists and hacks make their living off the system, they have a stake in assembling durable coalitions, in retaining power over time, and in keeping the government in functioning order. Slash-and-burn protests and quixotic ideological crusades are luxuries they can't afford. Insurgents and renegades have a role, which is to jolt the system with new energy and ideas; but professionals also have a role, which is to safely absorb the energy that insurgents unleash. Think of them as analogous to antibodies and white blood cells, establishing and patrolling the barriers between the body politic and would-be hijackers on the outside. As with biology, so with politics: When the immune system works, it is largely invisible. Only when it breaks down do we become aware of its importance.

Beginning early in the 20th century, and continuing right up to the present, reformers and the public turned against every aspect of insider politics: professional politicians, closed-door negotiations, personal favors, party bosses, financial ties, all of it. Progressives accused middlemen of subverting the public interest; populists accused them of obstructing the people's will; conservatives accused them of protecting and expanding big government.

To some extent, the reformers were right. They had good intentions and valid complaints. Back in the 1970s, as a teenager in the post-Watergate era, I was on their side. Why allow politicians ever to meet behind closed doors? Sunshine is the best disinfectant! Why allow private money to buy favors and distort policy making? Ban it and use Treasury funds to finance elections! It was easy, in those days, to see that there was dirty water in the tub. What was not so evident was the reason the water was dirty, which was the baby. So we started reforming.

We reformed the nominating process. The use of primary elections instead of conventions, caucuses, and other insider-dominated processes dates to the era of Theodore Roosevelt, but primary elections and party influence coexisted through the 1960s; especially in congressional and state races, party leaders had many ways to influence nominations and vet candidates. According to Jon Meacham, in his biography of George H. W. Bush, here is how Bush's father, Prescott Bush, got started in politics: "Samuel F. Pryor, a top Pan Am executive and a mover in Connecticut politics, called Prescott to ask whether Bush might like to run for Congress. 'If you would,' Pryor said, 'I think we can assure you that you'll be the nominee.'" Today, party insiders can still jawbone a little bit, but, as the 2016 presidential race has made all too clear, there is startlingly little they can do to influence the nominating process.

Primary races now tend to be dominated by highly motivated extremists and interest groups, with the perverse result of leaving moderates and broader, less well-organized constituencies underrepresented. According to the Pew Research Center, in the first 12 presidential-primary contests of 2016, only 17 percent of eligible voters participated in Republican primaries, and only 12 percent in Democratic primaries. In other words, Donald Trump seized the lead in the primary process by winning a mere plurality of a mere fraction of the electorate. In off-year congressional primaries, when turnout is even lower, it's even easier for the tail to wag the dog. In the 2010 Delaware Senate race, Christine "I am not a witch" O'Donnell secured the Republican nomination by winning just a sixth of the state's registered Republicans, thereby handing a competitive seat to the Democrats. Surveying congressional primaries for a 2014 Brookings Institution report, the journalists Jill Lawrence and Walter Shapiro observed: "The universe of those who actually cast primary ballots is small and hyper-partisan, and rewards candidates who hew to ideological orthodoxy." By contrast, party hacks tend to shop for candidates who exert broad appeal in a general election and who will sustain and build the party's brand, so they generally lean toward relative moderates and team players.

Moreover, recent research by the political scientists Jamie L. Carson and Jason M. Roberts finds that party leaders of yore did a better job of encouraging qualified mainstream candidates to challenge incumbents. "In congressional districts across the country, party leaders were able to carefully select candidates who would contribute to the collective good of the ticket," Carson and Roberts write in their 2013 book, *Ambition,*

Competition, and Electoral Reform: The Politics of Congressional Elections Across Time. "This led to a plentiful supply of quality candidates willing to enter races, since the potential costs of running and losing were largely underwritten by the party organization." The switch to direct primaries, in which contenders generally self-recruit and succeed or fail on their own account, has produced more oddball and extreme challengers and thereby made general elections less competitive. "A series of reforms that were intended to create more open and less 'insider' dominated elections actually produced more entrenched politicians," Carson and Roberts write. The paradoxical result is that members of Congress today are simultaneously less responsive to mainstream interests and harder to dislodge.

Was the switch to direct public nomination a net benefit or drawback? The answer to that question is subjective. But one effect is not in doubt: Institutionalists have less power than ever before to protect loyalists who play well with other politicians, or who take a tough congressional vote for the team, or who dare to cross single-issue voters and interests; and they have little capacity to fend off insurgents who owe nothing to anybody. Walled safely inside their gerrymandered districts, incumbents are insulated from general-election challenges that might pull them toward the political center, but they are perpetually vulnerable to primary challenges from extremists who pull them toward the fringes. Everyone worries about being the next Eric Cantor, the Republican House majority leader who, in a shocking upset, lost to an unknown Tea Partier in his 2014 primary. Legislators are scared of voting for anything that might increase the odds of a primary challenge, which is one reason it is so hard to raise the debt limit or pass a budget.

In March, when Republican Senator Jerry Moran of Kansas told a Rotary Club meeting that he thought President Obama's Supreme Court nominee deserved a Senate hearing, the Tea Party Patriots immediately responded with what has become activists' go-to threat: "It's this kind of outrageous behavior that leads Tea Party Patriots Citizens Fund activists and supporters to think seriously about encouraging Dr. Milton Wolf"—a physician and Tea Party activist—"to run against

Sen. Moran in the August GOP primary." (Moran hastened to issue a statement saying that he would oppose Obama's nominee regardless.) Purist issue groups often have the whip hand now, and unlike the elected bosses of yore, they are accountable only to themselves and are able merely to prevent legislative action, not to organize it.

We reformed political money. Starting in the 1970s, large-dollar donations to candidates and parties were subject to a tightening web of regulations. The idea was to reduce corruption (or its appearance) and curtail the power of special interests—certainly laudable goals. Campaign-finance rules did stop some egregious transactions, but at a cost: Instead of eliminating money from politics (which is impossible), the rules diverted much of it to private channels. Whereas the parties themselves were once largely responsible for raising and spending political money, in their place has arisen a burgeoning ecology of deep-pocketed donors, super PACs, 501(c)(4)s, and so-called 527 groups that now spend hundreds of millions of dollars each cycle. The result has been the creation of an array of private political machines across the country: for instance, the Koch brothers' Americans for Prosperity and Karl Rove's American Crossroads on the right, and Tom Steyer's NextGen Climate on the left.

Private groups are much harder to regulate, less transparent, and less accountable than are the parties and candidates, who do, at the end of the day, have to face the voters. Because they thrive on purism, protest, and parochialism, the outside groups are driving politics toward polarization, extremism, and short-term gain. "You may win or lose, but at least you have been intellectually consistent—your principles haven't been defeated," an official with Americans for Prosperity told *The Economist* in October 2014. The parties, despite being called to judgment by voters for their performance, face all kinds of constraints and regulations that the private groups don't, tilting the playing field against them. "The internal conversation we've been having is 'How do we keep state parties alive?'" the director of a mountain-state Democratic Party organization told me and Raymond J. La Raja recently for a Brookings Institution report. Republicans told us the same story.

"We believe we are fighting for our lives in the current legal and judicial framework, and the super PACs and (c)(4)s really present a direct threat to the state parties' existence," a southern state's Republican Party director said.

The state parties also told us they can't begin to match the advertising money flowing from outside groups and candidates. Weakened by regulations and resource constraints, they have been reduced to spectators, while candidates and groups form circular firing squads and alienate voters. At the national level, the situation is even more chaotic—and ripe for exploitation by a savvy demagogue who can make himself heard above the din, as Donald Trump has so shrewdly proved.

We reformed Congress. For a long time, seniority ruled on Capitol Hill. To exercise power, you had to wait for years, and chairs ran their committees like fiefs. It was an arrangement that hardly seemed either meritocratic or democratic. Starting with a rebellion by the liberal post-Watergate class in the '70s, and then accelerating with the rise of Newt Gingrich and his conservative revolutionaries in the '90s, the seniority and committee systems came under attack and withered. Power on the Hill has flowed both up to a few top leaders and down to individual members. Unfortunately, the reformers overlooked something important: Seniority and committee spots rewarded teamwork and loyalty, they ensured that people at the top were experienced, and they harnessed hundreds of middle-ranking members of Congress to the tasks of legislating. Compounding the problem, Gingrich's Republican revolutionaries, eager to prove their anti-Washington bona fides, cut committee staffs by a third, further diminishing Congress's institutional horsepower.

Congress's attempts to replace hierarchies and middlemen with top-down diktat and ad hoc working groups have mostly failed. More than perhaps ever before, Congress today is a collection of individual entrepreneurs and pressure groups. In the House, disintermediation has shifted the balance of power toward a small but cohesive minority of conservative Freedom Caucus members who think nothing of wielding their power against their own leaders. Last year, as House Republicans struggled to agree on a new speaker, the conservatives did not blush at demanding "the right to oppose their leaders and vote down legislation without repercussions," as *Time* magazine reported. In the Senate, Ted Cruz made himself a leading presidential contender by engaging in debt-limit brinkmanship and deriding the party's leadership, going so far as to call Majority Leader Mitch McConnell a liar on the Senate floor. "The rhetoric—and confrontational stance—are classic Cruz," wrote Burgess Everett in *Politico* last October: "Stake out a position to the right of where his leaders will end up, criticize them for ignoring him and conservative grass-roots voters, then use the ensuing inter- necine fight to stoke his presidential bid." No wonder his colleagues detest him. But Cruz was doing what makes sense in an age of maxi- mal political individualism, and we can safely bet that his success will inspire imitation.

We reformed closed-door negotiations. As recently as the early 1970s, congressional committees could easily retreat behind closed doors and members could vote on many bills anonymously, with only the final tallies reported. Federal advisory committees, too, could meet off the record. Understandably, in the wake of Watergate, those practices came to be viewed as suspect. Today, federal law, congressional rules, and public expectations have placed almost all formal deliberations and many informal ones in full public view. One result is greater trans- parency, which is good. But another result is that finding space for delicate negotiations and candid deliberations can be difficult. Smoke- filled rooms, whatever their disadvantages, were good for brokering complex compromises in which nothing was settled until everything was settled; once gone, they turned out to be difficult to replace. In public, interest groups and grandstanding politicians can tear apart a compromise before it is halfway settled.

Despite promising to televise negotiations over health-care reform, President Obama went behind closed doors with interest groups to put the package together; no sane person would have negotiated in full public view. In 2013, Congress succeeded in approving a modest bipartisan budget deal in large measure because the House and Senate

Budget Committee chairs were empowered to "figure it out themselves, very, very privately," as one Democratic aide told Jill Lawrence
for a 2015 Brookings report. TV cameras, recorded votes, and public
markups do increase transparency, but they come at the cost of complicating candid conversations. "The idea that Washington would work
better if there were TV cameras monitoring every conversation gets it
exactly wrong," the Democratic former Senate Majority Leader Tom
Daschle wrote in 2014, in his foreword to the book *City of Rivals*. "The
lack of opportunities for honest dialogue and creative give-and-take lies
at the root of today's dysfunction."

We reformed pork. For most of American history, a principal goal of any
member of Congress was to bring home bacon for his district. Pork-
barrel spending never really cost very much, and it helped glue Congress
together by giving members a kind of currency to trade: You support
my pork, and I'll support yours. Also, because pork was dispensed by
powerful appropriations committees with input from senior congressional leaders, it provided a handy way for the leadership to buy votes
and reward loyalists. Starting in the '70s, however, and then snowball-
ing in the '90s, the regular appropriations process broke down, a casu-
alty of reforms that weakened appropriators' power, of "sunshine laws"
that reduced their autonomy, and of polarization that complicated negotiations. Conservatives and liberals alike attacked pork-barreling as
corrupt, culminating in early 2011, when a strange bedfellows coalition of Tea Partiers and progressives banned earmarking, the practice
of dropping goodies into bills as a way to attract votes—including,
ironically, votes for politically painful spending *reductions*.

Congress has not passed all its annual appropriations bills in 20
years, and more than $300 billion a year in federal spending goes
out the door without proper authorization. Routine business such as
passing a farm bill or a surface-transportation bill now takes years instead of weeks or months to complete. Today two-thirds of federal-
program spending (excluding interest on the national debt) runs on
formula-driven autopilot. This automatic spending by so-called entitlement programs eludes the discipline of being regularly voted on,

dwarfs old-fashioned pork in magnitude, and is so hard to restrain that it's often called the "third rail" of politics. The political cost has also been high: Congressional leaders lost one of their last remaining tools to induce followership and team play. "Trying to be a leader where you have no sticks and very few carrots is dang near impossible," the Republican former Senate Majority Leader Trent Lott told CNN in 2013, shortly after renegade Republicans pointlessly shut down the government. "Members don't get anything from you and leaders don't give anything. They don't feel like you can reward them or punish them."

Like campaign contributions and smoke-filled rooms, pork is a tool of democratic governance, not a violation of it. It can be used for corrupt purposes but also, very often, for vital ones. As the political scientist Diana Evans wrote in a 2004 book, *Greasing the Wheels: Using Pork Barrel Projects to Build Majority Coalitions in Congress*, "The irony is this: pork barreling, despite its much maligned status, gets things done." In 1964, to cite one famous example, Lyndon Johnson could not have passed his landmark civil-rights bill without support from House Republican leader Charles Halleck of Indiana, who named his price: a NASA research grant for his district, which LBJ was glad to provide. Just last year, Republican Senator John McCain, the chairman of the Senate Armed Services Committee, was asked how his committee managed to pass bipartisan authorization bills year after year, even as the rest of Congress ground to a legislative standstill. In part, McCain explained, it was because "there's a lot in there for members of the committees."

Party-dominated nominating processes, soft money, congressional seniority, closed-door negotiations, pork-barrel spending—put each practice under a microscope in isolation, and it seems an unsavory way of doing political business. But sweep them all away, and one finds that business is not getting done at all. The political reforms of the past 40 or so years have pushed toward disintermediation—by favoring amateurs and outsiders over professionals and insiders; by privileging populism and self-expression over mediation and mutual restraint; by stripping middlemen of tools they need to organize the political system. All of the reforms promote an individualistic, atomized model of politics in which there are candidates and there are voters, but there is nothing in between. Other, larger trends, to be sure, have also contributed to political disorganization, but the war on middlemen has amplified and accelerated them.

AMERICAN HUSTLER

by Franklin Foer

[MARCH 2018]

Paul Manafort was a well-known lobbyist and political consultant for four decades—and emphatically not the sort of middleman Jonathan Rauch had in mind. He may have been a middleman only in a technical sense: Manafort's true client was always himself. He thrived on the kind of atomized politics and boundless opportunity that Rauch's "chaos syndrome" created. In 2019, Manafort was sentenced to more than seven years in federal prison for a variety of financial crimes uncovered by Special Counsel Robert Mueller's investigation.

Franklin Foer, an *Atlantic* staff writer and the author of *World Without Mind: The Existential Threat of Big Tech* (2017), profiled Manafort in 2018. His article, excerpted here, is rich in detail—Manafort was a big spender whose profligate lifestyle pushed him ever more deeply into a moral morass that troubled him not in the least. Russian billionaires, Arab arms dealers, African warlords—this was his world, a universe away from the genteel Washington fixers of a more distant age. "Helping elect Donald Trump, in so many ways, represents the culmination of Paul Manafort's work," Foer wrote. "The president bears some likeness to the oligarchs Manafort long served: a businessman with a portfolio of shady deals, who benefited from a cozy relationship to government; a man whose urge to dominate, and to enrich himself, overwhelms any higher ideal." Foer rendered this final verdict: Manafort's "personal corruption is less significant, ultimately, than his lifetime role as a corrupter of the American system."

The clinic permitted Paul Manafort one 10-minute call each day. And each day, he would use it to ring his wife from Arizona, his voice often soaked in tears. "Apparently he sobs daily," his daughter Andrea, then 29, texted a friend. During the spring of 2015, Manafort's life had tipped into a deep trough. A few months earlier, he had intimated to his other daughter, Jessica, that suicide was a possibility. He would "be gone forever," she texted Andrea.

His work, the source of the status he cherished, had taken a devastating turn. For nearly a decade, he had counted primarily on a single client, albeit an exceedingly lucrative one. He'd been the chief political strategist to the man who became the president of Ukraine, Viktor Yanukovych, with whom he'd developed a highly personal relationship. Manafort would swim naked with his boss outside his *banya*, play tennis with him at his palace ("Of course, I let him win," Manafort made it known), and generally serve as an arbiter of power in a vast country. One of his deputies, Rick Gates, once boasted to a group of Washington lobbyists, "You have to understand, we've been working in Ukraine a long time, and Paul has a whole separate shadow government structure . . . In every ministry, he has a guy." Only a small handful of Americans—oil executives, Cold War spymasters—could claim to have ever amassed such influence in a foreign regime. The power had helped fill Manafort's bank accounts; according to his recent indictment, he had tens of millions of dollars stashed in havens like Cyprus and the Grenadines.

Manafort had profited from the sort of excesses that make a country ripe for revolution. And in the early months of 2014, protesters gathered on the Maidan, Kiev's Independence Square, and swept his patron from power. Fearing for his life, Yanukovych sought protective shelter in Russia. Manafort avoided any harm by keeping a careful distance from the enflamed city. But in his Kiev office, he'd left behind a safe filled with papers that he would not have wanted to fall into public view or the wrong hands.

Money, which had always flowed freely to Manafort and which he'd spent more freely still, soon became a problem. After the revolution, Manafort cadged some business from former minions of the ousted president, the ones who hadn't needed to run for their lives. But he complained about unpaid bills and, at age 66, scoured the world (Hungary, Uganda, Kenya) for fresh clients, hustling without any apparent luck. Andrea noted her father's "tight cash flow state," texting Jessica, "He is suddenly extremely cheap." His change in spending habits was dampening her wedding plans. For her "wedding weekend kick off" party, he suggested scaling back the menu to hot dogs and eliminated a line item for ice.

He seemed unwilling, or perhaps unable, to access his offshore accounts; an FBI investigation scrutinizing his work in Ukraine had begun not long after Yanukovych's fall. Meanwhile, a Russian oligarch named Oleg Deripaska had been after Manafort to explain what had happened to an $18.9 million investment in a Ukrainian company that Manafort had claimed to have made on his behalf.

Manafort had known Deripaska for years, so he surely understood the oligarch's history. Deripaska had won his fortune by prevailing in the so-called aluminum wars of the 1990s, a corpse-filled struggle, one of the most violent of all the competitions for dominance in a post-Soviet industry. In 2006, the U.S. State Department had revoked Deripaska's visa, reportedly out of concern over his ties to organized crime (which he has denied). Despite Deripaska's reputation, or perhaps because of it, Manafort had been dodging the oligarch's attempts to contact him. As Deripaska's lawyers informed a court in 2014 while attempting to claw back their client's money, "It appears that Paul Manafort and Rick Gates have simply disappeared."

Nine months after the Ukrainian revolution, Manafort's family life also went into crisis. The nature of his home life can be observed in detail because Andrea's text messages were obtained last year by a "hacktivist collective"—most likely Ukrainians furious with Manafort's meddling in their country—which posted the purloined material on the dark web. The texts extend over four years (2012–16) and 6 million words. Manafort has previously confirmed that his daughter's phone was hacked and acknowledged the authenticity of some texts quoted by *Politico* and *The New York Times*. Manafort and Andrea both declined to comment for this article. Jessica could not be reached for comment.

Collectively, the texts show a sometimes fraught series of relationships, by turns loving and manipulative. Manafort was generous with his family financially—he'd invested millions in Jessica's film projects, and millions more in her now-ex-husband's real-estate ventures. But when he called home in tears or threatened suicide in the spring of 2015, he was pleading for his marriage. The previous November, as the cache of texts shows, his daughters had caught him in an affair with a woman more than 30 years his junior. It was an expensive relationship. According to the text messages, Manafort had rented his mistress a $9,000-a-month apartment in Manhattan and a house in the Hamptons, not far from his own. He had handed her an American Express card, which she'd used to good effect. "I only go to luxury restaurants," she once declared on a friend's fledgling podcast, speaking expansively about her photo posts on social media: caviar, lobster, haute cuisine.

The affair had been an unexpected revelation. Manafort had nursed his wife after a horseback-riding accident had nearly killed her in 1997. "I always marveled at how patient and devoted he was with her during that time," an old friend of Manafort's told me. But after the exposure of his infidelity, his wife had begun to confess simmering marital issues to her daughters. Manafort had committed to couples therapy but, the texts reveal, that hadn't prevented him from continuing his affair. Because he clumsily obscured his infidelity—and because his mistress posted about their travels on Instagram—his family caught him again, six months later. He entered the clinic in Arizona soon after, according to Andrea's texts. "My dad," she wrote, "is in the middle of a massive emotional breakdown."

––––––––––

By the early months of 2016, Manafort was back in greater Washington, his main residence and the place where he'd begun his career as a political consultant and lobbyist. But his attempts at rehabilitation— of his family life, his career, his sense of self-worth—continued. He began to make a different set of calls. As he watched the U.S. presidential campaign take an unlikely turn, he saw an opportunity, and he badly wanted in. He wrote Donald Trump a crisp memo listing all the reasons he would be an ideal campaign consigliere—and then implored mutual friends to tout his skills to the ascendant candidate.

Shortly before the announcement of his job inside Trump's campaign, Manafort touched base with former colleagues to let them know of his professional return. He exuded his characteristic confidence, but they surprised him with doubts and worries. Throughout his long career, Manafort had advised powerful men—U.S. senators and foreign supreme commanders, imposing generals and presidents-for-life. He'd learned how to soothe them, how to bend their intransigent wills with his calmly delivered, diligently researched arguments. But Manafort simply couldn't accept the wisdom of his friends, advice that he surely would have dispensed to anyone with a history like his own—the imperative to shy away from unnecessary attention.

His friends, like all Republican political operatives of a certain age, could recite the legend of Paul Manafort, which they did with fascination, envy, and occasional disdain. When Manafort had arrived in Washington in the 1970s, the place reveled in its shabby glories, most notably a self-satisfied sense of high duty. Wealth came in the form of Georgetown mansions, with their antique imperfections and worn rugs projecting power so certain of itself, it needn't shout. But that old boarding-school establishment wasn't Manafort's style. As he made a name for himself, he began to dress differently from the Brooks Brothers crowd on K Street, more European, with funky, colorful blazers and collarless shirts. If he entertained the notion, say, of moving his backyard swimming pool a few feet, nothing stopped him from the expense. Colleagues, amused by his sartorial quirks and his cosmopolitan lifestyle, referred to him as "the Count of Monte Cristo."

His acts of rebellion were not merely aesthetic. Manafort rewrote the rules of his adopted city. In the early '80s, he created a consulting firm that ignored the conventions that had previously governed lobbying. When it came to taking on new clients, he was uninhibited by moral limits. In 2016, his friends might not have known the specifics of his Cyprus accounts, all the alleged off-the-books payments to him captured in Cyrillic ledgers in Kiev. But they knew enough to believe that he could never sustain the exposure that comes with running a presidential campaign in the age of opposition research and aggressive media. "The risks couldn't have been more obvious," one friend who attempted to dissuade him from the job told me. But in his frayed state, these warnings failed to register.

When Paul Manafort officially joined the Trump campaign, on March 28, 2016, he represented a danger not only to himself but to the political organization he would ultimately run. A lifetime of foreign adventures didn't just contain scandalous stories, it evinced the character of a man who would very likely commandeer the campaign to serve his own interests, with little concern for the collective consequences.

Over the decades, Manafort had cut a trail of foreign money and influence into Washington, then built that trail into a superhighway. When it comes to serving the interests of the world's autocrats, he's been a great innovator. His indictment in October after investigation by Special Counsel Robert Mueller alleges money laundering, false statements, and other acts of personal corruption. (He has pleaded not guilty to all charges.) But Manafort's role in Mueller's broader narrative remains carefully guarded, and unknown to the public. And his personal corruption is less significant, ultimately, than his lifetime role as a corrupter of the American system. That he would be accused of helping a foreign power subvert American democracy is a fitting coda to his life's story.

———————

In the spring of 1977, a 28-year-old Paul Manafort sat at a folding table in a hotel suite in Memphis. Photos from that time show him with a Tom Selleck mustache and meaningful sideburns. He was surrounded by phones that he'd specially installed for the weekend. The desk held his copious binders, which he called "whip books." Eight hundred delegates had gathered to elect a new leader of the Young Republicans organization, and Manafort, a budding kingmaker, had compiled a dossier on each one. Those whip books provided the basis for dealmaking. To wheedle and cajole delegates, it helped to have an idea of what job they wanted in return for their support.

Control over the Young Republicans—a political and social network for professionals ages 18 to 40—was a genuine prize in those days. Presidential hopefuls sought to harness the group. This was still the era of brokered presidential conventions, and Young Republicans could descend in numbers sufficient to dominate the state meetings that selected delegates. In 1964, the group's efforts had arguably secured Barry Goldwater the GOP nomination; by the '70s every Republican aspirant understood its potency. The attention paid by party elders yielded opportunities for Young Republican leaders. Patronage flowed in their direction. To seize the organization was to come into possession of a baby Tammany.

In Memphis, Manafort was working on behalf of his friend Roger Stone, now best known as a pioneer in opposition research and a promiscuous purveyor of conspiracy theories. He managed Stone's candidacy for chairman of the group. Stone, then 24, reveled in the fact that he'd received his political education during Richard Nixon's reelection campaign in 1972; he even admitted to playing dirty tricks to benefit his idol. Stone and Manafort had met through College Republicans. They shared a home state, an affection for finely tailored power suits, and a deeper love of power itself. Together, they campaigned with gleeful ruthlessness.

Even at this early stage in his career, Manafort had acquired a remarkable skill for managing a gathering of great size. He knew how to command an army of loyalists, who took his orders via walkie-talkie. And he knew how to put on a show. In Memphis that year, he rented a Mississippi River paddleboat for a booze cruise and dispatched his whips to work over wavering delegates within its floating confines. To the Young Republican elite, the faction Manafort controlled carried a name that conveyed his expectation of unfailing loyalty: the Team. And in the face of the Team's prowess, Stone's rival eventually quit the race, mid-convention. "It's all been scripted in the back room," he complained.

Manafort had been bred for politics. While he was in high school, his father, Paul Manafort Sr., became the mayor of New Britain, Connecticut, and Manafort Jr. gravitated toward the action—joining a mock city council, campaigning for the gubernatorial candidate Thomas

Meskill as part of his Kiddie Corps. For college and law school, he chose Georgetown University, a taxi ride from the big time.

In the '70s, the big time was embodied by James A. Baker III, the shrewdest Republican insider of his generation. During the epic Republican National Convention of 1976, Manafort holed up with Baker in a trailer outside the Kemper Arena, in Kansas City, Missouri. They attempted to protect Gerald Ford's renomination bid in the face of Ronald Reagan's energetic challenge; Manafort wrangled delegates on Baker's behalf. From Baker, he learned the art of ostentatious humility, how to use the knife to butter up and then stab in the back. "He was studying at the feet of the master," Jeff Bell, a Reagan campaign aide, remembers.

By the late '70s, Manafort and Stone could foresee Ronald Reagan's ascendance, and both intended to become players in his 1980 campaign. For Manafort, this was an audacious volte-face. By flipping his allegiance from the former Ford faction, he provoked suspicion among conservatives, who viewed him as a rank opportunist. There was little denying that the Young Republicans made an ideal vehicle for his ambitions.

These ambitions left a trail of damage, including an Alabama lawyer named Neal Acker. During the Memphis convention, Acker had served as a loyal foot soldier on the Team, organizing the southern delegates on Stone's behalf. In return, Manafort and Stone had promised to throw the Team behind Acker's campaign to replace Stone as the head of the Young Republicans two years later, in 1979. Manafort would manage the campaign himself.

But as the moment of Acker's coronation approached, Manafort suddenly conditioned his plan. If Acker wanted the job, he had to swear loyalty to Reagan. When Acker ultimately balked—he wanted to stay neutral—Manafort turned on him with fury, "an unprecedented 11th-hour move," the Associated Press reported. In the week leading up to the 1979 Young Republicans convention, Manafort and Stone set out to destroy Acker's candidacy. At Manafort's urging, the delegates who were pledged to Acker bolted—and Manafort took over his opponent's campaign. In a bravura projection of power that no one in the Reagan campaign could miss, Manafort swung the vote sharply against Acker, 465 to 180. "It was one of the great fuck jobs," a Manafort whip told me recently.

Not long after that, Stone and Manafort won the crucial positions in the Reagan operation that they'd coveted. Stone directed the campaign in the Northeast, Manafort in the South. The campaign had its share of infighting; both men survived factional schisms and purges. "They were known as the Young Republican whizzes," Jeff Bell told me. Their performance positioned them for inner-sanctum jobs in the Reagan administration, but they had even grander plans.

During the years that followed World War II, Washington's most effective lobbyists transcended the transactional nature of their profession. Men such as Abe Fortas, Clark Clifford, Bryce Harlow, and Thomas Corcoran were known not as grubby mercenaries but as elegant avatars of a permanent establishment, lauded as "wise men." Lobbying hardly carried a stigma, because there was so little of it. When the legendary lawyer Tommy Boggs registered himself as a lobbyist, in 1967, his name was only 64th on the active list. Businesses simply didn't consider lobbying a necessity. Three leading political scientists had studied the profession in 1963 and concluded: "When we look at the typical lobby, we find its opportunities to maneuver are sharply limited, its staff mediocre, and its typical problem not the influencing of Congressional votes but finding the clients and contributors to enable it to survive at all."

On the cusp of the Reagan era, Republican lobbyists were particularly enfeebled. Generations of Democratic majorities in Congress had been terrible for business. The scant tribe of Republican lobbyists working the cloakrooms included alumni of the Nixon and Ford administrations; operating under the shame-inducing cloud of Watergate, they were disinclined toward either ambition or aggression.

This was the world that brash novices like Manafort and Stone quickly came to dominate. The Reagan administration represented a break with the old Republican establishment. After the long expansion of the regulatory state, business finally had a political partner eager to dismantle it—which generated unprecedented demand for lobbyists. Manafort could convincingly claim to know the new administration better than anyone. During its transition to power, he had run the Office of Personnel Management, which meant that he'd stacked the incoming government with his people. Along with Stone and Charlie Black, another veteran of the Young Republican wars, he set up a firm, Black, Manafort and Stone, which soon compiled an imposing client list: Bethlehem Steel, the Tobacco Institute, Johnson & Johnson, Trans World Airlines.

Whereas other firms had operated in specialized niches—lobbying, consulting, public relations—Black, Manafort and Stone bundled all those services under one roof, a deceptively simple move that would eventually help transform Washington. *Time* magazine deemed the operation "the ultimate supermarket of influence peddling." Fred Wertheimer, a good-government advocate, described this expansive approach as "institutionalized conflict of interest."

The linkage of lobbying to political consulting—the creation of what's now known as a double-breasted operation—was the real break-through. Manafort's was the first lobbying firm to also house political consultants. (Legally, the two practices were divided into different companies, but they shared the same founding partners and the same office space.) One venture would run campaigns; the other would turn around and lobby the politicians whom their colleagues had helped elect. The consulting side hired the hard-edged operative Lee Atwater, notorious for pioneering race-baiting tactics on behalf of Strom Thurmond. "We're getting into servicing what we sell," Atwater told his friends. Just as imagined, the firm's political clients (Jesse Helms, Phil Gramm, Arlen Specter) became reliable warhorses when the firm needed them to promote the agendas of its corporate clients. With this evolution of the profession, the effectiveness and influence of lobbying grew in tandem.

In 1984, the firm reached across the aisle. It made a partner of Peter Kelly, a former finance chairman of the Democratic National Committee, who had earned the loyalty of lawmakers by raising millions for their campaigns. Some members of the firm worked for Democratic Senate candidates in Louisiana, Vermont, and Florida, even as operatives down the hall worked for their Republican foes. "People said, 'It's un-American,'" Kelly told me. "'They can't lose. They have both sides.' I kept saying, 'How is it un-American to win?'" This sense of invincibility permeated the lobbying operation, too. When Congress passed tax-reform legislation in 1986, the firm managed to get one special rule inserted that saved Chrysler-Mitsubishi $58 million; it wrangled another clause that reaped Johnson & Johnson $38 million in savings. *Newsweek* pronounced the firm "the hottest shop in town."

Demand for its services rose to such heights that the firm engineered a virtual lock on the 1988 Republican primary. Atwater became the chief strategist for George H. W. Bush; Black worked with Bob Dole; Stone advised Jack Kemp. A congressional staffer joked to *Time*, "Why have primaries for the nomination? Why not have the candidates go over to Black, Manafort and Stone and argue it out?" Manafort cultivated this perception. In response to a questionnaire in *The Washington Times*, he declared Machiavelli the person he would most like to meet.

Despite his young age, Manafort projected the sort of confidence that inspires others to have confidence, a demeanor often likened to that of a news anchor. "He is authoritative, and you never see a chink in the armor," one of his longtime deputies, Philip Griffin, told me. Manafort wrote well, especially in proposals to prospective clients, and excelled at thinking strategically. Name-dropping never substituted for concrete steps that would bolster a client. "If politics has done anything, it's taught us to treat everything as a campaign," he once declared. He toiled for clients with unflagging intensity. His wife once quipped, according to the text messages, that Andrea was conceived between conference calls. He "hung up the phone, looked at his watch, and said, 'Okay, we have 20 minutes until the next one,'" Andrea wrote to her then-fiancé.

By the 1990s, the double-digit list of registered lobbyists that Tommy Boggs had joined back in 1967 had swelled to more than 10,000.

Black, Manafort, Stone and Kelly had greatly abetted that transformation, and stood to profit from the rising flood of corporate money into the capital. But by then, domestic politics had begun to feel a little small, a bit too unexotic, for Paul Manafort, whom Charlie Black described to me as a self-styled "adventurer."

Manafort had long befriended ambitious young diplomats at the trailhead to power, including Prince Bandar bin Sultan Al Saud, then the Saudi ambassador to Washington. When Bandar attended the 1984 Republican National Convention, Manafort dedicated a small group of advance men to smooth his way. Manafort arranged for Bandar to arrive at the presidential entrance, then had him whisked to seats in the vice-presidential box.

Foreign lobbying had certainly existed before the '80s, but it was limited in scale and operated under a penumbra of suspicion. Just before World War II, Congress had passed the Foreign Agents Registration Act, largely in response to the campaigns orchestrated by Ivy Lee, an American publicist hired by the German Dye Trust to soften the image of the Third Reich. Congress hadn't outlawed influence peddling on behalf of foreign interests, but the practice sat on the far fringes of K Street.

Paul Manafort helped change that. The Reagan administration had remade the contours of the Cold War, stepping up the fight against communism worldwide by funding and training guerrilla armies and right-wing military forces, such as the Nicaraguan contras and the Afghan mujahideen. This strategy of military outsourcing—the Reagan Doctrine—aimed to overload the Soviet Union with confrontations that it couldn't sustain.

All of the money Congress began spending on anti-communist proxies represented a vast opportunity. Ironfisted dictators and scruffy commandants around the world hoped for a share of the largesse. To get it, they needed help refining their image, so that Congress wouldn't look too hard at their less-than-liberal tendencies. Other lobbyists sought out authoritarian clients, but none did so with the focused intensity of Black, Manafort, Stone and Kelly. The firm would arrange for image-buffing interviews on American news programs; it would enlist allies in Congress to unleash money. Back home, it would help regimes acquire the whiff of democratic legitimacy that would bolster their standing in Washington.

The firm won clients because it adeptly marketed its ties to the Reagan administration, and then the George H. W. Bush administration after that. In one proposal, reported in *The New York Times* in 1988, the firm advertised its "personal relationships" with officials and promised to "upgrade" back channels "in the economic and foreign policy spheres." No doubt it helped to have a friend in James Baker, especially after he became the secretary of state under Bush. "Baker would send the firm clients," Kelly remembered. "He wanted us to help lead these guys in a better direction."

But moral improvement never really figured into Manafort's calculus. "Generally speaking, I would focus on how to bring the client in sync with Western European or American values," Kelly told me. "Paul took the opposite approach." (Kelly and Manafort have not spoken in recent years; the former supported Hillary Clinton in the last presidential campaign.) In her memoir, Riva Levinson, a managing director at the firm from 1985 to 1995, wrote that when she protested to her boss that she needed to believe in what she was doing, Manafort told her that it would "be my downfall in this business." The firm's client base grew to include dictatorial governments in Nigeria, Kenya, Zaire, Equatorial Guinea, Saudi Arabia, and Somalia, among others. Manafort's firm was a primary subject of scorn in a 1992 report issued by the Center for Public Integrity called "The Torturers' Lobby."

By the late 1980s, Manafort had a new friend from abroad, whom he mentioned to his partners more than any other, an arms dealer from Lebanon named Abdul Rahman Al Assir. "His name kept popping up," Peter Kelly remembered. While Al Assir never rated much attention in the American press, he had a familial connection who did. He was, for a time, the brother-in-law of the Saudi arms dealer Adnan Khashoggi, the middleman used in the arms-for-hostages scheme that became the Iran-Contra scandal. In the early '80s, Khashoggi was worth $4 billion; his biography, published in 1986, was titled *The Richest Man in the World*. Al Assir was the Khashoggi empire's representative in Spain and a broker of big weapons sales to African armies.

Manafort suggested to his partners that Al Assir might help connect the firm to clients around the world. He wanted to increase the firm's global reach. Manafort's exploration of the outermost moral frontiers of the influence business had already exposed him to kleptocrats, thugs, and other dubious characters. But none of these relationships imprinted themselves more deeply than his friendship and entrepreneurial partnership with Al Assir. By the '90s, the two had begun to put together big deals.

Manafort and Al Assir were more than business partners. "They were very brotherly," one mutual acquaintance of theirs told me. Manafort took Al Assir as his guest to George H. W. Bush's inauguration, in 1989. When Al Assir and his second wife had a child, Manafort became the godfather. Their families vacationed together near Cannes. Al Assir introduced Manafort to an aristocratic world that exceeded anything he had ever known. "There's money, and there's really big money," a friend of Manafort's told me. "Paul became aware of the difference between making $300,000 and $5 million. He discovered the south of France. Al Assir would show him how to live that life."

There were always suspicions among Manafort's colleagues in the firm that he was making money for himself without regard for his partners. Colleagues suspected the worst about Manafort because they had observed his growing mania for accumulating property, how he'd bought second, third, and fourth homes. "He would buy a house without ever seeing it," one former colleague told me. His Hamptons estate came with a putting green, a basketball court, a pool, and gardens. "He believed that suckers stay out of debt," the colleague told me. His unrestrained spending and pile of debt required a perpetual search for bigger paydays and riskier ventures.

In 1991, Black, Manafort, Stone and Kelly was purchased by the mega-public-affairs firm Burson-Marsteller, the second-largest agency in the world. It was a moment of consolidation in the industry, where the biggest players came to understand how much money could be made from the model that Manafort had created. But nearly as soon as Burson acquired the firm, Tom Bell, the head of its Washington office, began to notice the ways in which Manafort hadn't played by the rules. He'd been operating as a freelancer, working on projects that never went to the bottom line. In 1995, Manafort left Burson. Taking a handful of colleagues with him, he started a new firm—Davis, Manafort and Freedman—and a new chapter, one that would see him enter the sphere of the Kremlin.

During the 1980s and '90s, an arms dealer had stood at the pinnacle of global wealth. In the new century, post-Soviet oligarchs climbed closer to that position. Manafort's ambitions trailed that shift. His new firm found its way to a fresh set of titans, with the help of an heir to an ancient fortune.

In 2003, Rick Davis, a partner in Manafort's new firm, was invited to the office of a hedge fund in Midtown Manhattan. The summons didn't reveal the name of the man requesting his presence. When Davis arrived, he found himself pumping the hand of the Honorable Nathaniel Philip Victor James Rothschild, the British-born financier known as Nat. Throughout his young career, Nat had fascinated the London press with his love interests, his residences, and his shrewd investments. For his 40th birthday, he threw himself a legendary party in the Balkan state of Montenegro, which reportedly cost well over $1 million—a three-day festival of hedonism, with palm trees imported from Uruguay.

Russian oligarchs were drawn to Rothschild, whose name connoted power—and he to them. "He likes this wild world," Anders Åslund, a friend of Rothschild's, told me. Rothschild invested heavily in post-Communist economies and became a primary adviser (and a friend) to the young Russian billionaire Oleg Deripaska.

Rothschild and Deripaska fed off each other's grand ambitions. Like a pair of old imperialists, they imagined new, sympathetic governments across Eastern Europe that would accommodate and protect their investments. Their project required the type of expertise that Manafort had spent years accumulating. In 2004, Rothschild hired Manafort's new firm to resurrect the influence of an exiled Georgian politician, a former KGB operative and friend of Deripaska's then living in Moscow.

This made for a heavy lift because the operative had recently been accused in court as a central plotter in a conspiracy to assassinate the country's president, Eduard Shevardnadze. (He denied involvement.) The rehabilitation scheme never fully developed, but a few years later, Rick Davis triumphantly managed a referendum campaign that resulted in the independence of Montenegro—an effort that Deripaska funded with the hope of capturing the country's aluminum industry.

Deripaska's interests were not only financial. He was always looking to curry favor with the Russian state. An August 2007 email sent by Lauren Goodrich, an analyst for the global intelligence firm Stratfor, and subsequently posted on WikiLeaks, described Deripaska boasting to her about how he had set himself up "to be indispensable to Putin and the Kremlin." This made good business sense, since he had witnessed the Kremlin expropriate the vast empires of oligarchs such as Mikhail Khodorkovsky who'd dared to challenge Putin. In fact, the Kremlin came to consider Deripaska an essential proxy. When the United States denied Deripaska a visa, the Russians handed him a diplomatic passport, which permitted him to make his way to Washington and New York.

Manafort understood how highly Deripaska valued his symbiotic relationship with the Kremlin. According to the Associated Press, he pitched a contract in 2005, proposing that Deripaska finance an effort to "influence politics, business dealings and news coverage inside the United States, Europe and former Soviet Republics to benefit President Vladimir Putin's government." (Deripaska says he never took Manafort up on this proposal.)

The Kremlin's grip on its old Soviet sphere was especially precarious in the early aughts. President George W. Bush's democratic agenda espoused an almost messianic sense of how the United States could unleash a new age of freedom. The grandiloquent American rhetoric posed an existential threat to entrenched rulers of the region who were friendly to Russia, and who had become rich by plundering state resources. Suddenly, the threat of democratic revolution no longer felt theoretical.

The risks of popular uprising were very much on Rothschild's and

Deripaska's minds during the last months of 2004, when they handed Manafort a specific task. Ukraine had descended into political crisis, one that jeopardized business interests they'd already developed in the country (Rothschild had various private-equity investments; Deripaska had an aluminum smelter). They sent Manafort to Kiev to understand how they might minimize the dangers.

Of all Paul Manafort's foreign adventures, Ukraine most sustained his attention, ultimately to the exclusion of his other business. The country's politics are hardly as simple as commonly portrayed; corruption extends its tentacles into all the major parties. Still, the narrative of Manafort's time in Ukraine isn't terribly complicated. He worked on behalf of a clique of former gangsters from the country's east, oligarchs who felt linguistic and cultural affinity to Russia, and who wanted political control of the entire nation. When Manafort arrived, the candidate of this clique, Viktor Yanukovych, was facing allegations that he had tried to rig the 2004 presidential election with fraud and intimidation, and possibly by poisoning his opponent with dioxin. He lost the election anyway, despite having imported a slew of consultants from Moscow. After that humiliating defeat, Yanukovych and the oligarchs who'd supported him were desperate for a new guru.

By the time Manafort first entertained the possibility of working with Yanukovych, the defeated candidate had just returned to Kiev following a brief self-imposed exile at a Czech resort. They met at an old movie palace that had been converted into the headquarters for his political organization, the Party of Regions. When Manafort entered the grandiose building, the place was a mausoleum and Yanukovych a pariah. "People avoided him," Philip Griffin said. "He was radioactive."

Manafort groomed Yanukovych to resemble, well, himself. Åslund, who had advised the Ukrainian government on economic policy, told me, "Yanukovych and Manafort are almost exactly the same size. So they are big, tall men. He got Yanukovych to wear the same suits as he did and to comb the hair backwards as he does." Yanukovych had been wooden in public and in private, but "Manafort taught him how to smile and how to do small talk." And he did it all quietly, "from a back seat. He did it very elegantly."

He also directed Yanukovych's party to harp on a single theme each week—say, the sorry condition of pensioners. These were not the most-sophisticated techniques, but they had never been deployed in Ukraine. Yanukovych was proud of his American turn. After he hired Manafort, he invited U.S. Ambassador John Herbst to his office, placed a binder containing Manafort's strategy in front of him, and announced, "I'm going with Washington."

Manafort often justified his work in Ukraine by arguing that he hoped to guide the country toward Europe and the West. But his polling data suggested that Yanukovych should accentuate cultural divisions in the country, playing to the sense of victimization felt by Russian speakers in eastern Ukraine. And sure enough, his clients railed against NATO expansion. When a U.S. diplomat discovered a rabidly anti-American speech on the Party of Regions' website, Manafort told him, "But it isn't on the English version."

Yanukovych's party succeeded in the parliamentary elections beyond all expectations, and the oligarchs who'd funded it came to regard Manafort with immense respect. As a result, Manafort began spending longer spans of time in Ukraine. One of his greatest gifts as a businessman was his audacity, and his Ukrainian benefactors had amassed enormous fortunes. The outrageous amounts that Manafort billed, sums far greater than any he had previously received, seemed perfectly normal. An associate of Manafort's described the system this way: "Paul would ask for a big sum," Yanukovych would approve it, and then his chief of staff "would go to the other oligarchs and ask them to kick in. 'Hey, you need to pay a million.' They would complain, but Yanukovych asked, so they would give."

When Yanukovych won the presidency in 2010, he gave Manafort "walk in" privileges, allowing him to stroll into the inner sanctum of the presidential offices at any time.

———

Before everything exploded in Ukraine, Manafort saw the country as his golden land, the greatest of his opportunities. But his role as adviser, as powerful as it was, never quite matched his own buccaneering sense of self. After spending so much time in the company of Russian and Ukrainian oligarchs, he set out to become an oligarch himself. Rick Davis declared their firm to be mostly "in the deal business," according to James Harding's 2008 book, *Alpha Dogs: The Americans Who Turned Political Spin Into a Global Business.* "The thing I love," Davis said, "is that the political elites and the economic elites in every other country but the United States of America are the same." The elected officials and the people "running the elections are the richest people in the country, who own all the assets."

In 2006, Rick Gates, who'd begun as a wheel man at the old firm, arrived in Kiev. (Gates did not respond to multiple requests for comment on this article.) Manafort placed him at the helm of a new private equity firm he'd created called Pericles. He intended to raise $200 million to bankroll investments in Ukraine and Russia. "It was a virgin market in virtually any industry you wanted to pick up," Philip Griffin told me.

Manafort had always intended to rely on financing from Oleg Deripaska to fund Pericles. In 2007, Manafort persuaded him to commit $100 million to the project, a sum that would have hardly made a dent in the oligarch's fortune. On the eve of the 2008 global financial crisis, he was worth $28 billion.

Deripaska handed his money to Paul Manafort because he trusted him. Manafort repeatedly traveled to the oligarch's Moscow office, where they would sit for hours and tour the business and political horizon of the former Eastern Bloc. Deripaska had become a billionaire in his 30s, and acquired the noisy pretensions of young wealth. He wanted to become the global face of Russia, he said. But that would require overcoming the reputation that stalked him, and Manafort could help. In 2001, before Manafort and Deripaska met, the World Economic Forum in Davos had withdrawn its invitation to the oligarch, as a court examined his alleged misdeeds in the course of erecting his empire. (The case was eventually dismissed.) Five years after the Davos rejection, Rick Davis shepherded Deripaska around the elite confab, taking him to a party brimming with U.S. senators, including John McCain.

For Pericles's first deal, Manafort used Deripaska's money to buy a telecommunications firm in Odessa called Chorne More ("Black Seas," in English) at a cost of $18.9 million. He also charged a staggering $7.35 million in management fees for overseeing the venture.

But months after the Chorne More purchase, the 2008 financial crisis hit, gutting Deripaska's net worth. It plummeted so far that he needed a $4.5 billion bailout from the Russian state bank to survive. The loan included an interest payment in the form of abject humiliation: Putin traveled to one of Deripaska's factories and berated him on television.

As Deripaska's world came crashing down, his representatives asked Manafort to liquidate Pericles and give him back his fair share. Manafort had little choice but to agree. But that promise never translated to action. An audit of Chorne More that Rick Gates said was under way likewise never materialized. Then, in 2011, Manafort stopped responding to Deripaska's investment team altogether.

Deripaska wouldn't let go of the notion that Manafort owed him money. In 2015, his lawyers filed a motion in a Virginia court. They wanted the authority to track down more information on the deal, even though the initial papers for it had been filed in the Cayman Islands. The lawyers had already managed to get their hands on some of the documentation surrounding the deal, and they had extracted a belated explanation of what had happened from Gates. According to a spokeswoman for Deripaska, Gates said that Chorne More had defaulted on a $1 million loan that it had taken out to pay for capital expenditures, allegedly forfeiting the partnership's entire investment in the process. This explanation struck Deripaska's lawyers as wildly implausible. Deripaska began to publicly doubt whether Manafort had even bought the telecommunications company in the first place. "At present it seems that the Partnership never acquired any of the Chorne More entities," his lawyers argued.

All of the papers for the initial deal had included Rick Davis's name. They suggested that he would serve as Manafort's partner, and that shares would be divided evenly between the two. But Davis knew nothing of the Chorne More deal. While Manafort had been putting together Pericles, Davis had been on leave from Davis, Manafort and

Freedman, running John McCain's 2008 presidential campaign. Because Davis's connections to Manafort and Deripaska had caused him a public-relations headache at the outset of the campaign, he'd kept a healthy distance from both men. When Deripaska's lawyers asked him about the money he supposedly owed their client, Davis was gobsmacked. He soon discovered that Manafort had also registered a new company—Davis Manafort International—to continue trading on the old firm's name, while cutting him out of consulting fees. Upon returning from the campaign, and witnessing the extent to which Manafort had abused his trust, Davis left the firm they had created together.

Deripaska's attorneys had leveled a serious allegation—and true to his pattern, Manafort never filed a response. Those who have known Manafort the longest suggest that this reflects his tendency to run away from personal crises: "He'll get on a jet and fly off to Hawaii—and will come back when everything blows over," an old colleague told me, recalling Manafort's response to a scandal in the late '80s. But it was one thing to hide from reporters; it was another to hide from Oleg Deripaska. Though no longer the ninth-richest man in the world, he was still extremely powerful.

The fact is that by then, Manafort's options were tightly limited: Despite all the riches he had collected in Ukraine, it is unlikely that he could have paid Deripaska back. For years, according to his indictment, Manafort had found clever ways to transfer money that he'd stashed in foreign havens to the U.S. He'd used it to buy real estate, antique rugs, and fancy suits—all relatively safe vehicles for repatriating cash without paying taxes or declaring the manner in which it had been earned.

But in the summer of 2014, in the wake of the revolution that deposed Viktor Yanukovych, the FBI began scrutinizing the strongman's finances. The investigation came to cover Manafort's own dealings. Soon after the feds took an interest, interviewing Manafort in July 2014, the repatriations ceased. Meanwhile, Manafort struggled to collect the money owed him by Yanukovych's cronies. To finance his expensive life, he began taking out loans against his real estate—some $15 million over two years, his indictment says. This is not an uncommon tactic among money launderers—a bank loan allows the launderer to extract clean cash from property purchased with dirty money. But according to the indictment, some of Manafort's loans were made on the basis of false information supplied to the bank in order to inflate the sums available to him, suggesting the severity of his cash-flow problems. All of these loans would need to be paid back, of course. And one way or another, he would need to settle Deripaska's bill.

―――――――

"I really need to get to" Trump, Manafort told an old friend, the real-estate magnate Tom Barrack, in the early months of 2016. Barrack, a confidant of Trump for some 40 years, had known Manafort even longer. When Manafort asked for Barrack's help grabbing Trump's attention, he readily supplied it.

With the arrival of Donald Trump, Manafort smelled an opportunity to regain his losses, and to return to relevance. It was, in some ways, perfect: The campaign was a shambolic masterpiece of improvisation that required an infusion of technical knowledge and establishment credibility.

Barrack forwarded to Trump's team a memo Manafort had written about why he was the ideal match for the ascendant candidate. Old colleagues describe Manafort as a master pitchman with a preternatural ability to read his audience. He told Trump that he had "avoided the political establishment in Washington since 2005," and described himself as a lifelong enemy of Karl Rove, who represented the entrenched party chieftains conspiring to dynamite Trump's nomination. In other words, to get back on the inside, Manafort presented himself as the ultimate outsider—a strained case that would strike Trump, and perhaps only Trump, as compelling.

Manafort could write such a calibrated pitch because he had observed Trump over the decades. Back in the '80s, his firm had represented Trump when the mogul wanted to reroute planes flying over Mar-a-Lago, his resort in Palm Beach. Since 2006, Manafort had kept a pied-à-terre in Trump Tower, where he and Trump had occasionally seen each other and made small talk. This exposure yielded perhaps another crucial insight: Trump's parsimony. When Manafort offered

Trump his services, he resisted his tendency to slap a big price tag on them; he would provide his counsel, he said, free of charge. To his family, Manafort described this decision as a matter of strategy: If Trump viewed him as wealthy, then he would treat him as a near-equal, not as a campaign parasite.

But Manafort must have also believed that money would eventually come, just as it always had, from the influence he would wield in the campaign, and exponentially more so if Trump won. So might other favors and dispensations. These notions were very likely what led him to reach out to Oleg Deripaska almost immediately upon securing a post within the campaign, after having evaded him for years. Through one of his old deputies, a Ukrainian named Konstantin Kilimnik, he sent along press clippings that highlighted his new job. "How do we use to get whole," Manafort emailed Kilimnik. "Has OVD operation seen?" Manafort's spokesman has acknowledged that the initials refer to Oleg Vladimirovich Deripaska. In the course of the exchanges, Kilimnik expressed optimism that "we will get back to the original relationship" with the oligarch.

All of Manafort's hopes, of course, proved to be pure fantasy. Instead of becoming the biggest player in Donald Trump's Washington, he has emerged as a central villain in its central scandal. An ever-growing pile of circumstantial evidence suggests that the Trump campaign colluded with Russian efforts to turn the 2016 presidential election in its favor. Given Manafort's long relationship with close Kremlin allies including Yanukovych and Deripaska, and in particular his indebtedness to the latter, it is hard to imagine him as either a naive or passive actor in such a scheme—although Deripaska denies knowledge of any plan by Manafort to get back into his good graces. Manafort was in the room with Donald Trump Jr. when a Russian lawyer and lobbyist descended on Trump Tower in the summer of 2016, promising incriminating material on Hillary Clinton. That same summer, the Trump campaign, with Manafort as its manager, successfully changed the GOP's platform, watering down support for Ukraine's pro-Western, post-Yanukovych government, a change welcomed by Russia and previously anathema to Republicans.

When the Department of Justice indicted Paul Manafort in October—for failing to register as a foreign agent, for hiding money abroad—its portrait of the man depicted both avarice and desperation, someone who traffics in dark money and dark causes. It seems inevitable, in retrospect, that Robert Mueller, the special counsel, would treat Manafort's banking practices while in Ukraine as his first subject of public scrutiny, the obvious starting point for his investigation.

The sad truth is that all of the damning information contained within the Mueller indictment would have remained submerged if Manafort had withstood the temptation to seek out a role in Trump's campaign. Even if his record had become known, it would have felt unexceptional: Manafort's misdeeds, in our current era, would not have seemed so inconsistent with the run of global play.

From both the Panama Papers and the Paradise Papers, vast disclosures illuminating previously hidden offshore accounts of the rich and powerful worldwide, we can see the full extent to which corruption has become the master narrative of our times. We live in a world of smash-and-grab fortunes, amassed through political connections and outright theft. Paul Manafort, over the course of his career, was a great normalizer of corruption. The firm he created in the 1980s obliterated traditional concerns about conflicts of interest. It imported the ethos of the permanent campaign into lobbying and, therefore, into the construction of public policy.

And while Manafort is alleged to have laundered cash for his own benefit, his long history of laundering reputations is what truly sets him apart. He helped persuade the American political elite to look past the atrocities and heists of kleptocrats and goons. He took figures who should have never been permitted influence in Washington and softened their image just enough to guide them past the moral barriers to entry.

THE BATTLE FOR
NORTH CAROLINA

by Vann R. Newkirk II

[OCTOBER 2016]

There will always be individual opportunists, and they will always undermine the ability of good people to govern properly. An even bigger concern has to do with the machinery of governance: that is, whether the operations of democracy function as they must. At the turn of the twentieth century, North Carolina passed a suffrage amendment to the state constitution. It mandated poll taxes, literacy tests, and a variety of other measures designed to suppress voting by African Americans. The suffrage amendment achieved precisely what it set out to accomplish. It would take many generations—and federal intervention—before African Americans were able to vote freely in North Carolina. And vote they did. In 2012, the black voter-participation rate in the state (about 80 percent of eligible voters) exceeded that of whites (66 percent).

Shaken by such progress, the forces of rollback in the Republican state legislature stiffened their resolve. As staff writer Vann R. Newkirk II reported in *The Atlantic* in 2016, plans advanced rapidly both for gerrymandered districts and for new forms of voter suppression aimed at African Americans and other minorities. Those plans have been deflected, momentarily, by the courts (most recently in 2019). "In essence," Newkirk wrote of a Fourth Circuit decision on voting rights, "the court determined that Republican lawmakers had identified every voting provision that motivated high voter turnout among black voters, and then eliminated them, targeting black people with 'almost surgical precision.'"

Newkirk, who writes with a historian's eye, covers civil rights, environmental justice, and politics for *The Atlantic*. He is also the host of *Floodlines*, a 2020 *Atlantic* podcast about Hurricane Katrina and its aftermath.

In 1901, America was ascendant. Its victory over Spain, the reunification of North and South, and the closing of the frontier announced the American century. Americans awaited the inauguration of the 57th Congress, the first elected in the 20th century. All of the incoming members of Congress, like those they replaced, were white men, save one.

Representative George Henry White did not climb the steps of Capitol Hill on the morning of January 29 to share in triumph. The last black congressman elected before the era of Jim Crow, White, a Republican, took the House floor in defeat. He had lost his North Carolina home district after a state constitutional amendment disenfranchised black voters—most of his constituents. That law marked the end of black political power in North Carolina for nearly a century.

"This, Mr. Chairman, is perhaps the Negroes' temporary farewell to the American Congress," he declared, "but let me say: Phoenixlike he will rise up someday and come again. These parting words are in behalf of an outraged, heartbroken, bruised, and bleeding, but God-fearing people, faithful, industrious, loyal people—rising people, full of potential force."

White eulogized what the country had sacrificed for its newfound prosperity. "I am pleading for the life, the liberty, the future happiness, and manhood suffrage for one-eighth of the population of the United States," he told the House. His pleas fell on deaf ears.

Over the next century and a half, White's home state would see constant skirmishes over the same racial and political issues. Although

White admitted temporary defeat, the battle for North Carolina is still raging today.

––––––––––

In 2016, bitter and unyielding contests have placed the state at the center of national debates about race, civil rights, violence, and elections. In the span of a year, an anti-transgender "bathroom bill" sparked rallies and a fierce debate over civil rights, flames licked the streets of a resegregated Charlotte during protests over a police shooting, a local GOP office was firebombed, and a collection of new laws was enacted—and promptly challenged in court. But the most contentious and sustained rift has been in the arena of voting rights, where White's words resound most loudly.

I drove to one of the staging grounds of that battle in late August and watched as a stream of activists walked inside from the heat of a summer evening.

Sitting just outside of North Carolina State University's sprawling campus in Raleigh, Pullen Memorial Baptist Church is wholly unlike the hidebound Southern Baptist churches I grew up with in rural North Carolina. Inserts in the hymnals boasted of the church's commitment to racial, sexual, and gender inclusivity and advertised a training for sensitivity to transgender and gender-nonconforming folks. Scattered through the rows of the church sat an eclectic crowd of old-school civil-rights movement leaders, Latino college students, white clergymen, LGBTQ activists, state NAACP organizers, and first-timers who'd driven from the woods down state highways in pickup trucks.

After a round of call-and-response chants, the North Carolina NAACP president, Reverend William J. Barber II, took the pulpit to applause. With a seasoned preacher's pace, Barber launched into the kind of hybrid of political speech and sermon that marks pastors turned activists. "The Fourteenth Amendment says every person has a right to equal protection under the law," he told the crowd. "When you engage in intentional voter discrimination, you are robbing people of their equal protection under the law." His words were both a benediction and a battle cry.

Barber delights in connecting the dots between the country's past and its present. He has proclaimed this moment a "Third Reconstruction," and dubbed his protests "Moral Mondays." President Lyndon B. Johnson signed the Voting Rights Act in 1965, but its own limitations, and the backlash it sparked, led directly to the voting-rights problems facing North Carolina today.

Even after 1965, North Carolina still struggled mightily with racial equality at the ballot. Thirty-six percent of all eligible black adults were registered to vote in North Carolina in 1963; that number jumped to 50 percent after the passage of the Voting Rights Act but stalled there. Literacy tests remained active in the state until changes were made to the VRA in 1975. By 1980, the proportion of registered black voters had barely inched up to 52 percent. Adjustments made in 1982, including a new legal test for discrimination based on the effect of changes rather their intent, restored some momentum. In 1990, 63 percent of eligible black voters were registered, but the wide racial disparity in turnout still persisted in North Carolina through to the new millennium.

Why didn't—or couldn't—more black people vote once extended the franchise? One reason is that all the structural barriers to voting hadn't been eliminated. Research indicates that polling places tend to be less common in minority neighborhoods, and understaffed and underfunded relative to those in white neighborhoods, so longer lines are much more likely in minority areas. The latent difficulty of registering to vote in under-resourced areas compounds with other obstacles for minority voters—lower wages, higher unemployment, more rigid work schedules, and large racial disparities in car ownership—to depress turnout even in the absence of Jim Crow laws.

One simple way to increase turnout is to make voting easier. And North Carolina began doing just that in 1993, with a bipartisan push to establish early voting as an extension of on-site absentee voting. That was extended to statewide early voting in the 1999 session. The General Assembly also considered "no excuse" absentee voting by mail, preregistering teenagers, and expanding voter-registration locations. These proposals were intended to increase turnout among North

Carolinians of all races and party affiliations who struggle to make it to the polls on Election Day.

Economic and social frustrations deeply affected vulnerable people of color in North Carolina. Activists advocated closing the voter-turnout and -registration gaps as a way to push for greater unemployment benefits and expanded health-insurance coverage. One of those activists was William Barber.

"Moral Mondays came from the 'Moral Movement' that started in 2007 when Democrats were in office," Barber told me. "We came together—14 organizations that grew to 60—declaring that we needed a moral reset in the way in which we looked at public policy. We began to have what's called a 'People's Assembly.' The first time we gathered, more than 5,000 people showed up."

The Moral Movement coalition was instrumental in the passage of same-day voter registration in 2007. The measure was touted as a commonsense way to help the state's turnout across all races, but same-day registration provoked stiff Republican opposition. The bill's sponsor, then–State Representative Deborah Ross, now the Democratic challenger for Republican Richard Burr's Senate seat, joined with a coalition of liberal groups to pressure the Democratic leadership of the general assembly and Governor Mike Easley into adopting the provision. The movement had its first voting-rights victory.

North Carolina's presidential-election turnout increased 14 percentage points from 2000 to 2012, vaulting from 37th to 11th. The elections in 2008 saw historic turnout levels across the state. For the first time in the state's history, black voters outpaced white voters, and they did so again in 2012.

The one major wildcard in assessing the efficacy of voter laws in those elections was the candidacy of Barack Obama, who had the kind of paradigm-shifting effect on black registration and turnout as Emancipation and the Voting Rights Act. According to the state Board of Elections, Warren County, which has one of the highest proportions of black voters in the state, had a turnout rate greater than 80 percent in 2008.

That infusion of black voters—who mostly vote Democratic—

helped unseat Republican Senator Elizabeth Dole, deliver one of North Carolina's House seats to a Democrat, and give the party the general assembly and the offices of the governor, lieutenant governor, and attorney general. Obama himself won North Carolina by a razor-thin margin of just over 14,000 votes.

The causality of 2008 is still unclear: Did the Voting Rights Act and state voting expansions increase black voter turnout enough to hand the state to Democrats, or did Obama's historic appeal to people of color change the composition of North Carolina's electorate on its own? Republicans seemed to think both were factors, and the ensuing conservative backlash targeted black and Latino voters as well as Obama.

That backlash included a fundraising and organizing blitz that built the infrastructure for a political counterrevolution. The subsequent midterm election was crucial, not just for the congressional seats themselves, but because the 2010 Census would provide an opportunity to redraw both the state legislative and federal congressional district maps.

Through an initiative named "REDMAP," or the Redistricting Majority Project, Republicans coordinated party efforts across states to create Republican majorities in state legislatures. Operatives for the project poured money into obscure state-assembly races in backwoods across the South, overwhelming the traditional analog campaigns of once-safe Blue Dog Democrats and of Republicans it deemed insufficiently conservative. Its efforts were bolstered by the Tea Party wave of voters opposed to Obama and his agenda. The result, according to a REDMAP report, was a 700-seat swing among state legislatures nationwide, which the report describes as "more success than either party has seen in modern history."

In North Carolina, spending on state races increased by 20 percent from 2008 to 2010, an investment poured mostly into Republican campaigns. Almost all of the independent money spent on state races in 2010 came from the conservative millionaire and mega-donor Art Pope, his family, and allied groups, who spread more than $2 million across 22 races. Of those 22, Republicans won 18, creating GOP majorities in both chambers of the general assembly for the first time since

Reconstruction. Only this time, Republicans were focused on restricting the electorate rather than expanding it.

State Representative David Lewis was one of the Republican leaders responsible for consolidating gains in the general assembly with
the actual drawing of new political districts. During the record-setting
heat wave of summer 2011, Lewis and his partner, State Senator Bob
Rucho, got to work.

"We set about to draw districts that were fair and legal based on
the law," Lewis told me. "We held an unprecedented number of public hearings—36, I believe—before we released maps. We studied the
law very thoroughly . . . we complied with the Voting Rights Act as we
understood it, and as it had been interpreted by the Supreme Court of
the United States."

The Moral Movement geared up for protests immediately after
Rucho and Lewis unveiled the proposed maps, and registered official
comments in one of the largest series of feedback sessions the general
assembly has ever had on redistricting.

"They pass[ed] a redistricting plan that is not just worse than the
rest of the 20th century, they go all the way back to the 19th century,"
William Barber said. "It's what we called 'apartheid redistricting,' And
because they didn't remove any black districts, they didn't take away
any, then it really couldn't be stopped by preclearance," he said, referring to the provision in the Voting Rights Act that placed all voting-law
changes in certain counties and states under federal supervision.

Under authority created by the Voting Rights Act, both parties had
been creating "majority-minority" districts in redistricting plans. On
the one hand, these districts ensured the election of minority representatives en masse in many states for the first time since Reconstruction,
and new districts introduced new classes of black and Latino representation in Congress.

But on the other, Republicans across the South soon learned that
if enough black voters are packed into just enough majority-minority
districts to avoid triggering VRA protections, they could create a slew
of mostly white districts that reliably vote Republican without interference from their black neighbors. In legislative sessions, Lewis argued

that he'd actually been mandated by the Voting Rights Act into packing black voters into hyper-gerrymandered districts, saying they were "drawn with race as a consideration, as is required by" the VRA.

Key to the legality of majority-minority districts was the "Gingles test," a set of three preconditions based on a 1986 Supreme Court decision in a gerrymandering lawsuit—which also came out of North Carolina. Those three preconditions are "compactness," or whether a minority group is a coherent, massed geographic entity; the political cohesion of the minority group in question; and the presence of "racially-polarized voting," whereby local white voters have been determined to vote in a way that defeats minority-preferred candidates. That last condition is important, because it often signals the difference between packing minority voters in a district as a "shield" to protect them from racist voting, and packing them there as a way to diminish their political influence.

In July 2011, Lewis and Rucho revealed their new congressional map, and the improbable shapes of the resulting majority-minority districts alone made it difficult to imagine that the three most contentious districts might pass the Gingles test. The First Congressional District was a behemoth, connecting a dozen counties and crossing the entire length of the mostly black portion of the coastal plain, with a single feeler that reached down into Little Washington and New Bern like a creeper vine. The Twelfth Congressional District flowed like a river along a 100-mile stretch roughly coterminous with the I-85 corridor from Charlotte to Greensboro, with tributaries only branching off in search of nearby black neighborhoods. The "hanging claw" of the Fourth District was one of the most gerrymandered in the country, and at one point encompassed an area just wide enough to place a basketball court and bleachers. North Carolina isn't called the Tar Heel State for nothing.

Opponents of the law were left with no options, save one. "We had to go to court," said Barber. And so, at the end of 2011, two separate groups of plaintiffs—including the North Carolina NAACP—filed complaints to the state supreme court. After consolidating the two cases, the state court began hearing the trial in July of 2013.

Around the same time, a decision in Washington opened up a new front in the voting-rights fight. In *Shelby County v. Holder*, Chief Justice John Roberts argued that "things have changed dramatically. Largely because of the Voting Rights Act, 'voter turnout and registration rates' in covered jurisdictions 'now approach parity. Blatantly discriminatory evasions of federal decrees are rare. And minority candidates hold office at unprecedented levels.'"

While that argument might seem to illustrate the utility of the Voting Rights Act, the Roberts Court used it to nullify Section 4(b). That section outlined the congressional "preclearance" formula for determining Department of Justice oversight of precincts or states with histories of discriminatory voting laws. The *Shelby County* decision gutted federal oversight over election rules in areas where it had, arguably, been most effective.

Absent that federal oversight, Republicans in the South seemed bent on proving just why it was necessary in the first place. They passed a slate of new voting laws that likely would have been blocked just days before. North Carolina Republicans led the way. Although less than half of North Carolina's counties were covered under the original formula, preclearance would have been enough of a legal hurdle to make some proposed bills to eliminate early voting, establish voter ID, and end same-day registration—like the ominously named 2013 Senate Bill 666—a nightmare to implement.

Lewis, who also took the legislative lead in the general assembly to establish new voting laws in the immediate aftermath of *Shelby County*, argues that those prototypical bills were not discriminatory, but necessary. "I can show you Republican bills dating back to 2005 that institute voter ID," he told me. "And what happened in 2005 is the Carter-Baker Commission, chaired by former President Carter and Secretary of State Jim Baker, issued a report that said, 'We need a voter ID to improve election integrity.'" The Carter-Baker report does recommend standardized voter-ID requirements and procedures as a way to inspire confidence in elections. It also warns that such requirements "might prove a serious impediment to voting" if not implemented properly or in good faith.

According to Lewis, the goal of the new voting restrictions was not to take advantage of the sudden absence of federal oversight, but "to improve the real and perceived integrity of North Carolina's election system."

In anticipation of the *Shelby County* decision, the state House had already heavily revised an older voting bill—House Bill 589—to a form almost identical to Senate Bill 666, including strict voter-ID provisions, a reduction of the early-voting period from 17 days to 10, elimination of same-day registration, and an elimination of straight-ticket voting. That weeklong reduction came with a "same hours" provision that required counties to provide the same number of aggregate hours during the new 10-day early-voting period as they did during the original 17-day period—but counties could apply to have the requirement waived, and dozens did.

"The law provided for 10 days of early voting; 10 days is what the majority of states provide," Lewis told me. "I believe that our plan created more opportunities, more hours, more places, allowed more people to vote than had ever been allowed before."

The day of the *Shelby County* decision, State Senator Tom Apodaca announced to a local news station, WRAL, "Now we can go on with the full bill." Just four days later, the bill sat in front of Governor Pat McCrory. In less than a week, the Supreme Court and North Carolina had undone most of the election laws developed over decades to help the state move beyond its Jim Crow past.

———

Rosanell Eaton grew up in that dark age. Her home, on a country road outside of Louisburg, North Carolina, is filled with the artifacts from the fight for civil rights. Clippings of old newspapers lauding her work on voting rights mingle with photographs of civil-rights pioneers and commendations stamped with President Obama's seal. From a stately yellow armchair in the corner of a room, she regales visitors who sit on her plastic-covered couches with tales of voter-registration drives for black folks back when people like her were still lynched for voting. Very few—if any—living African Americans in North Carolina have fought for voting rights for as long as Eaton.

Born in rural Franklin County in April 1921, Eaton is the grand-daughter of people who were once enslaved. Black people in Franklin County just didn't try to vote much back then, and Eaton became motivated when she learned that it had not always been so. "You didn't hear much about voting in school, and I was interested in the history," she told me. "So I asked my ma one day about taking me to Louisburg to see about voting."

One morning in 1942, after Eaton's 21st birthday, she climbed on the family's mule-drawn wagon with her mother and brother and trav-eled the eight miles to the Louisburg courthouse. The three white men there were nonplussed.

"They asked me what was I there for," Eaton said. "And I told them that I came down to see about getting registered."

In order to even prove herself eligible to vote, Eaton recalled, she had to put her hands by her sides, stare straight ahead, and recite the Preamble to the Constitution, verbatim. Whether those three adminis-trators were aware of the staggering irony of their demand or not, she stood straight, stared at a spot behind them on the wall, and aced the recitation, word for word. Apparently, so few black people had been bold—or foolhardy—enough to take the test that the registrars had no thought of intimidation beyond that point. "You did a mighty good job," one man told Eaton. "Well, I reckon I have to have you to sign these papers."

While the early stirrings of the civil-rights movement—often re-ferred to as the Second Reconstruction—began in churches, bus de-pots, and lunch counters across the South, Eaton soon developed a reputation as an activist in her own right in her backwoods corner of Franklin County. Early on, she was given permission to register other people, and eventually led a small black-voter outreach team across the county and state.

Despite the draconian literacy tests and intimidation that kept most black voters away from the polls in the state for almost 30 years after her own registration, Eaton used the mounting social momentum of the era as motivation. Her work eventually intersected with the paths of better-known activists and movements in the '60s in Selma, Alabama, and Washington, D.C. Juggling life as a teacher and mother, she saved extra money and scrounged to take cross-state and cross-country trips to spread the gospel of the ballot. Eaton told me that she has probably registered close to 10,000 voters, and has voted in every election since her registration.

That record was put in peril with the passage of H.B. 589, which invalidated her existing identification because of a discrepancy between her voter registration and her driver's license. For a then-92-year-old woman, the task of traveling hundreds of miles from her home to almost a dozen agencies and banks to reconcile her license and registration bordered on Sisyphean.

As a longtime voting activist and teacher, Eaton possessed the knowledge necessary to navigate the process of reregistering. But she knew that if it was burdensome for her, then it could prove impossibly daunting to many others, including rural voters of color like her, in the same way it did during Jim Crow. "It was maybe harder for me to get to vote after the law than it was all the way back then," Eaton said.

After an appeal through the district court, a team of advocates and plaintiffs, including Eaton, won the ruling that they hoped for. In July 2016, the Fourth Circuit court found that the sweeping provisions of H.B. 589 not only possessed clear discriminatory impacts, but that they "were enacted with racially discriminatory intent." The ruling found that state legislators had requested racial data on early voting, out-of-precinct voting, voter ID, same-day registration, and provisional voting.

In essence, the court determined that Republican lawmakers had identified every voting provision that motivated high turnout among black voters, and then eliminated them, targeting black people with "almost surgical precision." The court also found that the speed of the general assembly's post–*Shelby County* maneuvering betrayed its true intentions. "Indeed, neither this legislature—nor, as far as we can tell, any other legislature in the Country—has ever done so much, so fast, to restrict access to the franchise," the opinion states.

Lewis was emphatic in denying the Fourth Circuit's claim of discriminatory intent. "There's no way in the world I would do anything that I felt denied folks the opportunity to vote, but at the same time I didn't want folks voting more than once, because that cheapens the vote," Lewis said. He stands by that rationale, despite a State Board of Elections report, presented to him in 2013, that found only two total allegations of in-person voter fraud in the entire state from 2000 to 2010.

Republicans faced another setback later in 2016, when a district-court ruling struck down Lewis and Rucho's redistricting plan. The court found that Lewis's map-drawing expert, Thomas Hofeller, had not even considered the "racially polarized voting" component of the Gingles test in the creation of the First District, and that black and white voters had actually worked together in electing minority candidates before the redistricting.

Between the Supreme Court's refusal to review the Fourth Circuit's decision on H.B. 589 and the district court's decision on the new state district maps, the winds seemed to shift against Republican maneuvering on voting rights. But for the North Carolina GOP, there was one last gambit.

In an August letter to county boards of elections—an unusual and controversial direct appeal—state GOP Executive Director Dallas Woodhouse told partisan board members that "Republicans can and should make party line changes to early voting."

Lewis argued that Republican reform efforts, including H.B. 589, were actually intended to make voting more accessible—and had included a provision to ensure that the overall number of voting hours could not be reduced. But with that bill struck down, Woodhouse urged Republican officials to do exactly that. His letter urged limiting hours during the 17 days mandated for early voting, reducing the number of early-voting sites, and eliminating strategically convenient sites on college campuses, in minority neighborhoods, and near churches. Lewis and Rucho released a subsequent letter urging boards of elections to not limit hours or polling places during the early-voting period.

After H.B. 589 was struck down, county election officials scrambled to submit new polling plans in time for the fall elections. Republicans pushed for restrictions that fell in line with Woodhouse's recommendations, including restricting polling places during the additional week of early voting reinstated when the court struck down the voting restrictions.

The Republicans' moves ignited opposition from their Democratic colleagues, who took their appeals to the State Board of Elections, with the hope that it would either accept their alternative plans to extend the full complement of early-voting polling places across all 17 days or offer a compromise.

That body, despite a Republican majority, ruled on September 8 to add more early-voting locations and hours in many of the counties with appeals. It ruled to adopt an alternative plan to include eight polling places across populous Wake County—including on the college campus and in the community center in the black neighborhood—during the additional week.

Aside from the handful of counties that changed early-voting regulations and did not appeal, Republican efforts to roll back the turnout-increasing voting laws across the state appeared to have met a dead end for this election cycle.

———

Although the Moral Movement and voting-rights activists won victories in the courts, the final outcome of voting rights in North Carolina and the century-old battle for its soul is far from settled. In the Supreme Court's 4–4 stalemate on McCrory's appeal and request to stay the lower court's injunction of H.B. 589, each of the conservative justices indicated that they would have granted the stay.

The future success of any appeal by the state will depend on the high court, and state legislators could always find new avenues for rolling back turnout. Without federal preclearance, in 2018, 2020, and beyond, county boards of elections are still vulnerable to the kind of coordinated partisan challenges that the state GOP offices attempted with their "party line" letter.

The issues surrounding the 2016 elections in North Carolina are fundamentally similar to the issues that framed the explosive politics of the Wilmington insurrection (in 1898) and Rosanell Eaton's time in the civil-rights movement, and the same probably holds nationwide. Instead of local firebrands, Donald Trump is the main force weaponizing white rage and grievance across the country, and his constant invocations of black and Latino criminality plot a course eerily similar to earlier invectives about "Negro rule" and rape.

It is possible that this turn of the wheel is different, and that the ghosts of Jim Crow really no longer haunt society or the fight over voting rights. Republicans in the state can point to their results over the past decade—a state that has increasingly turned red even as its demographics seem to shift blue—as proof that their goal is simply to win, and not to disenfranchise on the basis of race.

That's certainly the view of Carter Wrenn, a legendary Carolinian conservative strategist, commentator, and former aide to Senator Helms. "African American voters, going back to the '60s, voted overwhelmingly Democratic," he told me. "So, if you try to skew the voter laws against Democrats, African Americans are gonna suffer or they're gonna experience the skew disproportionately, because they vote heavily Democratic . . . I don't think Republicans sat down and said, 'Our goal is to make it harder for African Americans to vote for racial reasons.' I think they said, 'This will make it harder for Democrats to vote.' And that included African Americans naturally."

Wrenn did not have answers for the questions that seem to spring from his own explanation: Why do Republicans today seem to need to contract the electorate as much as possible to win, why does that contraction almost necessarily fall on lines of race, and can its necessity be separated from larger social friction about the loss of white electoral and social power?

If anything, history suggests that race and racism are perhaps the real answers here—not simple ancillaries to political maneuvering, but its first considerations. The concepts are inseparable, and disenfranchisement of black voters has been central to the duel between Republicans and Democrats since Emancipation.

The voting laws under which North Carolina operated for the vast majority of its history were dictated by white supremacy. That black voters historically turn out less than white voters is directly connected to the century-long campaign to disenfranchise them. That black voters overwhelmingly back Democrats is inseparable from the two parties' emphatic reversal on voting rights. That they turned out heavily for Barack Obama in 2008 must be considered within the context of a half-century drought of black political representation between the two Reconstructions.

Barber believes that this nationwide battle over voting rights, and the reawakening of fear and white rage across the country, are direct descendants of those moments. If Barber is right, history is mixed on the long-term prospects for racial progress, and civil-rights gains may be more precarious than they seem.

"I believe we're in the adolescent stages of a Third Reconstruction," he told me. "People are beginning to wake up in some ways and beginning to see that something is at stake when it comes to the very heart and soul of America."

Even if he's right, though, it's not clear whether it will prove more durable than its predecessors.

HOW AMERICA ENDS

by Yoni Appelbaum

[DECEMBER 2019]

The political battles in North Carolina are a harbinger of what will happen—is already happening—in many places as America faces its demographic future. As Yoni Appelbaum pointed out in "How America Ends," his contribution to a 2019 *Atlantic* special issue, "The United States is undergoing a transition perhaps no rich and stable democracy has ever experienced: Its historically dominant group is on its way to becoming a political minority—and its minority groups are asserting their co-equal rights and interests." While there is no true precedent, resonant parallels exist—for instance, the absorption of large waves of immigration—in the United States and elsewhere. In these cases, Appelbaum argues, a successful transition has depended on the response of the center-right. Did it become a welcome and welcoming voice for founding principles, national tradition, and institutional continuity, thereby serving as necessary ballast at an unsettling moment? Or did it retreat into snarling, ethnocentric, Canute-like efforts to sweep back the tide?

Appelbaum is a senior editor at *The Atlantic*, where he oversees the Ideas section. Before joining the magazine, he was a lecturer on history and literature at Harvard.

D emocracy depends on the consent of the losers. For most of the 20th century, parties and candidates in the United States have competed in elections with the understanding that electoral defeats are neither permanent nor intolerable. The losers could accept the result, adjust their ideas and coalitions, and move on to fight in the next election. Ideas and policies would be contested, sometimes viciously, but however heated the rhetoric got, defeat was not generally equated with political annihilation. The stakes could feel high, but rarely existential. In recent years, however, beginning before the election of Donald Trump and accelerating since, that has changed.

"Our radical Democrat opponents are driven by hatred, prejudice, and rage," Trump told the crowd at his reelection kickoff event in Orlando in June. "They want to destroy you and they want to destroy our country as we know it." This is the core of the president's pitch to his supporters: He is all that stands between them and the abyss.

In October, with the specter of impeachment looming, he fumed on Twitter, "What is taking place is not an impeachment, it is a COUP, intended to take away the Power of the People, their VOTE, their Freedoms, their Second Amendment, Religion, Military, Border Wall, and their God-given rights as a Citizen of The United States of America!" For good measure, he also quoted a supporter's dark prediction that impeachment "will cause a Civil War like fracture in this Nation from which our Country will never heal."

Trump's apocalyptic rhetoric matches the tenor of the times. The body politic is more fractious than at any time in recent memory. Over the past 25 years, both red and blue areas have become more deeply hued, with Democrats clustering in cities and suburbs and Republicans filling in rural areas and exurbs. In Congress, where the two caucuses once overlapped ideologically, the dividing aisle has turned into a chasm.

As partisans have drifted apart geographically and ideologically, they've become more hostile toward each other. In 1960, less than 5 percent of Democrats and Republicans said they'd be unhappy if their children married someone from the other party; today, 35 percent of Republicans and 45 percent of Democrats would be, according to a recent Public Religion Research Institute/*Atlantic* poll—far higher than the percentages that object to marriages crossing the boundaries of race and religion. As hostility rises, Americans' trust in political institutions, and in one another, is declining. A study released by the Pew Research Center in July found that only about half of respondents believed their fellow citizens would accept election results no matter who won. At the fringes, distrust has become centrifugal: Right-wing activists in Texas and left-wing activists in California have revived talk of secession.

Recent research by political scientists at Vanderbilt University and other institutions has found both Republicans and Democrats distressingly willing to dehumanize members of the opposite party. "Partisans are willing to explicitly state that members of the opposing party are like animals, that they lack essential human traits," the researchers found. The president encourages and exploits such fears. This is a dangerous line to cross. As the researchers write, "Dehumanization may loosen the moral restraints that would normally prevent us from harming another human being."

Outright political violence remains considerably rarer than in other periods of partisan divide, including the late 1960s. But overheated rhetoric has helped radicalize some individuals. Cesar Sayoc, who was arrested for targeting multiple prominent Democrats with pipe bombs, was an avid Fox News watcher; in court filings, his lawyers said he took inspiration from Trump's white-supremacist rhetoric. "It is impossible," they wrote, "to separate the political climate and [Sayoc's] mental illness." James Hodgkinson, who shot at Republican lawmakers (and badly wounded Representative Steve Scalise) at a baseball practice, was a member of the Facebook groups Terminate the Republican Party and The Road to Hell Is Paved With Republicans. In other instances, political protests have turned violent, most notably in Charlottesville, Virginia, where a Unite the Right rally led to the murder of a young woman. In Portland, Oregon, and elsewhere, the left-wing "antifa" movement has clashed with police. The violence of extremist groups provides ammunition to ideologues seeking to stoke fear of the other side.

What has caused such rancor? The stresses of a globalizing, postindustrial economy. Growing economic inequality. The hyperbolizing force of social media. Geographic sorting. The demagogic provocations of the president himself. As in *Murder on the Orient Express*, every suspect has had a hand in the crime.

But the biggest driver might be demographic change. The United States is undergoing a transition perhaps no rich and stable democracy has ever experienced: Its historically dominant group is on its way to becoming a political minority—and its minority groups are asserting their co-equal rights and interests. If there are precedents for such a transition, they lie here in the United States, where white Englishmen initially predominated, and the boundaries of the dominant group have been under negotiation ever since. Yet those precedents are hardly comforting. Many of these renegotiations sparked political conflict or open violence, and few were as profound as the one now under way.

Within the living memory of most Americans, a majority of the country's residents were white Christians. That is no longer the case, and voters are not insensate to the change—nearly a third of conservatives say they face "a lot" of discrimination for their beliefs, as do more than half of white evangelicals. But more epochal than the change that has already happened is the change that is yet to come: Sometime in the next quarter century or so, depending on immigration rates and the vagaries of ethnic and racial identification, nonwhites will become a majority in the U.S. For some Americans, that change will be cause for celebration; for others, it may pass unnoticed. But the transition is already producing a sharp political backlash, exploited and exacerbated by the president. In 2016, white working-class voters who said that discrimination against whites is a serious problem, or who said they felt like strangers in their own country, were almost twice as likely to vote for Trump as those who did not. Two-thirds of Trump voters agreed that "the 2016 election represented the last chance to stop America's decline." In Trump, they'd found a defender.

———

In 2002, the political scientist Ruy Teixeira and the journalist John Judis published a book, *The Emerging Democratic Majority*, which argued that demographic changes—the browning of America, along with the movement of more women, professionals, and young people into the Democratic fold—would soon usher in a "new progressive era" that would relegate Republicans to permanent minority political status. The book argued, somewhat triumphally, that the new emerging majority was inexorable and inevitable. After Barack Obama's reelection, in 2012, Teixeira doubled down on the argument in *The Atlantic*, writing, "The Democratic majority could be here to stay." Two years later, after the Democrats got thumped in the 2014 midterms, Judis partially recanted, saying that the emerging Democratic majority had turned out to be a mirage and that growing support for the GOP among the white working class would give the Republicans a long-term advantage. The 2016 election seemed to confirm this.

But now many conservatives, surveying demographic trends, have concluded that Teixeira wasn't wrong—merely premature. They can see the GOP's sinking fortunes among younger voters, and feel the culture turning against them, condemning them today for views that were commonplace only yesterday. They are losing faith that they can win elections in the future. With this comes dark possibilities.

The Republican Party has treated Trump's tenure more as an interregnum than a revival, a brief respite that can be used to slow its decline. Instead of simply contesting elections, the GOP has redoubled its efforts to narrow the electorate and raise the odds that it can win legislative majorities with a minority of votes. In the first five years after conservative justices on the Supreme Court gutted a key provision of the Voting Rights Act in 2013, 39 percent of the counties that the law had previously restrained reduced their number of polling places. And while gerrymandering is a bipartisan sin, over the past decade Republicans have indulged in it more heavily. In Wisconsin last year, Democrats won 53 percent of the votes cast in state legislative races, but just 36 percent of the seats. In Pennsylvania, Republicans tried to impeach the state Supreme Court justices who had struck down a GOP attempt to gerrymander congressional districts in that state. The Trump White House has tried to suppress counts of immigrants for the 2020 census, to reduce their voting power. All political parties maneuver for advantage, but only a party that has concluded it cannot win the votes of large swaths of the public will seek to deter them from casting those votes at all.

The history of the United States is rich with examples of once-dominant groups adjusting to the rise of formerly marginalized populations—sometimes gracefully, more often bitterly, and occasionally violently. Partisan coalitions in the United States are constantly reshuffling, realigning along new axes. Once-rigid boundaries of faith, ethnicity, and class often prove malleable. Issues gain salience or fade into irrelevance; yesterday's rivals become tomorrow's allies.

But sometimes, that process of realignment breaks down. Instead of reaching out and inviting new allies into its coalition, the political right hardens, turning against the democratic processes it fears will subsume it. A conservatism defined by ideas can hold its own against progressivism, winning converts to its principles and evolving with each generation. A conservatism defined by identity reduces the complex calculus of politics to a simple arithmetic question—and at some point, the numbers no longer add up.

Trump has led his party to this dead end, and it may well cost him his chance for reelection, presuming he is not removed through impeachment. But the president's defeat would likely only deepen the despair that fueled his rise, confirming his supporters' fear that the demographic tide has turned against them. That fear is the single greatest threat facing American democracy, the force that is already battering down precedents, leveling norms, and demolishing guardrails. When a group that has traditionally exercised power comes to believe that its eclipse is inevitable, and that the destruction of all it holds dear will follow, it will fight to preserve what it has—whatever the cost.

Adam Przeworski, a political scientist who has studied struggling democracies in Eastern Europe and Latin America, has argued that to survive, democratic institutions "must give all the relevant political forces a chance to win from time to time in the competition of interests and values." But, he adds, they also have to do something else, of equal importance: "They must make even losing under democracy more attractive than a future under nondemocratic outcomes." That conservatives—despite currently holding the White House, the Senate, and many state governments—are losing faith in their ability to win elections in the future bodes ill for the smooth functioning of American democracy. That they believe these electoral losses would lead to their destruction is even more worrying.

We should be careful about overstating the dangers. It is not 1860 again in the United States—it is not even 1850. But numerous examples from American history—most notably the antebellum South—offer a cautionary tale about how quickly a robust democracy can weaken when a large section of the population becomes convinced that it cannot continue to win elections, and also that it cannot afford to lose them.

The collapse of the mainstream Republican Party in the face of Trumpism is at once a product of highly particular circumstances and a disturbing echo of other events. In his recent study of the emergence of democracy in Western Europe, the political scientist Daniel Ziblatt zeroes in on a decisive factor distinguishing the states that achieved democratic stability from those that fell prey to authoritarian impulses: The key variable was not the strength or character of the political left, or of the forces pushing for greater democratization, so much as the viability of the center-right. A strong center-right party could wall off more extreme right-wing movements, shutting out the radicals who attacked the political system itself.

The left is by no means immune to authoritarian impulses; some of the worst excesses of the 20th century were carried out by totalitarian left-wing regimes. But right-wing parties are typically composed of people who have enjoyed power and status within a society. They might include disproportionate numbers of leaders—business magnates, military officers, judges, governors—upon whose loyalty and support the government depends. If groups that traditionally have enjoyed privileged positions see a future for themselves in a more democratic society, Ziblatt finds, they will accede to it. But if "conservative forces believe that electoral politics will permanently exclude them from government, they are more likely to reject democracy outright."

Ziblatt points to Germany in the 1930s, the most catastrophic collapse of a democracy in the 20th century, as evidence that the fate of democracy lies in the hands of conservatives. Where the center-right flourishes, it can defend the interests of its adherents, starving more radical movements of support. In Germany, where center-right parties faltered, "not their strength, but rather their *weakness*" became the driving force behind democracy's collapse.

Of course, the most catastrophic collapse of a democracy in the 19th century took place right here in the United States, sparked by the anxieties of white voters who feared the decline of their own power within a diversifying nation.

The slaveholding South exercised disproportionate political power in the early republic. America's first dozen presidents—excepting only those named Adams—were slaveholders. Twelve of the first 16 secretaries of state came from slave states. The South initially dominated Congress as well, buoyed by its ability to count three-fifths of the enslaved persons held as property for the purposes of apportionment.

Politics in the early republic was factious and fractious, dominated by crosscutting interests. But as Northern states formally abandoned slavery, and then embraced westward expansion, tensions rose between the states that exalted free labor and the ones whose fortunes were directly tied to slave labor, bringing sectional conflict to the fore. By the mid-19th century, demographics were clearly on the side of the free states, where the population was rapidly expanding. Immigrants surged across the Atlantic, finding jobs in Northern factories and settling on midwestern farms. By the outbreak of the Civil War, the foreign-born would form 19 percent of the population of the Northern states, but just 4 percent of the Southern population.

The new dynamic was first felt in the House of Representatives, the most democratic institution of American government—and the Southern response was a concerted effort to remove the topic of slavery from debate. In 1836, Southern congressmen and their allies imposed a gag rule on the House, barring consideration of petitions that so much as mentioned slavery, which would stand for nine years. As the historian Joanne Freeman shows in her recent book, *The Field of*

Blood: Violence in Congress and the Road to Civil War, slave-state representatives in Washington also turned to bullying, brandishing weapons, challenging those who dared disparage the peculiar institution to duels, or simply attacking them on the House floor with fists or canes. In 1845, an antislavery speech delivered by Ohio's Joshua Giddings so upset Louisiana's John Dawson that he cocked his pistol and announced that he intended to kill his fellow congressman. In a scene more Sergio Leone than Frank Capra, other representatives—at least four of them with guns of their own—rushed to either side, in a tense standoff. By the late 1850s, the threat of violence was so pervasive that members regularly entered the House armed.

As Southern politicians perceived that demographic trends were starting to favor the North, they began to regard popular democracy itself as a threat. "The North has acquired a decided ascendancy over every department of this Government," warned South Carolina's Senator John C. Calhoun in 1850, a "despotic" situation, in which the interests of the South were bound to be sacrificed, "however oppressive the effects may be." With the House tipping against them, Southern politicians focused on the Senate, insisting that the admission of any free states be balanced by new slave states, to preserve their control of the chamber. They looked to the Supreme Court—which by the 1850s had a five-justice majority from slaveholding states—to safeguard their power. And, fatefully, they struck back at the power of Northerners to set the rules of their own communities, launching a frontal assault on states' rights.

But the South and its conciliating allies overreached. A center-right consensus, drawing Southern plantation owners together with Northern businessmen, had long kept the Union intact. As demographics turned against the South, though, its politicians began to abandon hope of convincing their Northern neighbors of the moral justice of their position, or of the pragmatic case for compromise. Instead of reposing faith in electoral democracy to protect their way of life, they used the coercive power of the federal government to compel the North to support the institution of slavery, insisting that anyone providing sanctuary to slaves, even in free states, be punished: The Fugitive

Slave Act of 1850 required Northern law-enforcement officials to arrest those who escaped from Southern plantations, and imposed penalties on citizens who gave them shelter.

The persecution complex of the South succeeded where decades of abolitionist activism had failed, producing the very hostility to slavery that Southerners feared. The sight of armed marshals ripping apart families and marching their neighbors back to slavery roused many Northerners from their moral torpor. The push-and-pull of democratic politics had produced setbacks for the South over the previous decades, but the South's abandonment of electoral democracy in favor of counter-majoritarian politics would prove catastrophic to its cause.

Today, a Republican Party that appeals primarily to white Christian voters is fighting a losing battle. The Electoral College, Supreme Court, and Senate may delay defeat for a time, but they cannot postpone it forever.

The GOP's efforts to cling to power by coercion instead of persuasion have illuminated the perils of defining a political party in a pluralistic democracy around a common heritage, rather than around values or ideals. Consider Trump's push to slow the pace of immigration, which has backfired spectacularly, turning public opinion against his restrictionist stance. Before Trump announced his presidential bid, in 2015, less than a quarter of Americans thought legal immigration should be increased; today, more than a third feel that way. Whatever the merits of Trump's particular immigration proposals, he has made them less likely to be enacted.

For a populist, Trump is remarkably unpopular. But no one should take comfort from that fact. The more he radicalizes his opponents against his agenda, the more he gives his own supporters to fear. The excesses of the left bind his supporters more tightly to him, even as the excesses of the right make it harder for the Republican Party to command majority support, validating the fear that the party is passing into eclipse, in a vicious cycle.

The right, and the country, can come back from this. Our history is rife with influential groups that, after discarding their commitment to democratic principles in an attempt to retain their grasp on power, lost their fight and then discovered they could thrive in the political order they had so feared. The Federalists passed the Alien and Sedition Acts, criminalizing criticism of their administration; Redemption-era Democrats stripped black voters of the franchise; and Progressive Republicans wrested municipal governance away from immigrant voters. Each rejected popular democracy out of fear that it would lose at the polls, and terror at what might then result. And in each case democracy eventually prevailed, without tragic effect on the losers. The American system works more often than it doesn't.

The years around the First World War offer another example. A flood of immigrants, particularly from Eastern and Southern Europe, left many white Protestants feeling threatened. In rapid succession, the nation instituted Prohibition, in part to regulate the social habits of these new populations; staged the Palmer Raids, which rounded up thousands of political radicals and deported hundreds; saw the revival of the Ku Klux Klan as a national organization with millions of members, including tens of thousands who marched openly through Washington, D.C.; and passed new immigration laws, slamming shut the doors to the United States.

Under President Woodrow Wilson, the Democratic Party was at the forefront of this nativist backlash. Four years after Wilson left office, the party faced a battle between Wilson's son-in-law and Al Smith—a New York Catholic of Irish, German, and Italian extraction who opposed Prohibition and denounced lynching—for the presidential nomination. The convention deadlocked for more than 100 ballots, ultimately settling on an obscure nominee. But in the next nominating fight, four years after that, Smith prevailed, shouldering aside the nativist forces within the party. He brought together newly enfranchised women and the ethnic voters of growing industrial cities. The Democrats lost the presidential race in 1928—but won the next five, in one of the most dominant runs in American political history. The most effective way to protect the things they cherished, Democratic politicians belatedly discovered, wasn't by locking immigrants out of the party, but by inviting them in.

Whether the American political system today can endure without fracturing further, Daniel Ziblatt's research suggests, may depend on the choices the center-right now makes. If the center-right decides to accept some electoral defeats and then seeks to gain adherents via argumentation and attraction—and, crucially, eschews making racial heritage its organizing principle—then the GOP can remain vibrant. Its fissures will heal and its prospects will improve, as did those of the Democratic Party in the 1920s, after Wilson. Democracy will be maintained. But if the center-right, surveying demographic upheaval and finding the prospect of electoral losses intolerable, casts its lot with Trumpism and a far right rooted in ethnonationalism, then it is doomed to an ever smaller proportion of voters, and risks revisiting the ugliest chapters of our history.

Two documents produced after Mitt Romney's loss in 2012 and before Trump's election in 2016 lay out the stakes and the choice. After Romney's stinging defeat in the presidential election, the Republican National Committee decided that if it held to its course, it was destined for political exile. It issued a report calling on the GOP to do more to win over "Hispanic[s], Asian and Pacific Islanders, African Americans, Indian Americans, Native Americans, women, and youth[s]." There was an edge of panic in that recommendation; those groups accounted for nearly three-quarters of the ballots cast in 2012. "Unless the RNC gets serious about tackling this problem, we will lose future elections," the report warned. "The data demonstrates this."

But it wasn't just the pragmatists within the GOP who felt this panic. In the most influential declaration of right-wing support for Trumpism, the conservative writer Michael Anton declared in the *Claremont Review of Books* that "2016 is the Flight 93 election: charge the cockpit or you die." His cry of despair offered a bleak echo of the RNC's demographic analysis. "If you haven't noticed, our side has been losing consistently since 1988," he wrote, averring that "the deck is stacked overwhelmingly against us." He blamed "the ceaseless importation of Third World foreigners," which had placed Democrats "on the cusp of a permanent victory that will forever obviate [their] need to pretend to respect democratic and constitutional niceties."

The Republican Party faced a choice between these two competing visions in the last presidential election. The post-2012 report defined the GOP ideologically, urging its leaders to reach out to new groups, emphasize the values they had in common, and rebuild the party into an organization capable of winning a majority of the votes in a presidential race. Anton's essay, by contrast, defined the party as the defender of "a people, a civilization" threatened by America's growing diversity. The GOP's efforts to broaden its coalition, he thundered, were an abject surrender. If it lost the next election, conservatives would be subjected to "vindictive persecution against resistance and dissent."

Anton and some 63 million other Americans charged the cockpit. The standard-bearers of the Republican Party were vanquished by a candidate who had never spent a day in public office, and who oozed disdain for democratic processes. Instead of reaching out to a diversifying electorate, Donald Trump doubled down on core Republican constituencies, promising to protect them from a culture and a polity that, he said, were turning against them.

When Trump's presidency comes to its end, the Republican Party will confront the same choice it faced before his rise, only even more urgently. In 2013, the party's leaders saw the path that lay before them clearly, and urged Republicans to reach out to voters of diverse backgrounds whose own values matched the "ideals, philosophy and principles" of the GOP. Trumpism deprioritizes conservative ideas and principles in favor of ethnonationalism.

The conservative strands of America's political heritage—a bias in favor of continuity, a love for traditions and institutions, a healthy skepticism of sharp departures—provide the nation with a requisite ballast. America is at once a land of continual change and a nation of strong continuities. Each new wave of immigration to the United States has altered its culture, but the immigrants themselves have embraced and thus conserved many of its core traditions. To the enormous frustration of their clergy, Jews and Catholics and Muslims arriving on these shores became a little bit congregationalist, shifting power from the pulpits to the pews. Peasants and laborers became more entrepreneurial. Many new arrivals became more egalitarian. And all became more American.

By accepting these immigrants, and inviting them to subscribe to the country's founding ideals, American elites avoided displacement. The country's dominant culture has continually redefined itself, enlarging its boundaries to retain a majority of a changing population. When the United States came into being, most Americans were white, Protestant, and English. But the ineradicable difference between a Welshman and a Scot soon became all but undetectable. Whiteness itself proved elastic, first excluding Jews and Italians and Irish, and then stretching to encompass them. Established Churches gave way to a variety of Protestant sects, and the proliferation of other faiths made "Christian" a coherent category; that broadened, too, into the Judeo-Christian tradition. If America's white Christian majority is gone, then some new majority is already emerging to take its place—some new, more capacious way of understanding what it is to belong to the American mainstream.

So strong is the attraction of the American idea that it infects even our dissidents. The suffragists at Seneca Falls, Martin Luther King Jr. on the steps of the Lincoln Memorial, and Harvey Milk in front of San Francisco's city hall all quoted the Declaration of Independence. The United States possesses a strong radical tradition, but its most successful social movements have generally adopted the language of conservatism, framing their calls for change as an expression of America's founding ideals rather than as a rejection of them.

Even today, large numbers of conservatives retain the courage of their convictions, believing they can win new adherents to their cause. They have not despaired of prevailing at the polls and they are not prepared to abandon moral suasion in favor of coercion; they are fighting to recover their party from a president whose success was built on convincing voters that the country is slipping away from them.

The stakes in this battle on the right are much higher than the next election. If Republican voters can't be convinced that democratic elections will continue to offer them a viable path to victory, that they can thrive within a diversifying nation, and that even in defeat their basic rights will be protected, then Trumpism will extend long after Trump leaves office—and our democracy will suffer for it.

THE LAST TEMPTATION

by Michael Gerson

[APRIL 2018]

In today's America, evangelical Christians exert a major influence on the political right. But have Christians who have aligned themselves with Trump lost their way? "During the 2016 campaign, when the president of my university, Jerry Falwell Jr., endorsed a man who has lived in complete and unapologetic opposition to all the things I had been taught to value, I questioned my religion, I questioned my faith, and I questioned my God"—that was the response of a student at Liberty University to Michael Gerson's 2018 *Atlantic* cover story, "The Last Temptation," which sought to explain why evangelical Christians fell so hard for Donald Trump.

Gerson, a former speechwriter for President George W. Bush, traced the long history of evangelical Christianity in America: its slow disengagement from the mainstream, its adversarial stance toward the rest of society, and its growing involvement in politics as a bulwark of an angry and populist Republican Party. "Loyalty to Trump has involved progressively more difficult, self-abasing demands," Gerson observed. "And there appears to be no limit to what some evangelical leaders will endure ... They have basked in access to power and provided character references in the midst of scandal."

Gerson, now a syndicated columnist for *The Washington Post*, is the author of *Heroic Conservatism: Why Republicans Need to Embrace America's Ideals (And Why They Deserve to Fail If They Don't)* (2007) and a co-author of *City of Man: Religion and Politics in a New Era* (2010).

One of the most extraordinary things about our current politics—really, one of the most extraordinary developments of recent political history—is the loyal adherence of religious conservatives to Donald Trump. The president won four-fifths of the votes of white evangelical Christians. This was a higher level of support than either Ronald Reagan or George W. Bush, an outspoken evangelical himself, ever received.

Trump's background and beliefs could hardly be more incompatible with traditional Christian models of life and leadership. Trump's past political stances (he once supported the right to partial-birth abortion), his character (he has bragged about sexually assaulting women), and even his language (he introduced the words *pussy* and *shithole* into presidential discourse) would more naturally lead religious conservatives toward exorcism than alliance. This is a man who has cruelly publicized his infidelities, made disturbing sexual comments about his elder daughter, and boasted about the size of his penis on the debate stage. His lawyer reportedly arranged a $130,000 payment to a porn star to dissuade her from disclosing an alleged affair. Yet religious conservatives who once blanched at PG-13 public standards now yawn at such NC-17 maneuvers. We are a long way from *The Book of Virtues*.

Trump supporters tend to dismiss moral scruples about his behavior as squeamishness over the president's "style." But the problem is the distinctly non-Christian substance of his *values*. Trump's unapologetic materialism—his equation of financial and social success with human achievement and worth—is a negation of Christian teaching. His tribalism and hatred for "the other" stand in direct opposition to Jesus's radical ethic of neighbor love. Trump's strength-worship and contempt for "losers" smack more of Nietzsche than of Christ. *Blessed are the proud. Blessed are the ruthless. Blessed are the shameless. Blessed are those who hunger and thirst after fame.*

And yet, a credible case can be made that evangelical votes were a decisive factor in Trump's improbable victory. Trump himself certainly acts as if he believes they were. Many individuals, causes, and groups that Trump pledged to champion have been swiftly sidelined or sacrificed during Trump's brief presidency. The administration's outreach to white evangelicals, however, has been utterly consistent.

Trump-allied religious leaders have found an open door at the White House—what Richard Land, the president of the Southern Evangelical Seminary, calls "unprecedented access." In return, they have rallied behind the administration in its times of need. "Clearly, this Russian story is nonsense," explains the megachurch pastor Paula White-Cain, who is not generally known as a legal or cybersecurity expert. Pastor David Jeremiah has compared Jared Kushner and Ivanka Trump to Joseph and Mary: "It's just like God to use a young Jewish couple to help Christians." According to Jerry Falwell Jr., evangelicals have "found their dream president," which says something about the current quality of evangelical dreams.

Loyalty to Trump has involved progressively more difficult, self-abasing demands. And there appears to be no limit to what some evangelical leaders will endure. Figures such as Falwell and Franklin Graham followed Trump's lead in supporting Judge Roy Moore in the December Senate election in Alabama. These are religious leaders who have spent their entire adult lives bemoaning cultural and moral decay. Yet they publicly backed a candidate who was repeatedly accused of sexual misconduct, including with a 14-year-old girl.

In January, following reports that Trump had referred to Haiti and African nations as "shithole countries," Pastor Robert Jeffress came quickly to his defense. "Apart from the vocabulary attributed to him," Jeffress wrote, "President Trump is right on target in his sentiment." After reports emerged that Trump's lawyer paid hush money to the porn star Stormy Daniels to cover up their alleged sexual encounter, Graham vouched for Trump's "concern for Christian values." Tony Perkins, the president of the Family Research Council, argued that Trump should be given a "mulligan" for his past infidelity. One can only imagine the explosion of outrage if President Barack Obama had been credibly accused of similar offenses.

The moral convictions of many evangelical leaders have become a function of their partisan identification. This is not mere gullibility; it is utter corruption. Blinded by political tribalism and hatred for their political opponents, these leaders can't see how they are undermining the causes to which they once dedicated their lives. Little remains of a distinctly Christian public witness.

As the prominent evangelical pastor Tim Keller—who is not a Trump loyalist—recently wrote in *The New Yorker*, "'Evangelical' used to denote people who claimed the high moral ground; now, in popular usage, the word is nearly synonymous with 'hypocrite.'" So it is little wonder that last year the Princeton Evangelical Fellowship, an 87-year-old ministry, dropped the "E word" from its name, becoming the Princeton Christian Fellowship: Too many students had identified the term with conservative political ideology. Indeed, a number of serious evangelicals are distancing themselves from the word for similar reasons.

I find this desire understandable but not compelling. Some words, like strategic castles, are worth defending, and *evangelical* is among them. While the term is notoriously difficult to define, it certainly encompasses a "born-again" religious experience, a commitment to the authority of the Bible, and an emphasis on the redemptive power of Jesus Christ.

I was raised in an evangelical home, went to an evangelical church and high school, and began following Christ as a teen. After attending Georgetown University for a year, I transferred to Wheaton College in Illinois—sometimes called "the Harvard of evangelical Protestantism"— where I studied theology. I worked at an evangelical nonprofit, Prison Fellowship, before becoming a staffer for Senator Dan Coats of Indiana (a fellow Wheaton alum). On Capitol Hill, I found many evangelical partners in trying to define a "compassionate conservatism." And as a policy adviser and the chief speechwriter to President George W. Bush, I saw how evangelical leaders such as Rick and Kay Warren could be principled, tireless advocates in the global fight against AIDS.

Those experiences make me hesitant to abandon the word *evangelical*. They also make seeing the defilement of that word all the more painful. The corruption of a political party is regrettable. The corruption of a religious tradition by politics is tragic, shaming those who participate in it.

How did something so important and admirable become so disgraced? For many people, including myself, this question involves both intellectual analysis and personal angst. The answer extends back some 150 years, and involves cultural and political shifts that long predate Donald Trump. It is the story of how an influential and culturally confident religious movement became a marginalized and anxious minority seeking political protection under the wing of a man such as Trump, the least traditionally Christian figure—in temperament, behavior, and evident belief—to assume the presidency in living memory.

Understanding that evolution requires understanding the values that once animated American evangelicalism. It is a movement that was damaged in the fall from a great height.

My alma mater, Wheaton College, was founded by abolitionist evangelicals in 1860 under the leadership of Jonathan Blanchard, an emblematic figure in mid-19th-century Northern evangelicalism. Blanchard was part of a generation of radical malcontents produced by the Second Great Awakening, a religious revival that had touched millions of American lives in the first half of the 19th century. He was a Presbyterian minister, a founder of several radical newspapers, and an antislavery agitator.

In the years before the Civil War, a connection between moralism and a concern for social justice was generally assumed among Northern evangelicals. They variously militated for temperance, humane treatment of the mentally disabled, and prison reform. But mainly they militated for the end of slavery.

Indeed, Wheaton welcomed both African American and female students, and served as a stop on the Underground Railroad. In a history of the 39th Regiment of the Illinois Volunteer Infantry, the infantryman Ezra Cook recalled that "runaway slaves were perfectly safe in the College building, even when no attempt was made to conceal their presence."

Blanchard had explained his beliefs in an 1839 commencement address given at Oberlin College, titled "A Perfect State of Society." He preached that "every true minister of Christ is a universal reformer, whose business it is, so far as possible, to reform all the evils which press on human concerns." Elsewhere he argued that "slave-holding is not a solitary, but a social sin." He added: "I rest my opposition to slavery upon the one-bloodism of the New Testament. All men are equal, because they are of one equal blood."

During this period, evangelicalism was largely identical to mainstream Protestantism. Evangelicals varied widely in their denominational beliefs, but they uniformly agreed about the need for a personal decision to accept God's grace through faith in Christ. The evangelist Charles G. Finney, who was the president of Oberlin College from 1851 to 1866, described his conversion experience thusly: "I could feel the impression, like a wave of electricity, going through and through me. Indeed it seemed to come in waves and waves of liquid love."

In politics, evangelicals tended to identify New England, and then the whole country, with biblical Israel. Many a sermon described America as a place set apart for divine purposes. "Some nation," the evangelical minister Lyman Beecher said, "itself free, was needed, to blow the trumpet and hold up the light." (Beecher's daughter Harriet Beecher Stowe was among the founders of this magazine.) The burden of this calling was a collective responsibility to remain virtuous, in matters from ending slavery to ending Sabbath-breaking.

This was not advocacy for theocracy, and evangelical leaders were not blind to the risks of too close a relationship with worldly power. "The injudicious association of religion with politics, in the time of Cromwell," Beecher argued, "brought upon evangelical doctrine and piety, in England, an odium which has not ceased to this day." Yet few evangelicals would have denied that God's covenantal relationship with America required a higher standard of private and public morality, lest that divine blessing be forfeited.

Perhaps most important, prior to the Civil War, evangelicals were by and large postmillennialists—that is, they believed that the final millennium of human history would be a time of peace for the world and of expansion for the Christian Church, culminating in the Second Coming of Christ. As such, they were an optimistic lot who thought that human effort could help hasten the arrival of this promised era—a belief that encouraged both social activism and global missionary activity. "Evangelicals generally regarded almost any sort of progress as evidence of the advance of the kingdom," the historian George Marsden observes in *Fundamentalism and American Culture.*

In the mid-19th century, evangelicalism was the predominant religious tradition in America—a faith assured of its social position, confident in its divine calling, welcoming of progress, and hopeful about the future. Fifty years later, it was losing intellectual and social ground on every front. Twenty-five years beyond that, it had become a national joke.

———

The horrors of the Civil War took a severe toll on the social optimism at the heart of postmillennialism. It was harder to believe in the existence of a religious golden age that included Antietam. At the same time, industrialization and urbanization loosened traditional social bonds and created an impression of moral chaos. The mass immigration of Catholics and Jews changed the face and spiritual self-conception of the country. (In 1850, Catholics made up about 5 percent of the population. By 1906, they represented 17 percent.) Evangelicals struggled to envision a diverse, and some believed degenerate, America as the chosen, godly republic of their imagination.

But it was a series of momentous intellectual developments that most effectively drove a wedge between evangelicalism and elite culture. Higher criticism of the Bible—a scholarly movement out of Germany that picked apart the human sources and development of ancient texts—called into question the roots, accuracy, and historicity of the book that constituted the ultimate source of evangelical authority. At the same time, the theory of evolution advanced a new account of human origin. Advocates of evolution, as well as those who denied it most vigorously, took the theory as an alternative to religious accounts—and in many cases to Christian belief itself.

Religious progressives sought common ground between the Christian faith and the new science and higher criticism. Many combined their faith with the Social Gospel—a postmillennialism drained of the miraculous, with social reform taking the place of the Second Coming.

Religious conservatives, by contrast, rebelled against this strategy of accommodation in a series of firings and heresy trials designed to maintain control of seminaries. (Woodrow Wilson's uncle James lost his job at Columbia Theological Seminary for accepting evolution as compatible with the Bible.) But these tactics generally backfired, and seminary after seminary, college after college, fell under the influence of modern scientific and cultural assumptions. To contest progressive ideas, the religiously orthodox published a series of books called *The Fundamentals*. Hence the term *fundamentalism*, conceived in a spirit of desperate reaction.

Fundamentalism embraced traditional religious views, but it did not propose a return to an older evangelicalism. Instead it responded to modernity in ways that cut it off from its own past. In reacting against higher criticism, it became simplistic and overliteral in its reading of scripture. In reacting against evolution, it became anti-scientific in its general orientation. In reacting against the Social Gospel, it came to regard the whole concept of social justice as a dangerous liberal idea. This last point constituted what some scholars have called the "Great Reversal," which took place from about 1900 to 1930. "All progressive social concern," Marsden writes, "whether political or private, became suspect among revivalist evangelicals and was relegated to a very minor role."

This general pessimism about the direction of society was reflected in a shift away from postmillennialism and toward *pre*millennialism. In this view, the current age is tending not toward progress, but rather toward decadence and chaos under the influence of Satan. A new and better age will not be inaugurated until the Second Coming of Christ, who is the only one capable of cleaning up the mess. No amount of human effort can hasten that day, or ultimately save a doomed world. For this reason, social activism was deemed irrelevant to the most essential task: the work of preparing oneself, and helping others prepare, for final judgment.

The banishment of fundamentalism from the cultural mainstream culminated dramatically in a Tennessee courthouse in 1925. William

Jennings Bryan, the most prominent Christian politician of his time, was set against Clarence Darrow and the theory of evolution at the Scopes "monkey trial," in which a Tennessee educator was tried for teaching the theory in high school. Bryan won the case but not the country. The journalist and critic H. L. Mencken provided the account accepted by history, dismissing Bryan as "a tin pot pope in the Coca-Cola belt and a brother to the forlorn pastors who belabor half-wits in galvanized iron tabernacles behind the railroad yards." Fundamentalists became comic figures, subject to world-class condescension.

It has largely slipped the mind of history that Bryan was a peace activist as secretary of state under Woodrow Wilson and that his politics foreshadowed the New Deal. And Mencken was eventually revealed as a racist, an anti-Semite, and a eugenics advocate. In the fundamentalist–modernist controversy, there was only one winner. "In the course of roughly thirty-five years," the sociologist James Davison Hunter observes in *American Evangelicalism*, "Protestantism had moved from a position of cultural dominance to a position of cognitive marginality and political impotence." Activism and optimism were replaced by the festering resentment of status lost.

The fundamentalists were not passive in their exile. They created a web of institutions—radio stations, religious schools, outreach ministries—that eventually constituted a healthy subculture. The country, meanwhile, was becoming less secular and more welcoming of religious influence. (In 1920, church membership in the United States was 43 percent. By 1960, it was 63 percent.) A number of leaders, including the theologian Carl Henry and the evangelist Billy Graham (the father of Franklin Graham), bridled at fundamentalist irrelevance. Henry's book *The Uneasy Conscience of Modern Fundamentalism* was influential in urging greater cultural and intellectual engagement. This reemergence found its fullest expression in Graham, who left the fundamentalist ghetto, hobnobbed with presidents, and presented to the public a more appealing version of evangelicalism—a term that was deliberately employed as a contrast to the older, narrower fundamentalism.

Not everyone was impressed. When Graham planned mass evangelistic meetings in New York City in 1957, the theologian Reinhold Niebuhr editorialized against his "petty moralizing." But Niebuhr's attack on Graham provoked significant backlash, even in liberal theological circles. During a 16-week "crusade" that played to packed houses, Graham was joined one night at Madison Square Garden by none other than Martin Luther King Jr.

Over time, evangelicalism got a revenge of sorts in its historical rivalry with liberal Christianity. Adherents of the latter gradually found better things to do with their Sundays than attend progressive services. In 1972, nearly 28 percent of the population belonged to mainline-Protestant churches. That figure is now well below 15 percent. Over those four decades, however, evangelicals held steady at roughly 25 percent of the public (though this share has recently declined). As its old theological rival faded—or, more accurately, collapsed—evangelical endurance felt a lot like momentum.

With the return of this greater institutional self-confidence, evangelicals might have expected to play a larger role in determining cultural norms and standards. But their hopes ran smack into the sexual revolution, along with other rapid social changes. The Moral Majority appeared at about the same time that the actual majority was more and more comfortable with divorce and couples living together out of wedlock. Evangelicals experienced the power of growing numbers and healthy subcultural institutions even as elite institutions—from universities to courts to Hollywood—were decisively rejecting traditional ideals.

As a result, the primary evangelical political narrative is adversarial, an angry tale about the aggression of evangelicalism's cultural rivals. In a remarkably free country, many evangelicals view their rights as fragile, their institutions as threatened, and their dignity as assailed. The single largest religious demographic in the United States—representing about half the Republican political coalition—sees itself as a besieged and disrespected minority. In this way, evangelicals have become simultaneously more engaged and more alienated.

The overall political disposition of evangelical politics has remained decidedly conservative, and also decidedly reactive. After shamefully sitting out (or even opposing) the civil-rights movement, white evangelicals became activated on a limited range of issues. They defended Christian schools against regulation during Jimmy Carter's administration. They fought against Supreme Court decisions that put tight restrictions on school prayer and removed many state limits on abortion. The sociologist Nathan Glazer describes such efforts as a "defensive offensive"—a kind of morally indignant pushback against a modern world that, in evangelicals' view, had grown hostile and oppressive.

This attitude was happily exploited by the modern GOP. Evangelicals who were alienated by the pro choice secularism of Democratic presidential nominees were effectively courted to join the Reagan coalition. "I know that you can't endorse me," Reagan told an evangelical conference in 1980, "but I only brought that up because I want you to know that I endorse you." In contrast, during his presidential run four years later, Walter Mondale warned of "radical preachers," and his running mate, Geraldine Ferraro, denounced the "extremists who control the Republican Party." By attacking evangelicals, the Democratic Party left them with a relatively easy partisan choice.

The leaders who had emerged within evangelicalism varied significantly in tone and approach. Billy Graham was the uncritical priest to the powerful. (His inclination to please was memorialized on one of the Nixon tapes, in comments enabling the president's anti-Semitism.) James Dobson, the founder of Focus on the Family, was the prickly prophet, constantly threatening to bolt from the Republican coalition unless social-conservative purity was maintained. Jerry Falwell Sr. and Pat Robertson (the latter of whom ran for president himself in 1988) tried to be political kingmakers. And, following his dramatic conversion, Chuck Colson, of Watergate infamy, founded Prison Fellowship in an attempt to revive some of the old abolitionist spirit as an advocate of prison reform. Yet much of this variety was blurred in the public mind, with *religious right* used as a catchall epithet.

Where did this history leave evangelicals' political involvement?

For a start, modern evangelicalism has an important intellectual piece missing. It lacks a model or ideal of political engagement—an organizing theory of social action. Over the same century from Blanchard to Falwell, Catholics developed a coherent, comprehensive tradition of social and political reflection. Catholic social thought includes a commitment to solidarity, whereby justice in a society is measured by the treatment of its weakest and most vulnerable members. And it incorporates the principle of subsidiarity—the idea that human needs are best met by small and local institutions (though higher-order institutions have a moral responsibility to intervene when local ones fail).

In practice, this acts as an "if, then" requirement for Catholics, splendidly complicating their politics: If you want to call yourself pro-life on abortion, then you have to oppose the dehumanization of migrants. If you criticize the devaluation of life by euthanasia, then you must criticize the devaluation of life by racism. If you want to be regarded as pro-family, then you have to support access to health care. And vice versa. The doctrinal whole requires a broad, consistent view of justice, which—when it is faithfully applied—cuts across the categories and clichés of American politics. Of course, American Catholics routinely ignore Catholic social thought. But at least they have it. Evangelicals lack a similar tradition of their own to disregard.

So where do evangelicals get their theory of social engagement? It is cheating to say (as most evangelicals probably would) "the Bible." The Christian Bible, after all, can be a vexing document: At various points, it offers approving accounts of genocide and recommends the stoning of insubordinate children. Some interpretive theory must elevate the Golden Rule above Iron Age ethics and apply that higher ideal to the tragic compromises of public life. Lacking an equivalent to Catholic social thought, many evangelicals seem to find their theory merely by following the contours of the political movement that is currently defending, and exploiting, them. The voter guides of religious conservatives have often been suspiciously similar to the political priorities of movement conservatism. Fox News and talk radio are vastly greater influences on evangelicals' political identity than formal statements by religious denominations or from the National Association of

Evangelicals. In this Christian political movement, Christian theology is emphatically not the primary motivating factor.

The evangelical political agenda, moreover, has been narrowed by its supremely reactive nature. Rather than choosing their own agendas, evangelicals have been pulled into a series of social and political debates started by others. Why the asinine issue of spiritually barren prayer in public schools? Because of Justice Hugo Black's 1962 opinion rendering it unconstitutional. Why such an effort-wasting emphasis on a constitutional amendment to end abortion, which will never pass? Because in 1973 Justice Harry Blackmun located the right to abortion in the constitutional penumbra. Why the current emphasis on religious liberty? Because the 2015 *Obergefell v. Hodges* decision legalizing same-sex marriage has raised fears of coercion.

It is not that secularization, abortion, and religious liberty are trivial issues; they are extremely important. But the timing and emphasis of evangelical responses have contributed to a broad sense that evangelical political engagement is negative, censorious, and oppositional. This funneled focus has also created the damaging impression that Christians are obsessed with sex. Much of the secular public hears from Christians only on issues of sexuality—from contraceptive mandates to gay rights to transgender bathroom usage. And while religious people do believe that sexual ethics are important, the nature of contemporary religious engagement creates a misimpression about just how important they are relative to other crucial issues.

The upside potential of evangelical social engagement was illustrated by an important, but largely overlooked, initiative that I witnessed while working at the White House. The President's Emergency Plan for AIDS Relief (PEPFAR)—the largest initiative by a nation in history to fight a single disease—emerged in part from a sense of moral obligation informed by George W. Bush's evangelical faith. In explaining and defending the program, Bush made constant reference to Luke 12:48: "To whom much is given, much is required." PEPFAR also owes its existence to a strange-bedfellows political alliance of liberal global-health advocates and evangelical leaders, who had particular standing and sway with Republican members of Congress. Rather than being a response to secular aggression, this form of evangelical social engagement was the reaction to a massive humanitarian need and displayed a this-worldly emphasis on social justice that helped save millions of lives.

This achievement is now given little attention by secular liberals or religious conservatives. In the Trump era, evangelical leaders have seldom brought this type of issue to the policy front burner—though some have tried with criminal-justice reform and the fight against modern slavery. Individual Christians and evangelical ministries fight preventable disease, resettle refugees, treat addiction, run homeless shelters, and care for foster children. But such concerns find limited collective political expression.

Part of the reason such matters are not higher on the evangelical agenda is surely the relative ethnic and racial insularity of many white evangelicals. Plenty of African Americans hold evangelical theological views, of course, along with a growing number of Latinos. Yet evangelical churches, like other churches and houses of worship, tend to be segregated on Sunday. Nearly all denominations with large numbers of evangelicals are less racially diverse than the country overall.

Compare this with the Catholic Church, which is more than one-third Hispanic. This has naturally stretched the priorities of Catholicism to include the needs and rights of recent immigrants. In many evangelical communities, those needs remain distant and theoretical (though successful evangelical churches in urban areas are now experiencing the same diversity and broadening of social concern). Or consider the contrasting voting behaviors of white and African American evangelicals in last year's Senate race in Alabama. According to exit polls, 80 percent of white evangelicals voted for Roy Moore, while 95 percent of black evangelicals supported his Democratic opponent, Doug Jones. The two groups inhabit two entirely different political worlds.

———

Evangelicals also have a consistent problem with their public voice, which can be off-puttingly apocalyptic. "We are on the verge of losing"

America, proclaims the evangelical writer and radio host Eric Metaxas, "as we could have lost it in the Civil War." Franklin Graham declares, a little too vividly, that the country "has taken a nosedive off of the moral diving board into the cesspool of humanity." Such hyperbole may be only a rhetorical strategy, employing the apocalypse for emphasis. But the attribution of depravity and decline to America also reflects a consistent and (so far) disappointed belief that the Second Coming may be just around history's corner.

The difficulty with this approach to public life—other than its insanely pessimistic depiction of our flawed but wonderful country   is that it trivializes and undercuts the entire political enterprise. Politics in a democracy is essentially anti-apocalyptic, premised on the idea that an active citizenry is capable of improving the nation. But if we're already mere minutes from the midnight hour, then what is the point? The normal avenues of political reform are useless. No amount of negotiation or compromise is going to matter much compared with the Second Coming.

Moreover, in making their case on cultural decay and decline, evangelicals have, in some highly visible cases, chosen the wrong nightmares. Most notable, they made a crucial error in picking evolution as a main point of contention with modernity. "The contest between evolution and Christianity is a duel to the death," William Jennings Bryan argued. "If evolution wins . . . Christianity goes—not suddenly, of course, but gradually, for the two cannot stand together." Many people of his background believed this. But their resistance was futile, for one incontrovertible reason: Evolution is a fact. It is objectively true based on overwhelming evidence. By denying this, evangelicals made their entire view of reality suspect. They were insisting, in effect, that the Christian faith requires a flight from reason.

This was foolish and unnecessary. There is no meaningful theological difference between creation by divine intervention and creation by natural selection; both are consistent with belief in a purposeful universe, and with serious interpretation of biblical texts. Evangelicals have placed an entirely superfluous stumbling block before their neighbors and children, encouraging every young person who loves science to reject Christianity.

What if Bryan and others of his generation had chosen to object to eugenics rather than evolution, to social Darwinism rather than Darwinism? The textbook at issue in the Scopes case, after all, was titled *A Civic Biology*, and it urged sterilization for the mentally impaired. "Epilepsy, and feeble-mindedness," the text read, "are handicaps which it is not only unfair but criminal to hand down to posterity." What if this had been the focus of Bryan's objection? Mencken doubtless would still have mocked. But the moral and theological priorities of evangelical Christianity would have turned out differently. And evangelical fears would have been eventually justified by America's shameful history of eugenics, and by the more rigorous application of the practice abroad. Instead, Bryan chose evolution—and in the end, the cause of human dignity was not served by the obscuring of human origins.

The consequences, especially for younger generations, are considerable. According to a recent survey by Barna, a Christian research firm, more than half of churchgoing Christian teens believe that "the church seems to reject much of what science tells us about the world." This may be one reason that, in America, the youngest age cohorts are the least religiously affiliated, which will change the nation's baseline of religiosity over time. More than a third of Millennials say they are unaffiliated with any faith, up 10 points since 2007. Count this as an ironic achievement of religious conservatives: an overall decline in identification with religion itself.

———

By the turn of the millennium, many, including myself, were convinced that religious conservatism was fading as a political force. Its outsize leaders were aging and passing. Its institutions seemed to be declining in profile and influence. Bush's 2000 campaign attempted to appeal to religious voters on a new basis. "Compassionate conservatism" was designed to be a policy application of Catholic social thought—an attempt to serve the poor, homeless, and addicted by catalyzing the work of private and religious nonprofits. The effort was sincere but eventually undermined by congressional-Republican resistance and eclipsed by global crisis. Still, I believed that the old evangelical model of social engagement was exhausted, and that something more positive and principled was in the offing.

I was wrong. In fact, evangelicals would prove highly vulnerable to a message of resentful, declinist populism. Donald Trump could almost have been echoing the apocalyptic warnings of Metaxas and Graham when he declared, "Our country's going to hell." Or: "We haven't seen anything like this, the carnage all over the world." Given Trump's general level of religious knowledge, he likely had no idea that he was adapting premillennialism to populism. But when the candidate talked of an America in decline and headed toward destruction, which could be returned to greatness only by recovering the certainties of the past, he was strumming resonant chords of evangelical conviction.

Trump consistently depicts evangelicals as they depict themselves: a mistreated minority, in need of a defender who plays by worldly rules. Christianity is "under siege," Trump told a Liberty University audience. "Relish the opportunity to be an outsider," he added at a later date: "Embrace the label." Protecting Christianity, Trump essentially argues, is a job for a bully.

It is true that insofar as Christian hospitals or colleges have their religious liberty threatened by hostile litigation or government agencies, they have every right to defend their institutional identities—to advocate for a principled pluralism. But this is different from evangelicals regarding themselves, hysterically and with self-pity, as an oppressed minority that requires a strongman to rescue it. This is how Trump has invited evangelicals to view themselves. He has treated evangelicalism as an interest group in need of protection and preferences.

A prominent company of evangelical leaders—including Dobson, Falwell, Graham, Jeffress, Metaxas, Perkins, and Ralph Reed—has embraced this self-conception. Their justification is often bluntly utilitarian: All of Trump's flaws are worth his conservative judicial appointments and more-favorable treatment of Christians by the government. But they have gone much further than grudging, prudential calculation. They have basked in access to power and provided character references in the midst of scandal. Graham castigated the critics of Trump's response to the violence during a white-supremacist rally in

Charlottesville, Virginia ("Shame on the politicians who are trying to push blame on @POTUS"). Dobson has pronounced Trump a "baby Christian"—a political use of grace that borders on blasphemy. "Complaining about the temperament of the @POTUS or saying his behavior is not presidential is no longer relevant," Falwell tweeted. "[Donald Trump] has single-handedly changed the definition of what behavior is 'presidential' from phony, failed & rehearsed to authentic, successful & down to earth."

It is remarkable to hear religious leaders defend profanity, ridicule, and cruelty as hallmarks of authenticity and dismiss decency as a dead language. Whatever Trump's policy legacy ends up being, his presidency has been a disaster in the realm of norms. It has coarsened our culture, given permission for bullying, complicated the moral formation of children, undermined standards of public integrity, and encouraged cynicism about the political enterprise. Falwell, Graham, and others are providing religious cover for moral squalor—winking at trashy behavior and encouraging the unraveling of social restraints. Instead of defending their convictions, they are providing preemptive absolution for their political favorites. And this, even by purely political standards, undermines the causes they embrace. Turning a blind eye to the exploitation of women certainly doesn't help in making pro-life arguments. It materially undermines the movement, which must ultimately change not only the composition of the courts but the views of the public. Having given politics pride of place, these evangelical leaders have ceased to be moral leaders in any meaningful sense.

But setting matters of decency aside, evangelicals are risking their faith's reputation on matters of race. Trump has, after all, attributed Kenyan citizenship to Obama, stereotyped Mexican migrants as murderers and rapists, claimed unfair treatment in federal court based on a judge's Mexican heritage, attempted an unconstitutional Muslim ban, equivocated on the Charlottesville protests, claimed (according to *The New York Times*) that Nigerians would never "go back to their huts" after seeing America, and dismissed Haitian and African immigrants as undesirable compared with Norwegians.

For some of Trump's political allies, racist language and arguments are part of his appeal. For evangelical leaders, they should be sources of anguish. Given America's history of slavery and segregation, racial prejudice is a special category of moral wrong. Fighting racism galvanized the religious conscience of 19th-century evangelicals and 20th-century African American civil-rights activists. Perpetuating racism indicted many white Christians in the South and elsewhere as hypocrites. Americans who are wrong on this issue do not understand the nature of their country. Christians who are wrong on this issue do not understand the most-basic requirements of their faith.

Here is the uncomfortable reality: I do not believe that most evangelicals are racist. But every strong Trump supporter has decided that racism is not a moral disqualification in the president of the United States. And that is something more than a political compromise. It is a revelation of moral priorities.

If utilitarian calculations are to be applied, they need to be fully applied. For a package of political benefits, these evangelical leaders have associated the Christian faith with racism and nativism. They have associated the Christian faith with misogyny and the mocking of the disabled. They have associated the Christian faith with lawlessness, corruption, and routine deception. They have associated the Christian faith with moral confusion about the surpassing evils of white supremacy and neo-Nazism. The world is full of tragic choices and compromises. But for *this* man? For *this* cause?

Some evangelical leaders, it is worth affirming, are providing alternative models of social engagement. Consider Tim Keller, who is perhaps the most-influential advocate of a more politically and demographically diverse evangelicalism. Or Russell Moore, the president of the Ethics and Religious Liberty Commission of the Southern Baptist Convention, who demonstrates how moral conservatism can be both principled and inclusive. Or Gary Haugen, the founder of the International Justice Mission, who is one of the world's leading activists against modern slavery. Or Bishop Claude Alexander of the Park Church in North Carolina, who has been a strong voice for reconciliation and mercy. Or Francis Collins, the director of the National Institutes of Health, who shows the deep compatibility of authentic faith and authentic science. Or the influential Bible teacher Beth Moore, who has warned of the damage done "when we sell our souls to buy our wins." Or the writer Peter Wehner, who has ceased to describe himself as an evangelical even as he exemplifies the very best of the word.

Evangelicalism is hardly a monolithic movement. All of the above leaders would attest that a significant generational shift is occurring: Younger evangelicals are less prone to political divisiveness and bitterness and more concerned with social justice. (In a poll last summer, nearly half of white evangelicals born since 1964 expressed support for gay marriage.) Evangelicals remain essential to political coalitions advocating prison reform and supporting American global-health initiatives, particularly on AIDS and malaria. They do good work in the world through relief organizations such as World Vision and Samaritan's Purse (an admirable relief organization of which Franklin Graham is the president and CEO). They perform countless acts of love and compassion that make local communities more just and generous.

All of this is arguably a strong foundation for evangelical recovery. But it would be a mistake to regard the problem as limited to a few irresponsible leaders. Those leaders represent a clear majority of the movement, which remains the most loyal element of the Trump coalition. Evangelicals are broadly eager to act as Trump's shield and sword. They are his army of enablers.

WHY TECHNOLOGY FAVORS TYRANNY

by Yuval Noah Harari

[OCTOBER 2018]

Yuval Noah Harari, a historian and philosopher at the Hebrew University of Jerusalem, specializes in the long view: the
long view backward as well as the long view forward. He is
the author of, among other works, *Sapiens: A Brief History
of Humankind* (2014) and *Homo Deus: A Brief History of
Tomorrow* (2017). Here is what Harari worries about, looking
ahead: Artificial intelligence, by its very nature, could erode the
ideals of liberty and equality; at the same time, it could further
concentrate power among a small elite.

Harari recalls that, a generation ago, after most of the
world's Communist regimes had dissolved over a period of just
a few years, prominent voices announced the victory of liberal
democracy as the form of governance best suited to serve humanity ever onward. In his 2018 *Atlantic* article, "Why Technology Favors Tyranny," adapted from his book *21 Lessons
for the 21st Century* (2018), Harari raised the possibility of
a very different future. Exploring the relationship between
technology and political systems, Harari concludes that the
convergence of infotech and biotech could prove antitheti-
cal to liberal democratic forms of government. "Democracy,"
he notes, "distributes the power to process information and
make decisions among many people and institutions"—which
suited the 20th century, when the state of technology made it

inefficient "to concentrate too much information and power in one place." Artificial intelligence removes that constraint.

There is nothing inevitable about democracy. For all the success that democracies have had over the past century or more, they are blips in history. Monarchies, oligarchies, and other forms of authoritarian rule have been far more common modes of human governance.

The emergence of liberal democracies is associated with ideals of liberty and equality that may seem self-evident and irreversible. But these ideals are far more fragile than we believe. Their success in the 20th century depended on unique technological conditions that may prove ephemeral.

In the second decade of the 21st century, liberalism has begun to lose credibility. Questions about the ability of liberal democracy to provide for the middle class have grown louder; politics have grown more tribal; and in more and more countries, leaders are showing a penchant for demagoguery and autocracy. The causes of this political shift are complex, but they appear to be intertwined with current technological developments. The technology that favored democracy is changing, and as artificial intelligence develops, it might change further.

Information technology is continuing to leap forward; biotechnology is beginning to provide a window into our inner lives—our emotions, thoughts, and choices. Together, infotech and biotech will create unprecedented upheavals in human society, eroding human agency and, possibly, subverting human desires. Under such conditions, liberal democracy and free-market economics might become obsolete.

Ordinary people may not understand artificial intelligence and biotechnology in any detail, but they can sense that the future is passing them by. In 1938 the common man's condition in the Soviet Union, Germany, or the United States may have been grim, but he was constantly told that he was the most important thing in the world, and that he was the future (provided, of course, that he was an "ordinary man," rather than, say, a Jew or a woman). He looked at the propaganda posters—which typically depicted coal miners and steelworkers in heroic poses—and saw himself there: "I am in that poster! I am the hero of the future!"

In 2018 the common person feels increasingly irrelevant. Lots of mysterious terms are bandied about excitedly in TED Talks, at government think tanks, and at high-tech conferences—*globalization, blockchain, genetic engineering, AI, machine learning*—and common people, both men and women, may well suspect that none of these terms is about them.

In the 20th century, the masses revolted against exploitation and sought to translate their vital role in the economy into political power. Now the masses fear irrelevance, and they are frantic to use their remaining political power before it is too late. Brexit and the rise of Donald Trump may therefore demonstrate a trajectory opposite to that of traditional socialist revolutions. The Russian, Chinese, and Cuban revolutions were made by people who were vital to the economy but lacked political power; in 2016, Trump and Brexit were supported by many people who still enjoyed political power but feared they were losing their economic worth. Perhaps in the 21st century, populist revolts will be staged not against an economic elite that exploits people but against an economic elite that does not need them anymore. This may well be a losing battle. It is much harder to struggle against irrelevance than against exploitation.

The revolutions in information technology and biotechnology are still in their infancy, and the extent to which they are responsible for the current crisis of liberalism is debatable. Most people in Birmingham, Istanbul, St. Petersburg, and Mumbai are only dimly aware, if they are aware at all, of the rise of AI and its potential impact on their lives. It is undoubtable, however, that the technological revolutions now gathering momentum will in the next few decades confront humankind with the hardest trials it has yet encountered.

———

Let's start with jobs and incomes, because whatever liberal democracy's philosophical appeal, it has gained strength in no small part thanks to a practical advantage: The decentralized approach to decision making that is characteristic of liberalism—in both politics and economics—has allowed liberal democracies to outcompete other states, and to deliver rising affluence to their people.

Liberalism reconciled the proletariat with the bourgeoisie, the faithful with atheists, natives with immigrants, and Europeans with Asians by promising everybody a larger slice of the pie. With a constantly growing pie, that was possible. And the pie may well keep growing. However, economic growth may not solve social problems that are now being created by technological disruption, because such growth is increasingly predicated on the invention of more and more disruptive technologies.

Fears of machines pushing people out of the job market are, of course, nothing new, and in the past such fears proved to be unfounded. But artificial intelligence is different from the old machines. In the past, machines competed with humans mainly in manual skills. Now they are beginning to compete with us in cognitive skills. And we don't know of any third kind of skill—beyond the manual and the cognitive—in which humans will always have an edge.

At least for a few more decades, human intelligence is likely to far exceed computer intelligence in numerous fields. Hence as computers take over more routine cognitive jobs, new creative jobs for humans will continue to appear. Many of these new jobs will probably depend on cooperation rather than competition between humans and AI. Human–AI teams will likely prove superior not just to humans, but also to computers working on their own.

However, most of the new jobs will presumably demand high levels of expertise and ingenuity, and therefore may not provide an answer to the problem of unemployed unskilled laborers, or workers employable only at extremely low wages. Moreover, as AI continues to improve, even jobs that demand high intelligence and creativity might gradually disappear. The world of chess serves as an example of where things might be heading. For several years after IBM's computer Deep Blue defeated Garry Kasparov in 1997, human chess players still flourished; AI was used to train human prodigies, and teams composed of humans plus computers proved superior to computers playing alone.

Yet in recent years, computers have become so good at playing chess that their human collaborators have lost their value and might soon become entirely irrelevant. On December 6, 2017, another crucial milestone was reached when Google's AlphaZero program defeated the Stockfish 8 program. Stockfish 8 had won a world computer chess championship in 2016. It had access to centuries of accumulated human experience in chess, as well as decades of computer experience. By contrast, AlphaZero had not been taught any chess strategies by its human creators—not even standard openings. Rather, it used the latest machine-learning principles to teach itself chess by playing against itself. Nevertheless, out of 100 games that the novice AlphaZero played against Stockfish 8, AlphaZero won 28 and tied 72—it didn't lose once. Since AlphaZero had learned nothing from any human, many of its winning moves and strategies seemed unconventional to the human eye. They could be described as creative, if not downright genius.

Can you guess how long AlphaZero spent learning chess from scratch, preparing for the match against Stockfish 8, and developing its genius instincts? Four hours. For centuries, chess was considered one of the crowning glories of human intelligence. AlphaZero went from utter ignorance to creative mastery in four hours, without the help of any human guide.

AlphaZero is not the only imaginative software out there. One of the ways to catch cheaters in chess tournaments today is to monitor the level of originality that players exhibit. If they play an exceptionally creative move, the judges will often suspect that it could not possibly be a human move—it must be a computer move. At least in chess, creativity is already considered to be the trademark of computers rather than humans! So if chess is our canary in the coal mine, we have been duly warned that the canary is dying. What is happening today to human–AI teams in chess might happen down the road to human–AI teams in policing, medicine, banking, and many other fields.

What's more, AI enjoys uniquely nonhuman abilities, which makes the difference between AI and a human worker one of kind rather than merely of degree. Two particularly important nonhuman abilities that AI possesses are connectivity and updatability.

For example, many drivers are unfamiliar with all the changing traffic regulations on the roads they drive, and they often violate them. In addition, since every driver is a singular entity, when two vehicles approach the same intersection, the drivers sometimes miscommunicate their intentions and collide. Self-driving cars, by contrast, will know all the traffic regulations and never disobey them on purpose, and they could all be connected to one another. When two such vehicles approach the same junction, they won't really be two separate entities, but part of a single algorithm. The chances that they might miscommunicate and collide will therefore be far smaller.

Similarly, if the World Health Organization identifies a new disease, or if a laboratory produces a new medicine, it can't immediately update all the human doctors in the world. Yet even if you had billions of AI doctors in the world—each monitoring the health of a single human being—you could still update all of them within a split second, and they could all communicate to one another their assessments of the new disease or medicine. These potential advantages of connectivity and updatability are so huge that at least in some lines of work, it might make sense to replace *all* humans with computers, even if individually some humans still do a better job than the machines.

All of this leads to one very important conclusion: The automation revolution will not consist of a single watershed event, after which the job market will settle into some new equilibrium. Rather, it will be a cascade of ever-bigger disruptions. Old jobs will disappear and new jobs will emerge, but the new jobs will also rapidly change and vanish. People will need to retrain and reinvent themselves not just once, but many times.

Just as in the 20th century governments established massive education systems for young people, in the 21st century they will need to establish massive reeducation systems for adults. But will that be enough? Change is always stressful, and the hectic world of the early 21st century has produced a global epidemic of stress. As job volatility increases, will people be able to cope? By 2050, a useless class might emerge, the result not only of a shortage of jobs or a lack of relevant education but also of insufficient mental stamina to continue learning new skills.

As many people lose their economic value, they might also come to lose their political power. The same technologies that might make billions of people economically irrelevant might also make them easier to monitor and control.

AI frightens many people because they don't trust it to remain obedient. Science fiction makes much of the possibility that computers or robots will develop consciousness—and shortly thereafter will try to kill all humans. But there is no particular reason to believe that AI will develop consciousness as it becomes more intelligent. We should instead fear AI because it will probably always obey its human masters, and never rebel. AI is a tool and a weapon unlike any other that human beings have developed; it will almost certainly allow the already powerful to consolidate their power further.

Consider surveillance. Numerous countries around the world, including several democracies, are busy building unprecedented systems of surveillance. For example, Israel is a leader in the field of surveillance technology, and has created in the occupied West Bank a working prototype for a total-surveillance regime. Already today whenever Palestinians make a phone call, post something on Facebook, or travel from one city to another, they are likely to be monitored by Israeli microphones, cameras, drones, or spy software. Algorithms analyze the gathered data, helping the Israeli security forces pinpoint and neutralize what they consider to be potential threats. The Palestinians may administer some towns and villages in the West Bank, but the Israelis command the sky, the airwaves, and cyberspace. It therefore takes surprisingly few Israeli soldiers to effectively control the roughly 2.5 million Palestinians who live in the West Bank.

In one incident in October 2017, a Palestinian laborer posted to his private Facebook account a picture of himself in his workplace, alongside a bulldozer. Adjacent to the image he wrote, "Good morning!" A

Facebook translation algorithm made a small error when transliterating the Arabic letters. Instead of *Ysabechhum* (which means "Good morning"), the algorithm identified the letters as *Ydbachhum* (which means "Hurt them"). Suspecting that the man might be a terrorist intending to use a bulldozer to run people over, Israeli security forces swiftly arrested him. They released him after they realized that the algorithm had made a mistake. Even so, the offending Facebook post was taken down—you can never be too careful. What Palestinians are experiencing today in the West Bank may be just a primitive preview of what billions of people will eventually experience all over the planet.

Imagine, for instance, that the current regime in North Korea gained a more advanced version of this sort of technology in the future. North Koreans might be required to wear a biometric bracelet that monitors everything they do and say, as well as their blood pressure and brain activity. Using the growing understanding of the human brain and drawing on the immense powers of machine learning, the North Korean government might eventually be able to gauge what each and every citizen is thinking at each and every moment. If a North Korean looked at a picture of Kim Jong Un and the biometric sensors picked up telltale signs of anger (higher blood pressure, increased activity in the amygdala), that person could be in the gulag the next day.

And yet such hard-edged tactics may not prove necessary, at least much of the time. A facade of free choice and free voting may remain in place in some countries, even as the public exerts less and less actual control. To be sure, attempts to manipulate voters' feelings are not new. But once somebody (whether in San Francisco or Beijing or Moscow) gains the technological ability to manipulate the human heart—reliably, cheaply, and at scale—democratic politics will mutate into an emotional puppet show.

We are unlikely to face a rebellion of sentient machines in the coming decades, but we might have to deal with hordes of bots that know how to press our emotional buttons better than our mother does and that use this uncanny ability, at the behest of a human elite, to try to sell us something—be it a car, a politician, or an entire ideology. The bots might identify our deepest fears, hatreds, and cravings and use them against us. We have already been given a foretaste of this in recent elections and referendums across the world, when hackers learned how to manipulate individual voters by analyzing data about them and exploiting their prejudices. While science-fiction thrillers are drawn to dramatic apocalypses of fire and smoke, in reality we may be facing a banal apocalypse by clicking.

———————

The biggest and most frightening impact of the AI revolution might be on the relative efficiency of democracies and dictatorships. Historically, autocracies have faced crippling handicaps in regard to innovation and economic growth. In the late 20th century, democracies usually outperformed dictatorships, because they were far better at processing information. We tend to think about the conflict between democracy and dictatorship as a conflict between two different ethical systems, but it is actually a conflict between two different data-processing systems. Democracy distributes the power to process information and make decisions among many people and institutions, whereas dictatorship concentrates information and power in one place. Given 20th-century technology, it was inefficient to concentrate too much information and power in one place. Nobody had the ability to process all available information fast enough and make the right decisions. This is one reason the Soviet Union made far worse decisions than the United States, and why the Soviet economy lagged far behind the American economy.

However, artificial intelligence may soon swing the pendulum in the opposite direction. AI makes it possible to process enormous amounts of information centrally. In fact, it might make centralized systems far more efficient than diffuse systems, because machine learning works better when the machine has more information to analyze. If you disregard all privacy concerns and concentrate all the information relating to a billion people in one database, you'll wind up with much better algorithms than if you respect individual privacy and have in your database only partial information on a million people. An authoritarian government that orders all its citizens to have their DNA sequenced and to share their medical data with some central authority would gain an immense advantage in genetics and medical research over societies in which medical data are strictly private. The main handicap of authoritarian regimes in the 20th century—the desire to concentrate all information and power in one place—may become their decisive advantage in the 21st century.

New technologies will continue to emerge, of course, and some of them may encourage the distribution rather than the concentration of information and power. Blockchain technology, and the use of cryptocurrencies enabled by it, is currently touted as a possible counterweight to centralized power. But blockchain technology is still in the embryonic stage, and we don't yet know whether it will indeed counterbalance the centralizing tendencies of AI. Remember that the internet, too, was hyped in its early days as a libertarian panacea that would free people from all centralized systems—but is now poised to make centralized authority more powerful than ever.

Even if some societies remain ostensibly democratic, the increasing efficiency of algorithms will still shift more and more authority from individual humans to networked machines. We might willingly give up more and more authority over our lives because we will learn from experience to trust the algorithms more than our own feelings, eventually losing our ability to make many decisions for ourselves. Just think of the way that, within a mere two decades, billions of people have come to entrust Google's search algorithm with one of the most important tasks of all: finding relevant and trustworthy information. As we rely more on Google for answers, our ability to locate information independently diminishes. Already today, "truth" is defined by the top results of a Google search. This process has likewise affected our physical abilities, such as navigating space. People ask Google not just to find information but also to guide them around. Self-driving cars and AI physicians would represent further erosion: While these innovations would put truckers and human doctors out of work, their larger import lies in the continuing transfer of authority and responsibility to machines.

Humans are used to thinking about life as a drama of decision making. Liberal democracy and free-market capitalism see the individual as an autonomous agent constantly making choices about the world. Works of art—be they Shakespeare plays, Jane Austen novels, or cheesy Hollywood comedies—usually revolve around the hero having to make some crucial decision. To be or not to be? To listen to my wife and kill King Duncan, or listen to my conscience and spare him? To marry Mr. Collins or Mr. Darcy? Christian and Muslim theology similarly focus on the drama of decision making, arguing that everlasting salvation depends on making the right choice.

What will happen to this view of life as we rely on AI to make ever more decisions for us? Even now we trust Netflix to recommend movies and Spotify to pick music we'll like. But why should AI's helpfulness stop there?

Every year millions of college students need to decide what to study. This is a very important and difficult decision, made under pressure from parents, friends, and professors who have varying interests and opinions. It is also influenced by students' own individual fears and fantasies, which are themselves shaped by movies, novels, and advertising campaigns. Complicating matters, a given student does not really know what it takes to succeed in a given profession, and doesn't necessarily have a realistic sense of his or her own strengths and weaknesses.

It's not so hard to see how AI could one day make better decisions than we do about careers, and perhaps even about relationships. But once we begin to count on AI to decide what to study, where to work, and whom to date or even marry, human life will cease to be a drama of decision making, and our conception of life will need to change. Democratic elections and free markets might cease to make sense. So might most religions and works of art. Imagine Anna Karenina taking out her smartphone and asking Siri whether she should stay married to Karenin or elope with the dashing Count Vronsky. Or imagine your favorite Shakespeare play with all the crucial decisions made by a Google algorithm.

Hamlet and Macbeth would have much more comfortable lives, but what kind of lives would those be? Do we have models for making sense of such lives?

———

Can parliaments and political parties overcome these challenges and forestall the darker scenarios? At the current moment this does not seem likely. Technological disruption is not even a leading item on the political agenda. During the 2016 U.S. presidential race, the main reference to disruptive technology concerned Hillary Clinton's email debacle, and despite all the talk about job loss, neither candidate directly addressed the potential impact of automation. Donald Trump warned voters that Mexicans would take their jobs, and that the U.S. should therefore build a wall on its southern border. He never warned voters that algorithms would take their jobs, nor did he suggest building a firewall around California.

So what should we do?

For starters, we need to place a much higher priority on understanding how the human mind works—particularly how our own wisdom and compassion can be cultivated. If we invest too much in AI and too little in developing the human mind, the very sophisticated artificial intelligence of computers might serve only to empower the natural stupidity of humans, and to nurture our worst (but also, perhaps, most powerful) impulses, among them greed and hatred. To avoid such an outcome, for every dollar and every minute we invest in improving AI, we would be wise to invest a dollar and a minute in exploring and developing human consciousness.

More practically, and more immediately, if we want to prevent the concentration of all wealth and power in the hands of a small elite, we must regulate the ownership of data. In ancient times, land was the most important asset, so politics was a struggle to control land. In the modern era, machines and factories became more important than land, so political struggles focused on controlling these vital means of production. In the 21st century, data will eclipse both land and machinery as the most important asset, so politics will be a struggle to control data's flow.

Unfortunately, we don't have much experience in regulating the ownership of data, which is inherently a far more difficult task than regulating land or machines. Data are everywhere and nowhere at the same time, they can move at the speed of light, and you can create as many copies of them as you want. Do the data collected about my DNA, my brain, and my life belong to me, or to the government, or to a corporation, or to the human collective?

The race to accumulate data is already on, and is currently headed by giants such as Google and Facebook and, in China, Baidu and Tencent. So far, many of these companies have acted as "attention merchants"— they capture our attention by providing us with free information, services, and entertainment, and then they resell our attention to advertisers. Yet their true business isn't merely selling ads. Rather, by capturing our attention they manage to accumulate immense amounts of data about us, which are worth more than any advertising revenue. We aren't their customers—we are their product.

Ordinary people will find it very difficult to resist this process. At present, many of us are happy to give away our most valuable asset— our personal data—in exchange for free email services and funny cat videos. But if, later on, ordinary people decide to try to block the flow of data, they are likely to have trouble doing so, especially as they may have come to rely on the network to help them make decisions, and even for their health and physical survival.

Nationalization of data by governments could offer one solution; it would certainly curb the power of big corporations. But history suggests that we are not necessarily better off in the hands of overmighty governments. So we had better call upon our scientists, our philosophers, our lawyers, and even our poets to turn their attention to this big question: How do you regulate the ownership of data?

Currently, humans risk becoming similar to domesticated animals. We have bred docile cows that produce enormous amounts of milk but are otherwise far inferior to their wild ancestors. They are less agile, less curious, and less resourceful. We are now creating tame humans who produce enormous amounts of data and function as efficient chips in a huge data-processing mechanism, but they hardly maximize their human potential. If we are not careful, we will end up with downgraded humans misusing upgraded computers to wreak havoc on themselves and on the world.

If you find these prospects alarming—if you dislike the idea of living in a digital dictatorship or some similarly degraded form of society—then the most important contribution you can make is to find ways to prevent too much data from being concentrated in too few hands, and also find ways to keep distributed data processing more efficient than centralized data processing. These will not be easy tasks. But achieving them may be the best safeguard of democracy.

IN CASE OF EMERGENCY

by Elizabeth Goitein

[JANUARY/FEBRUARY 2019]

The legal expert Elizabeth Goitein's concern is not concentrations of data but concentrations of power—specifically, emergency power given to the president of the United States. Goitein, a co director of the Brennan Center for Justice's Liberty & National Security Program and the author of *The New Era of Secret Law* (2016), acknowledges that the power of a president to declare a "national emergency" is long established. Less well understood is how broad that power is and how many different kinds of authority become available with such a declaration—not just authority to use military force but authority over the economy, over communications, over criminal justice. Congress is supposed to keep watch, but doesn't.

In her 2019 article "In Case of Emergency," Goitein reported that some 30 declarations of national emergency by past presidents were still in force. (More have been put in place since her article appeared, including the declaration by President Trump of a national emergency in order to build a wall on the southern border.) As Goitein saw it, only the "reticence" of previous presidents, and their commitment to liberal democracy, had prevented grave abuse.

What happens if the occupant of the Oval Office is not a person of reticence, or lacks a commitment to liberal democracy? Goitein invoked Justice Robert Jackson's famous dissent in *Korematsu v. United States*, the case that upheld the right of the Roosevelt administration to subject Japanese Americans to internment: Each emergency power "lies about like a loaded weapon, ready for the hand of any authority that can bring forward a plausible claim of an urgent need."

Unknown to most Americans, a parallel legal regime allows the president to sidestep many of the constraints that the law usually imposes on executive action. The moment the president declares a "national emergency"—a decision that is entirely within his discretion—more than 100 special provisions become available to him. While many of these tee up reasonable responses to genuine emergencies, some appear dangerously suited to a leader bent on amassing or retaining power. For instance, the president can, with the flick of his pen, activate laws allowing him to shut down many kinds of electronic communications inside the United States or freeze Americans' bank accounts. Other powers are available even without a declaration of emergency, including laws that allow the president to deploy troops inside the country to subdue domestic unrest.

This edifice of extraordinary powers has historically rested on the assumption that the president will act in the country's best interest when using them. With a handful of noteworthy exceptions, this assumption has held up. But what if a president, backed into a corner and facing electoral defeat or impeachment, were to declare an emergency for the sake of holding on to power? In that scenario, our laws and institutions might not save us from a presidential power grab. They might be what takes us down.

The premise underlying emergency powers is simple: The government's ordinary powers might be insufficient in a crisis, and amending the law to provide greater ones might be too slow and cumbersome. Emergency powers are meant to give the government a temporary boost until the emergency passes or there is time to change the law through normal legislative processes.

Unlike the modern constitutions of many other countries, which specify when and how a state of emergency may be declared and which rights may be suspended, the U.S. Constitution itself includes no comprehensive separate regime for emergencies. Those few powers it does contain for dealing with certain urgent threats, it assigns to Congress, not the president. For instance, it lets Congress suspend the writ of habeas corpus—that is, allow government officials to imprison people without judicial review—"when in Cases of Rebellion or Invasion the public Safety may require it" and "provide for calling forth the Militia to execute the Laws of the Union, suppress Insurrections and repel Invasions."

Nonetheless, some legal scholars believe that the Constitution gives the president inherent emergency powers by making him commander in chief of the armed forces, or by vesting in him a broad, undefined "executive Power." At key points in American history, presidents have cited inherent constitutional powers when taking drastic actions that were not authorized—or, in some cases, were explicitly prohibited—by Congress. Notorious examples include Franklin D. Roosevelt's internment of U.S. citizens and residents of Japanese descent during World War II and George W. Bush's programs of warrantless wiretapping and torture after the 9/11 terrorist attacks. Abraham Lincoln conceded that his unilateral suspension of habeas corpus during the Civil War was constitutionally questionable, but defended it as necessary to preserve the Union.

The Supreme Court has often upheld such actions or found ways to avoid reviewing them, at least while the crisis was in progress. Rulings such as *Youngstown Sheet & Tube Company v. Sawyer*, in which the Court invalidated President Harry Truman's bid to take over steel mills during the Korean War, have been the exception. And while those exceptions have outlined important limiting principles, the outer boundary of the president's constitutional authority during emergencies remains poorly defined.

Presidents can also rely on a cornucopia of powers provided by Congress, which has historically been the principal source of emergency authority for the executive branch. Throughout the late 18th and 19th centuries, Congress passed laws to give the president additional leeway during military, economic, and labor crises. A more formalized approach evolved in the early 20th century, when Congress legislated powers that would lie dormant until the president activated them by declaring a national emergency. These statutory authorities began to pile up—and because presidents had little incentive to terminate states of emergency once declared, these piled up too. By the 1970s, hundreds of statutory emergency powers, and four clearly obsolete states of emergency, were in effect. For instance, the national emergency that Truman declared in 1950, during the Korean War, remained in place and was being used to help prosecute the war in Vietnam.

Aiming to rein in this proliferation, Congress passed the National Emergencies Act in 1976. Under this law, the president still has complete discretion to issue an emergency declaration—but he must specify in the declaration which powers he intends to use, issue public updates if he decides to invoke additional powers, and report to Congress on the government's emergency-related expenditures every six months. The state of emergency expires after a year unless the president renews it, and the Senate and the House must meet every six months while the emergency is in effect "to consider a vote" on termination.

By any objective measure, the law has failed. Thirty states of emergency are in effect today—several times more than when the act was passed. Most have been renewed for years on end. And during the 40 years the law has been in place, Congress has not met even once, let alone every six months, to vote on whether to end them.

As a result, the president has access to emergency powers contained in 123 statutory provisions, as recently calculated by the Brennan Center for Justice at NYU School of Law, where I work. These laws address a broad range of matters, from military composition to agricultural exports to public contracts. For the most part, the president is free to use any of them; the National Emergencies Act doesn't require that the powers invoked relate to the nature of the emergency. Even if the crisis at hand is, say, a nationwide crop blight, the president may activate the law that allows the secretary of transportation to requisition any privately owned vessel at sea. Many other laws permit the executive branch to take extraordinary action under specified conditions, such as war and domestic upheaval, regardless of whether a national emergency has been declared.

This legal regime for emergencies—ambiguous constitutional limits combined with a rich well of statutory emergency powers—would seem to provide the ingredients for a dangerous encroachment on American civil liberties. Yet so far, even though presidents have often advanced dubious claims of constitutional authority, egregious abuses on the scale of the Japanese American internment or the post-9/11 torture program have been rare, and most of the statutory powers available during a national emergency have never been used.

But what's to guarantee that this president, or a future one, will show the reticence of his predecessors? To borrow from Justice Robert Jackson's dissent in *Korematsu v. United States*, the 1944 Supreme Court decision that upheld the internment of Japanese Americans, each emergency power "lies about like a loaded weapon, ready for the hand of any authority that can bring forward a plausible claim of an urgent need."

———————

Like all emergency powers, the laws governing the conduct of war allow the president to engage in conduct that would be illegal during ordinary times. This conduct includes familiar incidents of war, such as the killing or indefinite detention of enemy soldiers. But the president can also take a host of other actions, both abroad and inside the United States.

These laws vary dramatically in content and scope. Several of them authorize the president to make decisions about the size and composition of the armed forces that are usually left to Congress. Although such measures can offer needed flexibility at crucial moments, they are subject to misuse. For instance, George W. Bush leveraged the state of emergency after 9/11 to call hundreds of thousands of reservists and members of the National Guard into active duty in Iraq, for a war that had nothing to do with the 9/11 attacks. Other powers are chilling under any circumstances: Take a moment to consider that during a declared war or national emergency, the president can unilaterally suspend the law that bars government testing of biological and chemical agents on unwitting human subjects.

One power poses a singular threat to democracy in the digital era. In 1942, Congress amended Section 706 of the Communications Act of 1934 to allow the president to shut down or take control of "any facility or station for wire communication" upon his proclamation "that there exists a state or threat of war involving the United States," resurrecting a similar power Congress had briefly provided Woodrow Wilson during World War I. At the time, "wire communication" meant telephone calls or telegrams. Given the relatively modest role that electronic communications played in most Americans' lives, the government's assertion of this power during World War II (no president has used it since) likely created inconvenience but not havoc.

We live in a different universe today. Although interpreting a 1942 law to cover the internet might seem far-fetched, some government officials recently endorsed this reading during debates about cybersecurity legislation. Under this interpretation, Section 706 could effectively function as a "kill switch" in the U.S.—one that would be available to the president the moment he proclaimed a mere threat of war. It could also give the president power to assume control over U.S. internet traffic.

The potential impact of such a move can hardly be overstated. In August, in an early-morning tweet, Trump lamented that search engines were "RIGGED" to serve up negative articles about him. Later that day the administration said it was looking into regulating the big internet companies. "I think that Google and Twitter and Facebook, they're really treading on very, very troubled territory. And they have to be careful," Trump warned. If the government were to take control of U.S. internet infrastructure, Trump could accomplish directly what he threatened to do by regulation: ensure that internet searches always return pro-Trump content as the top results. The government also would have the ability to impede domestic access to particular websites, including social-media platforms. It could monitor emails or prevent them from reaching their destination. It could exert control over computer systems (such as states' voter databases) and physical devices (such as Amazon's Echo speakers) that are connected to the internet.

To be sure, the fact that the internet in the United States is highly decentralized—a function of a relatively open market for communications devices and services—would offer some protection. Achieving the level of government control over internet content that exists in places such as China, Russia, and Iran would likely be impossible in the U.S. Moreover, if Trump were to attempt any degree of internet takeover, an explosion of lawsuits would follow. Based on its First Amendment rulings in recent decades, the Supreme Court seems unlikely to permit heavy-handed government control over internet communication.

But complacency would be a mistake. Complete control of internet content would not be necessary for Trump's purposes; even with less comprehensive interventions, he could do a great deal to disrupt political discourse and hinder effective, organized political opposition. And the Supreme Court's view of the First Amendment is not immutable. For much of the country's history, the Court was willing to tolerate significant encroachments on free speech during wartime. "The progress we have made is fragile," Geoffrey R. Stone, a constitutional-law scholar at the University of Chicago, has written. "It would not take much to upset the current understanding of the First Amendment." Indeed, all it would take is five Supreme Court justices whose commitment to presidential power exceeds their commitment to individual liberties.

———————

Next to war powers, economic powers might sound benign, but they are among the president's most potent legal weapons. All but two of the emergency declarations in effect today were issued under the International Emergency Economic Powers Act, or IEEPA. Passed in 1977, the law allows the president to declare a national emergency "to deal with any unusual and extraordinary threat"—to national security, foreign policy, or the economy—that "has its source in whole or in substantial part outside the United States." The president can then order a range of economic actions to address the threat, including freezing assets and blocking financial transactions in which any foreign nation or foreign national has an interest.

In the late 1970s and '80s, presidents used the law primarily to impose sanctions against other nations, including Iran, Nicaragua, South Africa, Libya, and Panama. Then, in 1983, when Congress failed to renew a law authorizing the Commerce Department to control certain exports, President Ronald Reagan declared a national emergency in order to assume that control under IEEPA. Subsequent presidents followed his example, transferring export control from Congress to the White House. President Bill Clinton expanded IEEPA's usage by targeting not just foreign governments but foreign political parties, terrorist organizations, and suspected narcotics traffickers.

President George W. Bush took matters a giant step further after 9/11. His Executive Order 13224 prohibited transactions not just with any suspected foreign terrorists, but with any foreigner *or any U.S. citizen* suspected of providing them with support. Once a person is "designated" under the order, no American can legally give him a job, rent him an apartment, provide him with medical services, or even sell him a loaf of bread unless the government grants a license to allow the transaction. The Patriot Act gave the order more muscle, allowing the government to trigger these consequences merely by opening an investigation into whether a person or group should be designated.

Designations under Executive Order 13224 are opaque and extremely difficult to challenge. The government needs only a "reasonable basis" for believing that someone is involved with or supports terrorism in order to designate him. The target is generally given no advance notice and no hearing. He may request reconsideration and submit evidence on his behalf, but the government faces no deadline to respond. Moreover, the evidence against the target is typically classified, which means he is not allowed to see it. He can try to challenge the action in court, but his chances of success are minimal, as most judges defer to the government's assessment of its own evidence.

Americans have occasionally been caught up in this Kafkaesque system. Several Muslim charities in the U.S. were designated or investigated based on the suspicion that their charitable contributions overseas benefited terrorists. Of course if the government can show, through judicial proceedings that observe due process and other constitutional rights, that an American group or person is funding terrorist activity, it should be able to cut off those funds. But the government shut these charities down by freezing their assets without ever having to prove its charges in court.

In other cases, Americans were significantly harmed by designations that later proved to be mistakes. For instance, two months after 9/11, the Treasury Department designated Garad Jama, a Somalian-born American, based on an erroneous determination that his money-wiring business was part of a terror-financing network. Jama's office was shut down and his bank account frozen. News outlets described him as a suspected terrorist. For months, Jama tried to gain a hearing with the government to establish his innocence and, in the meantime, obtain the government's permission to get a job and pay his lawyer. Only after he filed a lawsuit did the government allow him to work as a grocery-store cashier and pay his living expenses. It was several more months before the government reversed his designation and unfroze his assets. By then he had lost his business, and the stigma of having been publicly labeled a terrorist supporter continued to follow him and his family.

Despite these dramatic examples, IEEPA's limits have yet to be fully tested. After two courts ruled that the government's actions against American charities were unconstitutional, Barack Obama's administration chose not to appeal the decisions and largely refrained from further controversial designations of American organizations and citizens. Thus far, President Trump has followed the same approach.

That could change. In October, in the lead-up to the midterm elections, Trump characterized the caravan of Central American migrants headed toward the U.S. border to seek asylum as a "National Emergency." Although he did not issue an emergency proclamation, he could do so under IEEPA. He could determine that any American inside the U.S. who offers material support to the asylum seekers—or, for that matter, to undocumented immigrants inside the United States— poses "an unusual and extraordinary threat" to national security, and authorize the Treasury Department to take action against them.

Such a move would carry echoes of a law passed recently in Hungary that criminalized the provision of financial or legal services to undocumented migrants; this has been dubbed the "Stop Soros" law, after the Hungarian American philanthropist George Soros, who funds migrants'-rights organizations. Although an order issued under IEEPA would not land targets in jail, it could be implemented without legislation and without affording targets a trial. In practice, identifying every American who has hired, housed, or provided paid legal representation to an asylum seeker or undocumented immigrant would be impossible—but all Trump would need to do to achieve the desired political effect would be to make high-profile examples of a few. Individuals targeted by the order could lose their jobs, and find their bank accounts frozen and their health insurance canceled. The battle in the courts would then pick up exactly where it left off during the Obama administration—but with a newly reconstituted Supreme Court making the final call.

————

The idea of tanks rolling through the streets of U.S. cities seems fundamentally inconsistent with the country's notions of democracy and freedom. Americans might be surprised, therefore, to learn just how readily the president can deploy troops inside the country.

The principle that the military should not act as a domestic police force, known as "posse comitatus," has deep roots in the nation's history, and it is often mistaken for a constitutional rule. The Constitution, however, does not prohibit military participation in police activity. Nor does the Posse Comitatus Act of 1878 outlaw such participation; it merely states that any authority to use the military for law-enforcement purposes must derive from the Constitution or from a statute.

The Insurrection Act of 1807 provides the necessary authority. As amended over the years, it allows the president to deploy troops upon the request of a state's governor or legislature to help put down an insurrection within that state. It also allows the president to deploy troops unilaterally, either because he determines that rebellious activity has made it "impracticable" to enforce federal law through regular means, or because he deems it necessary to suppress "insurrection, domestic violence, unlawful combination, or conspiracy" (terms not defined in the statute) that hinders the rights of a class of people or "impedes the course of justice."

Presidents have wielded the Insurrection Act under a range of circumstances. Dwight Eisenhower used it in 1957 when he sent troops into Little Rock, Arkansas, to enforce school desegregation. George H. W. Bush employed it in 1992 to help stop the riots that erupted in Los Angeles after the verdict in the Rodney King case. George W. Bush considered invoking it to help restore public order after Hurricane Katrina, but opted against it when the governor of Louisiana resisted federal control over the state's National Guard. While controversy surrounded all these examples, none suggests obvious overreach.

And yet the potential misuses of the act are legion. When Chicago experienced a spike in homicides in 2017, Trump tweeted that the city must "fix the horrible 'carnage'" or he would "send in the Feds!" To carry out this threat, the president could declare a particular street gang—say, MS-13—to be an "unlawful combination" and then send troops to the nation's cities to police the streets. He could characterize sanctuary cities—cities that refuse to provide assistance to immigration-enforcement officials—as "conspiracies" against federal authorities, and order the military to enforce immigration laws in those places. Conjuring the specter of "liberal mobs," he could send troops to suppress alleged rioting at the fringes of anti-Trump protests.

How far could the president go in using the military within U.S. borders? The Supreme Court has given us no clear answer to this question. Take *Ex parte Milligan*, a famous ruling from 1866 invalidating the use of a military commission to try a civilian during the Civil War. The case is widely considered a high-water mark for judicial constraint on executive action. Yet even as the Court held that the president could not use war or emergency as a reason to bypass civilian courts, it noted that martial law—the displacement of civilian authority by the military—would be appropriate in some cases. If civilian courts were closed as a result of a foreign invasion or a civil war, for example, martial law could exist "until the laws can have their free course." The message is decidedly mixed: Claims of emergency or necessity cannot legitimize martial law . . . until they can.

Presented with this ambiguity, presidents have explored the outer limits of their constitutional emergency authority in a series of directives known as Presidential Emergency Action Documents, or PEADs. PEADs, which originated as part of the Eisenhower administration's plans to ensure continuity of government in the wake of a Soviet nuclear attack, are draft executive orders, proclamations, and messages to Congress that are prepared in advance of anticipated emergencies. PEADs are closely guarded within the government; none has ever been publicly released or leaked. But their contents have occasionally been described in public sources, including FBI memorandums that were obtained through the Freedom of Information Act as well as agency manuals and court records. According to these sources, PEADs drafted from the 1950s through the 1970s would authorize not only martial law but the suspension of habeas corpus by the executive branch, the revocation of Americans' passports, and the roundup and detention of "subversives" identified in an FBI "Security Index" that contained more than 10,000 names.

Less is known about the contents of more recent PEADs and equivalent planning documents. But in 1987, *The Miami Herald* reported that Lieutenant Colonel Oliver North had worked with the Federal Emergency Management Agency to create a secret contingency plan authorizing "suspension of the Constitution, turning control of the United States over to FEMA, appointment of military commanders to run state and local governments and declaration of martial law during a national crisis." A 2007 Department of Homeland Security report lists "martial law" and "curfew declarations" as "critical tasks" that local, state, and federal government should be able to perform in emergencies. In 2008, government sources told a reporter for *Radar* magazine that a version of the Security Index still existed under the code name Main Core, allowing for the apprehension and detention of Americans tagged as security threats.

Since 2012, the Department of Justice has been requesting and receiving funds from Congress to update several dozen PEADs first developed in 1989. The funding requests contain no indication of what these PEADs encompass, or what standards the department intends to apply in reviewing them. But whatever the Obama administration's intent, the review has now passed to the Trump administration. It will fall to Jeff Sessions's successor as attorney general to decide whether to rein in or expand some of the more frightening features of these PEADs. And, of course, it will be up to President Trump whether to actually use them—something no previous president appears to have done.

———————

What would the Founders think of these and other emergency powers on the books today, in the hands of a president like Donald Trump? In *Youngstown*, the case in which the Supreme Court blocked President Truman's attempt to seize the nation's steel mills, Justice Jackson observed that broad emergency powers were "something the forefathers omitted" from the Constitution. "They knew what emergencies were, knew the pressures they engender for authoritative action, knew, too, how they afford a ready pretext for usurpation," he wrote. "We may also suspect that they suspected that emergency powers would tend to kindle emergencies."

In the past several decades, Congress has provided what the Constitution did not: emergency powers that have the potential for creating emergencies rather than ending them. Presidents have built on these powers with their own secret directives. What has prevented the wholesale abuse of these authorities until now is a baseline commitment to liberal democracy on the part of past presidents.

Under a president who doesn't share that commitment, what might we see?

THE ENEMY WITHIN

by James Mattis

[DECEMBER 2019]

Much of what keeps a democracy firmly on the right path (to express the challenge positively) or prevents a democracy from degenerating into mayhem (to express it negatively) is not written down and possesses no force of law. It is simply a set of norms and values that governs how we think about one another and how we act as citizens. In a 2019 *Atlantic* essay, "The Enemy Within," James Mattis, a retired Marine Corps general, argued that letting go of those norms and values—and failing to teach them to new generations—is the surest path to national decline.

Mattis served as Donald Trump's secretary of defense until January 1, 2019. In his letter of resignation the month before, he cited disagreements over matters of principle, stating that the president deserved to have a secretary whose views were "better aligned" with those of the commander in chief. The lack of alignment was clear: Mattis possessed a "resolute and unambiguous" belief in maintaining strong alliances with countries that shared America's values, and in taking an unequivocal stand against major adversaries. The president did not.

In his *Atlantic* article, Mattis looked back at American history for enduring lessons that all Americans could unite around. "Here is what we seem to have forgotten," he wrote.

I n 1838, Abraham Lincoln gave a speech to the Young Men's Ly-
ceum in Springfield, Illinois. The subject was citizenship and the
preservation of America's political institutions. The backdrop was
the threat posed to those institutions by the evil of slavery. Lincoln
warned that the greatest danger to the nation came from within. All the
armies of the world could not crush us, he maintained, but we could
still "die by suicide."

And now, today, we look around. Our politics are paralyzing the
country. We practice suspicion or contempt where trust is needed, imposing a sentence of anger and loneliness on others and ourselves. We
scorch our opponents with language that precludes compromise. We
brush aside the possibility that a person with whom we disagree might
be right. We talk about what divides us and seldom acknowledge what
unites us. Meanwhile, the docket of urgent national issues continues
to grow—unaddressed and, under present circumstances, impossible
to address.

Contending viewpoints and vocal dissent are inevitable, and not the
issue. A year ago I stepped down from the best job in the world, as our
secretary of defense, over a matter of principle because of grave policy
differences with the administration—stating my reasons in a letter that
left no room for doubt. What is dangerous is not that people have
serious differences. It is the tone—the snarl, the scorn, the lacerating
despair.

Are we unaware of the consequences of national fracturing and disunity? Do we want to bequeath such a country to our children? Have
we taught them the principles that citizens of this democracy must live
by? Do we even remember those principles ourselves?

———————

Here is what we seem to have forgotten:

*America is not some finished work or failed project but an ongoing experi-
ment.* And it is an experiment that, by design, will never end. If parts of
the machine are broken, then the responsibility of citizens is to fix the
machine—not throw it away. The Founders, with their unsentimental

assessment of human nature, brought forth a constitutional system robust enough to withstand great stress and yet capable of profound correction to address injustice. (The Thirteenth Amendment, which abolished slavery. The Nineteenth Amendment, which gave women the right to vote.) The scale of the Founders' achievement was unprecedented. Except in small pockets here and there, a democratic system such as ours had never before been tried; the Founders applied it to a nation that would soon span a continent. I think of our own document's durable capacity when I consider the travails of the United Kingdom, which lacks a written constitution. The lesson is not that we can sit back in relief. It is that we must continue conducting the experiment.

Defects are part of the human condition. In a way, this is good news. Our imperfections can—and ought to—draw us together in humility, realism, patience, and determination. No one has a monopoly on wisdom or is free from error. Everyone benefits from understanding other points of view. The foundational virtue of democracy is trust— not trust in one's own rectitude or opinion, but trust in the capacity of collective deliberation to move us forward. That kind of trust is diminishing. About two-thirds of Americans in a recent Pew survey expressed the view that declining trust—in government, in one another—is hampering our ability to confront the country's problems. Yet trust is not gone. It binds the military, as I've seen firsthand in locales as varied as Fallujah and Kandahar, Fort Bragg and Coronado. It exists, in my personal experience, among members of the Intelligence Committee in the Senate and members of the Armed Services Committees of both houses on Capitol Hill—remarkable outliers in an otherwise poisonous environment. Trust is not some weather system over which we have no control. It is a decision about conducting the nation's business that each of us has the power to make. Building trust means listening to others rather than shutting them down. It also means looking for the right way to define a given problem—asking questions the right way so as to enlist opponents rather than provoke them. There's a famous observation attributed to Einstein: "If I had an hour to solve a problem, I'd spend 55 minutes thinking about the problem and five minutes

thinking about solutions." Too often we define our great national challenges—climate change, immigration, health care, guns—in a way that
guarantees division into warring camps. Instead we should be asking
one another: What could "better" look like?

*Acting wisely means acting with a time horizon not of months or years
but of generations.* Short-term thinking tends toward the selfish: *Better
get mine while I can!* Long-term thinking plays to higher ideals. Thomas
Jefferson's idea of "usufruct"—in his metaphor, the responsibility to
preserve fertile topsoil from landowner to landowner—embodied an
obligation of stewardship and intergenerational fairness. Our Founders
thought in centuries. Such thinking discourages shortsighted temptations (such as passing an immense burden of national debt onto our
descendants) and encourages the effective management of intractable
problems. It conditions us to take heart from the slow accretion of small
improvements—the slow accretion that gave us paved roads, public
schools, and electrification. I remember being a boy in Washington
State and the sense of wonder I felt as bridges replaced ferries on the
Columbia River. I remember my grandfather pointing out new power
lines extending into our rural part of the state. I think often of the
long history of nuclear-arms control. Steady diplomatic engagement
with Moscow over five decades—pursued until recently—ultimately
gave us an approximately three-quarters reduction in nuclear arsenals,
and greater security. Here's the not-so-secret recipe, applicable to members of Congress and community activists alike: Set a strategic goal
and keep at it. Former Secretary of State George Shultz, using his own
Jeffersonian metaphor, likened the effort to gardening: a continual,
never-ending process of tilling, planting, and weeding.

Cynicism is cowardice. We all know cynics. From time to time, we
all fall prey to cynicism. But cynicism is corrosive when it saturates a
society—as it has long saturated Russia's, and as it has saturated too
much of ours. Cynicism fosters a distrust of reality. It is nothing less
than a form of surrender. It provokes a suspicion that hidden malign
forces are at play. It instills a sense of victimhood. It may be psychically
gratifying in the moment, but it solves nothing.

Leadership doesn't mean someone riding in on a white horse. We're deluding ourselves if we think one person has all the answers. In a democracy, real leadership is slow, quiet, diplomatic, collegial, and often frustrating. I will always associate these qualities with General Colin Powell, a personal mentor who understood that to lead also means to serve. A leader, Dwight Eisenhower noted, is not someone who barks "Rise" or "Sit down." Leadership, he said, is "the art of getting someone else to do something that you want done because he *wants* to do it." And it's a two-way street. As Eisenhower put it, one thing every leader needs is "the inspiration he gets from the people he leads."

Achieving results nationally means participating locally. The scale of the country's challenges can seem so vast that only grand solutions offer any hope of meeting them. We give up on singles and doubles, hoping some slugger will come along and swing for the fences. This is wrong on two counts. First, the steep decline of democratic participation is itself one of our central challenges, reflecting a loss of conviction that government is actually in our hands. Only participation can solve the participation problem. Second, the impact of participation trickles up. Rosa Parks didn't start out by taking on all of Jim Crow; she started out by taking a seat on a local bus. National efforts on the environment, health care, highways, the minimum wage, workplace safety—all got their start in one state or another. And Washington isn't synonymous with America anyway. Community life is sustained locally, not only through government but through a wealth of civic associations that depend on the participation of ordinary people. The president famously possesses a bully pulpit, but the impetus for change just as often comes from the pews.

The "bonds of affection" Lincoln spoke about are paramount. Maybe it's a by-product of our success as a nation that Americans take for granted what we have in common. The freedoms we enjoy. The traditions we celebrate. Our rough-and-tumble sense of humor. We need one another the most at moments of crisis, and historically we have come together at such moments—after Pearl Harbor, after 9/11. The adversity of economic depression and world war served as a crucible for an entire generation of men and women, who created and sustained a stable world for half a century. Today we are coping with the consequences of pent-up neglect and intensifying tribal warfare, not of sudden attack. But we face a crisis nonetheless. The surest path to catastrophe is to sever those bonds of affection.

Our core institutions have value, even if all institutions are flawed. We live in an anti-institutional age. The favorability numbers of virtually every institution except the military are low, and dropping. (John McCain once told me that the only people who liked Congress were family members and salaried employees. His wife, Cindy, turned to him and jokingly said, "Don't count on family members.") For all their imperfections, institutions are the best way to transmit what is good down the corridors of time. Civilization is more fragile than one might think; during my career in the military, I saw it destroyed in front of my eyes. We need to make institutions better and stronger, not tear them down. Virulent, take-no-prisoners attacks on the media, the judiciary, labor unions, universities, teachers, scientists, civil servants—pick your target—don't help anyone. When you tear down institutions, you tear down the scaffolding on which society is built. Allowing institutions to erode—as we have allowed our educational system to erode—is as bad as tearing them down.

I have visited schools and spoken with students. I worry not only about budget cutbacks and funding inequities but also about classroom content. A proper understanding of our national story is absent. Students come away well versed in our flaws and shortcomings. They do not come away with an understanding of our higher ideals, our manifest contributions, our revolutionary aspirations. They do not come away with an understanding of the basic principles I have outlined. Or with an appreciation of how a thoughtful and clear-eyed person can also be—and indeed must be—a patriot.

Every generation since the Revolution has added to the legacy of the Founders in the endless quest to make the union "more perfect." And every generation shoulders a responsibility to pass along our freedoms, and the wherewithal to secure and enhance them, to the next generation. Having traveled during the past few months to every corner of the country, I know that Americans in general are better—kinder, more thoughtful, more respectful—than our political leadership.

But are we truly doing our duty by future generations? For too many, *e pluribus unum* is just a Latin phrase on the coins in their hands—not a concept with a powerful moral charge. It is hard work, building a country. In a democracy, it is noble work that all of us have to do.

III. THE AGE
OF TRUMP

To render even a semi-definitive historical judgment on a president before his (or, theoretically, her) term of office has expired is considered premature. In the case of Donald Trump, this popular understanding is wrong.

Trump will not have his Robert Caro treatment for decades. But his abdication of responsibility during the coronavirus pandemic—perhaps the most serious national challenge since World War II—will not cease to be a fact, and by itself merits a directed verdict. Trump has called himself a "wartime" president, but FDR did not leave the war to the governors. He certainly did not dismiss the threat posed to the U.S. by Japan *after* Pearl Harbor.

The basic contours of the Trump presidency are already knowable: the elevation of a politics based on racial division, with an agenda driven by personal hatred of the first black president; the systematic hollowing out of a functional, professional federal government, department by department; the disregard for seasoned, expert advice in the realm of military, foreign, and scientific affairs; the desire, frequently consummated, to divert the course of impartial justice and subject it to political control; the addition of cruelty to the federal-policy toolkit pertaining to people of color, immigrants, the poor, the sick, and many others; the willingness to sway opinion through lies, fear, and mockery; and the attacks on the press as an "enemy of the people," recycling Orwellian language to discredit independent sources of objective information and actual truth.

THE CORONAVIRUS CALLED AMERICA'S BLUFF

by Anne Applebaum

[MARCH 2020]

Even before it reached its peak, the coronavirus pandemic had made a number of things clear. One was that the United States was not as good at dealing with an emergency of this kind as we had thought we would be—and was not as good as many other countries. Another was that the administration did not excel at long-term planning or troubleshooting, and did not value the public-health bureaucracy. The president ignored the crisis for more than a month. Confronted with its severity, he failed to acquire needed equipment; left states to fend for themselves; and lost patience with the steady and sustained measures that experts advocated—even encouraging his supporters to protest against them.

The coronavirus pandemic has illustrated what happens when a culture of blind fear and fawning loyalty saturates the highest reaches of government—a culture in this instance demanded by the president himself. "Within a loyalty cult," wrote *Atlantic* staff writer Anne Applebaum in the early days of the crisis, "no one will tell the president that starting widespread emergency testing would be prudent, because anyone who does is at risk of losing the president's favor, even of being fired. Not that it matters, because Trump has very few truth-tellers around him anymore."

On July 8, 1853, Commodore Matthew Perry of the U.S. Navy sailed into Tokyo Bay with two steamships and two sailing vessels under his command. He landed a squadron of heavily armed sailors and marines; he moved one of the ships ostentatiously up the harbor, so that more people could see it. He delivered a letter from President Millard Fillmore demanding that the Japanese open up their ports to American trade. As they left, Perry's fleets fired their guns into the ether. In the port, people were terrified: "It sounded like distant thunder," a contemporary diarist wrote at the time, "and the mountains echoed back the noise of the shots. This was so formidable that the people in Edo [modern Tokyo] were fearful."

But the noise was not the only thing that frightened the Japanese. The Perry expedition famously convinced them that their political system was incapable of coping with new kinds of threats. Secure in their island homeland, the rulers of Japan had been convinced for decades of their cultural superiority. Japan was unique, special, the homeland of the gods. "Japan's position, at the vertex of the earth, makes it the standard for the nations of the world," the nationalist thinker Aizawa Seishisai wrote nearly three decades before Perry's arrival. But the steamships and the guns changed all that. Suddenly, the Japanese realized that their culture, their political system, and their technology were out of date. Their samurai-warrior leaders and honor culture were not able to compete in a world dominated by science.

————————

The coronavirus pandemic is in its early days. But the scale and force of the economic and medical crisis that is about to hit the United States may turn out to be as formidable as Perry's famous voyage was. Two weeks ago—it already seems like an infinity—I was in Italy, writing about the first signs of the virus. Epidemics, I wrote, "have a way of revealing underlying truths about the societies they impact." This one has already done so, and with terrifying speed. What it reveals about the United States—not just this administration, but also our health-care system, our bureaucracy, our political system itself—should make

Americans as fearful as the Japanese who heard the "distant thunder" of Perry's guns.

Not everybody has yet realized this, and indeed, it will take some time, just as it has taken time for the nature of the virus to sink in. At the moment, many Americans are still convinced that, even in this crisis, our society is more capable than others. Quite a lot was written about the terrifying and reckless behavior of the authorities in Wuhan, China, who initially threatened doctors who began posting information about the new virus, forcing them into silence.

On the very day that one of those doctors, Li Wenliang, contracted the virus, the Wuhan Municipal Health Commission issued a statement declaring, "So far no infection [has been] found among medical staff, no proof of human-to-human transmission." Only three weeks after the initial reports were posted did authorities begin to take the spread of the disease seriously, confirming that human-to-human transmission had in fact occurred. And only three days later did the lockdown of the city, and eventually the entire province, actually begin.

This story has been told repeatedly—and correctly—as an illustration of what's wrong with the Chinese system: The secrecy and mania for control inside the Communist Party lost the government many days during which it could have put a better plan into place. But many of those recounting China's missteps have become just a little bit too smug.

The United States also had an early warning of the new virus—but it, too, suppressed that information. In late January, just as instances of COVID-19, the disease caused by the coronavirus, began to appear in the United States, an infectious-disease specialist in Seattle, Helen Y. Chu, realized that she had a way to monitor its presence. She had been collecting nasal swabs from people in and around Seattle as part of a flu study, and proposed checking them for the new virus. State and federal officials rejected that idea, citing privacy concerns and throwing up bureaucratic obstacles related to lab licenses.

Finally, at the end of February, Chu could stand the intransigence no longer. Her lab performed some tests and found the coronavirus in a local teenager who had not traveled overseas. That meant the disease was already spreading in the Seattle region among people who had never been abroad. If Chu had found this information a month earlier, lives might have been saved and the spread of the disease might have slowed—but even after the urgency of her work became evident, her lab was told to stop testing.

———

Chu was not threatened by the government, like Li had been in Wuhan. But she was just as effectively silenced by a rule-bound bureaucracy that was insufficiently worried about the pandemic—and by officials at the Food and Drug Administration and the Centers for Disease Control and Prevention who may even have felt political pressure not to take this disease as seriously as they should.

We all now know that COVID-19 diagnostic tests are in scarce supply. South Korea, which has had exactly the same amount of time as the U.S. to prepare, is capable of administering 10,000 tests every day. The United States, with a population more than six times larger, had only tested about 10,000 people in total as of March 13. Vietnam, a poor country, has tested more people than the United States. During congressional testimony on March 12, Anthony Fauci, the most distinguished infectious-disease doctor in the nation, described the American testing system as "failing." "The idea of anybody getting [tested] easily the way people in other countries are doing it? We're not set up for that," he said. "Do I think we should be? Yes, but we're not."

And why not? Once again, no officials from the Chinese Communist Party instructed anyone in the United States not to carry out testing. Nobody prevented American public officials from ordering the immediate production of a massive number of tests. Nevertheless, they did not. We don't know all the details yet, but one element of the situation cannot be denied: The president himself did not want the disease talked of too widely, did not want knowledge of it to spread, and, above all, did not want the numbers of those infected to appear too high. He said so himself, while explaining why he didn't want a cruise ship full of infected Americans to dock in California. "I like the numbers being where they are," he said. "I don't need to have the numbers double because of one ship that wasn't our fault."

Donald Trump, just like the officials in Wuhan, was concerned about the numbers—the optics of how a pandemic looks. And everybody around him knew it. There are some indications that Alex Azar, the former pharmaceutical-industry executive and lobbyist who heads the Department of Health and Human Services, was not keen on telling the president things he did not want to hear. Here is how Dan Diamond, a *Politico* reporter who writes about health policy, delicately described the problem in a radio interview: "My understanding is [that Azar] did not push to do aggressive additional testing in recent weeks, and that's partly because more testing might have led to more cases being discovered of coronavirus outbreak, and the president had made clear—the lower the numbers on coronavirus, the better for the president, the better for his potential reelection this fall."

Once again: Nobody threatened Azar. But fear of offending the president may have led him to hesitate to push for aggressive testing nevertheless.

Without the threats and violence of the Chinese system, in other words, we have the same results: scientists not allowed to do their job; public-health officials not pushing for aggressive testing; preparedness delayed; all because too many people feared that it might damage the political prospects of the leader. I am not writing this in order to praise Chinese communism—far from it. I am writing this so that Americans understand that our government is producing some of the same outcomes as Chinese communism. This means that our political system is in far, far worse shape than we have hitherto understood.

What if it turns out, as it almost certainly will, that other nations are far better than we are at coping with this kind of catastrophe? Look at Singapore, which immediately created an app that could physically track everyone who was quarantined, and that energetically tracked down all the contacts of everyone identified to have the disease. Look at South Korea, with its proven testing ability. Look at Germany, where Chancellor Angela Merkel managed to speak honestly and openly about the disease—she predicted that 70 percent of Germans would get it—and yet did not crash the markets.

The United States, long accustomed to thinking of itself as the best, most efficient, and most technologically advanced society in the world, is about to be proved an unclothed emperor. When human life is in peril, we are not as good as Singapore, as South Korea, as Germany. And the problem is not that we are behind technologically, as the Japanese were in 1853. The problem is that American bureaucracies, and the antiquated, hidebound, unloved federal government of which they are part, are no longer up to the job of coping with the kinds of challenges that face us in the 21st century. Global pandemics, cyberwarfare, information warfare—these are threats that require highly motivated, highly educated bureaucrats; a national health-care system that covers the entire population; public schools that train students to think both deeply and flexibly; and much more.

The failures of the moment can be partly ascribed to the loyalty culture that Trump himself has spent three years building in Washington. Only two weeks ago, he named his 29-year-old former bodyguard, a man who was previously fired from the White House for financial shenanigans, to head up a new personnel-vetting team. Its role is to ensure that only people certifiably loyal are allowed to work for the president. Trump also fired, ostentatiously, the officials who testified honestly during the impeachment hearings, an action that sends a signal to others about the danger of truth-telling.

––––––––––

These are only the most recent manifestations of an autocratic style that has been described, over and over again, by many people. And now we see why, exactly, that style is so dangerous, and why previous American presidents, of both political parties, have operated much differently. Within a loyalty cult, no one will tell the president that starting widespread emergency testing would be prudent, because anyone who does is at risk of losing the president's favor, even of being fired. Not that it matters, because Trump has very few truth-tellers around him anymore. The kinds of people who would dare make the president angry have left the upper ranks of the Cabinet and the bureaucracy already.

But some of what we are seeing is unrelated to Trump. American dysfunction is also the result of our bifurcated health-care system, which is both the best in the world and the worst in the world, and is simply not geared up for any kind of collective national response. The present crisis is the result of decades of underinvestment in civil service, of undervaluing bureaucracy in public health and other areas, and, above all, of underrating the value of long-term planning.

Back from 2001 to 2003, I wrote multiple editorials for *The Washington Post* about biological warfare and pandemic preparedness—issues that were at the top of everyone's agenda in the wake of 9/11 and the brief anthrax scare. At the time, some very big investments were made into precisely those issues, especially into scientific research. We will now benefit from them. But in recent years, the subjects fell out of the news. Senators, among them the vaunted Republican moderate Susan Collins of Maine, knocked "pandemic preparedness" out of spending bills. New flu epidemics didn't scare people enough. More recently, Trump eliminated the officials responsible for international health from the National Security Council because this kind of subject didn't interest him—or very many other people in Washington, really.

As a nation, we are not good at long-term planning, and no wonder: Our political system insists that every president be allowed to appoint thousands of new officials, including the kinds of officials who think about pandemics. Why is that necessary? Why can't expertise be allowed to accumulate at the highest levels of agencies such as the CDC? I've written before about the problem of discontinuity in foreign policy: New presidents arrive and think they can have a "reset" with other nations, as if other nations are going to forget everything that happened before their arrival—as if we can cheerfully start all relationships from scratch. But the same is true on health, the environment, and other policy issues. Of course there should be new Cabinet members every four or eight years. But should all their deputies change? And their deputies' deputies? And their deputies' deputies' deputies? Because that's often how it works right now.

All of this happens on top of all the other familiar pathologies: the profound polarization; the merger of politics and entertainment; the loss of faith in democratic institutions; the blind eyes turned to corruption, white-collar crime, and money laundering; the growth of inequality; the conversion of social media and a part of the news media into for-profit vectors of disinformation. These are all part of the deep background to this crisis too.

The question, of course, is whether this crisis will shock us enough to change our ways. The Japanese did eventually react to Commodore Perry's squadron of ships with something more than fear. They stopped talking about themselves as the vertex of the Earth. They overhauled their education system. They adopted Western scientific methods, reorganized their state, and created a modern bureaucracy. This massive change, known as the Meiji Restoration, is what brought Japan, for better or for worse, into the modern world. Naturally, the old samurai-warrior class fought back against it, bitterly and angrily.

But by then the new threat was so obvious that enough people got it, enough people understood that a national mobilization was necessary, enough people understood that things could not go on that way indefinitely. Could it happen here, too?

DONALD TRUMP
AND THE POLITICS
OF FEAR

by Molly Ball

[SEPTEMBER 2016]

Revisiting the period before Donald Trump was elected offers a reminder that fear, in one form or another, has been bound up with his message and persona from the beginning. On the debate stage, other Republican presidential candidates shrank before Trump's bullying and bluster. During the campaign, Trump played on many kinds of fear: fear of immigrants, fear of Muslims, fear of terrorism, fear of change.

Molly Ball, *Time* magazine's national political correspondent and a former staff writer at *The Atlantic*, described how American politicians in the past have exploited fear ("Fear is easy," one veteran political ad maker told her). Writing before the 2016 election, Ball speculated that a campaign built around fear—in all its many guises—might be the only way for Trump to win.

"People are scared," Donald Trump said recently, and he was not wrong.

Fear is in the air, and fear is surging. Americans are more afraid today than they have been in a long time: Polls show majorities of Americans worried about being victims of terrorism and crime, numbers that have surged over the past year to highs not seen for more than a decade. Every week seems to bring a new large- or small-scale terrorist attack, at home or abroad. Mass shootings form a constant drumbeat. Protests have shut down large cities repeatedly, and some have turned violent. Overall crime rates may be down, but a sense of disorder is constant.

Fear pervades Americans' lives—and American politics. Trump is a master of fear, invoking it in concrete and abstract ways, summoning and validating it. More than most politicians, he grasps and channels the fear coursing through the electorate.

———————

Fear and anger are often cited in tandem as the sources of Trump's particular political appeal, so frequently paired that they become a refrain: *fear and anger, anger and fear*. But fear is not the same as anger; it is a unique political force. Its ebbs and flows through American political history have pulled on elections, reordering and destabilizing the electoral landscape.

On August 31, Trump delivered a speech on immigration that depicted outsiders as a frightening threat. "Countless innocent American lives have been stolen because our politicians have failed in their duty to secure our borders," he said. His acceptance speech at the Republican National Convention similarly made clear the extent to which his message revolves around fear. "The attacks on our police, and the terrorism in our cities, threaten our very way of life," Trump thundered. "Any politician who does not grasp this danger is not fit to lead our country. Americans watching this address tonight have seen the recent images of violence in our streets and the chaos in our communities. Many have witnessed this violence personally; some have even been its victims."

Notes of uplift were few and far between in the convention speech, and commentators were duly shocked by its dark tone. (The conservative writer Reed Galen called Trump's convention "a fear-fueled acid trip.") Trump summons fear in the conventional way, by describing in concrete terms the threats Americans face. But he also, in a more unusual maneuver, summons fear in the abstract: *There's something going on, folks.*

The critics who accuse Trump of cheap fear-mongering may be failing to recognize that the fear percolating in society is real, and somewhat justified; politicians who fail to validate it risk falling out of step with the zeitgeist. They are likely right, however, that ratcheting up fear helps Trump. This is the way fear works, according to social scientists: It makes people hold more tightly to what they have and regard the unfamiliar more warily. It makes them want to be protected. The fear reaction is a universal one to which everyone is susceptible. It might even be the only way Trump could win.

If the normal categories hold in this election—the patterns of turnout, the states in play, the partisan and demographic divides—Trump will find it almost impossible to prevail. The current polls show him losing in just such a predictable way, dogged by his offenses against various groups. But fear, history shows, has the power to jar voters out of their normal categories.

Trump paints a fearful picture, and events validate his vision. This is what happened in the Republican primary: When back-to-back terror attacks hit Paris in November and San Bernardino, California, in December, he pointed to them as proof that his warnings about Muslims were justified, and voters flocked to him, boosting and solidifying his polling lead in the final stretch before primary voting began. Trump's standing in the polls rose about 7 percentage points in the aftermath of the attacks, buoying him to the level necessary to win primary contests.

Trump supporters, recent polling has shown, are disproportionately fearful. They fear crime and terror far more than other Americans; they are also disproportionately wary of foreign influence and social change. (They are not, however, any more likely than other Americans to express economic anxiety.)

"I used to fly a lot, but now I don't get on an airplane unless I have to," Pat Garverick, a retired tech worker, told me at a recent Trump rally in Northern Virginia. "There's that little voice in the back of your head that says, 'Is this safe?' I try to stay away from crowds. There are so many people trying to hurt us or stir up violence."

Not all the Trump supporters I have asked in recent months say they feel afraid. One woman told me, "I'm not scared; I'm pissed off." Others cited less immediate fears: They say they are afraid for their country or their children's future. But many cited a visceral sense of insecurity. "I am terrified," confided Jonnianne Ridzelski, whom I met at a Trump rally in Alabama in April. She had, she said, been making preparations for disaster, including stocking up on canned food.

What, exactly, was she afraid of? She couldn't say, and that was perhaps the most frightening thing of all. "I don't know what's going to happen," she said.

While anger makes people aggressive, prone to lash out, fear makes them cower from the unfamiliar and seek refuge and comfort. Trump channels people's anger, but he salves their fear with promises of protection, toughness, strength. It is a feedback loop: He stirs up people's latent fears, then offers himself as the only solution.

Frightened people come to Trump for reassurance, and he promises to make them feel safe. "I'm scared," a 12-year-old girl told the candidate at a rally in North Carolina in December. "What are you going to do to protect this country?"

"You know what, darling?" Trump replied. "You're not going to be scared anymore. *They're* going to be scared."

———

To the seasoned political practitioner, fear is a handy tool. "Fear is easy," Rick Wilson, a Florida-based Republican ad maker, told me recently. "Fear is the simplest emotion to tweak in a campaign ad. You associate your opponent with terror, with fear, with crime, with causing pain and uncertainty."

Wilson has plenty of experience. In 2002, he made a commercial that criticized Democratic Senator Max Cleland, who had lost three limbs in Vietnam, while showing images of Saddam Hussein and Osama bin Laden. In 2008, Wilson made ads attacking Barack Obama by showing the incendiary statements of his former pastor, Jeremiah Wright. "I wanted to scare the living shit out of white people in Pennsylvania and Ohio," Wilson said. "Today, they would all be Trump voters, I'm sure."

Fear-based appeals hit people on a primitive level, Wilson said. "When people are under stress, the hind brain takes over," he said. Trump, Wilson believes, has expertly manipulated many people's latent fear of the other. "Fear of Mexicans, fear of the Chinese, fear of African Americans—Donald Trump has very deliberately stoked it and inflamed it and made it a centerpiece of his campaign," he told me.

A majority of Americans now worry that they or their families will be victims of terrorism, up from a third less than two years ago, according to a survey by the Public Religion Research Institute. Nearly two-thirds worry about being victims of violent crime. Another poll, by Gallup, found that concern about crime and violence is at its highest level in 15 years.

Trump supporters are more concerned than most. According to further PRRI data, 65 percent of Trump supporters fear being victims of terrorism, versus 51 percent of all Americans. Three-fourths of Trump supporters fear being victims of crime, versus 63 percent overall. Trump supporters also disproportionately fear foreign influence: 83 percent say the American way of life needs to be protected from it, versus 55 percent overall. Two-thirds of Trump supporters also worry that they or a family member will become unemployed, but this is not much different than the 63 percent of non–Trump supporters who have the same concern. Economic anxiety, while widespread in America today, is not a distinguishing characteristic of Trump supporters; other anxieties are.

Trump's audience of conservative-leaning voters may be particularly susceptible to fear-based appeals. Researchers have found that those who are more sensitive to threats and more wary of the unfamiliar tend to be more politically conservative. "The common basis for all the various components of the conservative attitude syndrome is a generalized susceptibility to experiencing threat or anxiety in the face of uncertainty," the British psychologist G. D. Wilson wrote in his 1973 book, *The Psychology of Conservatism*. In other words, an innate fear of uncertainty tends to correlate to people's level of conservatism.

Subsequent experiments have confirmed this idea. In a 2003 paper reviewing five decades of research across 12 different countries, the psychologist John Jost and his collaborators found "the psychological management of uncertainty and fear" to be strongly and consistently correlated with politically conservative attitudes. (This "fear of threat," however, is not the same as anxiety in the sense of neuroticism, which correlates strongly with liberal political attitudes.)

In study after study, the characteristic most predictive of a person's political leanings is his or her tolerance for ambiguity. "The more intolerant of ambiguity you are—the more you seek control over your surroundings, certainty, clear answers to things—the more you tend toward conservative preferences," Anat Shenker, a liberal communications consultant and cognitive-linguistics researcher, told me.

But it is not only conservatives who are susceptible to fear. Almost all of us exist somewhere on the continuum between the extremes of "totally averse to the unfamiliar" and "totally enthusiastic about the unknown." Experiments find that everyone's political views become more conservative when they are provoked to become more fearful. In one study, liberal subjects who had just been confronted with a threat immediately reported more conservative views on abortion, capital punishment, and gay rights.

If fear is strong enough, it can accomplish something exceedingly rare: It can override people's preexisting partisan commitments. This happened in the wake of the September 11 attacks: Political scientists say Republicans' success in the 2002 and 2004 elections can be largely attributed to Americans' increased fear of terrorism. "There is evidence from 2002 and 2004 that people's concern about terror was a very good predictor of their voting habits, even apart from partisanship," Shana Gadarian, a political scientist at Syracuse University and the author of *The Politics of Threat: How Terrorism News Shapes Foreign Policy Attitudes*, told me. (Democrats, Gadarian notes, also use fear to push their agenda on issues with which they're associated, like climate change and health care.)

Shenker makes the case that the world is changing these days more quickly than any of us are inherently equipped to handle. "The modern condition of life is pretty much an assault on our brains," she told me. "We're experiencing change and ambiguity at a rate unprecedented in human history. Think about how long it took to get from the agricultural revolution to the industrial revolution. And now all of a sudden the climate is changing, women are becoming men, I'm talking to you on a little sliver of plastic and metal. We have change in every dimension faster than our brains have evolved to deal with it." In studying Trump voters on behalf of MoveOn.org, Shenker found that they responded strongly to the idea that he would bring order and control to a chaotic world.

Gadarian, the political scientist, said, "When people feel anxious, they want to be protected." Trump's policies, she pointed out, are a literal answer to this desire: protectionist economics; a wall that physically protects the country from outsiders. "How do you overcome the threat of terror, of crime, of immigration? You say, 'We will protect the country by building a wall.'"

Here is a case study in the power of fear in politics. Immigration reform has seemed ripe for bipartisan compromise ever since President George W. Bush tried to pass it during his second term. Majorities of voters consistently say they support allowing undocumented immigrants to become citizens, and oppose mass deportation. Yet the policy has been derailed by intense, concentrated, visceral opposition. Meanwhile, the reaction to mass migration has upended the politics of virtually every European nation, including the U.K., France, and the Scandinavian countries.

Frank Sharry, a proponent of immigration reform who heads the group America's Voice, has worked on the issue since the 1980s, but the rise of Trump forced him to revise his understanding. What had always seemed to him like a policy dispute now strikes him as something more profound and primal, he told me.

"Ten years ago, when [John] McCain and [Ted] Kennedy were working together on comprehensive immigration reform and George W. Bush supported it, I really thought this was a rational policy disagreement that was headed toward a logical compromise," Sharry told me recently. "Now I see it as deeply cultural. It's racially charged, it's

tribalism, it's us-versus-them. It's a referendum on the face of globalization, on a moment of demographic and cultural change."

There are legitimate policy arguments against increasing immigration or legalizing the undocumented, but Sharry came to believe that
they were not the drivers of opposition to the issue. Once you see fear
as an axis, it resonates across any number of political debates. The fearful mind sees immigrants as an invasion force, refugees as terrorists,
rising crime as a threat to one's family, drugs as a threat to one's children, and social change as a threat to one's way of life. Almost everyone
is somewhat susceptible to fear's appeal; those naturally inclined to be
conservative are somewhat more so. But it takes a particular type of
politician to push the buttons in human nature that activate these fears.

"Some people's sense of who we are as a country is threatened to the
core," Sharry said. "Trump speaks to our id, something latent in all of
us to different degrees. This is not a political campaign. It's an identity
campaign."

THE FIRST WHITE PRESIDENT

by Ta-Nehisi Coates

[OCTOBER 2017]

The fears stoked by Donald Trump during his presidential campaign and now in his presidency cannot be separated from appeals to white voters that carry the stain and lash of racism—that is the case made by Ta-Nehisi Coates in "The First White President," an article published as part of a 2017 special issue of *The Atlantic*, "The Trump Presidency: A Damage Report."

Coates is the author of the best-selling books *The Beautiful Struggle: A Father, Two Sons, and an Unlikely Road to Manhood* (2008); *Between the World and Me* (2015); and *We Were Eight Years in Power: An American Tragedy* (2017), from which the article here was adapted. In a relentless and haunting indictment, Coates argued in *The Atlantic* that Donald Trump's presidency has been predicated almost entirely on the negation of a black president. He rejected the idea that Trump rode into office primarily on pent-up working-class resentment over economic dislocation and decline.

And he warned that the constituencies Trump activated are not going away. "To Trump," Coates wrote, "whiteness is neither notional nor symbolic but is the very core of his power. In this, Trump is not singular. But whereas his forebears carried whiteness like an ancestral talisman, Trump cracked the glowing amulet open, releasing its eldritch energies."

It is insufficient to state the obvious of Donald Trump: that he is a white man who would not be president were it not for this fact. With one immediate exception, Trump's predecessors made their way to high office through the passive power of whiteness—that bloody heirloom which cannot ensure mastery of all events but can conjure a tailwind for most of them. Land theft and human plunder cleared the grounds for Trump's forefathers and barred others from it. Once upon the field, these men became soldiers, statesmen, and scholars; held court in Paris; presided at Princeton; advanced into the Wilderness and then into the White House. Their individual triumphs made this exclusive party seem above America's founding sins, and it was forgotten that the former was in fact bound to the latter, that all their victories had transpired on cleared grounds. No such elegant detachment can be attributed to Donald Trump—a president who, more than any other, has made the awful inheritance explicit.

His political career began in advocacy of birtherism, that modern recasting of the old American precept that black people are not fit to be citizens of the country they built. But long before birtherism, Trump had made his worldview clear. He fought to keep blacks out of his buildings, according to the U.S. government; called for the death penalty for the eventually exonerated Central Park Five; and railed against "lazy" black employees. "Black guys counting my money! I hate it," Trump was once quoted as saying. "The only kind of people I want counting my money are short guys that wear yarmulkes every day." After his cabal of conspiracy theorists forced Barack Obama to present his birth certificate, Trump demanded the president's college grades (offering $5 million in exchange for them), insisting that Obama was not intelligent enough to have gone to an Ivy League school, and that his acclaimed memoir, *Dreams from My Father*, had been ghostwritten by a white man, Bill Ayers.

It is often said that Trump has no real ideology, which is not true—his ideology is white supremacy, in all its truculent and sanctimonious power. Trump inaugurated his campaign by casting himself as the defender of white maidenhood against Mexican "rapists," only to be later alleged by multiple accusers, and by his own proud words, to be a sexual violator himself. White supremacy has always had a perverse sexual tint. Trump's rise was shepherded by Steve Bannon, a man who mocks his white male critics as "cucks." The word, derived from *cuckold*, is specifically meant to debase by fear and fantasy—the target is so weak that he would submit to the humiliation of having his white wife lie with black men. That the slur *cuck* casts white men as victims aligns with the dicta of whiteness, which seek to alchemize one's profligate sins into virtue. So it was with Virginia slaveholders claiming that Britain sought to make slaves of them. So it was with marauding Klansmen organized against alleged rapes and other outrages. So it was with a candidate who called for a foreign power to hack his opponent's email and who now, as president, is claiming to be the victim of "the single greatest witch hunt of a politician in American history."

In Trump, white supremacists see one of their own. Only grudgingly did Trump denounce the Ku Klux Klan and David Duke, one of its former grand wizards—and after the clashes between white supremacists and counterprotesters in Charlottesville, Virginia, in August, Duke in turn praised Trump's contentious claim that "both sides" were responsible for the violence.

To Trump, whiteness is neither notional nor symbolic but is the very core of his power. In this, Trump is not singular. But whereas his forebears carried whiteness like an ancestral talisman, Trump cracked the glowing amulet open, releasing its eldritch energies. The repercussions are striking: Trump is the first president to have served in no public capacity before ascending to his perch. But more telling, Trump is also the first president to have publicly affirmed that his daughter is a "piece of ass." The mind seizes trying to imagine a black man extolling the virtues of sexual assault on tape ("When you're a star, they let you do it"), fending off multiple accusations of such assaults, immersed in multiple lawsuits for allegedly fraudulent business dealings, exhorting his followers to violence, and then strolling into the White House. But that is the point of white supremacy—to ensure that that which all others achieve with maximal effort, white people (particularly white men) achieve with minimal qualification. Barack Obama delivered to black people the hoary message that if they work twice as hard as white people, anything is possible. But Trump's counter is persuasive: Work half as hard as black people, and even more is possible.

For Trump, it almost seems that the fact of Obama, the fact of a black president, insulted him personally. The insult intensified when Obama and Seth Meyers publicly humiliated him at the White House Correspondents' Dinner in 2011. But the bloody heirloom ensures the last laugh. Replacing Obama is not enough—Trump has made the negation of Obama's legacy the foundation of his own. And this, too, is whiteness. "Race is an idea, not a fact," the historian Nell Irvin Painter has written, and essential to the construct of a "white race" is the idea of not being a nigger. Before Barack Obama, niggers could be manufactured out of Sister Souljahs, Willie Hortons, and Dusky Sallys. But Donald Trump arrived in the wake of something more potent—an entire nigger presidency with nigger health care, nigger climate accords, and nigger justice reform, all of which could be targeted for destruction or redemption, thus reifying the idea of being white. Trump truly is something new—the first president whose entire political existence hinges on the fact of a black president. And so it will not suffice to say that Trump is a white man like all the others who rose to become president. He must be called by his rightful honorific—America's first white president.

—————

The scope of Trump's commitment to whiteness is matched only by the depth of popular disbelief in the power of whiteness. We are now being told that support for Trump's "Muslim ban," his scapegoating of immigrants, his defenses of police brutality are somehow the natural outgrowth of the cultural and economic gap between Lena Dunham's America and Jeff Foxworthy's. The collective verdict holds that the Democratic Party lost its way when it abandoned everyday economic issues like job creation for the softer fare of social justice. The indictment continues: To their neoliberal economics, Democrats and liberals have married a condescending elitist affect that sneers at blue-collar culture and mocks the white man as history's greatest monster and prime-time television's biggest doofus. In this rendition, Donald Trump is not the product of white supremacy so much as the product of a backlash against contempt for white working-class people.

"We so obviously despise them, we so obviously condescend to them," the conservative social scientist Charles Murray, who co-wrote *The Bell Curve*, recently told *The New Yorker*, speaking of the white working class. "The only slur you can use at a dinner party and get away with is to call somebody a redneck—that won't give you any problems in Manhattan."

"The utter contempt with which privileged Eastern liberals such as myself discuss red-state, gun-country, working-class America as ridiculous and morons and rubes," charged the celebrity chef Anthony Bourdain, "is largely responsible for the upswell of rage and contempt and desire to pull down the temple that we're seeing now."

That black people, who have lived for centuries under such derision and condescension, have not yet been driven into the arms of Trump does not trouble these theoreticians. After all, in this analysis, Trump's racism and the racism of his supporters are incidental to his rise. Indeed, the alleged glee with which liberals call out Trump's bigotry is assigned even more power than the bigotry itself. Ostensibly assaulted by campus protests, battered by arguments about intersectionality, and oppressed by new bathroom rights, a blameless white working class did the only thing any reasonable polity might: elect an orcish reality-television star who insists on taking his intelligence briefings in picture-book form.

Asserting that Trump's rise was primarily powered by cultural resentment and economic reversal has become de rigueur among white pundits and thought leaders. But evidence for this is, at best, mixed. In a study of pre-election polling data, the Gallup researchers Jonathan Rothwell and Pablo Diego-Rosell found that "people living in areas with diminished economic opportunity" were "somewhat more likely to support Trump." But the researchers also found that voters in their study who supported Trump generally had a higher mean household income ($81,898) than those who did not ($77,046). Those who approved of Trump were "less likely to be unemployed and less likely to be employed part-time" than those who did not. They also tended to be from areas that were very white: "The racial and ethnic isolation of whites at the zip code level is one of the strongest predictors of Trump support."

An analysis of exit polls conducted during the presidential primaries estimated the median household income of Trump supporters to be about $72,000. But even this lower number is almost double the median household income of African Americans, and $15,000 above the American median. Trump's white support was not determined by income. According to Edison Research, Trump won whites making less than $50,000 by 20 points, whites making $50,000 to $99,999 by 28 points, and whites making $100,000 or more by 14 points. This shows that Trump assembled a broad white coalition that ran the gamut from Joe the Dishwasher to Joe the Plumber to Joe the Banker. So when white pundits cast the elevation of Trump as the handiwork of an inscrutable white working class, they are being too modest, declining to claim credit for their own economic class. Trump's dominance among whites across class lines is of a piece with his larger dominance across nearly every white demographic. Trump won white women (+9) and white men (+31). He won white people with college degrees (+3) and white people without them (+37). He won whites ages 18–29 (+4), 30–44 (+17), 45–64 (+28), and 65 and older (+19). Trump won whites in midwestern Illinois (+11), whites in mid-Atlantic New Jersey (+12), and whites in the Sun Belt's New Mexico (+5). In no state that Edison polled did Trump's white support dip below 40 percent. Hillary Clinton's did, in states as disparate as Florida, Utah, Indiana, and Kentucky. From the beer track to the wine track, from soccer moms to NASCAR dads, Trump's performance among whites was dominant. According to *Mother Jones*, based on pre-election polling data, if you tallied the popular vote of only white America to derive 2016 electoral votes, Trump would have defeated Clinton 389 to 81, with the remaining 68 votes either a toss-up or unknown.

Part of Trump's dominance among whites resulted from his running as a Republican, the party that has long cultivated white voters. Trump's share of the white vote was similar to Mitt Romney's in 2012. But unlike Romney, Trump secured this support by running against his party's leadership, against accepted campaign orthodoxy, and against all notions of decency. By his sixth month in office, embroiled in scandal after scandal, a Pew Research Center poll found Trump's approval rating underwater with every single demographic group. Every demographic group, that is, except one: people who identified as white.

The focus on one subsector of Trump voters—the white working class—is puzzling, given the breadth of his white coalition. Indeed, there is a kind of theater at work in which Trump's presidency is pawned off as a product of the white working class as opposed to a product of an entire whiteness that includes the very authors doing the pawning. The motive is clear: escapism. To accept that the bloody heirloom remains potent even now, some five decades after Martin Luther King Jr. was gunned down on a Memphis balcony—even after a black president; indeed, strengthened by the fact of that black president—is to accept that racism remains, as it has since 1776, at the heart of this country's political life. The idea of acceptance frustrates the left. The left would much rather have a discussion about class struggles, which might entice the white working masses, instead of about the racist struggles that those same masses have historically been the agents and beneficiaries of. Moreover, to accept that whiteness brought us Donald Trump is to accept whiteness as an existential danger to the country and the world. But if the broad and remarkable white support for Donald Trump can be reduced to the righteous anger of a noble class of smallville firefighters and evangelicals, mocked by Brooklyn hipsters and womanist professors into voting against their interests, then the threat of racism and whiteness, the threat of the heirloom, can be dismissed. Consciences can be eased; no deeper existential reckoning is required.

This transfiguration is not novel. It is a return to form. The tightly intertwined stories of the white working class and black Americans go back to the prehistory of the United States—and the use of one as a cudgel to silence the claims of the other goes back nearly as far. Like the black working class, the white working class originated in bondage—the former in the lifelong bondage of slavery, the latter in the temporary bondage of indenture. In the early 17th century, these two classes were remarkably, though not totally, free of racist enmity. But by the 18th century, the country's master class had begun etching race into law while phasing out indentured servitude in favor of a more en-during labor solution. From these and other changes of law and econ-omy, a bargain emerged: The descendants of indenture would enjoy the full benefits of whiteness, the most definitional benefit being that they would never sink to the level of the slave. But if the bargain protected white workers from slavery, it did not protect them from near-slave wages or backbreaking labor to attain them, and always there lurked a fear of having their benefits revoked. This early white working class "expressed soaring desires to be rid of the age-old inequalities of Europe and of any hint of slavery," according to David R. Roediger, a professor of American studies at the University of Kansas. "They also expressed the rather more pedestrian goal of simply not being mistaken for slaves, or 'negers' or 'negurs.'"

Roediger relates the experience, around 1807, of a British investor who made the mistake of asking a white maid in New England whether her "master" was home. The maid admonished the investor, not merely for implying that she had a "master" and thus was a "sarvant" but for his basic ignorance of American hierarchy. "None but negers are sarvants," the maid is reported to have said. In law and economics and then in custom, a racist distinction not limited to the household emerged between the "help" (or the "freemen," or the white workers) and the "servants" (the "negers," the slaves). The former were virtuous and just, worthy of citizenship, progeny of Jefferson and, later, Jackson. The latter were servile and parasitic, dim-witted and lazy, the children of African savagery. But the dignity accorded to white labor was situa-tional, dependent on the scorn heaped upon black labor—much as the honor accorded a "virtuous lady" was dependent on the derision di-rected at a "loose woman." And like chivalrous gentlemen who claim to honor the lady while raping the "whore," planters and their apologists could claim to honor white labor while driving the enslaved.

And so George Fitzhugh, a prominent 19th-century Southern pro-slavery intellectual, could in a single stroke deplore the exploita-tion of free whites' labor while defending the exploitation of enslaved blacks' labor. Fitzhugh attacked white capitalists as "cannibals," feeding off the labor of their fellow whites. The white workers were "'slaves without masters;' the little fish, who were food for all the larger." Fitzhugh inveighed against a "professional man" who'd "amassed a fortune" by exploiting his fellow whites. But whereas Fitzhugh imagined white workers as devoured by capital, he imagined black workers as elevated by enslavement. The slaveholder "provided for them, with almost parental affection"—even when the loafing slave "feigned to be unfit for labor." Fitzhugh proved too explicit—going so far as to argue that white laborers might be better off if enslaved. ("If white slavery be morally wrong," he wrote, "the Bible cannot be true.") Nevertheless, the argument that America's original sin was not deep-seated white supremacy but rather the exploitation of white labor by white capitalists—"white slavery"—proved durable. Indeed, the panic of white slavery lives on in our politics today. Black workers suffer because it was and is our lot. But when white workers suffer, something in nature has gone awry. And so an opioid epidemic among mostly white people is greeted with calls for compassion and treatment, as all epidemics should be, while a crack epidemic among mostly black people is greeted with scorn and mandatory minimums. Sympathetic op-ed columns and articles are devoted to the plight of working-class whites when their life expectancy plummets to levels that, for blacks, society has simply accepted as normal. White slavery is sin. Nigger slavery is natural. This dynamic serves a very real purpose: the consistent awarding of grievance and moral high ground to that class of workers which, by the bonds of whiteness, stands closest to America's aristocratic class.

This is by design. Speaking in 1848, Senator John C. Calhoun saw slavery as the explicit foundation for a democratic union among whites, working and not:

> With us the two great divisions of society are not the rich and poor, but white and black; and all the former, the poor as well as the rich, belong to the upper class, and are respected and treated as equals.

On the eve of secession, Jefferson Davis, the eventual president of the Confederacy, pushed the idea further, arguing that such equality between the white working class and white oligarchs could not exist at all without black slavery:

> I say that the lower race of human beings that constitute the sub-stratum of what is termed the slave population of the South, elevates every white man in our community . . . It is the presence of a lower caste, those lower by their mental and physical organization, controlled by the higher intellect of the white man, that gives this superiority to the white laborer. Menial services are not there performed by the white man. We have none of our brethren sunk to the degradation of being menials. That belongs to the lower race—the descendants of Ham.

Southern intellectuals found a shade of agreement with Northern white reformers who, while not agreeing on slavery, agreed on the nature of the most tragic victim of emerging capitalism. "I was formerly like yourself, sir, a very warm advocate of the abolition of slavery," the labor reformer George Henry Evans argued in a letter to the abolitionist Gerrit Smith. "This was before I saw that there was *white* slavery." Evans was a putative ally of Smith and his fellow abolitionists. But still he asserted that "the landless white" was worse off than the enslaved black, who at least enjoyed "surety of support in sickness and old age."

Invokers of "white slavery" held that there was nothing unique in the enslavement of blacks when measured against the enslavement of all workers. What evil there was in enslavement resulted from its status as a subsidiary of the broader exploitation better seen among the country's noble laboring whites. Once the larger problem of white exploitation was solved, the dependent problem of black exploitation could be confronted or perhaps would fade away. Abolitionists focused on slavery were dismissed as "substitutionists" who wished to trade one form of slavery for another. "If I am less troubled concerning the Slavery prevalent in Charleston or New-Orleans," wrote the reformer Horace Greeley, "it is because I see so much Slavery in New-York, which appears to claim my first efforts."

Firsthand reports by white Union soldiers who witnessed actual slavery during the Civil War rendered the "white slavery" argument ridiculous. But its operating premises—white labor as noble archetype, and black labor as something else—lived on. This was a matter of rhetoric, not fact. The noble-white-labor archetype did not give white workers immunity from capitalism. It could not, in itself, break monopolies, alleviate white poverty in Appalachia or the South, or bring a decent wage to immigrant ghettos in the North. But the model for America's original identity politics was set. Black lives literally did not matter and could be cast aside altogether as the price of even incremental gains for the white masses. It was this juxtaposition that allowed Theodore Bilbo to campaign for the Senate in the 1930s as someone who would "raise the same kind of hell as President Roosevelt" and later endorse lynching black people to keep them from voting.

The juxtaposition between the valid and even virtuous interests of the "working class" and the invalid and pathological interests of black Americans was not the province merely of blatant white supremacists like Bilbo. The acclaimed scholar, liberal hero, and future senator Daniel Patrick Moynihan, in his time working for President Richard Nixon, approvingly quoted Nixon's formulation of the white working class: "A new voice" was beginning to make itself felt in the country. "It is a voice that has been silent too long," Nixon claimed, alluding to working-class whites. "It is a voice of people who have not taken to the streets before, who have not indulged in violence, who have not broken the law."

It had been only 18 years since the Cicero riots; eight years since Daisy and Bill Myers had been run out of Levittown, Pennsylvania; three years since Martin Luther King Jr. had been stoned while walking through Chicago's Marquette Park. But as the myth of the virtuous white working class was made central to American identity, its sins needed to be rendered invisible. The fact was, working-class whites had been agents of racist terrorism since at least the draft riots of 1863; terrorism could not be neatly separated from the racist animus found in every class of whites. Indeed, in the era of lynching, the daily newspapers often whipped up the fury of the white masses by invoking the last species of property that all white men held in common—white women. But to conceal the breadth of white racism, these racist outbursts were often disregarded or treated not as racism but as the unfortunate side effect of legitimate grievances against capital. By focusing on that sympathetic laboring class, the sins of whiteness itself were, and are still being, evaded.

When David Duke, the former grand wizard of the Ku Klux Klan, shocked the country in 1990 by almost winning one of Louisiana's seats in the U.S. Senate, the apologists came out once again. They elided the obvious—that Duke had appealed to the racist instincts of a state whose schools are, at this very moment, still desegregating—and instead decided that something else was afoot. "There is a tremendous amount of anger and frustration among working-class whites, particularly where there is an economic downturn," a researcher told the *Los Angeles Times*. "These people feel left out; they feel government is not responsive to them." By this logic, postwar America—with its booming economy and low unemployment—should have been an egalitarian utopia and not the violently segregated country it actually was.

But this was the past made present. It was not important to the apologists that a large swath of Louisiana's white population thought it was a good idea to send a white supremacist who once fronted a terrorist organization to the nation's capital. Nor was it important that blacks in Louisiana had long felt left out. What was important was the fraying of an ancient bargain, and the potential degradation of white workers to the level of "negers." "A viable left must find a way to differentiate itself strongly from such analysis," David Roediger, the University of Kansas professor, has written.

That challenge of differentiation has largely been ignored. Instead, an imagined white working class remains central to our politics and to our cultural understanding of those politics, not simply when it comes to addressing broad economic issues but also when it comes to addressing racism. At its most sympathetic, this belief holds that most Americans—regardless of race—are exploited by an unfettered capitalist economy. The key, then, is to address those broader patterns that afflict the masses of all races; the people who suffer from those patterns more than others (blacks, for instance) will benefit disproportionately from that which benefits everyone. "These days, what ails working-class and middle-class blacks and Latinos is not fundamentally different from what ails their white counterparts," Senator Barack Obama wrote in 2006:

> Downsizing, outsourcing, automation, wage stagnation, the dismantling of employer-based health-care and pension plans, and schools that fail to teach young people the skills they need to compete in a global economy.

Obama allowed that "blacks in particular have been vulnerable to these trends"—but less because of racism than for reasons of geography and job-sector distribution. This notion—raceless antiracism—marks the modern left, from the New Democrat Bill Clinton to the socialist Bernie Sanders. Few national liberal politicians have shown any recognition that there is something systemic and particular in the relationship between black people and their country that might require specific policy solutions.

In 2016, Hillary Clinton acknowledged the existence of systemic racism more explicitly than any of her modern Democratic predecessors. She had to—black voters remembered too well the previous Clinton administration, as well as her previous campaign. While her husband's administration had touted the rising-tide theory of economic growth, it did so while slashing welfare and getting "tough on crime," a phrase that stood for specific policies but also served as rhetorical bait for white voters. One is tempted to excuse Hillary Clinton from having to answer for the sins of her husband. But in her 2008 campaign, she evoked the old dichotomy between white workers and loafing blacks, claiming to be the representative of "hardworking Americans, white Americans." By the end of the 2008 primary campaign against Barack Obama, her advisers were hoping someone would uncover an apocryphal "whitey tape," in which an angry Michelle Obama was alleged to have used the slur. During Bill Clinton's presidential-reelection campaign in the mid-1990s, Hillary Clinton herself had endorsed the "super-predator" theory of William J. Bennett, John P. Walters, and John J. DiIulio Jr. This theory cast "inner-city" children of that era as "almost completely unmoralized" and the font of "a new generation of street criminals . . . the youngest, biggest and baddest generation any society has ever known." The "baddest generation" did not become super-predators. But by 2016, they were young adults, many of whom judged Hillary Clinton's newfound consciousness to be lacking.

It's worth asking why the country has not been treated to a raft of sympathetic portraits of this "forgotten" young black electorate, forsaken by a Washington bought off by Davos elites and special interests. The unemployment rate for young blacks (20.6 percent) in July 2016 was double that of young whites (9.9 percent). And since the late 1970s, William Julius Wilson and other social scientists following in his wake have noted the disproportionate effect that the decline in manufacturing jobs has had on African American communities. If anyone should be angered by the devastation wreaked by the financial sector and a government that declined to prosecute the perpetrators, it is African Americans—the housing crisis was one of the primary drivers in the past 20 years of the wealth gap between black families and the rest of the country. But the cultural condescension toward and economic anxiety of black people is not news. Toiling blacks are in their proper state; toiling whites raise the specter of white slavery.

Moreover, a narrative of long-neglected working-class black voters, injured by globalization and the financial crisis, forsaken by out-of-touch politicians, and rightfully suspicious of a return of Clintonism, does not serve to cleanse the conscience of white people for having elected Donald Trump. Only the idea of a long-suffering white working class can do that. And though much has been written about the distance between elites and "Real America," the existence of a class-transcending, mutually dependent tribe of white people is evident.

Joe Biden, then the vice president, last year:

"They're all the people I grew up with . . . And they're not racist. They're not sexist."

Bernie Sanders, senator and former candidate for president, last year:

"I come from the white working class, and I am deeply humiliated that the Democratic Party cannot talk to the people where
I came from."

Nicholas Kristof, the *New York Times* columnist, in February of this
year:

"My hometown, Yamhill, Ore., a farming community, is Trump
country, and I have many friends who voted for Trump. I think
they're profoundly wrong, but please don't dismiss them as hateful bigots."

These claims of origin and fidelity are not merely elite defenses of an
aggrieved class but also a sweeping dismissal of the concerns of those
who don't share kinship with white men. "You can't eat equality," asserts
Joe Biden—a statement worthy of someone unthreatened by the loss of
wages brought on by an unwanted pregnancy, a background-check box
at the bottom of a job application, or the deportation of a breadwinner.
Within a week of Sanders lambasting Democrats for not speaking to
"the people" where he "came from," he was making an example of a
woman who dreamed of representing the people where she came from.
Confronted with a young woman who hoped to become the second
Latina senator in American history, Sanders responded with a parody of
the Clinton campaign: "It is not good enough for someone to say, 'I'm a
woman! Vote for me!' No, that's not good enough . . . One of the struggles that you're going to be seeing in the Democratic Party is whether
we go beyond identity politics." The upshot—attacking one specimen
of identity politics after having invoked another—was unfortunate.

Other Sanders appearances proved even more alarming. On MSNBC,
he attributed Trump's success, in part, to his willingness to "not be politically correct." Sanders admitted that Trump had "said some outrageous
and painful things, but I think people are tired of the same old, same
old political rhetoric." Pressed on the definition of political correctness,

Sanders gave an answer Trump surely would have approved of. "What it means is you have a set of talking points which have been poll-tested and focus-group-tested," Sanders explained. "And that's what you say rather than what's really going on. And often, what you are not allowed to say are things which offend very, very powerful people."

This definition of political correctness was shocking coming from a politician of the left. But it matched a broader defense of Trump voters. "Some people think that the people who voted for Trump are racists and sexists and homophobes and just deplorable folks," Sanders said later. "I don't agree." This is not exculpatory. Certainly not every Trump voter is a white supremacist, just as not every white person in the Jim Crow South was a white supremacist. But every Trump voter felt it acceptable to hand the fate of the country over to one.

One can, to some extent, understand politicians' embracing a self-serving identity politics. Candidates for high office, such as Sanders, have to cobble together a coalition. The white working class is seen, understandably, as a large cache of potential votes, and capturing these votes requires eliding uncomfortable truths. But journalists have no such excuse. Again and again in the past year, Nicholas Kristof could be found pleading with his fellow liberals not to dismiss his old comrades in the white working class as bigots—even when their bigotry was evidenced in his own reporting. A visit to Tulsa, Oklahoma, finds Kristof wondering why Trump voters support a president who threatens to cut the programs they depend on. But the problem, according to Kristof's interviewees, isn't Trump's attack on benefits so much as an attack on *their* benefits. "There's a lot of wasteful spending, so cut other places," one man tells Kristof. When Kristof pushes his subjects to identify that wasteful spending, a fascinating target is revealed: "Obama phones," the products of a fevered conspiracy theory that turned a long-standing government program into a scheme through which the then-president gave away free cellphones to undeserving blacks. Kristof doesn't shift his analysis based on this comment and, aside from a one-sentence fact-check tucked between parentheses, continues on as though it were never said.

Observing a Trump supporter in the act of deploying racism does not much perturb Kristof. That is because his defenses of the innate goodness of Trump voters and of the innate goodness of the white working class are in fact defenses of neither. On the contrary, the white working class functions rhetorically not as a real community of people so much as a tool to quiet the demands of those who want a more inclusive America.

Mark Lilla's *New York Times* essay "The End of Identity Liberalism," published not long after last year's election, is perhaps the most profound example of this genre. Lilla denounces the perversion of liberalism into "a kind of moral panic about racial, gender and sexual identity," which distorted liberalism's message "and prevented it from becoming a unifying force capable of governing." Liberals have turned away from their working-class base, he says, and must look to the "pre-identity liberalism" of Bill Clinton and Franklin D. Roosevelt. You would never know from this essay that Bill Clinton was one of the most skillful identity politicians of his era—flying home to Arkansas to see a black man, the lobotomized Ricky Ray Rector, executed; upstaging Jesse Jackson at his own conference; signing the Defense of Marriage Act. Nor would you know that the "pre-identity" liberal champion Roosevelt depended on the literally lethal identity politics of the white-supremacist "solid South." The name Barack Obama does not appear in Lilla's essay, and he never attempts to grapple, one way or another, with the fact that it was identity politics—the possibility of the first black president—that brought a record number of black voters to the polls, winning the election for the Democratic Party, and thus enabling the deliverance of the ancient liberal goal of national health care. "Identity politics . . . is largely expressive, not persuasive," Lilla claims. "Which is why it never wins elections—but can lose them." That Trump ran and won on identity politics is beyond Lilla's powers of conception. What appeals to the white working class is ennobled. What appeals to black workers, and all others outside the tribe, is dastardly identitarianism. All politics are identity politics—except the politics of white people, the politics of the bloody heirloom.

White tribalism haunts even more-nuanced writers. George Packer's *New Yorker* essay "The Unconnected" is a lengthy plea for liberals to focus more on the white working class, a population that "has succumbed to the ills that used to be associated with the black urban 'underclass.'" Packer believes that these ills, and the Democratic Party's failure to respond to them, explain much of Trump's rise. Packer offers no opinion polls to weigh white workers' views on "elites," much less their views on racism. He offers no sense of how their views and their relationship to Trump differ from other workers' and other whites'.

That is likely because any empirical evaluation of the relationship between Trump and the white working class would reveal that one adjective in that phrase is doing more work than the other. In 2016, Trump enjoyed majority or plurality support among every economic branch of whites. It is true that his strongest support among whites came from those making $50,000 to $99,999. This would be something more than working-class in many nonwhite neighborhoods, but even if one accepts that branch as the working class, the difference between how various groups in this income bracket voted is revealing. Sixty-one percent of whites in this "working class" supported Trump. Only 24 percent of Hispanics and 11 percent of blacks did. Indeed, the plurality of all voters making less than $100,000 and the majority making less than $50,000 voted for the Democratic candidate. So when Packer laments the fact that "Democrats can no longer really claim to be the party of working people—not white ones, anyway," he commits a kind of category error. The real problem is that Democrats aren't the party of white people—working or otherwise. White workers are not divided by the fact of labor from other white demographics; they are divided from all other laborers by the fact of their whiteness.

Packer's essay was published before the election, and so the vote tally was not available. But it should not be surprising that a Republican candidate making a direct appeal to racism would drive up the numbers among white voters, given that racism has been a dividing line for the national parties since the civil-rights era. Packer finds inspiration for his thesis in West Virginia—a state that remained Democratic through the 1990s before turning decisively Republican, at least at the level of presidential politics. This relatively recent rightward movement evinces, to Packer, a shift "that couldn't be attributed just to the politics of race." This is likely true—the politics of race are, themselves, never attributable "just to the politics of race." The history of slavery is also about the growth of international capitalism; the history of lynching must be seen in light of anxiety over the growing independence of women; the civil-rights movement can't be disentangled from the Cold War. Thus, to say that the rise of Donald Trump is about more than race is to make an empty statement, one that is small comfort to the people—black, Muslim, immigrant—who live under racism's boot.

The dent of racism is not hard to detect in West Virginia. In the 2008 Democratic primary there, 95 percent of the voters were white. Twenty percent of those—one in five—openly admitted that race was influencing their vote, and more than 80 percent voted for Hillary Clinton over Barack Obama. Four years later, the incumbent Obama lost the primary in 10 counties to Keith Judd, a white felon incarcerated in a federal prison; Judd racked up more than 40 percent of the Democratic-primary vote in the state. A simple thought experiment: Can one imagine a black felon in a federal prison running in a primary against an incumbent white president doing so well?

But racism occupies a mostly passive place in Packer's essay. There's no attempt to understand why black and brown workers, victimized by the same new economy and cosmopolitan elite that Packer lambastes, did not join the Trump revolution. Like Kristof, Packer is gentle with his subjects. When a woman "exploded" and told Packer, "I want to eat what I want to eat, and for them to tell me I can't eat French fries or Coca-Cola—no way," he sees this as a rebellion against "the moral superiority of elites." In fact, this elite conspiracy dates back to 1894, when the government first began advising Americans on their diets. As recently as 2002, President George W. Bush launched the HealthierUS initiative, urging Americans to exercise and eat healthy food. But Packer never allows himself to wonder whether the explosion he witnessed had anything to do with the fact that similar advice now came from the country's first black first lady. Packer concludes that Obama was leaving the country "more divided and angrier than most Americans can remember," a statement that is likely true only because most Americans identify as white. Certainly the men and women forced to live in the wake of the beating of John Lewis, the lynching of Emmett Till, the firebombing of Percy Julian's home, and the assassinations of Martin Luther King Jr. and Medgar Evers would disagree.

The triumph of Trump's campaign of bigotry presented the problematic spectacle of an American president succeeding at best in spite of his racism and possibly because of it. Trump moved racism from the euphemistic and plausibly deniable to the overt and freely claimed. This presented the country's thinking class with a dilemma. Hillary Clinton simply could not be correct when she asserted that a large group of Americans was endorsing a candidate because of bigotry. The implications—that systemic bigotry is still central to our politics; that the country is susceptible to such bigotry; that the salt-of-the-earth Americans whom we lionize in our culture and politics are not so different from those same Americans who grin back at us in lynching photos; that Calhoun's aim of a pan-Caucasian embrace between workers and capitalists still endures—were just too dark. Leftists would have to cope with the failure, yet again, of class unity in the face of racism. Incorporating all of this into an analysis of America and the path forward proved too much to ask. Instead, the response has largely been an argument aimed at emotion—the summoning of the white working class, emblem of America's hardscrabble roots, inheritor of its pioneer spirit, as a shield against the horrific and empirical evidence of trenchant bigotry.

Packer dismisses the Democratic Party as a coalition of "rising professionals and diversity." The dismissal is derived from, of all people, Lawrence Summers, the former Harvard president and White House economist, who last year labeled the Democratic Party "a coalition of the cosmopolitan élite and diversity." The inference is that the party has forgotten how to speak on hard economic issues and prefers discussing presumably softer cultural issues such as "diversity." It's worth unpacking what, precisely, falls under this rubric of "diversity"—resistance to the monstrous incarceration of legions of black men, resistance to the destruction of health providers for poor women, resistance to the effort to deport parents, resistance to a policing whose sole legitimacy is rooted in brute force, resistance to a theory of education that preaches "no excuses" to black and brown children, even as excuses are proffered for mendacious corporate executives "too big to jail." That this suite of concerns, taken together, can be dismissed by both an elite economist like Summers and a brilliant journalist like Packer as "diversity" simply reveals the safe space they enjoy. Because of their identity.

When Barack Obama came into office, in 2009, he believed that he could work with "sensible" conservatives by embracing aspects of their policy as his own. Instead he found that his very imprimatur made that impossible. Senate Minority Leader Mitch McConnell announced that the GOP's primary goal was not to find common ground but to make Obama a "one-term president." A health-care plan inspired by Romneycare was, when proposed by Obama, suddenly considered socialist and, not coincidentally, a form of reparations. The first black president found that he was personally toxic to the GOP base. An entire political party was organized around the explicit aim of negating one man. It was thought by Obama and some of his allies that this toxicity was the result of a relentless assault waged by Fox News and right-wing talk radio. Trump's genius was to see that it was something more, that it was a hunger for revanche so strong that a political novice and accused rapist could topple the leadership of one major party and throttle the heavily favored nominee of the other.

"I could stand in the middle of Fifth Avenue and shoot somebody and I wouldn't lose any voters," Trump bragged in January 2016. This statement should be met with only a modicum of skepticism. Trump has mocked the disabled, withstood multiple accusations of sexual violence (all of which he has denied), fired an FBI director, sent his minions to mislead the public about his motives, personally exposed those lies by boldly stating his aim to scuttle an investigation into his possible collusion with a foreign power, then bragged about that same obstruction to representatives of that same foreign power. It is utterly impossible to conjure a black facsimile of Donald Trump—to imagine Obama, say, implicating an opponent's father in the assassination of an American president or comparing his physical endowment with that of another candidate and then successfully capturing the presidency. Trump, more than any other politician, understood the valence of the bloody heirloom and the great power in not being a nigger.

But the power is ultimately suicidal. Trump evinces this, too. In a recent *New Yorker* article, a former Russian military officer pointed out that interference in an election could succeed only where "necessary conditions" and an "existing background" were present. In America, that "existing background" was a persistent racism, and the "necessary condition" was a black president. The two related factors hobbled America's ability to safeguard its electoral system. As late as July 2016, a majority of Republican voters doubted that Barack Obama had been born in the United States, which is to say they did not view him as a legitimate president. Republican politicians acted accordingly, infamously denying his final Supreme Court nominee a hearing and then, fatefully, refusing to work with the administration to defend the country against the Russian attack. Before the election, Obama found no takers among Republicans for a bipartisan response, and Obama himself, underestimating Trump and thus underestimating the power of whiteness, believed the Republican nominee too objectionable to actually win. In this Obama was, tragically, wrong. And so the most powerful country in the world has handed over all its affairs—the prosperity of its entire economy; the security of its 300 million citizens; the purity of its water, the viability of its air, the safety of its food; the future of its vast system of education; the soundness of its national highways, airways, and railways; the apocalyptic potential of its nuclear arsenal—to a carnival barker who introduced the phrase *grab 'em by the pussy* into the national lexicon. It is as if the white tribe united in demonstration to say, "If a black man can be president, then any white man—no matter how fallen—can be president." And in that perverse way, the democratic dreams of Jefferson and Jackson were fulfilled.

The American tragedy now being wrought is larger than most imagine and will not end with Trump. In recent times, whiteness as an overt political tactic has been restrained by a kind of cordiality that held that its overt invocation would scare off "moderate" whites. This has proved to be only half true at best. Trump's legacy will be exposing the patina of decency for what it is and revealing just how much a demagogue can get away with. It does not take much to imagine another politician, wiser in the ways of Washington and better schooled in the methodology of governance—and now liberated from the pretense of antiracist civility—doing a much more effective job than Trump.

It has long been an axiom among certain black writers and thinkers that while whiteness endangers the bodies of black people in the immediate sense, the larger threat is to white people themselves, the shared country, and even the whole world. There is an impulse to blanch at this sort of grandiosity. When W. E. B. Du Bois claims that slavery was "singularly disastrous for modern civilization" or James Baldwin claims that whites "have brought humanity to the edge of oblivion: because they think they are white," the instinct is to cry exaggeration. But there really is no other way to read the presidency of Donald Trump. The first white president in American history is also the most dangerous president—and he is made more dangerous still by the fact that those charged with analyzing him cannot name his essential nature, because they, too, are implicated in it.

THE REPUBLICAN PARTY MOVES FROM FAMILY VALUES TO WHITE NATIONALISM

by Alex Wagner

[JUNE 2018]

Donald Trump pledged during his presidential campaign to build a physical barrier along the U.S.-Mexico border to stem the flow of migrants into the country. At his rallies, he led crowds in ritual chants of "Build that wall!" Four years into his presidency, only a few miles of new wall have been built. What has been put into place instead is a policy of harsh enforcement, epitomized by the separation of children of some migrants from their parents. From the summer of 2017 through late 2019, more than 5,400 children were separated from parents at the border. In many cases, no provision was made for keeping track of children and parents, making family reunification difficult or impossible.

In a 2018 article, written as the full reality of the family-separation regime was becoming clear, Alex Wagner recalled a time when the Republican Party stood loudly for "family values." Wagner, a contributing writer at *The Atlantic* and a co-host of Showtime's *The Circus*, is the author of *Futureface: A Family Mystery, an Epic Quest, and the Secret to Belonging* (2018). The migrant crisis, she wrote, signaled an end to one era for the GOP—and the start of a tragic new one.

S itting in the Cabinet Room, surrounded by a largely white, male group of Republican lawmakers and administration officials, President Trump attempted to defuse a bomb of his own making. "We have compassion, we want to keep families together," he said as he signed an executive order ending the family separations that commenced at his own administration's directive. "It's very important."

The fit of compassion did not last long—not even through the end of the president's remarks. A few moments later, Trump added, "But we still have to maintain toughness or our country will be overrun by people, by crime, by all of the things that we don't stand for—and that we don't want."

Much as the unrepentant issue an apology before backsliding into retribution, Trump knew, politically, that he had to signal concern for the plight of these families, but could not, emotionally, make the sale. By that evening, at a rally in Minnesota, the president's vitriol was back at full throttle. "They're not sending their finest," he said of the asylum seekers. "We're sending them the hell back. That's what we're doing."

The plight of these migrant families is wrenching, but it is also instructive—revealing a fundamental shift in the priorities of the Republican Party. "Family values" once defined the GOP, informing its embrace of the pro-life platform (protecting unborn children) and its resistance to marriage equality (the union between a husband and wife was sacrosanct). Conservative lawyers led the campaign to censor rap lyrics, and evangelicals condemned extramarital affairs—conservative foot soldiers, for a time, marched under the banner of protecting children and preserving the institution of the family.

But in the Trump era, it is clear that these values no longer define the movement. Family values would never have permitted the separation of babies from their mothers and fathers, the incarceration of toddlers, the placement of grade-schoolers in shelters with histories of sexual and physical abuse. Nor would family values have allowed the disregard of families already separated: There is no plan in place to reunite the 2,342 children who have been taken from their parents. A former director of Immigration and Customs Enforcement, John

Sandweg, told my colleague Priscilla Alvarez that it is entirely possible these children and their parents will remain permanently separated. But to hear it in conservative news outlets, such concern—*what will happen to these children now?*—is a tedium of leftist whining.

Family values, further, would not permit policies likely to ensure that families will be kept apart: In early May, the administration announced its intention to begin screening sponsor families for their citizenship status—this includes extended family seeking to take in immigrant children who have been separated from their mothers and fathers (such screening would include biometric data, like fingerprinting). To place the specter of deportation over an immigrant family is to practically guarantee that its members will remain in the shadows, leaving unaccompanied children to find a home elsewhere—likely in foster care, with strangers. It is to ensure that the family unit, once broken, remains broken.

Trump has instead redefined his party around white nationalism, which deems brown-skinned men, women, and children to be of degraded humanity—and therefore absent any inherent value and unworthy of protection. You could see that as the president compared immigrant men, women, and children to vermin (they want to "infest our country," he tweeted). You could see it when, according to one *New York Times* account, his deputy Stephen Miller painted migrants as menaces—not candidates for asylum, but rather incarceration:

> Reading from a list of arrests in Philadelphia in May 2017, Mr. Miller recounted the crimes committed by illegal immigrants: murder, child neglect, negligent manslaughter, car theft, prostitution, racketeering, rape. "It is impossible to take moral lectures from people like the mayor of Philadelphia, who dance in jubilant celebration over 'sanctuary cities,' when you had innocent Americans, U.S.-born and foreign, who are victimized on a daily basis because of illegal immigration," Mr. Miller said.

You could see it when Trump's former campaign manager, Corey Lewandowski, responded to the proposition of a 10-year-old migrant child with Down syndrome being separated from her mother and kept in a cage. "Womp womp," said Lewandowski—half-cheer, half-IDGAF. How could a human not care about a child in such dire straits? Deny the child's humanity? Lewandowski would not apologize.

You could see it among Trump's supporters, who seem to have rationalized the spectacularly cruel treatment of Central American migrant families by calculating that they somehow need—and deserve—less:

> "I don't think we're mistreating them," Ms. Lagleder said. "It'd be different if they were put in a doghouse or something like that."

You could even see it in the condemnation. Evangelicals and Methodist leaders broke with the president to condemn his zero-tolerance policy; members of Congress, usually wary of running afoul of the White House, spoke out against it; roughly a third of self-identified Republicans told pollsters from Quinnipiac and CNN that they opposed the practice. Yet despite all of this—despite the photos of the 5-year-olds in cages and the stories about stolen children, despite the inescapable and bipartisan emotional anguish—a majority of Republicans still stood by the president and his policy. Here, finally, was the measure of how thoroughly Trump has redefined his party—and how far he has inverted its commitment to family values. No one else matters, no other thing matters. This is his party now.

There have been many indications that this—a white-nationalist takeover of Republicanism—was coming. In Puerto Rico, when a natural disaster ripped through homes and destroyed the lives of countless families—Hispanic ones—Trump's response was, effectively, *You brought this on yourselves*: "Texas & Florida are doing great but Puerto Rico, which was already suffering from broken infrastructure & massive debt, is in deep trouble," he tweeted.

Racial animus has been at the heart of policy prescriptions including mass incarceration and partisan gerrymandering and voter-ID laws, all of which disadvantage Americans of color. It informs the White House responses to Muslim hate crimes and police brutality, or a lack thereof. It remains, consistently, at the core of the worst moments of this presidency—from Charlottesville, Virginia, to Colin Kaepernick—which, coincidentally, are also some of its most defining moments, for detractors and supporters alike.

The migrant crisis signals an official end to one chapter of conservatism and the beginning of a terrifying new one. After all, a party cannot applaud the wailing screams of innocents as a matter of course and hope to ever reclaim the moral high ground. Trump seemed to know that, perhaps, sitting in the Cabinet Room, surrounded by a table of white officials. The compassion that he spoke of wasn't really for the children torn from their parents—it was for his own party and its struggle to contain them.

AM I AN AMERICAN?

by Ibram X. Kendi

[JULY 2019]

A quick check using Google Trends reveals that the appearance in public sources of the phrase *lashes out*—a headline-writing convention for conveying the tenor of comments by Donald Trump—has climbed steadily during the past several years. In July 2019, Trump lashed out at four freshman Democratic representatives—Alexandria Ocasio-Cortez of New York, Ilhan Omar of Minnesota, Rashida Tlaib of Michigan, and Ayanna Pressley of Massachusetts—who are all women of color. He tweeted: "Why don't they go back and help fix the totally broken and crime infested places from which they came"—the reference being to the countries the four women "originally" came from. Omar was born in Somalia and is a naturalized citizen. The other three women were born in the United States. Ibram X. Kendi wrote "Am I an American?" immediately after Trump made his comments.

Kendi is a contributing writer at *The Atlantic* and the author of *Stamped from the Beginning: The Definitive History of Racist Ideas in America* (2016), which won the National Book Award, and *How to Be an Antiracist* (2019).

I live in envy. I envy the people who know their nationality. All the people whose nationality has never been a question in their mind.

I can imagine the woman staring at her reflection in the Volta River who knows she's Ghanaian, like her ancestors who liberated their people in 1957 and chose the mighty precolonial "Ghana" as the name of their new nation. I can imagine the woman flying into Frankfurt who knows she's German, who knows she's arriving back home. I can imagine the man working on his antique car outside his home in Biloxi, forehead covered by the prized blood-red baseball cap he purchased at a rally back in November, a man who has never been told, "Go back to your country!" If somehow someone did tell him, it would confuse him as much as it would the Ghanaian or the German woman. It would be like someone driving by his house and shouting at him, "Go back to your home!"

That he is at home, that he is in his country, is as much a fact of his existence as the tool clenched in his hand, as the sunrays shooting past the Mississippi trees hovering above his sweaty hat and its four beaming white words.

Nothing is more certain to him than that he is an American—and that I am not. My living here, being born here, and being a citizen here—none of those fine details matter. To him, to millions like him, to their white-nationalist father in the White House, I am not an American. They want me to prove, like all the Barack Obamas, that I'm really an American.

This blend of nativism, racism, and nationalism is central to Trumpism, to their worldview. They view me as, they disregard me as, an illegal alien, like those four progressive congresswomen of color. I am tolerated until I am not. I can dine on American soil until I demand a role in remaking the menu that is killing me, like those four progressive congresswomen of color.

House Speaker Nancy Pelosi has told Representatives Ilhan Omar of Minnesota, Ayanna S. Pressley of Massachusetts, Rashida Tlaib of Michigan, and Alexandria Ocasio-Cortez of New York to get in line to be a Democrat, in the way I'm told by moderates away from Capitol Hill to get in line to be an American. I hear the moderate message of compliance, of assimilation, of being happy just dining. And I hear the message from the man with the blood-red hat defending the moderate and giving me an ultimatum.

"So interesting to see 'Progressive' Democrat Congresswomen, who originally came from countries whose governments are a complete and total catastrophe, the worst, most corrupt and inept anywhere in the world (if they even have a functioning government at all), now loudly and viciously telling the people of the United States, the greatest and most powerful Nation on earth, how our government is to be run," Donald Trump tweeted Sunday. "Why don't they go back and help fix the totally broken and crime infested places from which they came. Then come back and show us how it is done. These places need your help badly, you can't leave fast enough."

But Pelosi and her moderate lieutenants do not desire this type of defense, this white-nationalist brand of American exceptionalism. They quickly and rightly stood up for the Americanness of these four women. "When @realDonaldTrump tells four American Congresswomen to go back to their countries," Pelosi tweeted, "he affirms his plan to 'Make America Great Again' has always been about making America white again." They quickly and rightly classified Trump's MAGA attack as "a racist tweet from a racist president," as the assistant speaker of the House, Ben Ray Luján, tweeted.

But their defenses and affirmations of my Americanness—that my black, Puerto Rican, Somalian, and Palestinian sisters are indeed Americans—did little to quiet the question screaming in my soul for an answer. And I suspect in the souls of millions more.

———

I can't stop the screams. Am I an American? It is a question I have never been able to answer.

I can't stop the shouts: "Go back to your country!" It is a statement I have never been able to answer.

Is this my country? Am I an American?

Ocasio-Cortez—like Trump, like me—was born in New York City. Tlaib was born in Detroit, and Pressley in Cincinnati. Omar's family immigrated to the U.S. from Somalia when she was a child. They are all U.S. citizens, like me.

"WE are what democracy looks like," Pressley tweeted. "And we're not going anywhere."

But they are not white like the Slovene-born Melania Trump. Is an American essentially white? I do not know. I do not know if I'm still three-fifths of an American, as my ancestors were written into the U.S. Constitution. Or fully American. Or not American at all.

What I do know is that historically, people like me have only truly been all-American—if all-American is not constantly being told to "go back to your country" or "act like an American"—when we did not resist enslavement on a plantation, or in poverty, or in a prison with or without bars shackling our human potential and cultural flowering. Perhaps we were Americans when we did not resist our bodies being traded, our wombs being assaulted, and our bent backs and our hands being bloodied picking and cleaning and manufacturing white America's wealth.

Perhaps we were Americans when we did not resist how the self-identified white allies were trying to civilize us, telling us to slow down, telling us our anti-racist demands were impractical or impossible, instructing us how to get free. We were rarely told to go back to our country when we did kneel, when we did not kneel, when we did as told by the slaveholder and the abolitionist, by the segregator and racial reformer, by the American mentor telling us to pull up or pull down our pants.

Am I an American only when I act like a slave?

What Trump told those four congresswomen is hardly unorthodox for a U.S. president if we extend recent memory backwards. The year 1787, when the U.S. Constitution was drafted, was also the year that Thomas Jefferson published his influential *Notes on the State of Virginia*. Enslaved Africans should be emancipated, civilized, and "colonized to such place as the circumstances of the time should render most proper," he wrote.

Colonization emerged as the most popular solvent of the race problem before the Civil War, advocated by nearly every president from Jefferson to Abraham Lincoln. Slaveholders increasingly desired to rid the nation of the emancipated Negro. And moderate Americans increasingly advocated gradual emancipation and colonization, telling the anti-racists that immediate emancipation was impractical and impossible in the way that anti-racists are told immediate equality is impractical and impossible today.

At the founding of the American Colonization Society in 1816, Representative Henry Clay of Kentucky, the future presidential candidate and "Great Compromiser," gave voice to what we now call Trumpism, the savaging of people of color and the countries of people of color to hold up white Americanness.

"Can there be a nobler cause than that which, whilst it proposes to rid our country of a useless and pernicious, if not dangerous portion of its population, contemplates the spreading of the arts of civilized life, and the possible redemption from ignorance and barbarism of a benighted quarter of the globe!"

The moderate strategized then, as the moderate still do now, based on what was required to soothe white sensibilities. As the clergyman Robert Finley wrote in *Thoughts on the Colonization of Free Blacks* in 1816, through colonization, "the evil of slavery will be diminished and in a way so gradual as to prepare the whites for the happy and progressive change."

Some black people advocated back-to-Africa campaigns or relocated there, convinced American racism was permanent, convinced they could create a better life for themselves alongside their African kin. But many, perhaps most, black people resisted colonization schemes from their beginning. This is "the land of our nativity," thousands of black Philadelphians resolved in 1817. Still colonization recycled through time, on the basis that the black race could never "be placed on an equality with the white race," as Lincoln lectured a delegation of black men on August 14, 1862. The abolitionist William Lloyd Garrison corrected Lincoln: "It is not their color, but their being free, that makes their presence here intolerable."

President Andrew Johnson did everything he could to keep us slaves. His successor, Ulysses S. Grant, tired of alienating racist Americans from the Republican Party every time he sent federal troops to defend our right to live, vote, thrive, and hold political office from Ku Klux Klansmen led by men such as Nathan Bedford Forrest, whom Tennessee honored with his own day on Saturday.

In the so-called Compromise of 1877, northerners retained the White House in exchange for allowing racist southerners to treat us like anything but Americans over the next century. Or were we Americans all along, despite what the lynchings and pogroms did to our bodies, and what Jim Crow did to our political economy? Or did we become Americans through court rulings and congressional acts in the 1940s, 1950s, and 1960s? Or were we still not Americans in 1968, when the Kerner Commission's study of America's racial landscape concluded, "Our nation is moving towards two societies, one black, one white—separate and unequal."

Were the two societies—instead of black and white—the American society of legal patriots and the un-American society of illegal aliens? Did the Latinx, Muslim, Asian, and black immigrants who arrived in the United States since the 1960s join the people of color and anti-racist whites in the un-American society? Have people of color been allowed to enter American society and become Americans when they submitted to racist power and policy and inequality and injustice—when they became "my African American"? Have rebellious "un-Americans" of color been demonized as criminals and deported back to our countries or to more and more prisons like Angola in Louisiana?

Am I an American?

———

Blood-red-hatted segregationists say no, never, unless we submit to slavery. Assimilationists say we can be Americans if we stop speaking Spanish, stop wearing hijabs, cut our long hair, stop acting out against them—if we follow their gradual lead.

Anti-racist blacks have divided over this question as fiercely as segregationists and assimilationists. I am an American, and because I'm an American, I deserve to be free. I am not an American, because if I were an American, I'd be free.

"I, too, am America," Langston Hughes wrote in perhaps his most famous poem, first published in 1926.

"I'm not a Republican, nor a Democrat, nor an American—and got sense enough to know it," Malcolm X orated at a Detroit church on April 12, 1964.

Both ring true to me. I do not know whether I'm an American. But I do know it is up to me to answer this question based on how I define *American*, based on how I am treated by America. I don't care whether or not anyone thinks I am an American. I am not about persuading anyone to see how American I am. I do not write stories that show white people all the ways people of color contributed to America. I will not battle with anyone over who is an American. There is a greater battle for America.

Maybe that is the point. Maybe I had the question wrong all along. Maybe I should not live in envy; I should live in struggle. Maybe I should have been asking, "Who controls America?" instead of "Am I an American?" Because who controls America determines who is an American.

THE WORLD BURNS. SARAH SANDERS SAYS THIS IS FINE.

by Megan Garber

[JULY 2018]

Stephen Colbert launched the concept of "truthiness"—"the quality of seeming or being felt to be true, even if not necessarily true"—in 2005. With its implication that seeming to be true is still somehow important, the word today seems quaint. Sarah Sanders was appointed White House press secretary in 2017, succeeding Sean Spicer, who never quite recovered from lying, during his first full day on the job, about the size of the crowd at Trump's inauguration. In the midst of that controversy, Kellyanne Conway, a counselor to the president, insisted that the false statements were not lies but "alternative facts." As *Atlantic* staff writer Megan Garber noted in a 2018 essay, Sarah Sanders bestrode the world of alternative facts: "In a Sanders briefing, even the most straightforward questions are often met with obfuscation and indignation. Even the most basic matters of fact are disputed." Sanders served in the job for nearly two years, eventually reducing the number of news briefings, which in previous administrations were held an average of 10 times a month, to zero.

Note: The reference in Garber's article to the number of "known" lies spoken in public by Donald Trump is out of date. As of July 2020, *The Washington Post*'s "Fact Checker" tabulation of his "false or misleading" statements stood above 19,000.

On July 18, two representatives of the United States government held press briefings, both of them touching on one of the most astonishing news stories of the Trump presidency—a series of events that had begun two days earlier, when Donald Trump traveled to Helsinki to meet, behind closed doors, with Russian President Vladimir Putin.

Here was the White House Press Secretary Sarah Huckabee Sanders responding to a question from *The New York Times*'s Maggie Haberman about the notion that Putin had raised about a group of U.S. officials, including the former ambassador to Russia Michael McFaul, being interrogated by Russia: "The president is going to meet with his team, and we'll let you know when we have an announcement on that."

Here, on the other hand, was Heather Nauert, the State Department spokesperson, on the same issue: "The overall assertions are absolutely absurd—the fact that they want to question 11 American citizens and the assertions that the Russian government is making about those American citizens. We do not stand by those assertions."

It was a striking juxtaposition, this tale of two briefings: the one spokesperson outraged that the United States would entertain the idea of handing over its citizens to a nation that is an autocracy and an adversary; the other offering, in response to the suggestion, a pro forma "We'll let you know if there's an announcement on that front." *The Stakes of Diplomacy* chafing against *The Art of the Deal*. A house divided, live on C-SPAN.

What the collision makes clear, though, is how readily the spokesperson standing behind the White House briefing lectern also stands behind her boss. It is a well-worn cliché of the Trump presidency—which is also to say, it is a well-worn cliché about the Trump psyche—that, within a White House as vertically integrated as this one, loyalty counts above all. And Sarah Sanders, the press secretary who will have been on the job, this week, for one year—the White House announced her promotion to the role in July of 2017—performs that loyalty every time she meets the press.

This is a White House that prioritizes the scoring of points over the complexities of compromise. Sanders, on behalf of the president she works for—a happy warrior in a culture war that has found a front in the James S. Brady Press Briefing Room at 1600 Pennsylvania Avenue—takes for granted an assumption that would be shocking were it not so common in the American culture of the early 21st century: There are things that are more important than truth.

Things like, for example, the claiming of victory against the other side. Things like, for example, the owning of libs and the trolling of Dems and the ability to victor-write history so thoroughly that you can claim, with an air of annoyance about being asked to make such a clarification in the first place, that the president's long history of commentary on Russia has now been nullified because the president had, in a single public event, "misspoken." All of which made Wednesday's briefing—*the president will work with his team*—both deeply typical and astounding: Here was one of the most prominent representatives of the White House choosing partisanship over patriotism. Winning above all.

———

There are, in Sarah Sanders's briefing room, a series of predictable punch lines. Even the blandest of informational updates—as in the announcement that *the president will be traveling to Kansas City, Missouri, next Tuesday to address the Veterans of Foreign Wars' 119th Annual Convention, because he is committed to our veterans and has worked to reform the VA and to ensure veterans are given the care and support they deserve*—tend to be punctuated with familiar end notes: the greatness of President Trump, the undeniable success of his presidency, the foolishness of those who might question those priors. Sometimes far fewer words are required. Sometimes standing by the president—supporting Team Trump from within—comes down to subtler work: taking Trump's actions and coating them with the palatable veneer of evident normalcy. Michael McFaul, Bill Browder, Vladimir Putin, the notion that the United States might decide to use its citizens as bargaining chips in order to make deals with a despotic regime known for murdering dissidents: *We'll let you know if there's an announcement on that front.*

It is an approach that bumps up against world history and American foreign policy and, as Nauert's statement reminded us, Trump's own State Department. But it is also an approach that is wholly consistent with the Trumpian worldview—one that valorizes strength above all (he has "great control over his country," the president has mused of Putin), one that is populated by a collective of *us*es and *them*s, one whose sum, always, is zero. Ivana Trump tells the story of the birth of Don Jr. on New Year's Eve of 1977: She wanted to name the boy after his father, Donald's first wife recalls; Donald the elder, however, balked at the notion. "What if he's a loser?" the future president said.

A world of winners and a world, consequently, of losers: It is perhaps the clearest distillation of Trumpism. This White House, whether it is taking on health care or gun policy or tax policy or immigration policy, assumes everything is a competition—and reveres, to the general exclusion of the alternative, #winning. Sickness is weakness. Poverty is weakness. Otherness is weakness. And Trump understands the world according to one crucial insight: He himself is not weak. He is strong. He is a very fine person, fine enough to be the consummate winner. This is a White House that subscribes to the incontrovertible realities of the world according to one man. *Donaldpolitik.*

It is this world—it is this worldview—that Sarah Sanders, every day, helps to spin. Her handling of Maggie Haberman's McFaul-related question was not a gaffe; it was, in fact, a tidy reminder of one of the ways that Sanders has transformed the job of the press secretary itself in the year that she has spent as its occupant. Gone are the tense cordialities that defined the tenures of the Obama administration press secretaries Robert Gibbs and Jay Carney and Josh Earnest; gone, too, are the shouted lies of Sean Spicer and the swaggering camp of Anthony Scaramucci, who served under Trump.

Instead, briefing by briefing, Sanders strides to the lectern in the Brady briefing room and makes an argument about who belongs among the world's winners (Trump and those in his orbit, the forgotten Americans who will be helped by Trump's work, North Koreans, the participants in the upcoming Veterans of Foreign Wars' 119th Annual Convention in Kansas City, Missouri) and who must be counted among its losers (congressional Democrats, Democrats in general,

Barack Obama, Hillary Clinton, Nancy Pelosi, members of the American news media who are not on the payroll of the Fox News Channel). Sanders recently responded to a question from CNN's Jim Acosta by saying, "I know it's hard for you to understand even short sentences."

This kind of thing seeks to justify itself through the argument that Jim Acosta is "fake news," and that therefore Jim Acosta is a loser, and that therefore Jim Acosta needs to be mocked by the White House press secretary on national television. It's partisanship, all the way down. (Many times, when reporters point out that the president lies—more than 2,000 known ones at this point—Sanders responds by accusing them of being agents of an anti-Trump agenda.)

In a Sanders briefing, even the most straightforward questions tend to be met with obfuscation and indignation. Even the most basic matters of fact are disputed. The logic of the battlefield wins out, and the assigned teams face off, and it becomes clear, if you watch for long enough, that the thing being fought for is reality itself: facts, truths, common knowledge. The content and the contours of the world as we agree to understand it.

———————

In the summer of 1954, a group of 22 boys, all of them rising sixth graders, were invited to spend time at a summer camp in the Sans Bois Mountains, in southeastern Oklahoma. While there, the idea went, the kids would swim and boat and run and play and otherwise do the things you'd expect might be done at a summer camp tailored to the tendencies of 11-year-old boys. The campers were separated into two cabins—two separate camps, effectively—that were located far enough apart to be beyond seeing and hearing distance of each other. Neither group was aware, at first, of the other one. Nor were they aware that their idyllic camp was also a psychological test—the one that would come to be known as the Robbers Cave experiment.

It went like this: The boys, extremely similar but strategically separated, were initially left to bond among themselves, within their 11-member cabins; then, once a group identity had set in, each group was made aware of the fact that there was another cabin—a different cabin—nearby. With remarkable efficiency, as the psychologists Muzafer Sherif and Carolyn Wood Sherif and their team of counselor/assistants observed it, the logic of the team took over: The boys—they had been selected for similarities not only in age, but also in ethnicity and class and intellect—immediately wanted to compete with the members of the other cabin. And the competitions were not the friendly kinds you might associate with summer camp. Members of each group started to call the strangers of the other taunting names. They conducted raids on the other cabin, stealing some possessions and destroying others. One group, attempting to lay claim to the baseball diamond the two cabins shared, staked a flag on the pitcher's mound. The other group burned it down.

Robbers Cave—*Lord of the Flies* but with better experimental design—remains a dire warning, not only when it comes to psychology, but also when it comes to democracy: a lurking suggestion of how readily humans can be convinced to turn against one another on the grounds of otherness itself. It has lingered throughout American history. James Madison worried about factions and Alexander Hamilton worried about demagogues and the Framers as a messy collective worried about the inevitable inertias of human pettiness—and it was because they understood intuitively what the events at Robbers Cave would suggest, centuries later, to be true: Citizens would be inclined, they realized, to argue not just in the best of ways, but in the worst. It would be exceedingly easy for their fragile new republic to lose itself in the temptations of partisanship.

That fear is realized every time the person whose job it is to help the American people understand the daily doings of the executive branch instead mocks White House reporters to their face. That fear is realized every time Sanders, the daughter of a man who has made a career with the help of regular denigrations of the "media" (a collective to which, through a TV show broadcast to the masses, he insists he does not belong), uses her pulpit to promote the president's "fake news awards." That fear is realized every time Sanders accuses reporters of "purposely putting out information you know is false" and "purposefully misleading the American people"—offenses that, anyone familiar with the workings of the press will know, are grounds for instant firing. That fear is realized every time Sanders compares professional White House reporters to her three small children.

And that fear is realized every time Sanders takes a question about a specific matter of public policy—the state of diplomacy with North Korea, the fate of the Affordable Care Act, the White House attitude toward presidential self-pardons, the use of an American diplomat as a pawn to ratify the dealmaking capabilities of the 45th president—and, instead of offering an answer, twists the reply to make sure it endorses the familiar talking points: the stubbornness of the Democrats, the venality of the media, the manifest greatness of Donald Trump. Team above all. Victory at all costs.

American politics, overall, has ceded so much to the logic of warfare: This is a time of factions, of widespread bad faith, of normalized trolling, of the plodding weaponization of everything. But Sanders, for her part, serves as an omen in real time: a reminder of what happens when the airy ideals of republican government—compromise, commonality, objective truth—get refracted through competition and resentment and battle. The daily victories claimed by political Darwinism.

Last fall, when she was still settling into the press-secretary job after taking it over from Scaramucci, *The New York Times* asked Sanders, who is very much an evangelical Christian, what led her to want to work for Donald Trump, who is very much not. Sanders replied, matter-of-factly: "I thought he could win."

HOW TO DESTROY A GOVERNMENT

by George Packer

[APRIL 2020]

One small indication of the outsize role the job of president has acquired in the public mind is the use of the acronym POTUS for "President of the United States." A generation ago, few people were aware of the term; today, almost everyone is. *POTUS*, suggesting power, has symbolic resonance. The phrase the Founders used for the job was more workmanlike: Chief Executive. The government performs essential functions, and much of the president's job, regardless of party, is to manage them effectively. Crises and ceremonies may get the attention, but running the government takes up most of a typical president's time.

This is the part of the job in which Donald Trump takes no interest. Worse, as *Atlantic* staff writer George Packer demonstrated in a devastating 2020 investigation, he is undermining and hollowing out entire departments, destroying the civil service while bending what remains of government to his will. Packer's article, "How to Destroy a Government," appeared just as the coronavirus pandemic hit America with full force, and at a moment when key federal agencies were depleted.

Packer is the author, most recently, of *Our Man: Richard Holbrooke and the End of the American Century* (2019), which was a finalist for the 2020 Pulitzer Prize in Biography. His 2020 *Atlantic* article, which focused on the Department of Justice and the State Department, is presented here in abridged form.

When Donald Trump came into office, there was a sense that he would be outmatched by the vast government he had just inherited.

The new president was impetuous, bottomlessly ignorant, almost chemically inattentive, while the bureaucrats were seasoned, shrewd, protective of themselves and their institutions. They knew where the levers of power lay and how to use them or prevent the president from doing so. Trump's White House was chaotic and vicious, unlike anything in American history, but it didn't really matter as long as "the adults" were there to wait out the president's impulses and deflect his worst ideas and discreetly pocket destructive orders lying around on his desk.

After three years, the adults have all left the room—saying just about nothing on their way out to alert the country to the peril—while Trump is still there.

James Baker, the former general counsel of the FBI, and a target of Trump's rage against the state, acknowledges that many government officials, not excluding himself, went into the administration convinced "that they are either smarter than the president, or that they can hold their own against the president, or that they can protect the institution against the president because they understand the rules and regulations and how it's supposed to work, and that they will be able to defend the institution that they love or served in previously against what they perceive to be, I will say neutrally, the inappropriate actions of the president. And I think they are fooling themselves. They're fooling themselves. He's light-years ahead of them."

The adults were too sophisticated to see Trump's special political talents—his instinct for every adversary's weakness, his fanatical devotion to himself, his knack for imposing his will, his sheer staying power. They also failed to appreciate the advanced decay of the Republican Party, which by 2016 was far gone in a nihilistic pursuit of power at all costs. They didn't grasp the readiness of large numbers of Americans to accept, even relish, Trump's contempt for democratic norms and basic decency. It took the arrival of such a leader to reveal how many things that had always seemed engraved in monumental stone turned out to depend on those flimsy norms, and how much the norms depended on public opinion. Their vanishing exposed the real power of the presidency. Legal precedent could be deleted with a keystroke; law enforcement's independence from the White House was optional; the separation of powers turned out to be a gentleman's agreement; transparent lies were more potent than solid facts. None of this was clear to the political class until Trump became president.

But the adults' greatest miscalculation was to overestimate themselves—particularly in believing that other Americans saw them as selfless public servants, their stature derived from a high-minded commitment to the good of the nation.

When Trump came to power, he believed that the regime was his, property he'd rightfully acquired, and that the 2 million civilians working under him, most of them in obscurity, owed him their total loyalty. He harbored a deep suspicion that some of them were plotting in secret to destroy him. He had to bring them to heel before he could be secure in his power. This wouldn't be easy—the permanent government had defied other leaders and outlasted them. In his inexperience and rashness—the very qualities his supporters loved—he made early mistakes. He placed unreliable or inept commissars in charge of the bureaucracy, and it kept running on its own.

But a simple intuition had propelled Trump throughout his life: Human beings are weak. They have their illusions, appetites, vanities, fears. They can be cowed, corrupted, or crushed. A government is composed of human beings. This was the flaw in the brilliant design of the Framers, and Trump learned how to exploit it. The wreckage began to pile up. He needed only a few years to warp his administration into a tool for his own benefit. If he's given a few more years, the damage to American democracy will be irreversible.

This is the story of how a great republic went soft in the middle, lost the integrity of its guts, and fell in on itself—told through government officials whose names under any other president would have remained unknown, who wanted no fame, and who faced existential questions when Trump set out to break them.

Erica Newland went to work at the Department of Justice in the last summer of the Obama administration. She was 29 and arrived with the highest blessings of the meritocracy—a degree from Yale Law School and a clerkship with Judge Merrick Garland of the D.C. Court of Appeals, whom President Obama had recently nominated to the Supreme Court (and who would never get a Senate hearing). Newland became an attorney-adviser in the Office of Legal Counsel, the department's brain trust, where legal questions about presidential actions go to be answered, usually in the president's favor. The office had approved the most extreme wartime powers under George W. Bush, including torture, before rescinding some of them. Newland was a civil libertarian and a skeptic of broad presidential power. Her hiring showed that the Obama Justice Department welcomed heterodox views.

The election in November changed her, freed her, in a way that she understood only much later. If Hillary Clinton had won, Newland likely would have continued as an ambitious, risk-averse government lawyer on a fast track. She would have felt pressure not to antagonize her new bosses, because elite Washington lawyers keep revolving through one another's lives—these people would be the custodians of her future, and she wanted to rise within the federal government. But after the election she realized that her new bosses were not likely to be patrons of her career. They might even see her as an enemy.

She decided to serve under Trump. She liked her work and her colleagues, the 20 or so career lawyers in the office, who treated one another with kindness and respect. Like all federal employees, she had taken an oath to support the Constitution, not the president, and to discharge her office "well and faithfully." Those patriotic duties implied certain values, and they were what kept her from leaving. In her mind, they didn't make her a conspirator of the "deep state." She wouldn't try to block the president's policies—only hold them to a high standard of fact and law. She doubted that any replacement would do the same.

Days after Trump's inauguration, Newland's new boss, Curtis Gannon, the acting head of the Office of Legal Counsel, gave a seal of approval to the president's ban, bigoted if not illegal, on travelers from seven majority-Muslim countries. At least one lawyer in the office went out to Dulles Airport that weekend to protest it. Another spent a day crying behind a closed office door. Others reasoned that it wasn't the role of government lawyers to judge the president's motives.

Employees of the executive branch work for the president, and a central requirement of their jobs is to carry out the president's policies. If they can't do so in good conscience, then they should leave. At the same time, there's good reason not to leave over the results of an election. A civil service that rotates with the party in power would be a reversion to the 19th-century spoils system, whose notorious corruption led to the 1883 Pendleton Act, which created the modern merit-based, politically insulated civil service.

In Trump's first year an exodus from the Justice Department began, including some of Newland's colleagues. Some left in the honest belief that they could no longer represent their client, whose impulsive tweets on matters such as banning transgender people from the military it became the office's business to justify, but they largely kept their reasons to themselves. Almost every consideration—future job prospects, relations with former colleagues, career officials' long conditioning in anonymity—goes against a righteous exit.

Newland didn't work on the travel ban. Perhaps this distance allowed her to hold on to the idea that she could still achieve some good if she stayed inside. Her obligation was to the country, the Constitution. She felt she was fighting to preserve the credibility of the Justice Department. That first year, she saw her memos and arguments change outcomes.

Things got worse in the second year. It seemed as if more than half of the Office of Legal Counsel's work involved limiting the rights of noncitizens. The atmosphere of open discussion dissipated. The political appointees at the top, some of whom had voiced skepticism early on about the legality of certain policies, were readier to make excuses for Trump, to give his fabrications the benefit of the doubt. Among career officials, fear set in. They saw what was happening to colleagues in the FBI who had crossed the president during the investigation into Russian election interference—careers and reputations in ruins. For those with security clearances, speaking up, or even offering a snarky

eye roll, felt particularly risky, because the bar for withdrawing a clearance was low. Steven Engel, appointed to lead the office, was a Trump
loyalist who made decisions without much consultation. Newland's
colleagues found less and less reason to advance arguments that they
knew would be rejected. People began to shut up.

One day in May 2018, Newland went into the lunchroom carrying a printout of a White House press release titled "What You Need
to Know About the Violent Animals of MS-13." At a meeting about
Central American gangs a few days earlier, Trump had used the word
animals to describe undocumented immigrants, and in the face of criticism the White House was digging in. *Animals* appeared 10 times in
the short statement. Newland wanted to know what her colleagues
thought about it.

Eight or so lawyers were sitting around a table. They were all career
people—the politicals hadn't come to lunch yet. Newland handed the
printout to one of them, who handed it right back, as if he didn't want
to be seen with it. She put the paper faceup on the table, and another
lawyer turned it over, as if to protect Newland: "That way, if Steve
walks in . . ."

Newland turned it over again. "It's a White House press release and
I'm happy to explain why it bothers me." The conversation quickly
became awkward, and then muted. Colleagues who had shared Newland's dismay in private now remained silent. It was the last time she
joined them in the lunchroom.

No one risked getting fired. No one would become the target of a
Trump tweet. The danger might be a mediocre performance review or
a poor reference. "There was no sense that there was anything to be
gained by standing up within the office," Newland told me recently.
"The people who might celebrate that were not there to see it. You
wouldn't be able to talk about it. And if you're going to piss everyone
off within the department, you're not going to be able to get out" and
find a good job.

She hated going to work. In the lobby of the Justice Department
building, six blocks down Pennsylvania Avenue from the White House,
Newland had to pass under a large portrait of the president. Every

morning as she entered the building, she avoided looking at Trump, or she used side doors, where she wouldn't be confronted with his face. At night she slept poorly, plagued by regrets. Should she have pushed harder on a legal issue? Should she engage her colleagues in the lunchroom again? How could she live with the cruelty and bigotry of executive orders and other proposals, even legal ones, that crossed her desk? She was angry and miserable, and her friends told her to leave. She continued to find reasons to stay: worries about who would replace her, a determination not to abandon ship during an emergency, a sense of patriotism. Through most of 2018 she deluded herself that she could still achieve something by staying in the job.

In 1968, James C. Thomson, a former Asia expert in the Kennedy and Johnson administrations, published an essay in this magazine called "How Could Vietnam Happen? An Autopsy." Among the reasons Thomson gave for the war was "the 'effectiveness' trap"—the belief among officials that it's usually wisest to accept the status quo. "The inclination to remain silent or to acquiesce in the presence of the great men—to live to fight another day, to give on this issue so that you can be 'effective' on later issues—is overwhelming," he wrote. The trap is seductive, because it carries an impression of principled tough-mindedness, not cowardice. Remaining "effective" also becomes a reason never to quit.

As the executive orders and other requests for the office's approval piled up, many of them of dubious legality, one of Newland's supervisors took to saying, "We're just following orders." He said it without irony, as a way of reminding everyone, "We work for the president." He said it once to Newland, and when she gave him a look he added, "I know that's what the Nazis said, but we're not Nazis."

"The president has said that some of them are very fine people," Newland reminded him.

"Attorney General Sessions never said that," the supervisor replied. "Steve never said that, and I've never said that. We're not Nazis." That she could still have such an exchange with a supervisor seemed in itself like a reason not to leave.

But Newland, who is Jewish, sometimes asked herself: If she and her colleagues had been government lawyers in Germany in the 1930s, what kind of bureaucrat would each of them have been? There were the ideologues, the true believers, like one Clarence Thomas protégé. There were the opportunists who went along to get ahead. There were a handful of quiet dissenters. But many in the office just tried to survive by keeping their heads down. "I guess I know what kind I would have been," Newland told me. "I would have stayed in the Nazi administration initially and then fled." She thinks she would have been the kind of official who pushed for carve-outs in the Nuremberg Race Laws, preserving citizenship rights for Germans with only partial Jewish ancestry. She would have felt that this was better than nothing—that it justified having worked in the regime at the beginning.

Newland and her colleagues were saving Trump from his own lies. They were using their legal skills to launder his false statements and jury-rig arguments so that presidential orders would pass constitutional muster. When she read that producers of *The Apprentice* had had to edit episodes in order to make Trump's decisions seem coherent, she realized that the attorneys in the Office of Legal Counsel were doing something similar. Loyalty to the president was equated with legality. "There was hardly any respect for the other departments of government—not for the lower courts, not for Congress, and certainly not for the bureaucracy, for professionalism, for facts or the truth," she told me. "*Corruption* is the right word for this. It doesn't have to be pay-to-play to be corrupt. It's a departure from the oath."

In the fall of 2018, Newland learned that she and five colleagues would receive the Attorney General's Distinguished Service Award for their work on executive orders in 2017. The news made her sick to her stomach; her office probably thought she would feel honored by the award. She marveled at how the administration's conduct had been normalized. But she also suspected that department higher-ups were using the career people to justify policies such as the travel ban—at least, the award would be seen that way. Newland and another lawyer stayed away from the ceremony where the awards were presented, on October 24.

On October 27, an anti-Semitic extremist killed 11 people at a synagogue in Pittsburgh. Before the shooting, he berated Jews online for enabling "invaders" to enter the United States from Mexico. That same week, the Office of Legal Counsel was working on an order that, in response to the "threat" posed by a large caravan of Central Americans making its way north through Mexico, temporarily refused all asylum claims at the southern border. Newland, who could imagine being shot in a synagogue, felt that her office's work was sanctioning rhetoric that had inspired a mass killer.

She tendered her resignation three days later. By Thanksgiving she was gone. In the new year she began working at a nonprofit called Protect Democracy.

The asylum ban was the last public act of Attorney General Jeff Sessions. Trump fired him immediately after the midterm elections. Newland felt that Sessions—who had recused himself from the Russia investigation because he had spoken with Russian officials as an adviser in the Trump campaign—cared about protecting some democratic rights, but only for white Americans. He was eventually replaced by William Barr, a former attorney general with a reputation for intellect and competence. But Barr quickly made Sessions seem like a paragon of integrity. After watching him run her former department for a year, Newland wondered why she had stayed inside at all.

————————

Nothing constrained Trump more than independent law enforcement. Nothing would strengthen him like the power to use it for his own benefit. "The authoritarian leader simply has to get control over the coercive apparatus of the state," Susan Hennessey and Benjamin Wittes write in their new book, *Unmaking the Presidency.* "Without control of the Justice Department, the would-be tyrant's tool kit is radically incomplete."

When Trump nominated William Barr to replace Jeff Sessions as attorney general, the Washington legal establishment exhaled a collective sigh of relief. Barr had held the same job almost 30 years earlier, in the last 14 months of the first Bush presidency. He was now 68 and rich from years in the private sector. He had nothing to prove and nothing to gain. He was considered an "institutionalist"—quite conservative, an advocate of strong presidential power, but not an extremist. Because he was intimidatingly smart and bureaucratically skillful, he would protect the Justice Department from Trump's maraudings far better than the intellectually inferior Sessions and his ill-qualified temporary replacement, Matthew Whitaker. Barr told a friend that he agreed to come back because the department was in chaos and needed a leader with a bulletproof reputation.

Before Barr's confirmation hearings, Neal Katyal, a legal scholar who was acting solicitor general under Obama, warned a group of Democratic senators not to be fooled: Barr's views were well outside mainstream conservatism. He could prove more dangerous than any of his predecessors. And the reasons for concern could be found by anyone who took the trouble to study Barr's record, which was made of three durable, interwoven strands.

The first was his expansive view of presidential power, sometimes called the theory of the "unitary executive"—the idea that Article II of the Constitution gives the president sole and complete authority in the executive branch, with wide latitude to interpret laws and make war. When Barr became head of the Office of Legal Counsel under George H. W. Bush, in 1989, he wrote an influential memo listing 10 ways in which Congress had been trespassing on Article II, arguing, "Only by consistently and forcefully resisting such congressional incursions can executive branch prerogatives be preserved." He created and chaired an interagency committee to fight document requests and assert executive privilege.

One target of Barr's displeasure was the Office of the Inspector General, created by Congress in 1978 as an independent watchdog in executive-branch agencies. "For a guy like Barr, this goes to the core of the unitary executive—that there's this entity in there that reports to Congress," says Jack Goldsmith, a Harvard law professor who served as head of the Office of Legal Counsel under George W. Bush. When Barr became attorney general in 1991, he made sure that the inspector general's office in the Justice Department had as little power as possible to investigate misconduct.

Barr has even expressed skepticism about the guidelines, established after Watergate, that insulate the Justice Department from political interference by the White House. In a 2001 oral history Barr said, "I think it started picking up after Watergate, the idea that the Department of Justice has to be independent . . . My experience with the department is that the most political people in the Department of Justice are the career people, the least political are the political appointees." In Barr's view, political interference in law enforcement is almost a contradiction in terms. Since presidents (and their appointees) are subject to voters, they are better custodians of justice than the anonymous and unaccountable bureaucrats known as federal prosecutors and FBI investigators. Barr seemed unconcerned about what presidents might do between elections.

The Iran-Contra scandal that took place under Ronald Reagan shadowed Bush's presidency in the form of an investigation conducted by the independent counsel Lawrence Walsh. Barr despised independent counsels as trespasses on the unitary executive. A month before Bush left office, Barr persuaded the president to issue full pardons of several Reagan-administration officials who had been found guilty in the scandal, in addition to one—former Defense Secretary Caspar Weinberger—who had been indicted and might have provided evidence against Bush himself. The appearance of a cover-up didn't trouble Barr. But six years later, when the independent counsel Kenneth Starr was investigating President Bill Clinton for perjury and obstruction in a sex scandal, Barr, by then a corporate lawyer, criticized the Clinton White House for attacks on Starr that could impede the investigation and even intimidate jurors and witnesses.

Here is a glimpse of the second strand in Barr's thinking: partisanship. Less conspicuous than the first, which sheathes it in constitutional principles, it never disappears. Barr is a persistent critic of independent counsels—except when they're investigating a Democratic president. He's a vocal defender of presidential authority—when a Republican is in the White House.

This partisanship has to be understood in relation to the third enduring strand of Barr's thinking: He is a Catholic—a very conservative one. John R. Dunne, who ran the Justice Department's civil-rights division when Barr was attorney general under Bush, calls him "an authoritarian Catholic." Dunne and his wife once had dinner at Barr's house and came away with the impression of a traditional patriarch whom only the family dog disobeyed. Barr attended Columbia University at the height of the anti-war movement, and he drew a lesson from those years that shaped many other religious conservatives as well: The challenge to traditional values and authority in the 1960s sent the country into a long-term moral decline.

In 1992, as attorney general, Barr gave a speech at a right-wing Catholic conference in which he blamed "the long binge that began in the mid-1960s" for soaring rates of abortion, drug use, divorce, juvenile crime, venereal disease, and general immorality. "The secularists of today are clearly fanatics," Barr said. He called for a return to "God's law" as the basis for moral renewal. "There is a battle going on that will decide who we are as a people and what name this age will ultimately bear." One of Barr's speechwriters at the time was Pat Cipollone, who is now Trump's White House counsel and served as one of his defenders during impeachment. In 1995, as a private citizen, Barr published the same argument, with the same military metaphors, as an essay in the journal then called *The Catholic Lawyer*. "We are locked in a historic struggle between two fundamentally different systems of values," he wrote. "In a way, this is the end product of the Enlightenment." The secularists' main weapon in their war on religion, Barr continued, is the law. Traditionalists would have to fight back the same way.

What does this apocalyptic showdown have to do with Article II and the unitary executive? It raises the stakes of politics to eschatology. With nothing less than Christian civilization at stake, the faithful might well conclude that the ends justify the means.

Barr spent the quarter century between Presidents Bush and Trump in private practice, serving on corporate boards, and caring for the youngest of his three daughters as she battled lymphoma. Barr and Cipollone also sat together on the board of the Catholic Information Center, an office in Washington closely affiliated with Opus Dei, a far-right Catholic organization with influential connections in politics and business around the world. During those years, the Republican Party sank into its own swamp of moral relativism, hitting bottom with Trump's presidency.

Trump's arrival brought Barr out of semi-retirement as a reliable advocate. When Comey reopened the Clinton email investigation 11 days before the election, Barr wrote an approving op-ed. When Trump fired Comey six months later, supposedly for mishandling the same investigation, Barr published another approving op-ed. The only consistent principle seemed to be what benefited Trump. Then, in June 2018, Barr wrote a 19-page memo and sent it, unsolicited, to Rod Rosenstein. The memo argued that Robert Mueller could not charge Trump with obstructing justice for taking actions that came under the president's authority, including asking Comey to back off the Flynn investigation and then firing Comey. In Barr's expansive view of Article II, it was nearly impossible for Trump to obstruct justice at all.

Writing that memo was a strange thing for a former attorney general to do with his spare time. Six months later, Trump nominated Barr to his old job.

After Barr assumed office, his advocacy for Trump intensified. When Mueller completed his report, in March 2019, Barr rushed to tell the world not only that the report cleared Trump of conspiring with Russia, but that the lack of an "underlying crime" cleared the president of obstruction as well—despite 10 damning examples of possible crimes in the report, which Barr finally released, lightly redacted, three weeks later. Those extra weeks allowed Trump a crucial moment to claim complete exoneration. Then he turned his rhetorical gun on his pursuers. He wanted them brought down.

Two investigations of the investigators were already in the works—one by the Justice Department's inspector general, focusing on electronic surveillance of a Trump-campaign adviser (Barr called it "spying"), and a broader review by John Durham, the U.S. attorney for Connecticut, under Barr's supervision. In an interview with CBS in May, Barr prejudged the outcome of Durham's review, strongly implying that the Russia investigation had been flawed from the start. He located the misconduct in the deep state: "Republics have fallen because of [a] Praetorian Guard mentality where government officials get very arrogant, they identify the national interest with their own political preferences, and they feel that anyone who has a different opinion, you know, is somehow an enemy of the state. And, you know, there is that tendency that they know better and that, you know, they're there to protect as guardians of the people. That can easily translate into essentially supervening the will of the majority and getting your own way as a government official."

Even if this were true of the Russia case, the attorney general had no business foreshadowing the result of investigations. And when, in December, the inspector general released his report, finding serious mistakes in the applications for surveillance warrants but no political bias—no "Praetorian Guard"—in the Russia investigation, Barr wasn't satisfied. He announced that he disagreed with the report.

Barr uses his official platform to gaslight the public. In a speech to the conservative Federalist Society in Washington in November, he devoted six paragraphs to perhaps the most contemptuously partisan remarks an attorney general has ever made. Progressives are on a "holy mission" in which ends justify means, while conservatives "tend to have more scruple over their political tactics," Barr claimed. "One of the ironies of today is that those who oppose this president constantly accuse this administration of 'shredding' constitutional norms and waging a war on the rule of law. When I ask my friends on the other side, 'What exactly are you referring to?' I get vacuous stares, followed by sputtering about the travel ban or some such thing."

The core of the speech was a denunciation of legislative and judicial encroachments on the authority of the executive—as if presidential power hasn't grown enormously since 9/11, if not the New Deal, and as if Trump's conduct in office falls well within the boundaries of Article II. In October, at Notre Dame, the attorney general recycled his old jeremiad on religious war. For Barr the year is always 1975, Congress is holding hearings to enfeeble the presidency, and the secular left is destroying the American family. He is using his short time remaining onstage to hold off the coming darkness, and if Providence has played the cosmic joke of vesting righteous power in the radically flawed person of Donald Trump, Barr will do what he must to protect him: distort the Mueller report; impugn Justice Department officials; try to keep the Ukraine whistleblower's complaint from Congress via spurious legal arguments; give cover to White House stonewalling of the impeachment inquiry; create an official channel for the delivery of political dirt on the president's opponents; overrule his prosecutors on behalf of Trump's friend Roger Stone.

Barr and Trump are pursuing very different projects—the one a crusade to align government with his idea of religious authority, the other a venal quest for self-aggrandizement. But they serve each other's purpose by collaborating to destroy the independence of anything— federal agencies, the public servants who work in them, even the other branches of government—that could restrain the president.

"Barr is perhaps the most political attorney general we've ever had," a longtime government lawyer told me. He described the devastating effects on law enforcement of Trump's unending assault and Barr's complicity. "I know from talking to friends that many of the career people are distressed about two related things. One is the sense that legal decisions are being driven to an exceptional degree by politics." The Justice Department, disregarding the views of career lawyers, has taken extreme positions—for example, that the White House could refuse to provide any evidence in the impeachment hearings, and that neither the House of Representatives nor the Manhattan district at-torney can subpoena Trump's personal financial records. The other cause of distress, the lawyer said, is Barr's willingness to attack his own people, joining Trump in accusing government officials of conspiring against the president.

Even far afield from Washington, morale has suffered. A federal prosecutor in the middle of the country told me that he and his col-leagues can no longer count on their leaders to protect them from unfair accusations or political meddling. Any case with a hint of political risk is considered untouchable. The White House's agenda is driving more and more cases, especially those related to immigration. And there's a palpable fear of retaliation for any whiff of criticism. Prosecutors worry that Trump's attacks on law enforcement are having a corrosive effect

in courtrooms, because jurors no longer trust FBI agents or other government officers serving as witnesses.

As a result, many of the prosecutor's colleagues are thinking of leaving government service. "I hear a lot of people say, 'If there's a second
term, there's no possible way I can wait it out for another four.' A lot
of people feared how bad it could be, but we had no idea it would be
this bad. It's hard to weather that storm." What keeps this prosecutor
from leaving is a commitment to his cases, to the department's mission,
and to the thought "not so much that you could make a difference in
this administration, because that doesn't seem possible anymore, but so
you can be here in place when what we think will be a need to rebuild
comes."

When Trump launched his campaign, he was suspected of seeking only to enrich himself. The point of the presidency was more
high-paying guests at the Trump International Hotel, down the street
from the White House. If Trump's tax returns and financial records are
ever made public, we'll know just how much the presidency was worth
to him.

But Trump's ambitions have swelled since the election. He hasn't
crushed the independence of the Justice Department simply to be able
to squeeze more money out of his businesses. Financial self-interest "is
why he ran," Fred Wertheimer, of Democracy 21, says. "But power is
a drug. Power is an addiction—exercising power, flying around in Air
Force One, having motorcades, having people salute you. He thinks he
is the country."

———

As a candidate, Trump learned that a foreign country can provide
potent help in subverting an American election. As president, he has
the entire national-security bureaucracy under his command, but he
needed several years to find its weak spot—to figure out that the State
Department could be as corruptible as Justice, and as useful to his hold
on power.

When Mike Pompeo took over as secretary of state, in April 2018,
the State Department was already ailing. Diplomacy has been an

atrophying muscle of American power for several decades, and the status of Foreign Service officers has steadily diminished. In the mid-1970s, 60 percent of the positions at the level of assistant secretary and above were filled by career officials. By the time of the Obama administration, the figure was down to 30 percent, while ambassadorships had become a common way for presidents to thank big donors. "This wasn't invented in the beginning of 2017 with this administration," William Burns, a deputy secretary of state under Obama, told me. "Unqualified political appointees have been with us long before Donald Trump. As in so many areas, what he's done is accelerated that problem and made it a lot worse."

Rex Tillerson, Trump's first secretary of state, bled the department dry. To purge it of bloat, he tried to gut the budget, froze hiring, and pushed out a large cadre of senior diplomats. Offices and hallways in the headquarters on C Street grew deserted. When Pompeo became secretary, he promised to restore "swagger" to diplomacy. He ended the hiring freeze, promoted career officials, and began to fill empty positions at the top—but he brought in mostly political appointees. According to Ronald Neumann, a retired career ambassador who is now the president of the American Academy of Diplomacy, the politicization of the State Department represents "the destruction of a 100-year effort, from Teddy Roosevelt on, to build professional government separate from the spoils system." The destruction, Neumann told me, is a "deliberate process, based on the belief that the federal government is hostile, and now you have to put in loyal people across the board in senior positions to control the bastards—the career bureaucrats. In the past it has been primarily a frustration that the bureaucracy is sclerotic, that it is not agile. But it was not about loyalty, and that's what it's about now."

Under Pompeo, 42 percent of ambassadors are political appointees, an all-time high (before the Trump presidency the number was about 30 percent). They "are chosen for their loyalty to Trump," Elizabeth Jones, a retired career ambassador, told me. "They've learned that the only way to succeed is to be 100 percent loyal, 1,000 percent. The idea that you're out there to work for the American people is an alien idea."

Of the department's positions at the level of assistant secretary and above, only 8 percent are held by career officials, and only one Foreign Service officer has been confirmed by the Senate to a senior position since Trump took office—the others are in acting positions, a way for the administration to sap the independence of its senior officials. Many mid-level diplomats now look for posts outside Washington, in foreign countries that the president is unlikely to tweet about.

The story of how the first family, Rudy Giuliani, his two former business associates, a pair of discredited Ukrainian prosecutors, and the right-wing media orchestrated a smear campaign to force Ambassador Marie Yovanovitch out of her post in Kyiv because she stood in the way of their corrupt schemes has become famous as the origin of Trump's impeachment. The story of how Yovanovitch's colleagues in the State Department responded to the crisis is less well known. It reveals the full range of behavior among officials under unprecedented pressure from the top. It shows how an agency with a long, proud history can be hollowed out and broken by its own leaders.

Tom Malinowski, a Democratic congressman from New Jersey and former State Department official, was born in Communist Poland to a family that had lived through World War II. "I've often asked myself the alternative-history question of what might happen if the Nazis took over America," he told me. "Who would become, out of opportunism or maybe even shared outlook, one of them? Some people would. Most people would keep their head down. Some number of people would be courageous and do useful things. A smaller number would do recklessly useful things. And then some number, hopefully also small, would take advantage of the situation to help themselves."

Masha Yovanovitch had no public profile but was widely respected among colleagues. She joined the Foreign Service in 1986, when she was 28 years old, and rose through the ranks of the State Department to become the U.S. ambassador to Kyrgyzstan, then Armenia, and then, in 2016, Ukraine. At the embassy in Kyiv she became known as a dedicated fighter of the corruption rampant among Ukrainian political and business leaders. Her professionalism left her vulnerable when a gang of thugs set out to destroy her career. Corruption, the theme of her work in Ukraine, was also the theme of its abrupt end. "You're going to think that I'm incredibly naive," she told the House during her testimony, "but I couldn't imagine all the things that have happened."

In early March 2019, David Hale, the undersecretary of state for political affairs, paid a visit to the embassy in Kyiv. He asked Yovanovitch, who planned to end her tour that summer and then retire, to stay another year. With Ukrainian elections coming up, the embassy couldn't afford to be temporarily leaderless. She thought about it overnight and agreed.

Two weeks later, on March 20, *The Hill*, a Washington newspaper, published an interview with Yuriy Lutsenko, one of the dirty Ukrainian prosecutors who had been thwarted by Yovanovitch. Lutsenko accused her of trying to stop legitimate prosecutions. The article also reported that the ambassador was heard to have openly criticized Trump. The president retweeted the story, which was composed almost entirely of lies. It was followed by several more articles filled with conspiracy theories about Ukraine's interference in the 2016 election on behalf of Hillary Clinton. The reporter, John Solomon (who stands by his stories), was getting his information from Giuliani and his associates. Solomon had come to *The Hill* from *Circa News*, a right-wing site that two years earlier had published an identical falsehood about Andrew McCabe—that the former acting director of the FBI had openly trashed Trump in a meeting. McCabe, who helped launch a probe into Russian interference in U.S. politics, was ultimately fired. The Russia and Ukraine scandals are best understood as a single web of corruption and abuse of office, and Solomon is one of many strands connecting them.

Another is Joseph diGenova, a right-wing Washington lawyer, former appointee of Barr, and friend of Giuliani's who had asserted in 2016 that FBI agents were furious with James Comey for closing the Clinton investigation. On the same day the first *Hill* story about Yovanovitch was published, diGenova appeared on Sean Hannity's Fox News show and said that Yovanovitch "has bad-mouthed the president of the United States to Ukrainian officials and has told them not to listen or worry about Trump policy because he's going to be impeached.

This woman needs to be called home to the United States—" "Oh, immediately," Hannity interjected. Two nights later, Laura Ingraham repeated the story on her show. Victoria Toensing, diGenova's law partner (and wife) and a frequent Fox News guest, texted one of Giuliani's cronies: "Is the Wicket [sic] Witch gone?" On March 24, in a tweet, Donald Trump Jr. called Yovanovitch a "joker."

The State Department called *The Hill's* original story a "complete fabrication." But as the lies spread among conservative media, triggering a barrage of attacks, Yovanovitch found herself in a crisis. Hale, the department's No. 3 and its senior career diplomat, sent an email to two colleagues: "I believe Masha should deny on the record saying anything disrespectful and reaffirm her loyalty as Ambassador and FSO to POTUS and Constitution." Gordon Sondland, a Trump donor who, with no relevant experience, had been made ambassador to the European Union, gave her the same advice directly. "Tweet out there that you support the president, and that all these are lies," Yovanovitch recounted him saying during her impeachment testimony. "You know the sorts of things that he likes. Go out there battling aggressively and praise him."

Yovanovitch felt that she couldn't do it. Like Erica Newland, she had taken an oath to defend the Constitution, not the president. Instead of tweeting allegiance to Trump, Yovanovitch recorded a public-service announcement urging Ukrainians to vote in that country's upcoming presidential election. She tried to connect this civic duty to her role as a nonpartisan government official. "Diplomats like me make a pledge to serve whomever the American people, our fellow citizens, choose," she told the camera. Presidents Bush and Obama had both appointed her to ambassadorships, "and I promote and carry out the policies of President Trump and his administration. This is one of the marks of a true democracy."

Whatever impression this civics lesson made on Ukrainians, it did nothing to stop the vicious campaign against her back home. The United States was no longer the democracy that American diplomats hold up as a model to foreigners.

On March 24, unable to function in her post, Yovanovitch wrote a desperate email to David Hale. She asked for a statement from the secretary of state saying that she had his full confidence, that she spoke for the president and the country. Hale called Yovanovitch that afternoon and asked her to put her concerns in writing. She sent a longer email, describing the figures who were attacking her—including Giuliani and Lutsenko—and attempting to interpret their motives.

The next day, at a weekly meeting of senior officials in the secretary's office, Hale brought up Yovanovitch's request. Pompeo was confronted with a dilemma—stand up for his people or appease the White House. He solved it by punting, saying that no statement would be made on her behalf until Giuliani, Hannity, and others were asked for their evidence. Later that week Hale sent word to the European bureau: "No statement."

Yovanovitch herself never got an answer from Hale. "Basically, we moved on," Hale said during his testimony at the impeachment inquiry. "For whatever reason, we stopped working on that—at least, I stopped working on that issue. I was not involved in doing it, so I wasn't paying a great deal of attention to it." Expressing support for Yovanovitch might have made things worse, he noted. "One point of view was that it might even provoke a public reaction from the president himself about the ambassador."

A couple of bureaucratic levels below Hale, George Kent, the deputy assistant secretary of state for Europe, was fighting on behalf of the besieged ambassador. Kent had been her second in command at the embassy in Kyiv, where corruption had been his major focus. He knew all the Ukrainian players involved in the campaign against her, and he was outraged by the slanders, which had begun to tar his name as well. He had strengthened the original State Department response to the first *Hill* article, inserting the phrase *complete fabrication*, and when the attacks intensified he told Hale that the department needed to stand behind Yovanovitch. He spoke up despite his vulnerable status as a mid-level officer in line for a promotion to a senior position.

"Moments like this test people; they bring out one's true character," said Malinowski, who, as a member of the House Foreign Affairs Committee, heard days of testimony from ex-colleagues during the impeachment inquiry. "In normal times, it's hard to know who would do what under those circumstances." Kent's first impulse was to prevent American policy from being corrupted in Kyiv and Washington. Hale, in a more powerful job, put bureaucratic hierarchy and his own secure place in it first. As a result, Yovanovitch had no one to press the urgency of her case with her leadership.

"I believe moral courage is more difficult than physical courage," Ronald Neumann, the retired ambassador, told me. "I was an infantry officer in Vietnam. Some courageous officers on the battlefield became very cautious bureaucrats." Physical courage in battle is made easier by speed, adrenaline, comrades. "Moral courage—you have, in many cases, lots of time, it's a solitary act," he said. "You are fully aware of potential repercussions to your career, and it's harder. It shouldn't be harder—you're not going to get killed—but that's the way it is."

Things quieted down for a few weeks. On April 21 Volodymyr Zelensky, who ran on an anti-corruption platform, was elected president of Ukraine in a landslide. Right away, the White House let Pompeo know that Trump wanted Yovanovitch gone. The media storm kicked up again. On the evening of April 24, Yovanovitch hosted an embassy event to honor a young Ukrainian woman, an anti-corruption activist who had died after a sulfuric-acid attack and whose murder remained unsolved. After midnight, a call came in from the State Department: Yovanovitch was to get on the next plane home. She asked for a reason but was given none, other than concern for her security.

She was back in Washington on April 26. That was the day Pompeo, with great fanfare, unveiled his "Ethos" initiative, which included a new mission statement that the secretary himself recited before hundreds of Foreign Service officers: "I am a champion of American diplomacy . . . I act with uncompromising personal and professional integrity. I take ownership of and responsibility for my actions and decisions. And I show unstinting respect in word and deed for my colleagues and all who serve alongside me." Pompeo didn't meet with his ambassador to Ukraine after summarily recalling her, or ever again, nor did he say a public word on her behalf. Other officials told Yovanovitch that she had done nothing wrong but had somehow "lost the confidence of the president." The department found her a temporary teaching post at Georgetown, but her career as a diplomat was over.

"I, on a personal level, felt awful for her," Kent told the impeachment inquiry, "because it was within two months of us asking her—the undersecretary of state asking her—to stay another year." When, in late May, Giuliani resumed his campaign of lies, telling Ukrainian journalists that Yovanovitch and Kent were part of a plot against Trump led by George Soros, there was no rebuttal from the State Department. Hale sent word that Kent should keep his head down and lower his profile on Ukraine. Kent canceled several scheduled appearances at Washington think tanks.

By then America's Ukraine policy had fallen out of the regular State Department channels and into the hands of the "three amigos"— Ambassadors Gordon Sondland and Kurt Volker and Energy Secretary Rick Perry. Volker, the special envoy to Ukraine, wanted to arrange a meeting between Zelensky and Trump, and in July he told Kent that he was going to see Giuliani to discuss Ukrainian investigations of former Vice President Joe Biden's family and the 2016 election. Kent later said that when he asked Volker why he would do that, Volker replied, "If there's nothing there, what does it matter? And if there is something there, it should be investigated." Kent told him, "Asking another country to investigate a prosecution for political reasons undermines our advocacy of the rule of law." But if this principle had ever had currency in the Trump administration, it no longer did.

On July 25, after Ukraine's parliamentary elections, Trump called Zelensky and asked for "a favor"—an investigation of the Bidens that was tantamount to Ukrainian interference in the U.S. presidential campaign in exchange for the release of American military aid and a personal meeting in the Oval Office. A day or two later, Kent heard about the call from Lieutenant Colonel Alexander Vindman, the top Ukraine expert in the White House, who had been among those— including Pompeo—listening in. Vindman told Kent that Trump had called Yovanovitch "bad news," and that the conversation had gone into highly sensitive matters—so sensitive that Vindman couldn't share them with his colleague. Kent didn't try to learn more. For all his outspokenness in Yovanovitch's defense, Kent wasn't the type of official who wanted "to be in the middle of everything." In his impeachment testimony, he never mentioned writing a dissenting cable, or speaking to the inspector general. He carefully avoided the media.

The professional code of Foreign Service officers nearly kept the story of Trump's attempted shakedown of Zelensky a secret. "It's not in their DNA" to go public, Tom Malinowski said. Only one bureaucrat—the whistleblower—made it possible for the American people to find out about the quid pro quo. The complaint surfaced on September 9, just days before Zelensky was scheduled to meet CNN's Fareed Zakaria to discuss an interview, during which he likely would have announced the investigations that Trump wanted.

On September 25, the White House released a rough transcript of the July 25 call. In it, Trump said that "the former ambassador from the United States, the woman, was bad news" and "she's going to go through some things." During the impeachment inquiry Hale explained, in high bureaucratese, "That was not an operational comment that had been operationalized in any way."

At the State Department, Ambassador Michael McKinley read the transcript and had a visceral, almost physical reaction: He was appalled. McKinley was Pompeo's senior adviser, having been brought back from his post in Brazil to serve as a link between the secretary and the Foreign Service. He and Hale were the only career officers among the department's leadership, but he never made it into the secretary's inner circle of political appointees, which included Pompeo's former business partners. Until September 25, McKinley hadn't paid enough attention to connect the dots of the Ukraine story. Now he found that Trump's words spoke for themselves.

The next day, McKinley picked up where Kent had left off the previous spring. According to his impeachment testimony, he went to see Pompeo and asked, "Wouldn't it be good to put out a statement on Yovanovitch?" Pompeo listened, and then he said, "Thank you." The conversation lasted about three minutes.

In the last days of September, McKinley kept pushing for a statement praising Yovanovitch's professionalism and courage. He heard from eight or 10 colleagues that the State Department's silence in the face of an ugly presidential attack was demoralizing. On September 28 he emailed five senior colleagues, including Hale, insisting that the department needed to say something. Four wrote back agreeing. Hale didn't reply; he told a colleague that he didn't think McKinley's effort would go anywhere. A few hours later Pompeo's spokesperson informed McKinley that, in order to protect Yovanovitch from undue attention, the secretary would not release a statement.

The next day, a Sunday, McKinley told his wife that, after 37 years in the Foreign Service, he had to get out right away. Though he never spoke publicly until he was subpoenaed to appear before the House during the impeachment inquiry, his departure was so sudden that it had the quality of a resignation in protest. Pompeo, known in the department for his temper and bullying, spent 20 minutes on the phone from Europe with McKinley and gave him a tough time. Later, the secretary lied in an interview with ABC, saying that McKinley could have come to see him about Yovanovitch anytime but never had.

Before leaving, McKinley paid a visit to Hale and told him, one Foreign Service officer to another, that the department's silence was having a terrible effect on morale. Hale flatly disagreed—he asserted that morale was high. Afterward, Hale met with Pompeo and identified a different threat to morale—McKinley's negativity.

"I was flying solo," McKinley told the House during the impeachment inquiry. "I didn't know what the rules of engagement were. But I did know that, as a Foreign Service officer, I would be feeling pretty alone at this point." So he got in touch with Yovanovitch, whom he knew, and with Kent, whom he didn't. McKinley wanted to find out how they were doing. He was surprised to learn that he was the first senior official to contact them about the transcript of the Ukraine call. Kent was picking apples with his wife in Virginia when McKinley reached him. Afterward, he had to Google McKinley to find out who he was. "He appeared to me . . . to be a genuinely decent person who

was concerned about what was happening," Kent said in his impeachment testimony.

In early October, after House committees issued subpoenas for documents and scheduled depositions, the State Department ordered its
personnel not to cooperate. Pompeo sent a letter to Congress calling
the requests "an attempt to intimidate, bully, and treat improperly the
distinguished professionals of the Department of State." He also said
publicly that Congress had prevented Foreign Service officers from
talking to the department's lawyers, which wasn't true—the lawyers
wouldn't talk to Kent, who had received a subpoena and was willing to
testify. Kent felt bullied not by Congress, but by his own agency.

On October 3, the State Department's European bureau met to
discuss how to respond to the subpoenas. When Kent noted that the
department was being unresponsive to Congress, a department lawyer raised his voice at Kent in front of 15 colleagues, then called him
into the hall to yell some more. He was putting Kent on notice not to
cooperate. Kent wrote a memo about the encounter, which he gave
to McKinley, who sent it to Hale and others . . . and then the memo
disappeared into the files with all the other documents that the department refused to turn over to Congress.

The career people testified anyway. None of them had ever received
this kind of public scrutiny. Some were being regularly attacked by
name on social media and right-wing websites. All of them were facing
steep lawyers' bills. (Former colleagues set up a legal fund and raised
several hundred thousand dollars.) Pompeo and his State Department
continued to say nothing in their defense. But one after another they
came forward. Marie Yovanovitch, whose mother had just died, didn't
lose her composure when Representative Adam Schiff read aloud a
nasty tweet Trump had just written about her. George Kent testified
in a bow tie and matching pocket square like a throwback from an
era of great diplomacy, saying with a wry smile, "You can't promote
principled anti-corruption action without pissing off corrupt people."
David Hale, pale and terse, also testified. Toward the end of his testimony, Democratic Representative Denny Heck of Washington begged
Hale to say that Yovanovitch was a courageous patriot and that what

had happened to her was wrong. Hale's voice faltered as he replied, "I believe that she should have been able to stay at post and continue to do the outstanding work—"

Heck wasn't having it. "What happened to her was *wrong?*"

"That's right," Hale said.

"Thank you for clarifying the record. Because I wasn't sure where it was that she could go to set the record straight if it wasn't you, sir, or where she could go to get her good name and reputation back if it wasn't you, sir."

Tom Malinowski, listening to his former colleagues, thought that their testimony said something about what has happened to the State Department. "There's a lot of pent-up anger and trauma, and this was an outlet for the institution," he said. "These men and women were speaking for their colleagues about more than just what happened with Ukraine."

Bureaucrats never received such public praise as they did during the weeks of the impeachment inquiry. But the hearings left a misleading impression. The Ukraine story, like the Russia story before it, did not represent a morality tale in which truth and honor stood up to calumny and corruption and prevailed. Yovanovitch is gone, and so is her replacement, William Taylor Jr., and so are McKinley and others— Lieutenant Colonel Vindman was marched out of the White House in early February—while Pompeo is still there and, above him, so is the president. Trump is winning.

HOW TO BUILD
AN AUTOCRACY

by David Frum

[MARCH 2017]

Shortly after Donald Trump's inauguration, *Atlantic* staff writer David Frum laid out a blueprint for how the new president might, over time—with incremental actions, and always with the help of eager enablers in his own party—begin to dismantle the bearing walls of our constitutional structure. The title pulled no punches: "How to Build an Autocracy." Frum wrote: "Those citizens who fantasize about defying tyranny from within fortified compounds have never understood how liberty is actually threatened in a modern bureaucratic state: not by diktat and violence, but by the slow, demoralizing process of corruption and deceit. And the way that liberty must be defended is not with amateur firearms, but with an unwearying insistence upon the honesty, integrity, and professionalism of American institutions and those who lead them." Frum warned that the gravest threat to American democracy—and the quality that the president and his associates were counting on above all else—is public indifference.

"How to Build an Autocracy" became one of the most widely read magazine articles in *The Atlantic*'s 163-year history. Frum is the author of *Trumpocracy: The Corruption of the American Republic* (2018) and, most recently, *Trumpocalypse: Restoring American Democracy* (2020).

In an 1888 lecture, James Russell Lowell, a founder of this magazine, challenged the happy assumption that the Constitution was a "machine that would go of itself." Lowell was right. *Checks and balances* is a metaphor, not a mechanism.

No society, not even one as rich and fortunate as the United States has been, is guaranteed a successful future. When early Americans wrote things like "Eternal vigilance is the price of liberty," they did not do so to provide bromides for future bumper stickers. They lived in a world in which authoritarian rule was the norm, in which rulers habitually claimed the powers and assets of the state as their own personal property.

The United States is of course a very robust democracy. Yet no human contrivance is tamper-proof, a constitutional democracy least of all. Some features of the American system hugely inhibit the abuse of office: the separation of powers within the federal government; the division of responsibilities between the federal government and the states. Federal agencies pride themselves on their independence; the court system is huge, complex, and resistant to improper influence.

The American system is also perforated by vulnerabilities no less dangerous for being so familiar. Supreme among those vulnerabilities is reliance on the personal qualities of the man or woman who wields the awesome powers of the presidency. A British prime minister can lose power in minutes if he or she forfeits the confidence of the majority in Parliament. The president of the United States, on the other hand, is restrained first and foremost by his or her own ethics and public spirit. What happens if somebody comes to the high office lacking those qualities?

Over the past generation, we have seen ominous indicators of a breakdown of the American political system: the willingness of congressional Republicans to push the United States to the brink of a default on its national obligations in 2013 in order to score a point in budget negotiations; Barack Obama's assertion of a unilateral executive power to confer legal status upon millions of people illegally present in the United States—despite his own prior acknowledgment that no such power existed.

Donald Trump, however, represents something much more radical. A president who plausibly owes his office at least in part to a clandestine intervention by a hostile foreign intelligence service? Who uses the bully pulpit to target individual critics? Who creates blind trusts that are not blind, invites his children to commingle private and public business, and somehow gets the unhappy members of his own political party either to endorse his choices or shrug them off? If this were happening in Honduras, we'd know what to call it. It's happening here instead, and so we are baffled.

"Ambition must be made to counteract ambition." With those words, written more than 200 years ago, the authors of the Federalist Papers explained the most important safeguard of the American constitutional system. They then added this promise: "In republican government, the legislative authority necessarily predominates." Congress enacts laws, appropriates funds, confirms the president's appointees. Congress can subpoena records, question officials, and even impeach them. Congress can protect the American system from an overbearing president.

But will it?

As politics has become polarized, Congress has increasingly become a check only on presidents of the opposite party. Recent presidents enjoying a same-party majority in Congress—Barack Obama in 2009 and 2010, George W. Bush from 2003 through 2006—usually got their way. And congressional oversight might well be performed even less diligently during the Trump administration.

The first reason to fear weak diligence is the oddly inverse relationship between President Trump and the congressional Republicans. In the ordinary course of events, it's the incoming president who burns with eager policy ideas. Consequently, it's the president who must adapt to—and often overlook—the petty human weaknesses and vices of members of Congress in order to advance his agenda. This time, it will be Paul Ryan, the Speaker of the House, doing the advancing—and consequently the overlooking.

Trump has scant interest in congressional Republicans' ideas, does not share their ideology, and cares little for their fate. He can—and would—break faith with them in an instant to further his own interests. Yet here they are, on the verge of achieving everything they have hoped to achieve for years, if not decades. They owe this chance solely to Trump's ability to deliver a crucial margin of votes in a handful of states—Wisconsin, Michigan, and Pennsylvania—which has provided a party that cannot win the national popular vote a fleeting opportunity to act as a decisive national majority. The greatest risk to all their projects and plans is the very same X factor that gave them their opportunity: Donald Trump, and his famously erratic personality. What excites Trump is his approval rating, his wealth, his power. The day could come when those ends would be better served by jettisoning the institutional Republican Party in favor of an ad hoc populist coalition, joining nationalism to generous social spending—a mix that's worked well for authoritarians in places like Poland. Who doubts Trump would do it? Not Paul Ryan. Not Mitch McConnell, the Senate majority leader. For the first time since the administration of John Tyler in the 1840s, a majority in Congress must worry about their president defecting from *them* rather than the other way around.

A scandal involving the president could likewise wreck everything that Republican congressional leaders have waited years to accomplish. However deftly they manage everything else, they cannot prevent such a scandal. But there is one thing they can do: their utmost not to find out about it.

"Do you have any concerns about Steve Bannon being in the White House?" CNN's Jake Tapper asked Ryan in November. "I don't know Steve Bannon, so I have no concerns," answered the Speaker. "I trust Donald's judgment."

Asked on *60 Minutes* whether he believed Donald Trump's claim that "millions" of illegal votes had been cast, Ryan answered: "I don't know. I'm not really focused on these things."

What about Trump's conflicts of interest? "This is not what I'm concerned about in Congress," Ryan said on CNBC. Trump should handle his conflicts "however he wants to."

Ryan has learned his prudence the hard way. Following the airing of Trump's past comments, caught on tape, about his forceful sexual advances on women, Ryan said he'd no longer campaign for Trump. Ryan's net favorability rating among Republicans dropped by 28 points in less than 10 days. Once unassailable in the party, he suddenly found himself disliked by 45 percent of Republicans.

As Ryan's cherished plans move closer and closer to presidential signature, Congress's subservience to the president will likely intensify. Whether it's allegations of Russian hacks of Democratic Party internal communications, or allegations of self-enrichment by the Trump family, or favorable treatment of Trump business associates, the Republican caucus in Congress will likely find itself conscripted into serving as Donald Trump's ethical bodyguard.

The Senate historically has offered more scope to dissenters than the House. Yet even that institution will find itself under pressure. Two of the Senate's most important Republican Trump skeptics will be up for reelection in 2018: Arizona's Jeff Flake and Texas's Ted Cruz. They will not want to provoke a same-party president—especially not in a year when the president's party can afford to lose a seat or two in order to discipline dissenters. Mitch McConnell is an even more results-oriented politician than Paul Ryan—and his wife, Elaine Chao, has been offered a Cabinet position, which might tilt him further in Trump's favor.

Ambition will counteract ambition only until ambition discovers that conformity serves its goals better. At that time, Congress, the body expected to check presidential power, may become the president's most potent enabler.

Discipline within the congressional ranks will be strictly enforced not only by the party leadership and party donors, but also by the overwhelming influence of Fox News. Trump versus Clinton was not 2016's only contest between an overbearing man and a restrained woman. Just such a contest was waged at Fox, between Sean Hannity and Megyn Kelly. In both cases, the early indicators seemed to favor the women. Yet in the end it was the men who won, Hannity even more decisively than Trump. Hannity's show, which became an unapologetic infomercial for Trump, pulled into first place on the network in mid-October.

Kelly's show tumbled to fifth place, behind even *The Five*, a roundtable program that airs at 5 p.m. Kelly landed on her feet, of course, but Fox learned its lesson: Trump sells; critical coverage does not. Since the election, the network has awarded Kelly's former 9 p.m. time slot to Tucker Carlson, who is positioning himself as a Trump enthusiast in the Hannity mold.

From the point of view of the typical Republican member of Congress, Fox remains all-powerful: the single most important source of visibility and affirmation with the voters whom a Republican politician cares about. In 2009, in the run-up to the Tea Party insurgency, South Carolina's Bob Inglis crossed Fox, criticizing Glenn Beck and telling people at a town-hall meeting that they should turn his show off. He was drowned out by booing, and the following year, he lost his primary with only 29 percent of the vote, a crushing repudiation for an incumbent untouched by any scandal.

Fox is reinforced by a carrier fleet of supplementary institutions: super PACs, think tanks, and conservative web and social-media presences, which now include such former pariahs as Breitbart and Alex Jones. So long as the carrier fleet coheres—and unless public opinion turns sharply against the president—oversight of Trump by the Republican congressional majority will very likely be cautious, conditional, and limited.

———

Donald Trump will not set out to build an authoritarian state. His immediate priority seems likely to be to use the presidency to enrich himself. But as he does so, he will need to protect himself from legal risk. Being Trump, he will also inevitably wish to inflict payback on his critics. Construction of an apparatus of impunity and revenge will begin haphazardly and opportunistically. But it will accelerate. It will have to.

If Congress is quiescent, what can Trump do? A better question, perhaps, is what can't he do?

Newt Gingrich, the former Speaker of the House, who often articulates Trumpist ideas more candidly than Trump himself might think prudent, offered a sharp lesson in how difficult it will be to enforce laws against an uncooperative president. During a radio roundtable in December, on the topic of whether it would violate anti-nepotism laws to bring Trump's daughter and son-in-law onto the White House staff, Gingrich said: The president "has, frankly, the power of the pardon. It is a totally open power, and he could simply say, 'Look, I want them to be my advisers. I pardon them if anybody finds them to have behaved against the rules. Period.' And technically, under the Constitution, he has that level of authority."

That statement is true, and it points to a deeper truth: The United States may be a nation of laws, but the proper functioning of the law depends upon the competence and integrity of those charged with executing it. A president determined to thwart the law in order to protect himself and those in his circle has many means to do so.

The power of the pardon, deployed to defend not only family but also those who would protect the president's interests, dealings, and indiscretions, is one such means. The powers of appointment and removal are another. The president appoints and can remove the commissioner of the IRS. He appoints and can remove the inspectors general who oversee the internal workings of the Cabinet departments and major agencies. He appoints and can remove the 93 U.S. attorneys, who have the power to initiate and to end federal prosecutions. He appoints and can remove the attorney general, the deputy attorney general, and the head of the criminal division at the Department of Justice.

There are hedges on these powers, both customary and constitutional, including the Senate's power to confirm (or not) presidential appointees. Yet the hedges may not hold in the future as robustly as they have in the past.

Senators of the president's party traditionally have expected to be consulted on the U.S.-attorney picks in their states, a highly coveted patronage plum. But the U.S. attorneys of most interest to Trump—above all the ones in New York and New Jersey, the locus of many of his businesses and bank dealings—come from states where there are no Republican senators to take into account. And while the U.S. attorneys in Florida, home to Mar-a-Lago and other Trump properties, surely concern him nearly as much, if there's one Republican senator whom Trump would cheerfully disregard, it's Marco Rubio.

The traditions of independence and professionalism that prevail within the federal law-enforcement apparatus, and within the civil service more generally, will tend to restrain a president's power. Yet in the years ahead, these restraints may also prove less robust than they look. Republicans in Congress have long advocated reforms to expedite the firing of underperforming civil servants. In the abstract, there's much to recommend this idea. If reform is dramatic and happens in the next two years, however, the balance of power between the political and the professional elements of the federal government will shift, decisively, at precisely the moment when the political elements are most aggressive. The intelligence agencies in particular would likely find themselves exposed to retribution from a president enraged at them for reporting on Russia's aid to his election campaign. "As you know from his other career, Donald likes to fire people." So New Jersey Governor Chris Christie joked to a roomful of Republican donors at the party's national convention in July. It would be a mighty power—and highly useful.

The courts, though they might slowly be packed with judges inclined to hear the president's arguments sympathetically, are also a check, of course. But it's already difficult to hold a president to account for financial improprieties. As Donald Trump correctly told reporters and editors from *The New York Times* on November 22, presidents are not bound by the conflict-of-interest rules that govern everyone else in the executive branch.

Presidents from Jimmy Carter onward have balanced this unique exemption with a unique act of disclosure: the voluntary publication of their income-tax returns. At a press conference on January 11, Trump made clear that he will not follow that tradition. His attorney instead insisted that everything the public needs to know is captured by his annual financial-disclosure report, which is required by law for executive-branch employees and from which presidents are not exempt. But a glance at the reporting forms (you can read them yourself at www.oge.gov/web/278eguide.nsf) will show their inadequacy to

Trump's situation. They are written with stocks and bonds in mind, to capture mortgage liabilities and deferred executive compensation—not the labyrinthine deals of the Trump Organization and its ramifying networks of partners and brand-licensing affiliates. The truth is in the tax returns, and they will not be forthcoming.

Even outright bribe-taking by an elected official is surprisingly difficult to prosecute, and was made harder still by the Supreme Court in 2016, when it overturned, by an 8–0 vote, the conviction of former Virginia Governor Bob McDonnell. McDonnell and his wife had taken valuable gifts of cash and luxury goods from a favor seeker. McDonnell then set up meetings between the favor seeker and state officials who were in a position to help him. A jury had even accepted that the "quid" was indeed "pro" the "quo"—an evidentiary burden that has often protected accused bribe-takers in the past. The McDonnells had been convicted on a combined 20 counts.

The Supreme Court objected, however, that the lower courts had interpreted federal anti-corruption law too broadly. The relevant statute applied only to "official acts." The Court defined such acts very strictly, and held that "setting up a meeting, talking to another official, or organizing an event—without more—does not fit that definition of an 'official act.'"

Trump is poised to mingle business and government with an audacity and on a scale more reminiscent of a leader in a post-Soviet republic than anything ever before seen in the United States. Glimpses of his family's wealth-seeking activities will likely emerge during his presidency, as they did during the transition. Trump's Indian business partners dropped by Trump Tower and posted pictures with the then-president-elect on Facebook, alerting folks back home that they were now powers to be reckoned with. The Argentine media reported that Trump had discussed the progress of a Trump-branded building in Buenos Aires during a congratulatory phone call from the country's president. (A spokesman for the Argentine president denied that the two men had discussed the building on their call.) Trump's daughter Ivanka sat in on a meeting with the Japanese prime minister—a useful meeting for her, since a government-owned bank has a large ownership stake in the Japanese company with which she was negotiating a licensing deal.

Suggestive. Disturbing. But illegal, post-*McDonnell*? How many presidentially removable officials would dare even initiate an inquiry?

You may hear much mention of the Emoluments Clause of the Constitution during Trump's presidency: "No Title of Nobility shall be granted by the United States: And no Person holding any Office of Profit or Trust under them, shall, without the Consent of the Congress, accept of any present, Emolument, Office, or Title, of any kind whatever, from any King, Prince, or foreign State."

But as written, this seems to present a number of loopholes. First, the clause applies only to the president himself, not to his family members. Second, it seems to govern benefits only from foreign governments and state-owned enterprises, not from private business entities. Third, Trump's lawyers have argued that the clause applies only to gifts and titles, not to business transactions. Fourth, what does "the Consent of Congress" mean? If Congress is apprised of an apparent emolument, and declines to do anything about it, does that qualify as consent? Finally, how is this clause enforced? Could someone take President Trump to court and demand some kind of injunction? Who? How? Will the courts grant standing? The clause seems to presume an active Congress and a vigilant public. What if those are lacking?

It is essential to recognize that Trump will use his position not only to enrich himself; he will enrich plenty of other people, too, both the powerful and—sometimes, for public consumption—the relatively powerless. Venezuela, a stable democracy from the late 1950s through the 1990s, was corrupted by a politics of personal favoritism, as Hugo Chávez used state resources to bestow gifts on supporters. Venezuelan state TV even aired a regular program to showcase weeping recipients of new houses and free appliances. Americans recently got a preview of their own version of that show as grateful Carrier employees thanked then-President-Elect Trump for keeping their jobs in Indiana.

"I just couldn't believe that this guy . . . he's not even president yet and he worked on this deal with the company," T. J. Bray, a 32-year-old

Carrier employee, told *Fortune*. "I'm just in shock. A lot of the workers are in shock. We can't believe something good finally happened to us. It felt like a victory for the little people."

Trump will try hard during his presidency to create an atmosphere of personal munificence, in which graft does not matter, because rules and institutions do not matter. He will want to associate economic benefit with personal favor. He will create personal constituencies, and implicate other people in his corruption. That, over time, is what truly subverts the institutions of democracy and the rule of law. If the public cannot be induced to care, the power of the investigators serving at Trump's pleasure will be diminished all the more.

"The first task for our new administration will be to liberate our citizens from the crime and terrorism and lawlessness that threatens our communities." Those were Donald Trump's words at the Republican National Convention. The newly nominated presidential candidate then listed a series of outrages and attacks, especially against police officers.

> America was shocked to its core when our police officers in Dallas were so brutally executed. Immediately after Dallas, we've seen continued threats and violence against our law-enforcement officials. Law officers have been shot or killed in recent days in Georgia, Missouri, Wisconsin, Kansas, Michigan, and Tennessee.
>
> On Sunday, more police were gunned down in Baton Rouge, Louisiana. Three were killed, and three were very, very badly injured. An attack on law enforcement is an attack on all Americans. I have a message to every last person threatening the peace on our streets and the safety of our police: When I take the oath of office next year, I will restore law and order to our country.

You would never know from Trump's words that the average number of felonious killings of police during the Obama administration's tenure was almost one-third lower than it was in the early 1990s, a decline that tracked with the general fall in violent crime that has so blessed American society. There had been a rise in killings of police in 2014 and 2015 from the all-time low in 2013—but only back to the 2012 level. Not every year will be the best on record.

A mistaken belief that crime is spiraling out of control—that terrorists roam at large in America and that police are regularly gunned down—represents a considerable political asset for Donald Trump. Seventy-eight percent of Trump voters believed that crime had worsened during the Obama years.

In true police states, surveillance and repression sustain the power of the authorities. But that's not how power is gained and sustained in backsliding democracies. Polarization, not persecution, enables the modern illiberal regime.

By guile or by instinct, Trump understands this.

Whenever Trump stumbles into some kind of trouble, he reacts by picking a divisive fight. The morning after *The Wall Street Journal* published a story about the extraordinary conflicts of interest surrounding Trump's son-in-law, Jared Kushner, Trump tweeted that flag burners should be imprisoned or stripped of their citizenship. That evening, as if on cue, a little posse of oddballs obligingly burned flags for the cameras in front of the Trump International Hotel in New York. Guess which story dominated that day's news cycle?

Civil unrest will not be a problem for the Trump presidency. It will be a resource. Trump will likely want not to repress it, but to publicize it—and the conservative entertainment-outrage complex will eagerly assist him. Immigration protesters marching with Mexican flags; Black Lives Matter demonstrators bearing anti-police slogans—these are the images of the opposition that Trump will wish his supporters to see. The more offensively the protesters behave, the more pleased Trump will be.

Calculated outrage is an old political trick, but nobody in the history of American politics has deployed it as aggressively, as repeatedly, or with such success as Donald Trump. If there is harsh law enforcement by the Trump administration, it will benefit the president not to the extent that it quashes unrest, but to the extent that it enflames more of it, ratifying the apocalyptic vision that haunted his speech at the convention.

———————

At a rally in Grand Rapids, Michigan, in December, Trump got to talking about Vladimir Putin. "And then they said, 'You know he's killed reporters,'" Trump told the audience. "And I don't like that. I'm totally against that. By the way, I hate some of these people, but I'd never kill them. I hate them. No, I think, no—these people, honestly—I'll be honest, I'll be honest, I would never kill them. I would never do that. Ah, let's see—nah, no, I wouldn't. I would never kill them. But I do hate them."

In the early days of the Trump transition, Nic Dawes, a journalist who has worked in South Africa, delivered an ominous warning to the American media about what to expect. "Get used to being stigmatized as 'opposition,'" he wrote. "The basic idea is simple: to delegitimize accountability journalism by framing it as partisan."

The rulers of backsliding democracies resent an independent press, but cannot extinguish it. They may curb the media's appetite for critical coverage by intimidating unfriendly journalists, as President Jacob Zuma and members of his party have done in South Africa. Mostly, however, modern strongmen seek merely to discredit journalism as an institution, by denying that such a thing as independent judgment can exist. All reporting serves an agenda. There is no truth, only competing attempts to grab power.

By filling the media space with bizarre inventions and brazen denials, purveyors of fake news hope to mobilize potential supporters with righteous wrath—and to demoralize potential opponents by nurturing the idea that everybody lies and nothing matters. A would-be kleptocrat is actually better served by spreading cynicism than by deceiving followers with false beliefs: Believers can be disillusioned; people who expect to hear only lies can hardly complain when a lie is exposed. The inculcation of cynicism breaks down the distinction between those forms of media that try their imperfect best to report the truth, and those that purvey falsehoods for reasons of profit or ideology. *The New*

York Times becomes the equivalent of Russia's RT; *The Washington Post* of Breitbart; NPR of Infowars.

One story, still supremely disturbing, exemplifies the falsifying method. During November and December, the slow-moving California vote count gradually pushed Hillary Clinton's lead over Donald Trump in the national popular vote further and further: past 1 million, past 1.5 million, past 2 million, past 2.5 million. Trump's share of the vote would ultimately clock in below Richard Nixon's in 1960, Al Gore's in 2000, John Kerry's in 2004, Gerald Ford's in 1976, and Mitt Romney's in 2012—and barely ahead of Michael Dukakis's in 1988.

This outcome evidently gnawed at the president-elect. On November 27, Trump tweeted that he had in fact "won the popular vote if you deduct the millions of people who voted illegally." He followed up that astonishing, and unsubstantiated, statement with an escalating series of tweets and retweets.

It's hard to do justice to the breathtaking audacity of such a claim. If true, it would be so serious as to demand a criminal investigation at a minimum, presumably spanning many states. But of course the claim was not true. Trump had not a smidgen of evidence beyond his own bruised feelings and internet flotsam from flagrantly unreliable sources. Yet once the president-elect lent his prestige to the crazy claim, it became fact for many people. A survey by YouGov found that by December 1, 43 percent of Republicans accepted the claim that millions of people had voted illegally in 2016.

A clear untruth had suddenly become a contested possibility. When CNN's Jeff Zeleny correctly reported on November 28 that Trump's tweet was baseless, Fox's Sean Hannity accused Zeleny of media bias—and then proceeded to urge the incoming Trump administration to take a new tack with the White House press corps, and to punish reporters like Zeleny. "I think it's time to reevaluate the press and maybe change the traditional relationship with the press and the White House," Hannity said. "My message tonight to the press is simple: You guys are done. You've been exposed as fake, as having an agenda, as colluding. You're a fake news organization."

This was no idiosyncratic brain wave of Hannity's. The previous morning, Ari Fleischer, the former press secretary in George W. Bush's administration, had advanced a similar idea in a *Wall Street Journal* op-ed, suggesting that the White House could withhold credentials for its press conferences from media outlets that are "too liberal or unfair." Newt Gingrich recommended that Trump stop giving press conferences altogether.

Twitter, unmediated by the press, has proved an extremely effective communication tool for Trump. And the whipping-up of potentially violent Twitter mobs against media critics is already a standard method of Trump's governance. Megyn Kelly blamed Trump and his campaign's social-media director for inciting Trump's fans against her to such a degree that she felt compelled to hire armed guards to protect her family. I've talked with well-funded Trump supporters who speak of recruiting a troll army explicitly modeled on those used by Turkey's Recep Tayyip Erdoğan and Russia's Putin to take control of the social-media space, intimidating some critics and overwhelming others through a blizzard of doubt-casting and misinformation. The WikiLeaks Task Force recently tweeted—then hastily deleted—a suggestion that it would build a database to track personal and financial information on all verified Twitter accounts, the kind of accounts typically used by journalists at major media organizations. It's not hard to imagine how such compilations could be used to harass or intimidate.

Even so, it seems unlikely that President Trump will outright send the cameras away. He craves media attention too much. But he and his team are serving notice that a new era in government-media relations is coming, an era in which all criticism is by definition oppositional—and all critics are to be treated as enemies.

In an online article for *The New York Review of Books*, the Russian-born journalist Masha Gessen brilliantly noted a commonality between Donald Trump and the man Trump admires so much, Vladimir Putin. "*Lying is the message*," she wrote. "It's not just that both Putin and Trump lie, it is that they lie in the same way and for the same purpose: blatantly, to assert power over truth itself."

The lurid mass movements of the 20th century—communist, fascist, and other—have bequeathed to our imaginations an outdated image of what 21st-century authoritarianism might look like.

Whatever else happens, Americans are not going to assemble in parade-ground formations, any more than they will crank a gramophone or dance the turkey trot. In a society where few people walk to work, why mobilize young men in matching shirts to command the streets? If you're seeking to domineer and bully, you want your storm troopers to go online, where the more important traffic is. Demagogues need no longer stand erect for hours orating into a radio microphone. Tweet lies from a smartphone instead.

"Populist-fueled democratic backsliding is difficult to counter," wrote the political scientists Andrea Kendall-Taylor and Erica Frantz late last year. "Because it is subtle and incremental, there is no single moment that triggers widespread resistance or creates a focal point around which an opposition can coalesce . . . Piecemeal democratic erosion, therefore, typically provokes only fragmented resistance." Their observation was rooted in the experiences of countries ranging from the Philippines to Hungary. It could apply here, too.

If people retreat into private life, if critics grow quieter, if cynicism becomes endemic, the corruption will slowly become more brazen, the intimidation of opponents stronger. Laws intended to ensure accountability or prevent graft or protect civil liberties will be weakened.

If the president uses his office to grab billions for himself and his family, his supporters will feel empowered to take millions. If he successfully exerts power to punish enemies, his successors will emulate his methods.

If citizens learn that success in business or in public service depends on the favor of the president and his ruling clique, then it's not only American politics that will change. The economy will be corrupted, too, and with it the larger culture. A culture that has accepted that graft is the norm, that rules don't matter as much as relationships with those in power, and that people can be punished for speech and acts that remain theoretically legal—such a culture is not easily reoriented back to constitutionalism, freedom, and public integrity.

The oft-debated question "Is Donald Trump a fascist?" is not easy to answer. There are certainly fascistic elements to him: the subdivision of society into categories of friend and foe; the boastful virility and the delight in violence; the vision of life as a struggle for dominance that only some can win, and that others must lose.

Yet there's also something incongruous and even absurd about applying the sinister label of fascist to Donald Trump. He is so pathetically needy, so shamelessly self-interested, so fitful and distracted. Fascism fetishizes hardihood, sacrifice, and struggle—concepts not often associated with Trump.

Perhaps this is the wrong question. Perhaps the better question about Trump is not "What is he?" but "What will he do to us?"

By all early indications, the Trump presidency will corrode public integrity and the rule of law—and also do untold damage to American global leadership, the Western alliance, and democratic norms around the world. The damage has already begun, and it will not be soon or easily undone. Yet exactly how much damage is allowed to be done is an open question—the most important near-term question in American politics. It is also an intensely personal one, for its answer will be determined by the answer to another question: What will you do? And you? And you?

GENERAL CHAOS

by Mark Bowden

[NOVEMBER 2019]

When James Mattis resigned as secretary of defense in December 2018, it was widely assumed that Mattis's sharp differences with Donald Trump—among other things, over the president's decision to abruptly remove U.S. forces from Syria; his frequent disparagement of the NATO alliance; and his seeming warmth toward Russia's Vladimir Putin—reflected those of other officers at the highest reaches of the U.S. military. *Atlantic* contributing writer Mark Bowden's article "General Chaos," based on a series of candid interviews with top military leaders, all but one of whom had served under Trump, established the truth of that assumption. In the article, abridged here, the officers described the president's disdain for expertise, his trust in his own instincts, his lack of any coherent strategy, and his cartoonish view of what soldiering involves. Bowden is the author of *Black Hawk Down* (1999), *The Finish: The Killing of Osama bin Laden* (2012), and *Huê′ 1968* (2017).

For most of the past two decades, American troops have been deployed all over the world—to about 150 countries. During that time, hundreds of thousands of young men and women have experienced combat, and a generation of officers have come of age dealing with the practical realities of war. They possess a deep well of knowledge and experience. For the past three years, these highly trained professionals have been commanded by Donald Trump.

To get a sense of what serving Trump has been like, I interviewed officers up and down the ranks, as well as several present and former civilian Pentagon employees. Among the officers I spoke with were four of the highest ranks—three or four stars—all recently retired. All but one served Trump directly; the other left the service shortly before Trump was inaugurated. They come from different branches of the military, but I'll simply refer to them as "the generals." Some spoke only off the record, some allowed what they said to be quoted without attribution, and some talked on the record.

Military officers are sworn to serve whomever voters send to the White House. Cognizant of the special authority they hold, high-level officers epitomize respect for the chain of command, and are extremely reticent about criticizing their civilian overseers. That those I spoke with made an exception in Trump's case is telling, and much of what they told me is deeply disturbing. In 20 years of writing about the military, I have never heard officers in high positions express such alarm about a president. Trump's pronouncements and orders have already risked catastrophic and unnecessary wars in the Middle East and Asia, and have created severe problems for field commanders engaged in combat operations. Frequently caught unawares by Trump's statements, senior military officers have scrambled, in their aftermath, to steer the country away from tragedy. How many times can they successfully do that before faltering?

Amid threats spanning the globe, from nuclear proliferation to mined tankers in the Persian Gulf to terrorist attacks and cyberwarfare, those in command positions monitor the president's Twitter feed like field officers scanning the horizon for enemy troop movements. A new front line in national defense has become the White House Situation Room, where the military struggles to accommodate a commander in chief who is both ignorant and capricious. In May, after months of threatening Iran, Trump ordered the carrier group led by the USS *Abraham Lincoln* to shift from the Mediterranean Sea to the Persian Gulf. On June 20, after an American drone was downed there, he ordered a retaliatory attack—and then called it off minutes before it was to be launched. The next day he said he was "not looking for war" and wanted to talk with Iran's leaders, while also promising them "obliteration like you've never seen before" if they crossed him. He threatened North Korea with "fire and fury" and dispatched a three-aircraft-carrier flotilla to waters off the Korean peninsula—then he pivoted to friendly summits with Kim Jong Un, with whom he announced he was "in love"; canceled long-standing U.S. military exercises with South Korea; and dangled the possibility of withdrawing American forces from the country altogether. While the lovefest continues for the cameras, the U.S. has quietly uncanceled the canceled military exercises, and dropped any mention of a troop withdrawal.

The generals I spoke with didn't agree on everything, but they shared the following characterizations of Trump's military leadership.

He disdains expertise. Trump has little interest in the details of policy. He makes up his mind about a thing, and those who disagree with him—even those with manifestly more knowledge and experience—are stupid, or slow, or crazy.

As a personal quality, this can be trying; in a president, it is dangerous. Trump rejects the careful process of decision making that has long guided commanders in chief. Disdain for process might be the defining trait of his leadership. Of course, no process can guarantee good decisions—history makes that clear—but eschewing the tools available to a president is choosing ignorance. What Trump's supporters call "the deep state" is, in the world of national security—hardly a bastion of progressive politics—a vast reservoir of knowledge and global experience that presidents ignore at their peril. The generals spoke nostalgically of the process followed by previous presidents, who solicited advice from field commanders, foreign service and intelligence officers, and in some cases key allies before reaching decisions about military action. As different as George W. Bush and Barack Obama were in temperament and policy preferences, one general told me, they were remarkably alike in the Situation Room: Both presidents asked hard questions, wanted prevailing views challenged, insisted on a variety of options to consider, and weighed potential outcomes against broader goals. Trump doesn't do any of that. Despite commanding the most sophisticated intelligence-gathering apparatus in the world, this president prefers to be briefed by Fox News, and then arrives at decisions without input from others.

One prominent example came on December 19, 2018, when Trump announced, via Twitter, that he was ordering all American forces in Syria home.

"We have defeated ISIS in Syria, my only reason for being there during the Trump presidency," he tweeted. Later that day he said, "Our boys, our young women, our men, they are all coming back, and they are coming back now."

This satisfied one of Trump's campaign promises, and it appealed to the isolationist convictions of his core supporters. Forget the experts, forget the chain of command—they were the people who, after all, had kept American forces engaged in that part of the world for 15 bloody years without noticeably improving things. Enough was enough.

At that moment, however, American troops were in the final stages of crushing the Islamic State, which, contrary to Trump's assertion, was collapsing but had not yet been defeated. Its brutal caliphate, which had briefly stretched from eastern Iraq to western Syria, had been painstakingly dismantled over the previous five years by an American-led global coalition, which was close to finishing the job. Now they were to stop and come home?

Here, several of the generals felt, was a textbook example of ill-informed decision making. The downsides of a withdrawal were obvious: It would create a power vacuum that would effectively cede the fractured Syrian state to Russia and Iran; it would abandon America's local allies to an uncertain fate; and it would encourage a diminished ISIS to keep fighting. The decision—which prompted the immediate resignations of the secretary of defense, General James Mattis, and the U.S. special envoy to the mission, Brett McGurk—blindsided not only Congress and America's allies but the person charged with actually waging the war, General Joseph Votel, the commander of U.S. Central Command. He had not been consulted.

Trump's tweet put Votel in a difficult spot. Here was a sudden 180-degree turn in U.S. policy that severely undercut an ongoing effort. The American contingent of about 2,000 soldiers, most of them Special Forces, was coordinating with the Iraqi army; the Syrian Democratic Forces, or SDF, consisting primarily of Kurdish militias and Syrians opposed to President Bashar al-Assad; and representatives of NATO, the Arab League, and dozens of countries. This alliance had reduced ISIS's territory to small pockets of resistance inside Syria. America's troops were deep in the Euphrates Valley, a long way from their original bases of operation. An estimated 10,000 hard-core Islamist soldiers were fighting to the death. Months of tough combat lay ahead.

Votel's force in Syria was relatively small, but it required a steady supply of food, ammunition, parts, and medical supplies, and regular troop rotations. The avenue for these vital conveyances through hundreds of miles of hazardous Iraqi desert—was truck convoys, protected almost exclusively by the SDF. To protect its troops during a retreat, America could have brought in its own troops or replaced those truck convoys with airlifts, but either step would have meant suddenly escalating an engagement that the president had just pronounced finished.

For the American commander, this was a terrible logistical challenge. An orderly withdrawal of his forces would further stress supply lines, therefore necessitating the SDF's help even more. Votel found himself in the position of having to tell his allies, in effect, *We're screwing you, but we need you now more than ever.*

Field commanders are often given orders they don't like. The military must bow to civilian rule. The generals accept and embrace that. But they also say that no careful decision-making process would have produced Trump's abrupt about-face.

Votel decided to take an exceedingly rare step: He publicly contradicted his commander in chief. In an interview with CNN he said that no, ISIS was not yet defeated, and now was not the time to retreat. Given his responsibility to his troops and the mission, the general didn't have much choice.

Votel held everything together. He took advantage of the good relationship he had built with the SDF to buy enough time for Trump to be confronted with the consequences of his decision. A few days later, the president backed down—while predictably refusing to admit that he had done so. American forces would stay in smaller numbers (and France and the U.K. would eventually agree to commit more troops to the effort). The 180-degree turn was converted into something more like a 90-degree one. In the end, the main effects of Trump's tweet were bruising the trust of allies and heartening both Assad and ISIS.

He only trusts his own instincts. Trump believes that his gut feelings about things are excellent, if not genius. Those around him encourage that belief, or they are fired. Winning the White House against all odds may have made it unshakable.

Decisiveness is good, the generals agreed. But making decisions without considering facts is not.

Trump has, on at least one occasion, shown the swiftness and resolution commanders respect: On April 7, 2017, he responded to a chemical-warfare attack by Assad with a missile strike on Syria's Shayrat Airbase. But this was not a hard call. It was a onetime proportional retaliation unlikely to stir international controversy or wider repercussions. Few international incidents can be cleanly resolved by an air strike.

A case in point is the flare-up with Iran in June. The generals said Trump's handling of it was perilous, because it could have led to a shooting war. On June 20, Iran's air defenses shot down an American RQ-4A Global Hawk, a high-altitude surveillance drone the Iranians said had violated their airspace. The U.S. said the drone was in international airspace. (The disputed coordinates were about 12 miles apart—not a big difference for an aircraft moving hundreds of miles an hour.) In retaliation, Trump ordered a military strike on Iran—and then abruptly called it off after, he claimed, he'd been informed that it would kill about 150 Iranians. One general told me this explanation is highly improbable—any careful discussion of the strike would have considered potential casualties at the outset. But whatever his reasoning, the president's reversal occasioned such relief that it obscured the gravity of his original decision.

"How did we even get to that point?" the general asked me in astonishment. Given what a tinderbox that part of the world is, what kind of commander in chief would risk war with Iran over a drone?

Not only would a retaliatory strike have failed the litmus test of proportionality, this general said, but it would have accomplished little, escalated the dispute with Iran, and risked instigating a broad conflict. In an all-out war, the U.S. would defeat Iran's armed forces, but not without enormous bloodshed, and not just in Iran. Iran and its proxies would launch terrorist strikes on American and allied targets throughout the Middle East and beyond. If the regime were to fall, what would come next? Who would step in to govern a Shiite Muslim nation of 82 million steeped for generations in hatred of America? The mullahs owe their power to the American overthrow of Iran's elected government in 1953, an event widely regarded in Iran (and elsewhere) as an outrage. Conquering Americans would not be greeted by happy Persian crowds. The generals observed that those who predicted such parades in Baghdad following the ouster of Saddam Hussein instead got a decade-long bloodbath. Iran has more than twice Iraq's population, and is a far more developed nation. The Iraq War inspired the creation of ISIS and gave renewed momentum to al-Qaeda; imagine how war with Iran might mobilize Hezbollah, the richest and best-trained terrorist organization in the world.

Sometimes, of course, war is necessary. That's why we maintain the most expensive and professional military in the world. But a fundamental reason to own such power is to *avoid* wars—especially wars that are likely to create worse problems than they solve.

The real reason Trump reversed himself on the retaliatory strike, one general said, was not because he suddenly learned of potential casualties, but because someone, most likely General Joseph Dunford, the chairman of the Joint Chiefs of Staff, aggressively confronted him with the extended implications of an attack.

"I know the chairman very well," the general said. "He's about as fine an officer as I have ever spent time around. I think if he felt the president was really heading in the wrong direction, he would let the president know." He added that Secretary of State Mike Pompeo may have counseled against an attack as well. "Pompeo's a really bright guy. I'm sure he would intervene and give the president his best advice."

He resists coherent strategy. If there is any broad logic to Trump's behavior, it's *Keep 'em confused.* He believes that unpredictability itself is a virtue.

Keeping an enemy off-balance can be a good thing, the generals agreed, so long as you are not off-balance yourself. And it's a tactic, not a strategy. Consider Trump's rhetorical dance with the North Korean dictator Kim Jong Un. No president in modern times has made progress with North Korea. Capable of destroying Seoul within minutes of an outbreak of hostilities, Pyongyang has ignored every effort by the U.S. and its allies to deter it from building a nuclear arsenal.

Trump has gone back and forth dramatically on Kim. As a candidate in 2016, he said he would get China to make the North Korean dictator "disappear in one form or another very quickly." Once in office, he taunted Kim, calling him "Little Rocket Man," and suggested that the U.S. might immolate Pyongyang. Then he switched directions and orchestrated three personal meetings with Kim.

"That stuff is just crazy enough to work," one of the generals told me with a *what-the-hell?* chuckle. "We'll see what happens. If they can get back to some kind of discussion, if it can avert something, it will have been worth it. The unconventional aspect of that does have the opportunity to shake some things up."

In the long run, however, unpredictability is a problem. Without a coherent underlying strategy, uncertainty creates confusion and increases the chance of miscalculation—and miscalculation, the generals pointed out, is what starts most wars. John F. Kennedy famously installed a direct hotline to the Kremlin in order to lower the odds of blundering into a nuclear exchange. Invading Kuwait, Saddam Hussein stumbled into a humiliating defeat in the first Gulf War—a conflict that killed more than 100,000 people—after a cascading series of miscommunications and miscalculations led to a crushing international response.

Unpredictability becomes an impediment to success when it interferes with orderly process. "Say you're going to have an engagement with North Korea," a general who served under multiple presidents told me. "At some point you should have developed a strategy that says, *Here's what we want the outcome to be*. And then somebody is developing talking points. Those talking points are shared with the military, with the State Department, with the ambassador. Whatever the issue might be, before the president ever says *anything*, everybody should know what the talking points are going to be." To avoid confusion and a sense of aimlessness, "everybody should have at least a general understanding of what the strategy is and what direction we're heading in."

Which is frequently not the case now.

"If the president says 'Fire and brimstone' and then two weeks later says 'This is my best friend,' that's not necessarily bad—but it's bad if the rest of the relevant people in the government responsible for executing the strategy aren't aware that that's the strategy," the general said. Having a process to figure out the sequences of steps is essential. "The process tells the president what he should say. When I was working with Obama and Bush," he continued, "before we took action, we would understand what that action was going to be, we'd have done a Q&A on how we think the international community is going to respond to that action, and we would have discussed how we'd deal with that response."

To operate outside of an organized process, as Trump tends to, is to reel from crisis to rapprochement to crisis, generating little more than noise. This haphazard approach could lead somewhere good—but it could just as easily start a very big fire.

If the president eschews the process, this general told me, then when a challenging national-security issue arises, he won't have information at hand about what the cascading effects of pursuing different options might be. "He's kind of shooting blind." Military commanders find that disconcerting.

"The process is not a panacea—Bush and Obama sometimes made bad decisions even with all the options in front of them—but it does help."

He has a simplistic and antiquated notion of soldiering. Though he disdains expert advice, Trump reveres—perhaps fetishizes—the military. He began his presidency by stacking his administration with generals: Mattis, McMaster, Kelly, and, briefly, Michael Flynn, his first national security adviser. Appointing them so soon after their retirement from the military was a mistake, according to Don Bolduc, a retired brigadier general who is currently running as a Republican for the U.S. Senate in New Hampshire. Early on, the biggest difference Bolduc saw between the Trump administration and its predecessors, and one he felt was "going to be disruptive in the long term," was "the significant reliance, in the Pentagon, at least, on senior military leadership overriding and making less relevant our civilian oversight. That was going to be a huge problem. The secretary of defense pretty much surrounded himself with his former Marine comrades, and there was, at least from that group, a distrust of civilians that really negatively affected the Pentagon in terms of policy and strategy in Afghanistan, Syria, and Iraq, by following the same old failed operational approaches." Trump's reliance on military solutions is problematic because "there are limits to what the military can solve. I think initially the Trump administration held this idea that general officers somehow have all the answers to everything. I think the president discovered in short order that that's really not the case."

Bolduc also pointed out an unusual leadership challenge caused by having a general of McMaster's rank serve as national security adviser—he did not retire when he assumed the post. "McMaster, for whom I have tremendous respect, came in as a three-star general. Leaving him a three-star forces him on a daily basis to have to engage with four-star generals who see his rank as beneath theirs, even though his position is much more than that."

The problems posed by Trump's skewed understanding of the military extend beyond bad decision making to the very culture of our armed forces: He apparently doesn't think American soldiers accused of war crimes should be prosecuted and punished. In early May, he pardoned former Army Lieutenant Michael Behenna, who had been convicted of murdering an Iraqi prisoner. Two weeks later, he asked the Justice Department to prepare pardon materials for a number of American servicemen and contractors who were charged with murder and desecration of corpses, including Special Operations Chief Edward Gallagher, a Navy SEAL who stood accused by his own team members of fatally stabbing a teenage ISIS prisoner and shooting unarmed civilians. (He was ultimately acquitted of the murders but convicted of posing for photos with the boy's body.) Trump subsequently chastised the military attorneys who had prosecuted Gallagher, and directed that medals awarded to them be rescinded. All of the generals agreed that interfering with the military's efforts to police itself badly undermines command and control. When thousands of young Americans are deployed overseas with heavy weaponry, crimes and atrocities will sometimes occur. Failing to prosecute those who commit them invites behavior that shames everyone in uniform and the nation they serve.

"He doesn't understand the warrior ethos," one general said of the president. "The warrior ethos is important because it's sort of a sacred covenant not just among members of the military profession, but between the profession and the society in whose name we fight and serve. The warrior ethos transcends the laws of war; it governs your behavior. The warrior ethos makes units effective because of the values of trust and self-sacrifice associated with it—but the warrior ethos also makes wars less inhumane and allows our profession to maintain our self-respect and to be respected by others. Man, if the warrior ethos gets misconstrued into 'Kill them all . . .'" he said, trailing off. "Teaching soldiers about ethical conduct in war is not just about morality: "If you treat civilians disrespectfully, *you're working for the enemy!* Trump doesn't understand."

Having never served or been near a battlefield, several of the generals said, Trump exhibits a simplistic, badly outdated notion of soldiers as supremely "tough"—hard men asked to perform hard and sometimes ugly jobs. He also buys into a severely outdated concept of leadership.

The generals, all of whom have led troops in combat, know better than most that war is hard and ugly, but their understanding of "toughness" goes well beyond the gruff stoicism of a John Wayne movie. Good judgment counts more than toughness.

Bolduc said he came up in a military where it was accepted practice for senior leaders to blame their subordinates, lose their temper, pound on desks, and threaten to throw things, and the response to that behavior was "*He's a hard-ass*. Right? *He's tough*. That is not leadership. You don't get optimal performance being that way. You get optimal performance by being completely opposite of that."

Bolduc worries that, under Trump's command, a return to these antiquated notions of "toughness" will worsen the epidemic of PTSD plaguing soldiers who have served repeated combat tours. Senior military officers have learned much from decades of war—lessons Bolduc said are being discarded by a president whose closest brush with combat has been a movie screen.

The military is hard to change. This is bad, because it can be maddeningly slow to adapt, but also good, because it can withstand poor leadership at the top. In the most crucial areas, the generals said, the military's experienced leaders have steered Trump away from disaster. So far.

"The hard part," one general said, "is that he may be president for another five years."

INSIDE IVANKA'S DREAMWORLD

by Elaina Plott

[APRIL 2019]

The contrast between the behavior of the Trump administration and that of the first daughter could in some ways not be more stark. On the one hand: brutal messaging, callous incompetence, managerial chaos. On the other: a studied obliviousness; an intimation of perfection; an office decorated in tones of white on white; and the suggestion, neither articulated nor denied, that the occupant of that office is a "moderating force." As Elaina Plott observed in her 2019 profile of the president's elder daughter, excerpted here, "Succeeding as Ivanka Trump has always required a suspension of disbelief—on her part and on the part of others." Plott covered the White House as a staff writer for *The Atlantic* and is currently a national political reporter for *The New York Times*. Her reporting for "Inside Ivanka's Dreamworld" included interviews with nearly 50 people who know Ivanka (including the president, who revealed that he had considered nominating his daughter to lead the World Bank, "because she's very good with numbers"). The deepest misconception about Ivanka, in Plott's view, is this one: "Because she embraced the manners of polite society, she surely embraced its politics, too."

Y ou could tell by his eyes, the way they popped and gleamed and fixed on someone behind me. Only one person gets that kind of look from Donald Trump. "Oh!" the president said. "Ivanka!"

Ivanka Trump lifted her hands, astonished. "I *forgot* you guys were meeting—I was just coming by!" she said. "Uh-oh!"

The first daughter (though not the only daughter), wearing a fitted black mockneck and black pants, her golden hair fastened in a low twist, glided across the Oval Office. It was a Tuesday afternoon, and it was apparently vital to inform Trump, at that very moment, that Siemens had pledged to expand its education and training opportunities to more workers as part of Ivanka's workforce-development initiative. She also wanted to remind him that tomorrow would be the inaugural session of the program's advisory board, and that Tim Cook would be joining the meeting.

"She loves doing it," Trump said, presumably to me but while looking at Ivanka. "And she wants no credit. Just like me, she wants no credit." They both started laughing.

For months, I had tried to secure an on-the-record interview with Ivanka to talk about her White House role and her life in Washington, D.C., but she had repeatedly declined. So I was surprised to receive a call one morning from Sarah Sanders, the White House press secretary, telling me that the president himself was available to talk about his daughter. We had spent 20 minutes, until Ivanka walked in, doing just that.

In our conversation, the president wanted to be clear: He was very proud of *all* his children. "Barron is young, but he's got wonderful potential," he said. "And Tiffany's doing extremely well. Don is, uh, he's enjoying politics; actually, it's very good. And Eric is running the business along with Don, and also very much into politics. I mean, the children—the children have been very, very good."

But Ivanka, whom he sometimes calls "Baby" in official meetings, is "unique." If Trump sees any of his children as his heir apparent, it's Ivanka. "If she ever wanted to run for president," he said, "I think she'd be very, very hard to beat." At 37, she is old enough. But Ivanka has never talked with her friends about running for office, and the president said she has never expressed any interest about that to him. Still, while Don Jr. might be a hit at political rallies, Ivanka is the only child the president ever considered for an administration post. "She went into the whole helping-people-with-jobs, and I wasn't sure that was going to be the best use of her time, but I didn't know how successful she'd be," the president said. "She's created millions of jobs, and I had no idea she'd be that successful."

The "millions of jobs" claim is not true. (Through Ivanka's work as an adviser to the president, companies such as Walmart and IBM have pledged to provide re-skilling opportunities over the next five years, mainly to people with jobs already.) But it's true that when jobs open up in the Trump administration—a frequent occurrence—Ivanka is at the top of her father's mind. "She's a natural diplomat," Trump said. "She would've been great at the United Nations, as an example." I asked why he didn't nominate her. "If I did, they'd say nepotism, when it would've had nothing to do with nepotism. But she would've been incredible." Warming to the subject, he said, "I even thought of Ivanka for the World Bank . . . She would've been great at that because she's very good with numbers."

The president went on: "She's got a great calmness . . . I've seen her under tremendous stress and pressure. She reacts very well—that's usually a genetic thing, but it's one of those things, nevertheless." He added: "She's got a tremendous presence when she walks into the room."

The Oval Office drop-in did not come as much of a surprise. The world may have gone off script, but Ivanka still follows the teleprompter. When she ran her multimillion-dollar lifestyle brand, she worked relentlessly at "cultivating authenticity," as she put it. She dreamed up a world full of serendipitous moments and marvelous coincidences, with the pastel-hued bags and shoes to match. Ivanka told W magazine, at age 22, "There are very few things we can control in life, but how we project ourselves is one of them." That discipline has meant, as her brother Don Jr. told me, that "you can put Ivanka in virtually any environment and she'll thrive." In the White House, she has projected herself as a cosmopolitan peacemaker, dedicating her efforts largely to issues such as women's economic empowerment, workforce development, and the fight against human trafficking. She is not a conservative, she enjoys telling people. She is a "pragmatist."

One evening earlier this year, the former deputy national security adviser Dina Powell, on behalf of Ivanka, invited lawmakers, donors, and ambassadors to Washington's Metropolitan Club to celebrate the passage of the Women's Entrepreneurship and Economic Empowerment Act, an effort Ivanka had led to promote gender equality in the developing world. "People say Washington doesn't work," Ivanka told the gathering, according to an attendee who paraphrased her remarks. "But this room tells you bipartisanship is possible." She made no mention of the fact that, outside, thanks to her father's insistence on building a border wall despite bipartisan opposition, the U.S. government was mired in the longest shutdown in its history.

There were two competing reads on Ivanka that evening. Some of those present praised her to me as a serious adviser pushing positive change amid unending chaos. Others condemned her as a dutiful daughter content to pretend that the chaos doesn't exist. ("Then why did you go?" I asked one of her critics. "As a favor to Dina," this person insisted.) Ivanka has always been subject to unsavory interpretations— the price of being a Trump. But she has also been adept at defining herself apart from her father. There is an advantage to being surrounded by men people don't like. So when she moved to Washington, Ivanka deployed a version of her signature approach—planning "impromptu" visits at the White House instead of at Trump Tower; posing for "candid" Instagrams at international summits rather than at the Met Gala. What her friends say she couldn't understand was why, this time, many people weren't buying it—why it was no longer the authenticity they saw, but the cultivation.

———

Ivanka Trump begins most mornings at about 5:30 a.m., when Washington's Kalorama neighborhood is still dark. She shares a 6,870-square-foot white colonial home there with her husband, Jared Kushner, a senior adviser to the president, and their three children. Jared, who calls his wife "Ivanks," makes her coffee and breakfast, often crackers with cottage cheese and sliced fruit. Depending on the day, Ivanka might lead a hair stylist to her office, where the desk has been cleared so he can arrange his tools. Her request is almost always the same: sleek and straight, parted down the middle.

The branding education of Ivanka began in Aspen, Colorado, in 1989, just after Christmas. Donald Trump had taken his wife, Ivana, and their three children—11-year-old Don, 8-year-old Ivanka, and 5-year-old Eric—for a week-long stay at the Little Nell hotel. He had also brought along his 26-year-old mistress, Marla Maples, dispatching his airplane to pick her up in Tennessee and stashing her in a penthouse not far from his family. A few days into the trip, they all collided at a restaurant on the mountain. During the screaming match that ensued between her and Ivana, Maples let out a triumphant cry: "It's out! It's finally out!" The kids didn't say a word.

Talk of divorce was immediate back in New York. The tabloids were ravening. Reporters accosted Ivanka as she walked to school. In *The Trump Card*, the memoir she published at 27, Ivanka recalled one "idiot" asking, in the aftermath of the "Best Sex I've Ever Had" *New York Post* headline, whether Maples's claims were true.

Ivanka did not view her father's philandering as a personal betrayal. Her grievances were more cosmic. She mourned the breakdown of the order and routines she'd cherished. She dwelled less on the divorce itself than on the fact that she hadn't seen it coming. Traumatic as it was, Ivanka wrote in her memoir, she chose to use the experience as a way of giving her life "shape and meaning." The divorce might have educated her on all the things she couldn't control, but it also affirmed for her the one thing she could control, at least up to a point: her image.

According to her mother, Ivanka was destined to be disciplined, polished, and tactful—she made sure of it. "I did not spoil my kids," Ivana told me on the phone from Miami, where she spends the winter months. "They had no choice . . . I kept them busy, busy, busy." She signed her daughter up for skiing, ice-skating, and tennis lessons, as well as singing classes ("She was okay"). There were several years of ballet, including a role in *The Nutcracker* at Christmastime, which Ivana's "old friend Michael Jackson" came to watch. Ivana was careful never to give her children "too much money," because when "girls get too much money, they buy the drugs, they go to nightclubs—none of that Ivanka ever did." The craziest things ever got was probably the day a 14-year-old Ivanka came home with blue hair. "I freaked out," Ivana said. "I bought the Nice 'n Easy in the palest blond and put it all over."

In a *Seventeen* magazine feature in 1998, Ivanka showed off her dorm room at Choate Rosemary Hall, posing amid decor such as a sparkly Urban Outfitters lamp, a travel-size hairbrush, algebra and trigonometry textbooks, and a Robert Doisneau poster she'd gotten "on a street in France for about a buck." Around the same time Paris Hilton was emerging as the vacuous and club-happy heiress, Ivanka was blooming as her straitlaced foil.

It has been said that Donald Trump is a poor person's idea of a rich person—the hot blondes, the private jets and wine bottles and steaks bearing his name in big block letters. Ivanka presented herself as something closer to a rich person's idea of a rich person—a young Jackie Kennedy, whispery voice and all, who just happened to be trapped in a tacky gilded cage. After graduating from the University of Pennsylvania's Wharton School with an economics degree, she went on to enjoy success as an entrepreneur with a jewelry line and, later, a full fashion label. In interviews, she came across as a woman whose wealth never blinded her to the plight of others or the importance of hard work.

That Ivanka defied expectations was, at first, no more than a curiosity. Whether keeping her distance from the Trump brand was just a media-savvy calculation—a veneer masking deeper alignment—would matter more in the years to come. In 2011, Trump became the nation's most high-profile "birther." Over the next three years, he would question Barack Obama's citizenship on television and tweet that he'd been told by an "extremely credible source" that the president's birth certificate was a "fraud." There's no record of Ivanka ever commenting on Trump's conduct during those years, nor was she pressed, because *of course* she didn't agree with him. There was no need to even ask.

For all that, people close to the family understood Ivanka's devotion to her father. In the thick of his birther phase, Trump revisited the idea of running for office, either governor of New York or president of the

United States. Always by his side, every step of the way, was Ivanka. She was there on a series of afternoons in Trump Tower in 2013 and 2014, scribbling notes as a murderers' row of her father's confidants—Roger Stone, Michael Cohen, Michael Caputo—gamed out a potential campaign. "She was quiet in the meetings," Caputo told me, "but Mr. Trump would turn to her and ask her questions. It became clear to me that he trusted Ivanka more than anyone."

––––––––––

I first met Ivanka Trump in the summer of 2013, when I was interning for the *New York Observer*. This was when Jared Kushner owned the paper, though I had never seen him, or Ivanka, in the office. But they were at the Plaza Hotel one evening for an event marking the *Commercial Observer*'s annual ranking of the real-estate industry's most powerful people. We interns were checking coats.

When my shift was up, I ventured into the crowd. Ivanka was hard to miss—taller and prettier than everyone else. I was a fan, as were most girls I knew. We thought she had it all—her own company, a pretty family, a pretty apartment. When I saw an opening, I told her as much. She thanked me and told me she liked my dress. We took a photo together, which I posted on Instagram.

By 2015, when Donald Trump announced his bid for president, her company's profits suggested that many women saw Ivanka the way I did. If anything, her life had become even prettier. She had launched her clothing line, and had signed a contract for a book about how to be just like her. She was a Woman Who Worked; she would soon have her third child. All of which made for a somewhat jarring image that infamous June day when Trump came down the escalator to warn of a Mexican-rapist invasion while Ivanka, ever the fount of respectability, stood alongside him.

The founding myth of Ivanka Trump is that she is a "moderating force." It is difficult to trace how the idea took hold. Perhaps Trump himself unwittingly put it best when he described to me Ivanka's decision to get involved in his presidential campaign: "I think it just morphed into something that happened." During the election, Ivanka never said outright that she supported abortion rights, for example, or was concerned about climate change, yet many people felt sure of both. Ivanka did not offer an opinion on immigration or the need for a border wall, yet the conventional wisdom was that her views must be different from her father's. She wrote thank-you notes. She spoke in complete sentences. Because she embraced the manners of polite society, she surely embraced its politics, too.

Throughout the election, Ivanka maintained a pleasing blankness. According to a senior campaign official, she was not keen on taking part in campaign rallies. "She didn't want anything to do with them," the official told me, "even though she was by far the most requested surrogate." By saying nothing to anyone, Ivanka could be everything to everyone. Having Ivanka as a focus proved convenient to many Republicans, especially white suburban women, straining to rationalize support for a nominee whose style they detested. Following Trump's victory, even some Democrats pinned their hopes on Ivanka. Hadn't she met with Planned Parenthood? Al Gore? It all seemed reason enough to believe that the new first daughter would keep her father's worse impulses in check.

In August 2016, three months before the election, Ivanka posed for a multipage spread in *Harper's Bazaar*. By then, Donald Trump had already committed a series of disturbing offenses on the trail— denigrating women, insulting John McCain. Ivanka still managed to present a facsimile of separateness. "She is standing like a statue, a magnificent statue, in a Carolina Herrera gown, with a baby on one shoulder and a cell phone on the other," the *Bazaar* piece began. It referred to Ivanka as Wonder Woman.

Ivanka might have laughed had anyone predicted, as the stylist zipped her into that $6,990 Herrera gown, that in less than a year she would find herself rebuffed by a D.C. workout studio she hadn't yet heard of—Solidcore, a Pilates-based gym frequented by Michelle Obama. In February 2017, after Ivanka took a class there, the owner, Anne Mahlum, in a since-deleted Facebook post, accused President

Trump of "threatening the rights of many of my beloved clients and coaches." Suddenly, Ivanka was finding herself radioactive. Back in New York, when people had seen her at boutique workout sessions, they'd asked for selfies.

Don Jr. explained how life had changed for Ivanka. "She was loved by all the people in the world she wanted to be loved by," he told me. "I can't say she's not disappointed by them turning on her. After the election, I found 10,000 emails saying, 'Hey, buddy, we were with you all along,' and I'm like, *No you weren't, you piece of shit.* I just think I figured it out a little bit earlier than she did that people were going to see us differently after my father won."

The disdain deepened when Ivanka joined the White House as an adviser, in March 2017. No one understood what she had been brought on to do. Not even the president. During our interview, I asked Trump how he had envisioned Ivanka's role. "So I didn't know," he said without pause. "I'm not sure *she* knew."

Ivanka's first months were spent navigating the rollout of her book. A week before the election, Ivanka had handed in the manuscript for *Women Who Work*, a guide to "rewriting the rules for success." Her publisher was confident that the book, centered on what they understood to be her personal brand, would reach its intended audience of "working women in coastal cities," a source with knowledge of the discussions told me. Trump wasn't going to be elected, and Ivanka still seemed to have the cachet that had earned her a contract in the first place.

When Trump won, everything went to hell. According to the source, "We just really didn't know what would happen, because we were now publishing a book to a community who didn't like her dad very much." The silver lining was that the publicity team was flooded with requests for interviews with the first daughter. Then, three weeks before publication, government ethics lawyers weighed in: Ivanka could not do a single appearance or interview to promote the book. Sales were dismal. *Women Who Work* was widely panned. Reviewers did not just excoriate the book; they excoriated Ivanka. She herself hadn't changed: She was doling out the same #ITWiseWords she always had—"Prove smart is

sexy," "Seize the moments as they come," "'Now' is the new 'later.'"
But for the first time, Ivanka was unable to disassociate from her father.
She was no longer a Woman Who Worked. She was a Woman Who
Worked for Donald Trump.

———————

As the book's sales struggled, Ivanka turned her full attention—behind
the scenes—to the Paris Agreement. Her father had promised on the
campaign trail to withdraw the United States from the climate accord.
If Ivanka could change the president's mind, the planet might not be
the only beneficiary.

In lobbying her father, Ivanka had important allies: her senior-
adviser husband, Jared; National Economic Council Director Gary
Cohn; and Secretary of State Rex Tillerson. She also faced strong opposition: the chief strategist Steve Bannon; White House Counsel Don
McGahn; and Environmental Protection Agency Administrator Scott
Pruitt. Ivanka sat in on nearly every meeting about the accord. Her
strategy was to appeal to her father's obsession with good press. "It was
always 'This is going to look really bad. We're going to get killed by
the media,'" a former senior official told me. She phoned Tim Cook,
asking him to press her father personally to stay in the agreement.

Another former official recounted a meeting in the Situation Room.
McGahn, Pruitt, and Attorney General Jeff Sessions had come armed
with a "deeply technical" presentation on why the United States should
withdraw. After the three men wrapped up, Ivanka stood to offer her
own take. In tempered, breathy tones, she argued that the U.S. was
under no obligation to pay the billions that Obama had promised, and
referred to the deal several times as "aspirational." She sat back down.
"No one really knew how to respond," the former official recalled.
"Even Tillerson and others who wanted us to stay in were like, 'Okay,
thank you for that. Moving on.'"

Few things about the Trump administration are predictable, but it's
a safe bet that if the president makes a controversial move, an anonymously sourced reference to Ivanka's distress will circulate soon after. At
a Rose Garden ceremony in June 2017, President Trump announced

that the United States would indeed withdraw from the climate accord. Six days later, *Us Weekly* published a story about Ivanka. The glossy cover line read, "WHY I DISAGREE WITH MY DAD: Balancing her personal ideals with love and loyalty to her father, the president's daughter will always fight for what she believes in." Citing a "source close to Ivanka," the article said that she was "disappointed" by her father's decision.

My own sources close to Ivanka insisted to me recently that neither she nor her team had anything to do with the *Us Weekly* cover. "Those kinds of leaks always came from people who hated her and wanted to make her look like an asshole to the base," one person said. Still, the damage was done. The cover was instantly memed and mocked across the internet. I asked President Trump about his recollection of Ivanka's voice in the Paris negotiations. "Ivanka was in favor of staying in," the president said. "She expressed it, but I'm not sure she knew it as well as I did. I'm not sure she knew the costs of it . . . You know, that was one of my easier decisions, actually."

————————

The climate decision marked the start of what one of the former senior White House officials I spoke with referred to as Ivanka's "bunker period." It was as though she began fashioning a snow globe for herself to inhabit. It would include an issue portfolio—empowering women, energizing the workforce—whose contents she reserved the right to change should something beyond their scope spark bipartisan appeal. No longer would she insert herself into every debate. If it was not in her portfolio, it was not her concern.

Four former senior White House officials told me that Ivanka participated less in staff meetings as summer stretched into fall. On August 15, 2017, Trump caused an uproar when he delivered remarks from Trump Tower about the racist and anti-Semitic demonstrations in Charlottesville, Virginia. The president stated that "very fine people" had been among both the violent neo-Nazis and those who had opposed their presence—this after a white supremacist had driven his car into a crowd of protesters, killing one person and injuring about two dozen. Ivanka is a convert to Judaism, and her husband and his family are observant. But during the fallout from Trump's comments, Ivanka and Jared were quietly on vacation in Vermont.

Some in the White House resent the couple for their convenient absences in moments of crisis. But few things have helped Ivanka endear herself to her colleagues more than the simple fact of not being Jared. That John Kelly despised both Ivanka and Jared is no secret. When the retired Marine general was brought on as chief of staff, in July 2017, he saw a couple "playing government," a phrase he would utter frequently. "He kind of walked in and looked at Ivanka like, *What the fuck is Barbie doing in the West Wing?*" the source close to her said. But if Kelly saw Ivanka as a headache, Jared was a consciousness-altering migraine. Kelly had little idea what Jared did all day—he could be text-messaging Van Jones about criminal-justice reform or catching up with Saudi Crown Prince Mohammed bin Salman (implicated in the murder last fall of the journalist Jamal Khashoggi). Kelly struggled to hide his contempt. At one senior-staff meeting, when someone raised a question relating to foreign policy, Kelly, according to a person in the room, observed that having a clear read on the answer was hard for him, given that "we have about three secretaries of state now." Jared, who was present, remained silent.

"I think everyone started to appreciate that it was never like, 'Oh, here comes Ivanka to blow everything up and take over,' like it was with Jared," a former senior White House official told me. Sidelining herself on many issues might have helped Ivanka earn goodwill inside the White House, but it also fueled a public narrative that she was irrelevant. As recently as last month, CNN ran a story asking, "What does Ivanka Trump do?" She can point to several modest bipartisan accomplishments. She led the push to double the child tax credit in the GOP's December 2017 tax-cut bill. As noted, she launched the first government-wide approach to help 50 million women in developing countries gain access to capital and vocational training. And she's a key reason congressional Republicans are now debating paid family leave. "When I hear people say, 'Well, what are her qualifications? What does she think she can do?' it often comes from people who have done nothing, and who never will," Kentucky Governor Matt Bevin, who has worked closely with Ivanka on workforce development, told me. "Ivanka could literally save an elderly woman from getting hit by a train and the people would blame her for disrupting the travel time."

The specter of Jared's involvement in various business deals and campaign events, including those probed by Special Counsel Robert Mueller, has loomed large for more than two years, and has cast a shadow on Ivanka and her work. So have questions about how she received her security clearance and whether she conducted official business through her personal email account. In February, Ivanka told *The View*'s Abby Huntsman that her father "had no involvement pertaining to my clearance or my husband's clearance, zero." Since then, many outlets have reported that the president ordered Kelly to grant Ivanka and Jared top-secret clearances against the recommendation of security officials. (White House personnel logs I obtained show that the couple received their clearances on the same day: May 1, 2018.) In a recent interview, I asked a senior White House official whether Ivanka had spoken truthfully on *The View*. "Absolutely," this person said, adding the qualifier that there was no involvement by the president *as far as Ivanka or Jared knew.*

All the same, Ivanka has not presented nearly as big a target as her husband has. In the president's view, that's because she's "a very honest person," as he put it to me. A more likely reason is that Democrats are reluctant to go after the president's children, especially a daughter whom many lawmakers have come to regard, rightly or wrongly, as relatively benign. When House Democrats issued a demand for documents from 81 individuals and organizations in Trump's orbit, Ivanka was not on the list. An accommodating view of Ivanka has come to permeate the West Wing as well, which is perhaps what happens when you succeed in helping oust the bulk of officials who dislike you. By January 2019, Kelly was out of a job. (As for the East Wing, it is only as welcoming as it needs to be. Asked whether the first lady and first daughter get along, the source close to Ivanka told me that they have a "desire to be mutually respectful" but that their relationship is certainly not "affectionate." Ivana told me of Ivanka's feelings toward Melania:

"She likes her fine, because she didn't cause me to break up the marriage like the other one—I don't even want to pronounce her name." Stephanie Grisham, a spokeswoman for the first lady, added, "They've always shared a close relationship and still do today.")

Ask White House staffers today about Jared, and they'll gripe that he operates as the president's de facto chief of staff. Ask about Ivanka, and you'll hear how she always says hello in the hallway and asks after your children. You'll hear that she is a devoted mother. You'll hear about the time she saw a positive piece of press on a colleague, printed it out, had her father sign it, framed it, and delivered it to that person as a gift.

———————

Unlike other members of her family, Ivanka Trump declined to be interviewed on the record for this article. We did have an off-the-record conversation recently at the White House. Most offices in the West Wing are standard government-issue—black swivel chairs, walls an uninspiring beige. When Ivanka had settled into her second-floor quarters, she wanted everything to be white. White walls, white chairs, white window shades. One of the former senior White House officials compared entering Ivanka's office to "walking into an Apple store." Taped to the wall by her desk are letters that were cut out of construction paper in alternating colors—purple, neon orange, blue. The letters spell "JOBS CZAR."

On a small coffee table when I visited was a book called *Playa Fire*—about the Burning Man festival, as I'd later learn. Seeing it there revived many of the questions I've had about Ivanka and her inner life—questions that, after interviewing nearly 50 people who are close to her or know her, I still can't answer. A conversation with her betrays few hints. The quality that people say they admire most about Ivanka is her "poise"; I've heard the word used about her probably 100 times. And she *is* poised. Not a word or a hair out of place. When you ask a question, no matter how innocuous, her eyes narrow at each word, as though she is positioning herself on a tennis court to return an opponent's serve.

So I didn't know how to explain this book on Burning Man, a gathering that seems to represent the opposite of everything I had come to know about Ivanka. When I told a longtime friend of Ivanka's about the book, she laughed and said, "Really? Huh"—unsure, too, of what to make of it. It could be that Ivanka's secret self longs to escape her name and stop wearing sheath dresses and sway to EDM on hour three of an acid trip. It could be that Ivanka doesn't want to do any of those things but wants you to think she does, because it would be unexpected and thus build intrigue. It could be that Ivanka simply received the book as a gift. But even then, her choice to display it would have been intentional, because Ivanka's choices are only intentional. It could be none of these things. But when much of your life is a study in the art of projection, everything begins to feel like part of the project.

Ivanka may find it bizarre that, two years into the Trump presidency, many people regard her as party to what they see as destructive policies and hateful rhetoric. How is it her fault what the president ultimately decides to say or do? It would be impossible for her or anyone to moderate a man like Donald Trump out of his agenda. She feels like she was saddled with an unrealistic expectation from the outset—one that, according to former United Nations Ambassador Nikki Haley, who is close to Ivanka, she never had a chance of living up to. "If she is involved" in the president's decision making, "she's attacked. If she's not involved, she's attacked," Haley told me.

In any case, it's not clear that Ivanka disagrees with her father, for all the public perception of distance. When I spoke about Ivanka with Jared, the one comment from that conversation he was willing to make publicly had to do with how much she resembles her father. "She's like her dad in that she's very good at managing details. Her father is meticulous with details and has a great memory," he said in a recent interview in his office. "He really knows how to drive people, and I think she's the same way—results-oriented and also an excellent communicator."

Ivanka has come to disdain the notion that her father's agenda should be any different from what it is. She believes his critics have it all wrong. She is unwilling to concede that she ought to understand why someone might have interpreted her father's *Access Hollywood* comments as misogynistic, or his remarks after Charlottesville as tone-deaf, if not racist. Ivanka knows Trump probably better than anyone, and she knows him to be good. In Ivanka's snow globe, evidence to the contrary simply does not exist.

WILL BETH MOORE LOSE HER FLOCK?

by Emma Green

[OCTOBER 2018]

Beth Moore, the Houston-based evangelical preacher, has written books that sell by the tens of millions. She can pack an auditorium with the faithful and bring them to their feet. Life in a snow globe is not for her. But she might have wished for such a life after October 2016. Moore had built an empire by teaching Scripture to women—and being deferential to men. But faced with Donald Trump's degrading comments about women in the *Access Hollywood* tape, she felt compelled as a person of faith to speak up. Moore tweeted, "Wake up, Sleepers, to what women have dealt with all along in environments of gross entitlement & power. Are we sickened? Yes. Surprised? NO."

In that moment, as *Atlantic* staff writer Emma Green recounted in a 2018 profile, Beth Moore opened up a schism within evangelical ranks. Many male evangelical leaders condemned her for breaking with Trump. So did many of the faithful. But Moore herself, over time, has become increasingly emboldened in her statements and her choice of targets, including influential pastors caught up in sexual hypocrisy. "She has castigated the evangelical movement for selling its soul to buy political wins," Green wrote. "Moore is hopeful that a reckoning is finally under way."

When Beth Moore arrived in Houston in the 1980s, she found few models for young women who wanted to teach Scripture. Many conservative Christian denominations believed that women should not hold authority over men, whether in church or at home; many denominations still believe this. In some congregations, women could not speak from the lectern on a Sunday or even read the Bible in front of men. But Moore was resolute: God, she felt, had called her to serve. So she went where many women in Texas were going in the '80s: aerobics class. Moore kicked her way into ministry, choreographing routines to contemporary Christian music for the women of Houston's First Baptist Church.

At the time, most Texas seminaries weren't offering the kind of instruction she sought, so Moore found a private tutor. Slowly, she started getting invitations to speak at women's luncheons and study groups, in exchange for a plate of food or a potted plant. In tiny church social halls, she laid the cornerstone of an evangelical empire.

Moore's audience seemed to be starved for a teacher who understood their lives. To them, she was a revelation: a petite bottle blonde from Arkadelphia, Arkansas, who could talk seriously about Jesus one moment and the impossibility of finding decent child care the next. As charismatic as her male peers, she was also earnest and charmingly self-deprecating. Friends call her Beth La Ham.

In one of her most famous talks, Moore describes an encounter with a haggard, elderly man in an airport terminal. Suddenly, she feels called by God to brush the man's hair—not to bear witness to him, or even help him board his plane, but to smooth his tangled locks. Moore describes her embarrassment, recounting her inner dialogue with God, in which she tries to talk her way out of the divine directive. Ultimately, however, she obeys. What began as a comic set piece ends as a moving testament to faith and the power of intimate acts of kindness. The Lord knows what our need is, Moore says. "The man didn't need witnessing to. He needed his hair brushed!"

By the late '90s, women were packing sports arenas to hear Moore tell this and other parables. She earned speaking slots at big-name churches, including Hillsong and Saddleback, whose pastor, Rick Warren, calls her a dear friend. "She's a singularly influential figure among evangelicals as a woman leader," Ed Stetzer, the executive director of the Billy Graham Center at Wheaton College, the elite evangelical school outside of Chicago, told me. "Beth just is a category by herself."

A publishing career followed, further magnifying Moore's influence. She was the first woman to have a Bible study published by LifeWay, the Christian retail giant, and has since reached 22 million women, the most among its female authors. Today, her Bible studies are ubiquitous, guiding readers through scriptural passages with group-discussion questions and fill-in-the-blank workbooks. "It would be hard to find a church anywhere where at least some segment of the congregation has not been through at least one Beth Moore study," Russell Moore, the head of the political arm of the Southern Baptist Convention (and no relation to Beth) told me.

Moore's success was possible because she spent her career carefully mapping the boundaries of acceptability for female evangelical leaders. She rarely spoke to the press and made a point of keeping her politics to herself. Her persona embodies what a young fan described to me as the "Southern-belle white Christian woman."

Privately, however, Moore has never cared much for the delicate norms of Christian femininity. Her days are tightly scheduled and obsessively focused on writing. She spends hours alone in an office decorated with a Bible verse written in a swirling font ("I tell you, her many sins have been forgiven," Luke 7:47). Though she often performs domestic femininity for her audience, in her own life she has balanced motherhood with demanding professional ambitions. She traveled every other weekend while her two daughters were growing up—they told me they ate a lot of takeout. Like other Southern Baptists, Moore considers herself a complementarian: She believes the Bible teaches that men and women have distinctive roles and that men should hold positions of authority and leadership over women in the home and in the church. Yet her husband, Keith, a retired plumber, sees his vocation as helping his wife succeed. "That's what I do," he told me. "I lay blocks so O.J. can run."

For decades, Moore never broke stride. In the past few years, however, she has felt out of step with the evangelical community. During the 2016 campaign, many of its leaders not only excused Donald Trump's boorish behavior but painted him as a great defender of Christianity—evangelicals' "dream president," in the words of Jerry Falwell Jr. More recently, a series of high-profile pastors have been toppled by accusations of sexual misconduct. The deferential reserve that defined Moore's career has become harder for her to maintain.

On a chilly Texas evening recently, Moore and I sat in rocking chairs on her porch. It was the first time she had invited a reporter to visit her home, on the outskirts of Houston. Moore, who is 61, was the consummate hostess, fussing about feeding me and making sure I was warm enough beside the mesquite-wood fire. But as we settled into conversation, her demeanor changed. She fixed her perfectly mascaraed eyes on me. "The old way is over," she said. "The stakes are too high now."

Moore was flying home from a ministry event in October 2016 when she decided to compose the tweets that changed her life. That weekend, she had glimpsed headlines about Donald Trump's 2005 comments on the now-infamous *Access Hollywood* tape. But it wasn't until that plane ride, with newspapers and transcripts spread out in front of her, that Moore learned the full extent of it—including the reaction of some Christian leaders who, picking up a common line of spin, dismissed the comments as "locker-room talk."

"I was like, 'Oh, no. No. No,'" Moore told me. "I was so appalled." Trump's ugly boasting felt personal to her: Many of her followers have confided to her that they've suffered abuse, and Moore herself says she was sexually abused as a small child by someone close to her family—a trauma she has talked about publicly, though never in detail.

The next day, Moore wrote a few short messages to her nearly 900,000 followers. "Wake up, Sleepers, to what women have dealt with all along in environments of gross entitlement & power," she said in one tweet. "Are we sickened? Yes. Surprised? NO." Like other women,

Moore wrote, she had been "misused, stared down, heckled, talked naughty to." As pastors took to the airwaves to defend Trump, she was trying to understand how "some Christian leaders don't think it's that big a deal."

The tweets upended Moore's cheerful, feminine world. *Breitbart News* claimed that Moore was standing "in the gap for Hillary Clinton," borrowing a turn of phrase from the Book of Ezekiel. Moore did not support Clinton; she told me she voted for a third-party candidate in 2016. But she was horrified by church leaders' reflexive support of Trump. To Moore, it wasn't just a matter of hypocrisy, of making a deal with the devil that would deliver a Supreme Court seat, among other spoils. Moore believes that an evangelical culture that demeans women, promotes sexism, and disregards accusations of sexual abuse enabled Trump's rise.

Evangelicals, Moore said, have "clearer lines between men and women and how they serve." But sometimes, "that attitude is no longer about a role in a church. It becomes an attitude of gender superiority. And that has to be dealt with." Moore may be a complementarian, but she is adamant that Christian men should not treat women "any less than Jesus treated women in the Gospels: always with dignity, always with esteem, never as secondary citizens."

This may seem like an uncontroversial stance. But in the wake of her tweets, the staff at Living Proof Ministries, Moore's tight-knit organization, "could not hang up the phone for picking it up." She got messages from women who had read her Bible studies for years but said they'd never read another. Event attendance dropped.

A number of male evangelical leaders asked Moore to recant. A few days later, she returned to Twitter to clarify that she was not making an endorsement in the election. She felt depressed, she told me: "I can't tell you how many times . . . I faced toward heaven with tears streaming down my cheeks, thinking, *Have I lost my mind?*"

But her reproachful tweets seem all the more apt today. In recent months, several high-profile pastors—including Bill Hybels, the founder of the Chicagoland megachurch Willow Creek—have stepped down following accusations of sexual harassment, misconduct, or assault. (Hybels has denied the allegations against him.) Paige Patterson, the head of a Southern Baptist seminary, was pushed out after reports surfaced that he had downplayed women's physical and sexual abuse throughout his years in ministry, including encouraging them not to report allegations of rape and assault to the police.

These events have emboldened Moore. Whereas her criticisms of church leaders were once veiled, she now speaks her mind freely. She blogged icily about meeting a prominent male theologian who looked her up and down and told her she was prettier than another famous female Bible teacher. She has castigated the evangelical movement for selling its soul to buy political wins. Moore is hopeful that a reckoning is finally under way. "There is a very strong saying that Peter used himself, that judgment begins in the house of God. And I do believe that's what's happening."

———————

White evangelicals helped elect Donald Trump, and they may well decide his political future, as soon as the 2018 midterms. While it can seem as if the whole of evangelicalism has embraced the president, Trump has in fact exacerbated deep fracture lines within the movement. Christians of color have expressed rage over what they see as abandonment by their brothers and sisters in the faith; many have even left their congregations.

Among women, the picture is cloudier. Polling has suggested that at least some Christian women may share Moore's chagrin at the president's behavior. During his first year or so in office, Trump's approval rating among white evangelical women fell 13 points, compared with an eight-point drop among all women, according to Pew. Young Christians, in particular, may reshape evangelical politics. According to a study conducted by Pew, compared with their older peers, Millennial evangelicals are 12 percentage points more likely to favor stricter environmental regulations and 22 points more likely to support same-sex marriage. Young evangelical women may believe in male authority, but they're also not afraid to talk about sexual abuse.

For the moment, however, most evangelical women look like Beth

Moore's traditional fan base: white and middle-aged. Not long ago, I joined a line of these women—purses slung over their shoulders, Bibles in hand—as they waited outside a megachurch near Seattle. The event was billed as an "intimate" gathering, but 5,000 women sitting in a church auditorium is intimate only by contrast with the arena-size crowds Moore hosted in the past. Trips to the bathroom were a lost cause. As a worship band warmed up the room, the energy was somewhere between a pep rally and a slumber party. On her way to the stage, Moore worked the room in stiletto boots, greeting strangers like old friends.

Onstage, she gave the kind of performance that made her evangelical-famous, a manic outpouring that combined the rhythms of a tight stand-up routine and the earnestness of a Sunday-school lesson. "Some of you are here because you are trying to just get away from the children," she told the audience, which whooped obligingly. "Some of you are here to see if I'm as big a fruitcake as they say that I am, and"—here Moore emitted a theatrical little gasp-laugh, like helium escaping a balloon—"you probably already have your answer."

Debbie, 54, my seatmate, had been to eight Beth Moore events. She told me she was in the midst of the worst three years of her life, but that "God's always met me here." As the event wound down, women ran down the aisle of the auditorium, eager to claim their salvation, weeping as they threw their bodies across the floor. Moore walked slowly among them as if in a trance, pausing to rub a back or whisper a prayer.

Above all, what women seem to want from Moore is to be seen. Her work is mostly about drying tears and praying through daily suffering and struggle. In the public imagination, evangelicalism has become synonymous with political activism. But inside the evangelical world, many people are looking for something simpler: A community. A prayer. Hope.

Many of these same women have been put off by Moore's political turn, which was not in evidence onstage that night. Even those who might disdain Trump see her outspokenness as divisive and inappropriate for a Bible teacher. "I don't think this is the avenue for political discussions," said Shelly, 56. "I think it should stay focused on God."

Moore believes she *is* focused on God. The target of her scorn is an evangelical culture that downplays the voices and experiences of women. Her objective is not to evict Trump from the White House, but to clear the cultural rot in the house of God.

Moore has not become a liberal, or even a feminist. She's trying to help protect the movement she has always loved but that hasn't always loved her back—at least, not in the fullness of who she is. This mission has cost her, personally and professionally, but she told me her only regret is that she'd let others dictate what her place in the community should be: "What I feel a little sorry for, looking back over my shoulder, is how often I apologized for being there." She told me to note that she had a smile on her face. It was what she said during the most painful moments in our conversations.

THE CRUELTY
IS THE POINT

by Adam Serwer

[OCTOBER 2018]

"The Cruelty Is the Point." The title of this 2018 article by *Atlantic* staff writer Adam Serwer quickly went viral. *Slate*'s Dahlia Lithwick called it "the defining phrase of the Trump presidency." Joe Biden picked it up, noting that cruelty was not just the point but was the *only* point. Serwer's attention was focused mainly on immigration policy, but he ranged far more widely. His overall argument was simple: President Trump and his supporters find community by rejoicing in the suffering of those they hate and fear: "The cruelty of the Trump administration's policies, and the ritual rhetorical flaying of his targets before his supporters, are intimately connected."

The Museum of African-American History and Culture is in part a catalog of cruelty. Amid all the stories of perseverance, tragedy, and unlikely triumph are the artifacts of inhumanity and barbarism: the child-size slave shackles, the bright-red robes of the wizards of the Ku Klux Klan, the recordings of civil-rights protesters being brutalized by police.

The artifacts that persist in my memory, the way a bright flash does when you close your eyes, are the photographs of lynchings. But it's not the burned, mutilated bodies that stick with me. It's the faces of the white men in the crowd. There's the photo of the lynching of Thomas

Shipp and Abram Smith in Indiana in 1930, in which a white man can be seen grinning at the camera as he tenderly holds the hand of his wife or girlfriend. There's the undated photo from Duluth, Minnesota, in which grinning white men stand next to the mutilated, half-naked bodies of two men lashed to a post in the street—one of the white men is straining to get into the picture, his smile cutting from ear to ear. There's the photo of a crowd of white men huddled behind the smoldering corpse of a man burned to death; one of them is wearing a smart suit, a fedora hat, and a bright smile.

Their names have mostly been lost to time. But these grinning men were someone's brother, son, husband, father. They were human beings, people who took immense pleasure in the utter cruelty of torturing others to death—and were so proud of doing so that they posed for photographs with their handiwork, jostling to ensure they caught the eye of the lens, so that the world would know they'd been there. Their cruelty made them feel good, it made them feel proud, it made them feel happy. And it made them feel closer to one another.

The Trump era is such a whirlwind of cruelty that it can be hard to keep track. In the first week of October alone, the news broke that the Trump administration was seeking to ethnically cleanse more than 193,000 American children of immigrants whose temporary protected status had been revoked by the administration, that the Department of Homeland Security had lied about creating a database of children that would make it possible to unite them with the families the Trump administration had arbitrarily destroyed, that the White House was considering a blanket ban on visas for Chinese students, and that it would deny visas to the same-sex partners of foreign officials. At a rally in Mississippi, a crowd of Trump supporters cheered as the president mocked Christine Blasey Ford, the psychology professor who has said that Brett Kavanaugh, whom Trump has nominated to a lifetime appointment on the Supreme Court, attempted to rape her when she was a teenager. "Lock her up!" they shouted.

Ford testified to the Senate, utilizing her professional expertise to describe the encounter, that one of the parts of the incident she re-membered most was Kavanaugh and his friend Mark Judge laughing at her as Kavanaugh fumbled at her clothing. "Indelible in the hippo-campus is the laughter," Ford said, referring to the part of the brain that processes emotion and memory, "the uproarious laughter between the two, and their having fun at my expense." And then at his October 2 rally, the president made his supporters laugh at her.

Even those who believe that Ford fabricated her account, or was mistaken in its details, can see that the president's mocking of her tes-timony renders all sexual-assault survivors collateral damage. Anyone afraid of coming forward, afraid that she would not be believed, can now look to the president to see her fears realized. Once malice is em-braced as a virtue, it is impossible to contain.

The cruelty of the Trump administration's policies, and the ritual rhetorical flaying of his targets before his supporters, are intimately connected. As Lili Loofbourow wrote of the Kavanaugh incident in *Slate*, adolescent male cruelty toward women is a bonding mechanism, a vehicle for intimacy through contempt. The white men in the lynch-ing photos are smiling not merely because of what they have done, but because they have done it together.

We can hear the spectacle of cruel laughter throughout the Trump era. There were the border-patrol agents cracking up at the crying im-migrant children separated from their families, and the Trump adviser who delighted white supremacists when he mocked a child with Down syndrome who was separated from her mother. There were the po-lice who laughed uproariously when the president encouraged them to abuse suspects, and the Fox News hosts mocking a survivor of the Pulse Nightclub massacre (and in the process inundating him with threats), the survivors of sexual assault protesting to Senator Jeff Flake, the women who said the president had sexually assaulted them, and the teen survivors of the Parkland school shooting. There was the presi-dent mocking Puerto Rican accents shortly after thousands were killed and tens of thousands displaced by Hurricane Maria, the black athletes protesting unjustified killings by the police, the women of the #MeToo movement who have come forward with stories of sexual abuse, and the disabled reporter whose crime was reporting on Trump truthfully. It is not just that the perpetrators of this cruelty enjoy it; it is that they enjoy it with one another. Their shared laughter at the suffering of others is an adhesive that binds them to one another, and to Trump.

Taking joy in that suffering is more human than most would like to admit. Somewhere on the wide spectrum between adolescent teasing and the smiling white men in the lynching photographs are the Trump supporters whose community is built by rejoicing in the anguish of those they see as unlike them, who have found in their shared cruelty an answer to the loneliness and atomization of modern life.

The laughter undergirds the daily spectacle of insincerity, as the president and his aides pledge fealty to bedrock democratic principles they have no intention of respecting. The president who demanded the execution of five black and Latino teenagers for a crime they didn't commit decrying "false accusations," when his Supreme Court nominee stands accused; his supporters who fancy themselves champions of free speech meeting references to Hillary Clinton or a woman whose only crime was coming forward to offer her own story of abuse with screams of "Lock her up!" The political movement that elected a president who wanted to ban immigration by adherents of an entire religion, who encourages police to brutalize suspects, and who has destroyed thousands of immigrant families for violations of the law less serious than those of which he and his coterie stand accused, now laments the state of due process.

———————

This isn't incoherent. It reflects a clear principle: Only the president and his allies, his supporters, and their anointed are entitled to the rights and protections of the law, and if necessary, immunity from it. The rest of us are entitled only to cruelty, by their whim. This is how the powerful have ever kept the powerless divided and in their place, and enriched themselves in the process.

A blockbuster *New York Times* investigation published on October 2 reported that President Trump's wealth was largely inherited through fraudulent schemes, that he became a millionaire while still a child, and that his fortune persists in spite of his fumbling entrepreneurship, not because of it. The stories are not unconnected. The president and his advisers have sought to enrich themselves at taxpayer expense; they have attempted to corrupt federal law-enforcement agencies to protect themselves and their cohorts, and they have exploited the nation's darkest impulses in the pursuit of profit. But their ability to get away with this fraud is tied to cruelty.

Trump's only true skill is the con; his only fundamental belief is that the United States is the birthright of straight, white, Christian men, and his only real, authentic pleasure is in cruelty. It is that cruelty, and the delight it brings them, that binds his most ardent supporters to him, in shared scorn for those they hate and fear: immigrants, black voters, feminists, and treasonous white men who empathize with any of those who would steal their birthright. The president's ability to execute that cruelty through word and deed makes them euphoric. It makes them feel good, it makes them feel proud, it makes them feel happy, it makes them feel united. And as long as he makes them feel that way, they will let him get away with anything, no matter what it costs them.

THE LAST DAY
OF MY OLD LIFE

by Caitlin Flanagan

[JUNE 2020]

When *Atlantic* staff writer Caitlin Flanagan faced a recurrence of her cancer, a decade ago, a nurse shrewdly advised her to "get closer to the science." She did. Now confronting another recurrence, this time amid a global public-health crisis, Flanagan acknowledges the wisdom of what she was told by that wise practitioner. And she considers the nurse's words in the context of a president whose reaction to a grave national threat has been one of denial and mockery.

The good thing about having Stage IV cancer is that nobody thinks you're bellyaching when you complain about it. It's a field day for the discontented. You get to wander around muttering to yourself, "Stage IV cancer! Could it get any worse?"

Rilke taught us not to seek the answers but to love the questions. Good advice. Now I'm stuck in my house muttering, "Stage IV cancer during a pandemic! Could it get any—*oh, never mind.*"

I'm one of the people all of this social distancing is helping to stay alive, so far. I belong to the group of people—the infirm, the weak—who certain conservatives have said should offer themselves up to the coronavirus. I'm part of the "cure" that mustn't be worse than "the problem," according to Donald Trump. Glenn Beck seems to think we should show our patriotism by volunteering to be killed by the virus rather than "kill the country."

I've come close to dying a few times, and I'm not afraid anymore, just sad. I'm like a war correspondent or an assassin—all I need is the call, and I'll be gone in the night. I wish I had something helpful to say, now, about fear; for a long time, I was so terrified that I could hardly breathe. Somehow, you get used to it.

But if I die from the coronavirus, it will be one more unnecessary American death. Every epidemiologist in the world warned us the pandemic was coming, yet we were totally unprepared. And even after governors and public-health experts performed the astonishing feat of getting huge numbers of Americans to stay home, Trump continued to undermine them.

In March, he got bored and floated the idea that we'd all be sprung by Easter. In April, Central Park became a field hospital and refrigerated trucks were moving through New York City. Easter—victory over death—came and went. We tuned out the president, and listened only to experts. The experts said we weren't getting out anytime soon.

When I was diagnosed with cancer, there were no smartphones. Moms had efficient little cameras in their purses; fathers carried enormous cameras with zoom lenses, which were so complicated that the dads were always missing the big moment and begging kids to restage it. Because of a mom camera, I have a photograph of the very last day of my old life.

I was a chaperone for a preschool field trip to the Los Angeles Fire Department Museum. (Of course I was; I loved everything about having little kids. I loved going to the library and to the park and to the miniature railroad at Griffith Park, and I loved watching *Clifford the Big Red Dog* and lying on a blanket in the front yard past bedtime, looking at the stars.) On that field trip, a friend happened to snap a picture of me talking to one of my twin boys.

I still feel sad when I look at it. There I am, so happy and—as far as I knew—healthy. And there's my little boy on the very last day of his childhood before he had to understand frightening ideas and words. Joan Didion wrote, "It is easy to see the beginnings of things, and harder to see the ends." But in this case, the end of things was very clear: Our life changed—and stayed changed—the day after that field trip.

Since then I have counted my life in graduations. I sat in the back row of the preschool graduation trying not to cry, which meant stopping myself from saying the words *This could be the only graduation I go to.* Everyone else was so happy and bustling, but I was in a far place and couldn't get back.

The boys graduated from kindergarten the next year and I was there—knocked down from a year of treatment, bald, but starting to recover. I made it through first and second grade, and I thought maybe I could shoot for the elementary-school graduation, but when the boys were in third grade my cancer came back. That one should have got me. If it had happened a few years earlier, it probably would have. But the science was a big step ahead of me.

———

A long time ago, when I was still a young person without a single thought of cancer, a scientist named Dennis Slamon was sitting in his lab at UCLA and he had an idea: that one of the most aggressive forms of breast cancer, the kind marked by an overexpression of the gene HER2/neu, could be treated with an antibody called Herceptin. The story of his fight to get the research funded, and of the women who volunteered to take part in the clinical trials, has been told many times. It's the story of a stubborn scientist who was sure he was onto something, and who wouldn't stop until he had the funding and data to prove it.

When I was diagnosed, Herceptin had just been approved for limited use in my type of cancer. The practice where I was treated was allowed to give it to me under certain protocols: I received it with my chemo, and stayed on it for a year. That wasn't nearly long enough.

Five years after my diagnosis, my luck ran out: a metastatic recurrence with tumors in my lungs and chest wall and liver. I pretty much assumed that was it for me. But I got a couple of good tips.

The first was from a nurse at my oncology practice, who risked his job by closing the door of the exam room and suggesting that I get a second opinion. The second one, the one that saved my life, was from someone who knows a lot about cancer: "You have to get closer to the science."

The science was at UCLA, where Slamon and his team of researchers were changing the fates of millions of women. I left the private practice and became the patient of a brilliant young oncologist in Slamon's lab, Sara Hurvitz. My former oncologist had suggested sectioning my liver. Hurvitz had no intention of doing that. She would give me six treatments of chemotherapy; halfway through I would get a scan to see if it was working. In cancer treatment, the gold medal is finding out that the tumors are shrinking. Silver—and who wouldn't want a silver medal?—is that you are stable. There is no bronze.

The day my husband and I drove to the appointment where Hurvitz would tell us the results of the scan was an experience of anxiety and fear I can't convey. The fear you feel when you're waiting to hear the results of a cancer scan is different from when you're in physical danger. You have the same adrenaline overload but you can't go into fight-or-flight. You can't even freeze. You have to keep putting one foot after the other: out of the parking garage, into the lobby, into the elevator. You have to have a nurse check your vitals and you have to sit on the table with the white paper.

Sara Hurvitz came in. All of my tumors were gone. Undetectable on the scan.

My husband and I nearly fainted. We went to a hotel and had cocktails—which "aren't a good idea on chemo," I had been repeatedly told. Those cocktails were the best idea of my life.

I finished the treatments, and every three weeks I got an infusion of Herceptin. With these interventions, I enjoyed a full remission that lasted 11 years. Do you know what it's like for a mother of school-age children to be given an 11-year remission? And it was the direct consequence of the UCLA scientist who never gave up.

Now here I am—here we all are—with our health in the hands of Donald Trump, M.D. When the coronavirus appeared on the horizon, he did not get closer to the science. He mocked science. He said the panic around the virus and the criticism of his response were a big hoax;

he said the outbreak would end with warmer weather in April; he said the virus was no more serious than the common flu; he said there would be a vaccine soon; he said the virus would suddenly disappear "like a miracle"; he said there were plenty of "beautiful" tests and anyone who wanted one could have one; he said the number of U.S. infections was going "substantially down, not up." He said an antimalarial drug cured COVID-19 and the FDA had approved it for use by prescription. He said there were only 15 patients with COVID-19 in the U.S. and the number, "within a couple of days, is going to be down to close to zero."

He said, "That's a pretty good job we've done."

After I made it to my boys' sixth-grade and high-school graduations, I thought I'd have college in the bag. But I got sick again last year, when they were juniors. After the news of the bad scan, I told the doctor I'd see her in two weeks—I was on my way to Italy, to visit my son who was studying there. When you've had cancer long enough, you realize you can't put off anything.

A second recurrence of metastatic cancer is always a big deal, and I will be on treatment for the rest of my life. But the HER2 armamentarium now holds enough drugs that I could live for many years. The science has stayed a step ahead of me.

When I first learned I had cancer, a friend told me that even during chemo I would still have my life, that I would still go forward, still do the things I wanted to do. I didn't believe her. I recently looked through all of our photo albums—something I never do, because I feel so sad about what happened—and I was stunned by what I saw. I didn't see pictures of two sad boys. I saw picture after picture of two boys with huge smiles on their faces, pictures of vacations and soccer games and art classes and all the fun to be had on the big swing set I bought at Costco when I first got sick. In Costco, it had looked a reasonable size. In our small backyard, it looked like a condo building had gone up. It looked ridiculous. And the boys loved it. Looking at all of those pictures, I realized something: This was my life's work. I gave the boys the best childhood I possibly could.

A year ago, I sat on a couch with my phone in my hand, waiting to place a call: The Mount Vernon Grand Hotel, which is near Kenyon College, accepts reservations exactly one year before graduation, and books up in an hour. I got through and said something I'd never said before: "I'd like a suite, please." Reserving a hotel suite in central Ohio is not the grand gesture it would be in Venice, but it meant something to me. I'd made it.

Today my husband called to relinquish the suite, because the graduation ceremony is postponed. No one knows for how long. Maybe I'll get to my sons' college graduations, and maybe I won't.

Stage IV cancer during a pandemic when Donald Trump is the president! Could it get any worse? No.

BECOMING A PARENT IN THE AGE OF BLACK LIVES MATTER

by Clint Smith

[JUNE 2020]

On May 25, 2020, an unarmed 46-year-old African American man named George Floyd was arrested by four police officers in Minneapolis, Minnesota. Soon he was dead. Bystander video captured the entire episode: Floyd handcuffed and helpless on the ground, a police officer kneeling on his neck for nearly nine minutes as he gasped for breath.

The murder of George Floyd sparked protests across the nation against a pattern of police brutality toward black people. President Trump responded by threatening to send in the U.S. military to quell disturbances. Tear gas and rubber bullets were used to disperse a crowd of peaceful protesters outside the White House. Trump's deafness to pleas for racial justice and his threats of military force drew widely publicized rebukes from General James Mattis, Trump's former secretary of defense, and Admiral Mike Mullen, a former chairman of the Joint Chiefs of Staff—both writing in *The Atlantic*.

Floyd's death and the events that followed provide the context for Clint Smith's essay "Becoming a Parent in the Age of Black Lives Matter." Smith is a writer, teacher, and poet. He is the author of *Counting Descent* (2016), a collection of poetry, and of the forthcoming *How the Word Is Passed*, which

explores the ways different historical sites reckon with—or fail
to reckon with—their relationship to slavery.

I n a park about half a mile from my home is a wide-open field of
grass, whose thin, uneven blades rise up past my ankles. The play-
ground near the park is, like other playgrounds across the country,
no longer open, surrounded by the orange-plastic fencing that has become unsettlingly familiar. Swings and seesaws and monkey bars that
were once teeming with children sit in silence. Robins have begun
making a nest at the top of the slide, building a home in the empty
corner of the jungle gym's small deck.

I have a 3-year-old son who loves to sing songs from *The Lion King*
at the top of his lungs and a 1-year-old daughter who laughs like there
are fireworks in her belly. Almost every day over the past three months
of quarantine, I have taken my children to this field as the culmination
of our daily walks. We are almost always the only people there, and
relish the sweeping emptiness that surrounds us. We park the double
stroller in the center of the grass and build our own world around it.
We grab sticks from fallen branches and pretend to be wizards casting
spells that turn one another into farm animals. We play tag and chase
one another through the field as the tall grass licks our ankles. We bend
down low to the earth, take deep breaths, and blow the dandelion-seed
heads, watching their small, white parachute seeds spiral through the
wind.

My children are both respite from all the tragedy transpiring in the
world, and a reminder of how high the stakes are. When I am with
them—on our walks, playing in the field, reading them stories, giving them baths—I am not able to fall into the infinite hole of endless
scrolling that so often brings me to despair. But also when I am with
them, I am reminded of the brokenness of the world that their mother
and I have brought them into, and get lost in a labyrinth of anxiety
about how I might protect them from it.

I did not have children when the Movement for Black Lives was at its height. At protests following police killings six years ago, I moved through the night with brazen indifference about what might happen to me. I was governed by anger and thought little about the implications of what might happen if I were arrested, if I were hurt, or worse.

As is the case for many other parents, my children have pushed me to reprioritize, reevaluate, and reorient my relationship to the world. My decisions are no longer singularly centered on me. They are shaped by my commitment to these two small humans who think of me and my wife as their entire world. This is a new reality for many black parents who did not have children when the Movement for Black Lives began, but who have young children now in 2020. So much has changed in our lives even when it feels like so little in our country has. Our children have raised the stakes of this fight, while also shifting the calculus of how we move within it. It is one thing to be concerned for my own well-being, to navigate the country as a black man and to encounter its risks. It is another thing to be raising two black children and to consider both the dangers for yourself and the dangers that lie ahead for them.

A week ago, George Floyd was killed by the Minneapolis police officer Derek Chauvin after Chauvin kept his knee planted on Floyd's neck for nearly nine minutes. Floyd, in a distressing echo of Eric Garner's pleas five years ago, could be heard telling the officers around him that he could not breathe. Despite Floyd's appeals, according to a court document, "the defendant had his knee on Mr. Floyd's neck for 8 minutes and 46 seconds in total." It went on: "Two minutes and 53 seconds of this was after Mr. Floyd was non-responsive."

Floyd's death follows a string of recent incidents in which black people have been killed at the hands of police and vigilantes: Ahmaud Arbery, who was killed in South Georgia by a group of white men who chased him down while he was jogging and shot him as he struggled to escape. Breonna Taylor, who was killed when police officers in Louisville, Kentucky, entered her home with a search warrant looking for drugs that were being sold out of a house more than 10 miles away.

There was also the incident involving Amy Cooper, a white woman in New York City's Central Park who was captured on camera falsely claiming that a black man named Christian Cooper was attacking her. I imagine how easily a different story might have been told if Christian Cooper had not recorded the incident, if Amy Cooper's distressed 911 call was the only piece of evidence from that moment. I keep thinking about that shift in the register of Amy Cooper's voice, making it sound as if she was actively being attacked while on the phone—how she knew exactly what that inflection would signal to the person on the other end of the line.

So much of this feels heartbreakingly similar to what transpired a few years ago. People took to the streets to protest the deaths of Michael Brown, Eric Garner, Renisha McBride, Jordan Davis, Freddie Gray, and others. And yet an obvious difference exists between this moment and that one: Today, all of this is happening during a global pandemic that is disproportionately killing black people in America. While some may claim, implicitly or explicitly, that this disparity is simply a result of cultural or individual shortcomings, black coronavirus deaths are not the result of personal failings. They are the result of housing segregation, medical discrimination, low-wage jobs, and lack of access to health care; they are the result of history.

This is part of the story that my parents had to explain to me, and that I will one day explain to my own children—that so many in our community find themselves in these conditions not because black people have done something wrong, but because of all the wrong that has been done to black people. Many are now familiar with the other conversations that black parents have with their children, the conversations in which parents attempt to tread the line of making their children aware of the realities of the world without making them feel somehow at fault. I experienced these conversations as a child, and will one day have to find a way to have them with my own children. A conversation that is more central to my life at the moment, however, is the one that black parents are having with one another.

With many of my friends in their early 30s, an increasing number are beginning to have children. We are new to parenting, and almost everyone's children are under 3 years old. For the past few years our text-message threads have been filled with advice on how to get your child to sleep through the night, where you could find the best deal on diapers, and who was going to the toddler birthday party that weekend. More recently, our Zoom calls and group chats have largely centered on checking in with one another amid the isolation of quarantine and the stream of black deaths, from both vigilantes and the virus. A common theme is that the need to be present for our children, who are so young and so in need of our constant attention, has distracted us from the television screens and phones we might otherwise be glued to. How we are at once grateful to be pulled away and stressed by the fact that the world feels more dangerous than we have ever known it to be. As one of my friends put it when thinking about having a 2-year-old son in this moment, it's the "discomforting juxtaposition between the joy of seeing the world through his eyes and knowing how the world will see him one day."

In 2015, before I had children, I wrote a letter to the son I might one day have. In it I wrote, "I hope to teach you so much of what my father taught me, but I pray that you live in a radically different world from the one that he and I have inherited." Now I do have a son, and all the fears, anxieties, and joys I wrote about five years ago are no longer an abstraction. They exist in his curly hair, his soft face, and his voice full of songs and questions. I am not sure how different the world I entered is from the one he has, but the past several weeks—to say nothing of the past several years—have made clear how fragile the project of progress truly is.

As we were leaving the park last week, my son saw a butterfly fluttering across the field. "Caterpillar! Chrysalis! Butterfly!" he sang to himself, taking pride in having recently learned the animal's life cycle. My daughter clapped and swung her head from side to side as he repeated the words. I watched the butterfly rise and fall in the wind, its thin yellow wings carrying its body in an uneven pirouette through the air.

George Floyd had children of his own, two daughters, Gianna and Roxie. I am left wondering what their memories of their father will be. Did they run through open fields together? Blow dandelions into the wind? Play tag until they fell breathless and jubilant to the ground? I hope that any memories they carry will supersede those of their father on the ground, begging for his life.

IV. BECOMING
CITIZENS AGAIN

The *Atlantic* was founded in 1857, during a period of grave crisis. Within a few years, the United States was engulfed in the Civil War—our greatest national trauma. The Civil War would be followed by an attempt at Reconstruction, abandoned after scarcely a decade in a deal between both political parties. The murder of Reconstruction consigned African Americans to a regime of injustice and violence that would have legal sanction for a century.

But several things happened in the brief window between the end of the Civil War and the end of Reconstruction that have, in the years that followed, either kept us from falling or borne us aloft.

One was the passage of the Thirteenth, Fourteenth, and Fifteenth Amendments. Not only was slavery abolished but the provisions of the Bill of Rights were extended to cover the actions of state governments. The so-called Reconstruction Amendments redefined the nature of citizenship and represented a "second founding." Americans have invoked these amendments—successfully—time and again.

That same brief window gave us a speech by Frederick Douglass entitled "Our Composite Nationality," a work of literature and rhetoric that sought to define America's highest aspirations. Douglass's vision of the kind of society America might become entails a duty that Americans cannot shirk.

As writers note in the essays that follow, America has reinvented itself before—and has needed to. History offers no blueprint. It provides neither exact parallels nor off-the-shelf policy options. But it can remind us of the tools still at our disposal—values, outlooks, attitudes, instincts. It reminds us as well that aspiration itself can be a tool.

THE LESSONS OF THE GREAT DEPRESSION

by Lizabeth Cohen

[MAY 2020]

President Franklin Delano Roosevelt launched the New Deal nine decades ago, several years into the Great Depression. Americans have looked to that example ever since, especially during times of trauma and upheaval. It is by now a durable element of our national myth. What lessons can we draw from it in our present crisis? If the past is "usable," how do we make use of the New Deal?

As Lizabeth Cohen noted in her 2020 *Atlantic* article "The Lessons of the Great Depression," part of the challenge is understanding what the New Deal was and wasn't. The New Deal's legacy was immense, but some of the most important things to learn from it transcend the familiar "alphabet soup" of particular policies and programs: The essential role played by millions of ordinary citizens, empowering themselves and their communities through grassroots activity. The importance of empathy as not just a personal virtue but a political one. And the strategic necessity of a forward-leaning patience so that failure never stifles innovation.

Cohen is the Howard Mumford Jones Professor of American Studies and a Harvard University Distinguished Service Professor in the Department of History at Harvard. She is a two-time winner of the Bancroft Prize—for her books *Making a New Deal: Industrial Workers in Chicago, 1919–1939* (1990) and

Saving America's Cities: Ed Logue and the Struggle to Renew Urban America in the Suburban Age (2019).

Americans are out of work. More than 20 million lost their jobs in April alone. Lines at food banks stretch for miles. Businesses across the country are foundering. Headlines scream that the coronavirus has brought about the worst economic crisis since the Great Depression.

The economic collapse of the 1930s, one of the defining traumas of the 20th century, is still the benchmark against which recessions are measured. And, for many Americans, the New Deal, launched by President Franklin Delano Roosevelt, remains the standard for how the federal government should respond to a major national emergency. By the late 1940s, the United States had exited economic calamity and entered into an unparalleled period of national prosperity—with measurably greater income equality. America did not merely endure the Great Depression; its response transformed it into a richer and more equitable society.

Many hope to replicate that achievement today. But the success of the New Deal was built on more than all the agencies it spawned, or the specific programs it established—it rested on the spirit of those who brought it into being. The New Dealers learned to embrace experimentation, accepting failures along the path to success. They turned aside the ferocious opposition their bold proposals provoked. They organized supporters, and learned not just to lead, but to listen. And, perhaps above all, they pushed for unity and cultivated empathy.

The New Deal offers us more than a simple guide for returning to some semblance of normalcy. The larger lesson it offers is that recovery is a complex and painful process that requires the participation of many, not directives from a few. And that, ultimately, we're all in this together.

During the Great Depression, the nation's initial response to disaster was crippled by the negative view of government held by then-president Herbert Hoover and his Republican Party. At the beginning of the century, the Progressive Era had led to greater government oversight of interstate commerce and the processing of food and drugs. But as secretary of commerce in the 1920s, Hoover had promoted an alternative ideal of voluntary regulation, whereby professional organizations and American businesses monitored their own affairs instead of being regulated by the federal government. That arrangement, which the historian Ellis W. Hawley dubbed the "associative state," offered a sharp contrast with the progressivism that had preceded it.

Hoover was sworn in as president in March 1929, just months before the stock market crashed. But try as he might, he couldn't get his associative state to master the challenge of the Great Depression. His miserable failure paved the way for Roosevelt's landslide victory in November 1932.

Faced with a crisis of enormous proportion, Roosevelt reinvented how the nation did much of its business, most notably by involving the federal government in areas of American life that previously had belonged to cities, counties, or states—if to any governing authority at all. The New Deal succeeded in implementing policies at the federal level that had been percolating for years in reform circles, or that had been partly implemented by the most progressive states.

To ameliorate the immediate crisis, the federal government funded relief, jobs, and infrastructure. In the longer term, it established a new normal that included a national retirement system, unemployment insurance, disability benefits, minimum wages and maximum hours, public housing, mortgage protection, electrification of rural America, and the right of industrial labor to bargain collectively through unions.

These programs were rife with limitations. Social Security and unemployment insurance were tied to jobs, rather than citizenship; federal backing for mortgages redlined neighborhoods considered too nonwhite or immigrant; whole categories of workers were exempted from Social Security and fair-labor standards, such as those doing domestic and agricultural labor; and many necessities for a decent life, such as paid sick days and health coverage, were left to the discretion of employers or the bargaining brawn of unions. Yet flaws and all, the New Deal constructed a social safety net that undergirded a long period of growth and prosperity.

But if we want to use the New Deal as a model for creating opportunity out of catastrophe, we will need to understand more than just its policies and programs. Building a new and improved United States, post-coronavirus, will require understanding how Roosevelt and his associates, labor leaders and activists, and ordinary Americans combined their efforts during the bleakness of crisis to build a better future. We need to know not just what they did, but how they pulled it off.

———————

The New Deal was experimental and incremental—not ideological. Roosevelt and his advisers were far from the clairvoyant visionaries of legend. They never had a master plan. Rather, in the administration's first 100 days, they implemented a flurry of laws and regulations. If those programs worked, they remained. If they didn't, they were dropped, to be replaced by others.

The National Industrial Recovery Act, for example, with its voluntary codes of fair competition for prices and wages and limited encouragement of collective bargaining, proved inadequate, and then was ruled unconstitutional. The administration quickly developed alternatives, including the National Labor Relations Act (known as the Wagner Act), which offered a clearer path to unionization.

Not until after 1935 did the New Deal's welfare state of Social Security, unemployment insurance, and public housing emerge. And many of its initiatives failed, such as when a premature rollback of federal programs precipitated the "Roosevelt recession" of 1937, boosting unemployment back to frighteningly high levels. Even the Harvard professor Alvin Hansen, FDR's trusted economic adviser, admitted, "I really do not know what the basic principle of the New Deal is."

Indeed, disagreements rent the Roosevelt White House. For example, some economic planners wanted a recovery that revived the old Progressive-era crusade against monopoly, while others favored regulating businesses regardless of size, or taking a Keynesian approach of using the state's fiscal powers to increase consumption. By the late 1930s, the Keynesians had won out. John Kenneth Galbraith, then a young professor, recalled that, as late as 1936, the acceptance of the rules of classical economics was "a litmus by which the reputable economist was separated from the crackpot." A year later, "Keynes had reached Harvard with tidal force." The point is that no well-prepared road map set the New Deal's course.

Roosevelt was also remarkable for the manner in which he successfully disarmed most of his political opponents. It may be tempting today— with our stalemated politics, deeply divided electorate, and inflammatory media—to imagine that FDR, who won by landslides in 1932 and 1936 and by a comfortable margin even when seeking an unprecedented third term in 1940, enjoyed the luxury of a national consensus. Nothing could be further from the truth. The Roosevelt administration was attacked from the right by disapproving Republicans, business leaders who vowed to destroy the "socialist" New Deal, wary southern Democratic members of Congress, and the hugely popular Roman Catholic radio host Father Charles Coughlin. Coughlin's *Golden Hour of the Little Flower* program regularly drew an audience of more than 30 million into his anti-Roosevelt, anti-Communist, anti-Semitic, isolationist, and conspiratorial miasma.

On the left, Roosevelt faced small but effectively organized communist and socialist groups, as well as miscellaneous third parties like John Dewey and Paul H. Douglas's League for Independent Political Action. Much more threatening was Huey Long of Louisiana. The populist— and wildly popular—governor and then senator quickly abandoned Roosevelt as too cautious, mounting his more redistributive "Share Our Wealth" program. Long reached millions through a national network of clubs and his own radio broadcasts. Roosevelt feared Long as a dangerous demagogue until his assassination in September 1935, but Long's indisputable popularity likely pushed FDR leftward.

Roosevelt responded to these challenges from the right and the left by justifying the New Deal in uncontroversial, almost nonpartisan terms. Although his message could fluctuate depending on which enemies he aimed to vanquish—for example, denouncing capitalist elites as "economic royalists" in his 1936 speech to the Democratic National Convention so as not to be outflanked on the left—FDR typically justified the New Deal as the pursuit of "security against the hazards and vicissitudes of life" or the protection of the "four freedoms" of speech, worship, want, and fear. And not to be outdone by Father Coughlin or Long, Roosevelt became a master himself of the radio, brilliantly using his many fireside chats to establish an intimate relationship with the American people.

———————

Roosevelt also learned that to lead, he needed to listen. The social and political changes of the New Deal were built by mobilizing ordinary Americans as Democratic Party voters and rank-and-file union members. The New Deal was no top-down revolution. Democratic politicians as well as union organizers quickly discovered that they needed to focus on the real problems people faced, and to respond to their preferences.

Before the New Deal, many working people lived political lives circumscribed by their local party, whether Democratic or Republican. First- or second-generation immigrants were loyal partisans, if they voted at all. Few African Americans in the Jim Crow South could vote. Those who traveled north in the Great Migration of the 1910s and '20s spurned the Democratic Party as the instrument of their southern oppressors and the enemy of the party of Lincoln, which many of them now eagerly supported.

Within industrial workplaces, unions—to the extent they existed in the 1920s—were made up of elite craft workers, mostly white and native-born, who sought to limit the opportunity and mobility of the more numerous, and more vulnerable, nonunion workers. Labor organizers suffered a series of stinging defeats in 1919, after which unions seemed to hold little promise for the less-skilled workers who powered the mass production plants that were making the U.S. the 20th century's "workshop of the world."

Fearing reprises of the unionization drives that had followed World War I, some employers mounted paternalistic welfare programs in the 1920s, touting benefits such as paid sick leave and vacations, pensions, stock ownership, group life insurance, and employee representation plans. But companies rarely backed those promises with the level of financial investment required to deliver those benefits to more than a fraction of their workforce. Workers relied instead on inadequate safety nets provided by their ethnic, racial, and religious communities, which quickly failed under the strain of the Great Depression.

By the time Roosevelt won a second presidential term, in 1936, the world had transformed. Many of those in need were taking full advantage of federal relief and jobs programs sponsored by the array of New Deal agencies, including the FERA, CWA, PWA, WPA, NYA, and CCC. By addressing the needs of Americans, Roosevelt earned their support. Faced with the enormity of the Great Depression, working-class Americans were voting in record numbers—and they voted for the Democratic president. Black voters were even replacing the motto "Stick to Republicans because Lincoln freed you" with "Let Jesus lead you and Roosevelt feed you."

Working people also drove a massive effort to unionize industrial laborers across many sectors, coordinated by the newly founded Congress of Industrial Organizations (CIO), whose success was facilitated by the Wagner Act. By 1940, in the manufacturing stronghold of Chicago, one in three industrial workers belonged to a union, whereas 10 years earlier hardly any had. The story was much the same in Detroit and Flint in Michigan, Cleveland and Akron in Ohio, and in Minneapolis, Pittsburgh, and elsewhere. Workers who only a few years before had felt little connection to Washington, D.C., and felt excluded from national unions, now identified with the federal government and nationwide political and labor movements.

Through their participation in the Democratic Party and unions, workers helped to ideologically reorient both of these new centers of political gravity. Although leaders mattered, from local precincts to the Democratic Party headquarters and from shop floors to the CIO's inner circle, those with power had to contend with a rank and file that knew its own mind.

This was particularly evident in the labor movement. Left-wing activists were crucial organizers of Communist Unemployed Councils, socialist Workers' Committees on Unemployment, hunger marches, demonstrations outside relief offices, and emerging unions. But in the end, despite all the hardships of the Great Depression, few workers bought into the anti-capitalist message.

The Communist organizer Steve Nelson recalled how he and his comrades had begun by "agitating against capitalism and talking about the need for socialism." Quickly, however, they figured out that working-class people were more concerned with their daily struggles. "We learned to shift . . . to what might be called a grievance approach to the organizing," he said. "We began to raise demands for . . . immediate federal assistance to the unemployed, and a moratorium on mortgages, and finally we began to talk about the need for national employment insurance." In fact, partly inspired by the empty promises of their employers' welfare-capitalist schemes of the 1920s, working-class Americans came to embrace what I have elsewhere labeled "moral capitalism." While workers benefited from the organizing experience of radical leaders, they more often opted for liberal goals than for radicalism, preferring a more just capitalist order over any alternative.

————

The New Deal's success had one final, and crucial, ingredient: the cultivation of empathy.

For labor leaders, it was a practical necessity. Herbert March, a Communist organizer in Chicago, was typical in worrying that "it would not be possible to achieve unionism because you had the split of black and white and too many nationalities . . . that they [employers] would play against each other." These sorts of ethnic and racial divisions had helped doom the 1919 organizing drives. Unless unions could inculcate an ideal of racial inclusion and class solidarity, white working people might well retreat to their segmented ethnic and racial worlds and push their African American co-workers back into the arms of employers as strikebreakers.

To avoid that danger, the leftist leaders of the CIO worked hard to cultivate what I have called an inclusive "culture of unity" within the evolving union movement. Black packinghouse worker Jim Cole told an interviewer in 1939 that the CIO had "done the greatest thing in the world" by bringing workers together, and dispelling the "hate and bad feelings that used to be held against the Negro." Enlightened activists helped working people transcend their prejudices at a critical moment.

The New Deal, too, made this work central to its project. Along-side their many new and unfamiliar agencies, the New Dealers set out to document how Americans were weathering the Great Depression. These undertakings were spurred by multiple motives, including gen-erating publicity for New Deal programs and employment for out-of-work artists and actors. But most fundamentally, these projects educated people about their countrymen and -women and bred empa-thy. "We introduced America to Americans," is how the FSA head Roy Stryker put it many years later.

The Farm Security Administration images taken by such legendary photographers as Walker Evans, Dorothea Lange, Russell Lee, Gordon Parks, and Ben Shahn are probably the best-known such initiative, but almost every New Deal agency mounted its own photography project to document its impact on the American people. The WPA's Federal Writers' Project sponsored life and oral histories, ethnographies, and portraits of diverse cultural communities, including recent immigrants, Native Americans, and African Americans. And the Federal Theater Project produced documentary plays in its "Living Newspaper" per-formances.

If these lessons of the New Deal apply to our own moment, then so does one more: There will be no easy return to normalcy. Despite all of the New Deal's interventions, unemployment was still disturbingly high on the eve of World War II. The massive stimulus of global war was what finally lifted the United States out of depression, although that war brought with it additional years of deprivation and sacrifice. Moreover, many Americans would never overcome the trauma of the Depression, and would have to be prodded into a postwar era that depended more than ever on consumer spending to deliver widespread prosperity.

What form the economic recovery from COVID-19 shutdowns will take remains difficult to predict. The strategies and programs of the 2020s won't be the same as those of the 1930s. The enormous growth of consumption as a percentage of GDP, from a low of 49.5 percent in 1944 to roughly 70 percent today, has led policy makers to prioritize a ramping-up of consumption—often prematurely—over job creation. National leaders seem to prefer sending checks to the jobless over providing them with jobs. Brick-and-mortar stores, restaurants, and other vendors of personal services, which were already struggling with the shift to online shopping, have been particularly hard hit. Their slow recovery will not only remain a drag on the larger economy, but will also affect the vitality of public life that often revolves around commercial districts.

Moreover, there is a real risk that the downturn will exacerbate the inequalities already present in the American economy—in jobs, income, health care, housing, and education. Consumption could continue to shift toward the largest sellers, like Amazon, squeezing out smaller businesses. The nation's workforce might then become even more unequal, with small numbers of salaried executives at the top and armies of low-skilled, hourly warehouse employees and package deliverers with limited benefits at the bottom. Already, the COVID-19 crisis has made apparent shameful racial disparities that are taking an extraordinary toll on communities of color.

And the current disaster could also deepen our divisions. Perhaps the greatest obstacle to solving our social ills has been the intense partisanship and vicious scapegoating that has paralyzed the polity. We are fractured along many lines. What once were civil disagreements over the size of government, the reach of the safety net, or the relative benefits of taxing versus incentivizing business entrepreneurship have become unsurmountable divides.

But if we cannot simply copy the New Deal's programs and apply them to our contemporary challenges, we can still take inspiration from the spirit that animated them. We can set aside ideology in favor of experimentation, fend off partisan attacks with appeals to higher principles, focus on the needs of ordinary workers, and deliberately cultivate the unity and empathy required to forge an effective coalition to do battle with the coronavirus and economic devastation.

This last point is perhaps the most important, and it may be the most difficult. Empathy, after all, has been badly missing in the United States in recent decades.

Perhaps we've made a start. The iconic images of this pandemic are of nurses, doctors, and EMTs caring for the sick. Nightly displays of thanks echo in many parts of the country. Grocery-store clerks are recognized as heroes. The coronavirus's harsh lesson in our shared vulnerability to disease—that we are all safe only when everyone is healthy—could become the basis for a broader recognition of our shared fate as Americans. Learning that lesson may help us rebuild our society into one that treats everyone as essential.

THE ROAD FROM SERFDOM

by Danielle Allen

[DECEMBER 2019]

In her 2019 essay "The Road From Serfdom," which appeared as part of the *Atlantic* special issue "How to Stop a Civil War," the political philosopher Danielle Allen returned to George Washington's farewell address as a modern touchstone. Washington, she explained, had more than one reason for warning Americans away from the allure of "faction"—what today we would call "factionalism." Washington wrote, "The disorders and miseries which result gradually incline the minds of men to seek security and repose in the absolute power of an individual." But the problem goes deeper. Factionalism erodes unity, and a sense of unity—*we're all in this together*—is a prerequisite of compromise. Compromise is what enables a diverse people to organize and get important things done—which is what our Constitution was designed to enable us to do. In her essay, excerpted here, Allen argued that we have lost sight of these basic truths—and must reclaim them.

Danielle Allen is the James Bryant Conant University Professor at Harvard University and the director of Harvard's Edmond J. Safra Center for Ethics. She is the author of *Talking to Strangers: Anxieties of Citizenship since* Brown v. Board of Education (2004), *Our Declaration: A Reading of the Declaration of Independence in Defense of Equality* (2014), and *Cuz: The Life and Times of Michael A.* (2017).

As I think about our national paralysis, and the reasons for it, I find myself recalling George Washington's farewell address—the letter he wrote to the American people in 1796 after deciding not to run for a third presidential term. Washington wanted to issue a warning about the dangers of factionalism: what happens when a nation forgets that it is one country—that its citizens and values and processes, whatever the inevitable disagreements, are indivisible. Unity, he believed, had a moral dimension. It was also the best defense against bullying and tyranny, on the one hand, and gridlock, on the other. In recent decades, the fact that Washington owned slaves has obliterated his words from many minds. *Hamilton* notwithstanding, quoting slaveholders is out of fashion. But here is some of what Washington said:

> The alternate domination of one faction over another, sharpened by the spirit of revenge, natural to party dissension, which in different ages and countries has perpetrated the most horrid enormities, is itself a frightful despotism. But this leads at length to a more formal and permanent despotism. The disorders and miseries which result gradually incline the minds of men to seek security and repose in the absolute power of an individual; and sooner or later the chief of some prevailing faction, more able or more fortunate than his competitors, turns this disposition to the purposes of his own elevation on the ruins of public liberty.

This slave owner knew something about liberty and its preservation. It is a paradox that the embrace and maintenance of slavery at the nation's founding—its original sin—schooled early Americans in the lessons of freedom and equality. They didn't share freedom and equality with everyone, but they learned those lessons. Washington himself used the language of "freemen" and "slaves" to define the stakes in the contest with Britain. His audience knew firsthand what he meant.

Washington worried deeply about the prospects for the early American republic—and especially that factionalism might destroy it.

Faction—an old word, but better than *tribalism*—captures the idea not just of political parties but of parties ready to fight existentially, as if unto death. Washington spoke about the "artificial and extraordinary force" of faction. In particular, he cited its capacity

> to put in the place of the delegated will of the nation the will of a party, often a small but artful and enterprising minority of the community; and, according to the alternate triumphs of different parties, to make the public administration the mirror of the ill concerted and incongruous projects of faction, rather than the organ of consistent and wholesome plans digested by common councils and modified by mutual interests.

Washington's phrases sometimes creak like the old phaeton that carried him about in Philadelphia, but his meaning remains clear. In Washington's view, public liberty depended on a process of mutual consultation—adjusting the interests of various parties in relation to one another—with the aim of achieving "consistent and wholesome plans" that could provide stability of direction over the long haul. Our very political institutions, born of compromise and sketched in the Constitution, were this country's first plan. Washington believed that the business of government—of "public administration"—was to get important things done, that getting things done depended on compromise, that compromise was enabled by a commitment to unity, and that deciding what needed to be done required a long view of the public interest.

Sensible ideas. How did we ever misplace them?

———

Centuries from now, historians looking back at contemporary America will identify the 1970s as a moment when one era gave way to another. We are accustomed to focusing on how the advent of the digital age disrupted the world as we knew it. But for all of technology's impact, other changes have been even more disruptive: the changes to our values themselves. The '70s brought major shifts in the social, political, and economic domains, and brought them all at once. Now, in 2019, we sit on the far side of that transformation.

Consider, first, the social changes. The draft ended in 1973. The introduction of a professional, all-volunteer military put an end to a culture in which most adult men had a shared experience of service. The civil-rights movement, the widespread use of the pill, and the legalization of abortion overturned generations of old social hierarchies. These hierarchies had always served as the informal constitution for the country. They underpinned the legal Constitution by determining who could wield power through political institutions. The wielders of power had primarily been white men. In the final decades of the 20th century, large parts of the country, but not all, embraced the project of replacing the old informal constitution with a new, egalitarian one.

The social changes of the '70s have sometimes been described as bringing a decline in social capital and social activity. The political scientist Robert Putnam famously made this argument in a book pointedly titled *Bowling Alone*. He attributed shrinking membership in clubs such as the Rotary and the Jaycees to new commuting patterns, new forms of entertainment (such as television), the influx of women into the workforce, and "generational change." Yet what actually occurred from 1970 to 1990 was bigger than that. The U.S. rewrote the law of association, mainly through state action and Supreme Court decisions; for instance, new legislation and jurisprudence made the gender-exclusive membership policies of the Rotary, the Jaycees, and other groups illegal. In a society seeking to do away with hierarchies based on race and gender, some organizations had trouble adapting. Many faded away and were never replaced.

The 1970s widened divisions: between rich and poor, experts and nonexperts, veterans and nonveterans, young and old. An age of burden sharing gave way to an age of burden evasion, as those who reaped the benefits of our social arrangements and those who bore their costs separated into distinguishable subpopulations. Warring tribes faced off along yet another dividing line—one group seeking to establish an American social order on the basis of egalitarian norms, the other less sure that this new order was worth creating and in some cases actively working to retain the old social order. A battle was joined over how to define "Americanness." It is raging now.

Meanwhile—owing in part to the Vietnam War, in part to the Watergate scandal, in part to other factors—the country's respect for political institutions began a precipitous decline. There were attempts at reform and greater transparency. Political parties made their nominating process more democratic: thumbs-up for open primaries, thumbs-down for smoke-filled rooms. None of this restored the legitimacy or capability of our politics—unexpectedly, it eroded them further. As Jonathan Rauch argued in "What's Ailing American Politics?" [excerpted in Section II], political reforms in the name of democracy and transparency, combined with the advent of nonstop forms of new media, have done away with the power of political gatekeepers, the pragmatic brokers who organized the political system around relatively moderate, deal-cutting politicians. The result, he argued, has been "chaos syndrome," where politics is dominated by politicians who do not care about what other politicians think of them and who pander to their base of voters. Senator Ted Cruz of Texas is despised by members of both parties, but that is of little concern to him. He happily read *Green Eggs and Ham* on the Senate floor as part of a fake filibuster because he knew it would energize his supporters. The disappearance of gatekeepers has undermined the ability of politicians and citizens to "organize": to convene, to set a direction at the level of broad principle, to negotiate, and ultimately to come to a result that moves everyone—imperfectly and with some noses out of joint—toward an incrementally more desirable outcome. You can write whole tomes describing the basic work of democracy, but the single word *organize* will save you a lot of ink.

The Declaration of Independence makes use of this vocabulary. With respect to government, the Declaration charges citizens with the task of "organizing its powers in such form, as to them shall seem most likely to effect their safety and happiness." Citizens of democracies must know how to organize—not merely to secure power but to convert power into usable plans. This was the point made by George Washington, who understood that the only alternative would be "the ill concerted and incongruous projects of faction." But the democratic work of organizing is something that many Americans are no longer capable of doing. The Tea Party gave us the House Freedom Caucus, whose purpose is obstruction. Progressive activism is giving rise to the Justice Democrats, who hinder governance by insisting on perfection, as if that's an option. For most people, texts such as the Declaration of Independence and Washington's farewell address don't pulse with vitality anymore. We don't really *know* them, and we certainly don't use them as the handbooks they were meant to be—the owner's manuals that came with our new country.

All of this has left Americans to fight over the issues that are now most politicized—namely, social and cultural issues. Sometimes we do this brutally, when one faction believes it has the power to force its will—imposing draconian measures by referendum, confirming judges by partisan fiat. We have shed the burden of compromise because politics has become factional. This state of affairs was epitomized by a statement from Senate Majority Leader Mitch McConnell: "Winners make policy, and losers go home."

When we're not fighting, we slink away, sorting ourselves into ideological and residential enclaves. The Civil War, it turns out, didn't settle the question of secession; it outsourced the job to moving vans. If you know a zip code, you know whether you'll find an Applebee's or a gastropub in the neighborhood; you know whether the waiting list at the library will be for John Grisham or Jesmyn Ward; you know the odds on whether the local confectioner will bake a cake for a same-sex wedding.

———

The collapse of the old informal constitution, as yet not fully replaced, and the hollowing-out of our political institutions have left society disunited, disorganized, and raw. They have also left it defenseless against the consequences of a third major shift—in economic thinking and economic reality, and in who is at the table when decisions are made.

In the late 20th century, economics established itself firmly as the queen of the policy-making sciences. Up until then, before the emergence of digital computing power and the spread of numbers-based social science, people who were trained as lawyers, not as economists, had dominated policy making. The shift is documented in recent research by the sociologist Elizabeth Popp Berman. The difference in outlook between economists and lawyers is immense. Whereas economists seek out rules that are in theory universal—mathematical principles that apply everywhere, and are blind to context—legal thinking is fundamentally about the institutions of specific societies and about how institutions actually work in specific situations. This is not to say that we can always count on lawyers to see real people or that lawyers went away. The point is that a different way of thinking—emerging first in economics—has ascended across a wide range of professions.

In the utilitarian model that dominates economics, the goal of policy, in an abstract, mathematical sort of way, is to maximize happiness—or, to use the jargon you won't hear at most dinner tables, "utility"—for members of a society in the aggregate. In its crudest form, the effort to maximize aggregate utility relies on cost-benefit analyses linked not to the conditions of actual communities—small-town Nebraska, working-class Ohio, rural Mississippi—but to broad national measures of expenditure, income, and wealth. This way of thinking, detached from popular debate, has spread worldwide. It is evident in the behavior of central banks and in the demands made of developing countries in return for aid. It is linked to policies intended to enhance the size and efficiency of markets and create an integrated, "frictionless" global economy. The policies have done that, and helped many. But they have also disrupted the world's labor markets. They helped sink the Rust Belt and contributed to unprecedented levels of mass migration. At the same time, the unregulated behavior of the powerful financial sector brought on the Great Recession of 2008, which devastated ordinary Americans and for which virtually no one was held to account.

The kinds of economists involved most intimately with government and financial institutions by and large don't notice real people in real places—people who may be losing jobs and falling into despondency, addiction, and suicide. They tend not to see as relevant to their domains of expertise the millions of people on the move and the impact of mass migration on cultural cohesion. In recent years, they overlooked the warning signs indicating limits to the acceptance of their worldview, notably in the very communities suffering because of their economic policies. Elites on both the left and the right, with their well-thumbed passports and multicultural outlook, were no less blind. They did not see the pressures rising. In the immediate aftermath of the 2016 presidential election, I more than once heard an economist friend say something like the following: "We knew globalization would force transformations, but we never thought they would be localized in a specific subset of communities." And: "We knew that globalization would cause disruption over a 20-year period, but I never thought about what 20 years is like in the life of a specific person or community." The very language conveys remoteness—the sheer size of the chasm between the World Economic Forum and the actual world. This is what happens when the messy, mediating business of popular politics no longer functions properly—when it no longer serves as the membrane through which ideas must pass before they turn into action.

No one wants to feel buffeted in this way—subject to, and at the mercy of, the will of powerful others, to whom they are invisible. There's a word we can use to describe a condition when people feel helpless, whipsawed, and disconnected from the levers of personal and economic autonomy; when people feel trapped in a particular place and circumstance; when decisions about one's life and work and mode of cultural existence seem to rest in the hands of others; when even personal property seems to be evanescent, or nonexistent, or on loan. It's an extreme word, but let's put it on the table. The word is *serfdom*.

Freighted though it is, *serfdom* has a modern intellectual history. How did the present state of affairs come about? How were questions of political economy hived off from political debate?

The first part of the explanation lies in the work of Friedrich A. Hayek, an Austrian economist who spent most of his career after 1931 at the London School of Economics and the University of Chicago. In 1944, Hayek published a book called *The Road to Serfdom*—a condition he saw arising through a very different process from the one I've described. He had left continental Europe at a time when socialist movements of various kinds were growing in influence, and now believed he saw the same dynamic emerging in the English-speaking world. Since the onset of the Great Depression, American economists had been advocating for a managed-market economy in which the government played an essential regulatory role. They were following in the footsteps of the British political economist John Maynard Keynes, who bent monetary policy and government spending toward a target of full employment. This approach brought strength to labor unions and to legislatures, which played a role in both the short- and long-term management of the economy.

In the rise of Keynesian-style intervention, Hayek heard echoes of his past. He felt that, in some sense, by moving to Britain and then to the U.S., he was moving back through time. These countries, he believed, were heading in the same direction as socialist Europe, but were not too far down the path. Like a time traveler, he would use his experience of later stages of that process—his tussles with the fearsome socialist Morlocks—to warn his new compatriots of what he saw as a dangerous drift toward disaster.

At its core, the argument in *The Road to Serfdom* was an argument against "planning"—against the very idea that George Washington had celebrated as the essence of public administration. In particular, Hayek sought to ward off any sort of top-down decision making about the economy. His basic worry was that a planned economy, where a government nationalizes the means of production and makes centralized decisions about how to allocate resources, violates human freedom, distorts human activity, and damages economic productivity. The term *serfdom* captured this concern. Hayek, who won a Nobel Prize in 1974, was right to worry about the dangers of preemptive state control, as the record of communist countries has shown. And he was not some blinkered zealot. His economic theory rested on a rich and evocative account of human beings and human society, and on how to bring about the best outcomes for both on a foundation of freedom. That said, he made a fundamental mistake in thinking that free economic activity within a market system would, by itself, inevitably be good for society as a whole. He disregarded the clear evidence that human beings commonly use economic activity to pursue narrow interests, including domination over one another.

Hayek's anti-planning position was profoundly influential. It links him, in many minds, with another Nobel laureate, Milton Friedman. Friedman's work provides the second part of the explanation. Friedman disagreed with much of Hayek's economic theory, but he considered *The Road to Serfdom* to be of crucial political importance and adopted its anti-planning gospel wholeheartedly. It dovetailed with his vision of the purpose of monetary policy: to establish a stable frame for free-market transactions. He championed price stability—keeping inflation low—as the primary managerial target, not jobs, wages, equality, or anything else. Friedman's advocacy of a market economy, monetarism, and stable prices that secure the efficient functioning of markets rested on a set of propositions about human beings that have made their way, often in caricatured form, deep into the heart of our culture.

Friedman wrote with forceful confidence. He envisioned society as "a number of independent households—a collection of Robinson Crusoes, as it were," united only by relations of free exchange. There are, in his view, no larger national or social goals beyond the aggregate of "the goals that the citizens severally serve." His faith in the ultimately benign power of the free market—rational individuals pursuing their own ends in a ferment of competition—ran deep. Because competition worked so efficiently—bringing productivity, wealth, and social equilibrium—the job of government must be "to foster competitive markets." Further, this limited role for government had an immense corollary benefit: "By removing the organization of economic activity from the control of political authority, the market eliminates this source of coercive power." In conclusion: "A society that puts equality before freedom will get neither. A society that puts freedom before equality will get a high degree of both."

In time, propositions like these produced a broad policy framework that saw markets as the solution to every problem. The idea was that individual self-interest and wealth creation produce beneficial outcomes for everyone. Markets therefore need to be protected from the kind of political control that was built into Keynesian fiscal policy. Economic policy became a matter for economists and bankers. In the 1980s, the task of achieving price stability came to dominate the work of ever more powerful independent central banks. Institutions such as the Federal Reserve, which have formal independence from politics and considerable insulation from democratic accountability, grew stronger. Legislatures grew weaker. Republican and Democratic administrations alike fell into line. The liberation of markets from politics was understood to be a policy that put an end to planning—even though, of course, "putting an end to planning" is itself a kind of plan. It sets the rules of the game.

The final part of the explanation is the rise of a class of people whose job it is to make decisions for us. When it comes to government by technocrats, the center of gravity was once mainly in the economic sphere. And it must be said: Technocrats—or, better, democratically accountable experts—have a role to play. Central banks are necessary and can't be operated by plebiscite (though they could indeed be more accountable). But technocrats are not just setting interest rates. The technocratic way of thinking has affected everything from homeownership to the quality of schools, from income distribution to the rights of workers, from insurance rates to the legal system. All of these issues get talked about as if they were still the central domain of politics, and as if elected officials actually dealt with them, but in fact they are being addressed (or left unaddressed) by the technocratic class—the people sometimes derided as policy wonks. The sprawling nature of the modern state may have its roots in political decisions made, willy-nilly, at various points in the past, but its evolution and management are largely detached from politics. Indeed, in America, the modern state is even becoming detached from government, its functions outsourced to private-sector contractors, whose ranks have swelled by more than 1 million since 1996. (The federal payroll has held more or less constant.) Think about defense strategy, environmental regulation, privacy laws, prison building, and on and on: How much of the directional policy making about any of these, much less the implementation of policy, is any longer the outcome of an open, democratic process, as opposed to a few knowledgeable people deciding what to do?

The result of all this has been the erosion of our collective understanding of the work of public administration. We are descending again into a form of servitude, though not the kind that Hayek feared: assignment to this or that role in an excessively planned economy. This time our servitude is to those who have siphoned away the power of ordinary citizens, transferring major decisions about our future from a political to a technocratic realm.

———

By now, Americans pretty much take for granted modes of decision making that do not involve electoral politics. Looking back at the past two decades, the only major pieces of actual legislation that will seem significant 50 years from now are the Affordable Care Act, if it survives, and the post-9/11 legislation that gave the executive branch enhanced surveillance powers and a blank check to deploy the military—these last two representing a further separation of vital decisions from democratic will. We have come a long way from George Washington's "wholesome plans digested by common councils."

I keep coming back to Washington because his emphasis on collective accomplishment is the forgotten half of America's constitutional ethos. We all remember what the Founders said about electoral procedures, about checks and balances, about the basic rights of citizens. We forget that all these elements were part of a plan. We forget that they were supposed to be tools to help us create something. And we forget that politics and compromise are essential to the act of creation.

Americans must learn how to plan again—to plan in the way George Washington intended. This means recovering knowledge of how to create and operate democratic institutions, and putting experts back in their proper place as advisers to a decision-making people. Our dignity, our freedom, and our public liberty are at stake. Think about what planning in its visionary sense has done for us. The Northwest Ordinance. The canals and railroads. The land-grant college system. The Progressive-era reforms. Social Security and Medicare. The GI Bill. The highway system. The civil-rights revolution. None of them perfect. None of them easy. All of them achieved through democratic negotiation. All of them hard to imagine getting through Congress in today's climate.

A failure to understand the value of plans grows out of a failure to understand actual human beings—the one thing that true democratic politics, for all its flaws, really does take into account. People are not so much rational actors as purpose-driven ones. Human goals and values cannot always be represented in financial terms. Can you put a price on family? Empowerment? Self-sacrifice? Love? You cannot. As purpose-driven actors, we develop our values and learn to justify them within the context of communities that give our lives meaning and worth. Human moral equality flows from the human need to be the author of one's own life.

As a measure of human flourishing, empowerment is more important than wealth. Wealth is merely one possible source of empowerment. It cannot buy what makes nations flourish: social cohesion, freedom, and healthy institutions. Social cohesion is created by cooperation, and cooperation occurs only if individuals have equal standing. The role of government is not to stay out of the way of markets. It is to secure the rights that undergird empowerment, cohesion, and participation. Securing these rights requires combatting monopolies. We understand what monopoly power means in the economic sense. But the issue of monopoly power applies to the political and social domains, too. Gerrymandered districts create monopolistic political power. Our current approach to education funding, which tightly links it to property taxes, has allowed the socioeconomically advantaged to establish a near monopoly on genuine educational opportunities. People with money enjoy a position of privilege in the legal system. Corporations enjoy one when it comes to the quiet tweaking of bureaucracy and regulation. A proper role of government—nearly forgotten today, but the overriding concern of the Founders—is finding ways to prevent undue concentrations of power wherever they occur. Power tends toward self-perpetuation; where it is left undisturbed, it will draw further advantages to itself, shut out rivals, and mete out ever-bolder forms of injustice.

Undue concentrations of power sow division and factionalism. When Washington described public liberty as depending on the citizenry's ability to ward off the despotism of faction, he was offering a profound insight: The precondition of democratic decision making is unity. If a political system that relies heavily on majority rule cannot keep minorities affixed to it through loyalty, then every fresh, durable minority faction that comes into being will bring with it the threat of breakup. A first secession will provide grounds for a second, and on and on; the polity will face a threat to its very existence. The United Kingdom is living through a version of this nightmare right now.

From antiquity through the formation of the American republic and beyond, those who have looked closely at the question of what is required to maintain free institutions—from Livy to Machiavelli to Washington to Lincoln—repeated one lesson over and over again: *Choose unity.* A commitment to unity—an unswerving insistence on unity—induces citizens to seek out ways of adapting their purposes so as to get something done. Because if unity is not negotiable, then there is no other choice. Technocrats are oblivious to this. If you accept Hayek or Friedman, unity recedes as an essential factor—in fact, disunity is inevitable. But if you emphasize unity—and stipulate that it cannot be sacrificed—then it becomes a democratic tool. It encourages all sides to compromise. It is the opposite of executive decision making fueled by the self-interest or anger of one part of the electorate.

Compromise is what allows us to stay together in the space we share; discard it, and we're all condemned to our own private Bosnias. The goal is not unanimity; that is neither achievable nor desirable. Compromise entails embracing not Mitch McConnell's outlook—the winners make policy and the losers go home—but rather the view that the winners deserve a leadership role in steering the conversation toward the "wholesome plans" that Washington spoke of. The Old English root of the word *whole* means "healthy." That is what we seek—to be a healthy people.

In America, we have drifted far from that vision—to the point where many have no experience of its promise, much less its necessity. The findings of Yascha Mounk and Roberto Stefan Foa, published in the *Journal of Democracy*, are startling. Ask people born in the 1930s whether they believe it is "essential" to live in a democracy, and 72 percent will answer yes. Ask that same question of people born in the 1980s, and only 30 percent will say yes. Nearly half of Millennials in a recent Pew survey said they'd prefer to be governed by "experts" than by elected officials. This is more than a yellow warning light. It is a sign of catastrophic breakdown.

Americans today, across the political spectrum, have plenty of ideas about how to address our own great national challenges—health care and immigration, for example. But we have arrived at a point where no issue is as important as restoring the institutions of democratic participation—enabling those institutions to recognize the people's will and channel it toward a common purpose. Yes, one faction or another might strong-arm a "solution" to some grave problem, but the solution will never be seen as legitimate—and will never prove durable unless the decision-making process itself is seen as legitimate. I have strong views about what the nation should be doing when it comes to education, inequality, and economic development. But reviving political participation is by far the most urgent priority. If we do not address the corrosion of our democracy itself, we will have lost the essence of the American experiment. Nothing else will matter.

The challenges of participation and justice won't be met by markets working independently of politics, and they won't be met by the triumph of one faction over another. No great challenge can be met that way. As a nation, we have been called to be our best and most united selves by inspirational goals. The salvation of the democratic experiment must become such a goal. In the first half of the 20th century, reciting the Pledge of Allegiance on thousands of days, Americans in a segregated country spoke of being "one nation, indivisible." The language papered over a different reality. In 1954, Congress split the phrase by adding the words *under God* and divided the country along yet another line. The simple fact is we have lost the shared vocabulary that should bind us all as Americans. We fight over words like *patriotism, solidarity, loyalty*. Yet there is a word that defines our relationship. Lincoln knew what it was. The word is *union*. In a political sense, the word points to something concrete. It means talking honestly, fighting fairly, and planning together. It means "Choose unity."

It's time for all of us to become citizens again.

IN THE FALL OF ROME, GOOD NEWS FOR AMERICA

by James Fallows

[OCTOBER 2019]

The idea began as a conceit: Does new scholarship about the fate of the Roman Empire prompt fresh thinking about what may be in store for America? And is the news all bad? James Fallows, whose reporting has appeared in *The Atlantic* since the late 1970s, and who is currently a staff writer, was intrigued by the emerging portrait of late antiquity—a time of decay for centralized government that would give rise to extraordinary vitality in the old Roman Empire's many parts. Power abhors a vacuum. Today, as Washington remains paralyzed by gridlock and self-interest, many of America's smaller cities are reinventing themselves, without federal help. And many states are asserting themselves with new confidence. No one wishes for national collapse, Fallows wrote in his 2019 essay on the fall of Rome and its aftermath, but the shift of energy and innovation away from a dysfunctional capital is a phenomenon to welcome. Fallows and his wife, Deborah, are the authors of *Our Towns: A 100,000-Mile Journey Into the Heart of America* (2018).

It's time to think about the Roman empire again. But not the part of its history that usually commands attention in the United States: the long, sad path of Decline and Fall. It's what happened later that deserves our curiosity.

As a reminder, in A.D. 476, a barbarian general named Odoacer overthrew the legitimate emperor of the Western empire, Romulus Augustulus, who thus became the last of the emperors to rule from Italy.

The Eastern empire, ruled from Constantinople, chugged along for many more centuries. But the Roman progression—from republic to empire to ruin—has played an outsize role in tragic imagination about the United States. If a civilization could descend from Cicero and Cato to Caligula and Nero in scarcely a century, how long could the brave experiment launched by Madison, Jefferson, and company hope to endure?

The era that began with Rome's collapse—"late antiquity," as scholars call it—holds a hazier place in America's imagination and makes only rare cameo appearances in speeches or essays about the national prospect. Before, we have the familiar characters in togas; sometime after, knights in armor. But in between? And specifically: How did the diverse terrain that had been the Roman empire in the West respond when central authority gave way? When the last emperor was gone, how did that register in Hispania and Gaul? How did people manage without the imperial system that had built roads and aqueducts, and brought its laws and language to so much of the world?

The historians' view appears to be that they managed surprisingly well. "It is only too easy to write about the Late Antique world as if it were merely a melancholy tale," Peter Brown, of Princeton, wrote in his influential 1971 book, *The World of Late Antiquity*. But, he continued, "we are increasingly aware of the astounding new beginnings associated with this period." These included not only the breakup of empire into the precursors of what became modern countries but also "much that a sensitive European has come to regard as most 'modern' and valuable in his own culture," from new artistic and literary forms to self-governing civic associations.

In his new book, *Escape From Rome*, Walter Scheidel, of Stanford, goes further, arguing that "the Roman empire made modern development possible by going away and never coming back." His case, in boiled-down form, is that the removal of centralized control opened the way to a sustained era of creativity at the duchy-by-duchy and monastery-by-monastery level, which in turn led to broad cultural advancement and eventual prosperity. The dawn of the university and private business organizations; the idea of personal rights and freedoms—on these and other fronts, what had been Roman territories moved forward as imperial control disappeared. "From this developmental perspective, the death of the Roman empire had a much greater impact than its prior existence," Scheidel writes. He quotes Edward Gibbon's famous judgment that Rome's fall was "the greatest, perhaps, and most awful scene, in the history of mankind"—but disagrees with the "awful" part.

Might the travails of today's American governing system, and the strains on the empire-without-the-name it has tried to run since World War II, have a similar, perversely beneficial effect? Could the self-paralysis of American national governance somehow usher in a rebirth—our own Dark Ages, but in a good way?

Naturally my hope as an American is that the national government starts working better. And what I've learned from living through crisis cycles from the 1960s onward, plus studying those of the more distant past, is to always allow for the rebound capacity of this continually changing culture.

But what if faith in American resilience is now misplaced? What if it really is different this time? I've been asking historians, politicians, businesspeople, and civic leaders to imagine 21st-century America the way historians like Brown and Scheidel imagine late antiquity. How will things look for us, duchy by duchy and monastery by monastery, if the national government has broken in a way that can't be fixed?

Governmental "failure" comes down to an inability to match a society's resources to its biggest opportunities and needs. This is the clearest standard by which current U.S. national governance fails. In principle, almost nothing is beyond America's capacities. In practice, almost every big task seems too hard.

Yet for our own era's counterparts to duchies and monasteries—for state and local governments, and for certain large private organizations, including universities and some companies—the country is still mainly functional, in exactly the areas where national governance has failed.

Samuel Abrams, a political scientist at Sarah Lawrence, has been leading a multiyear national survey of "social capital" for the American Enterprise Institute. Among the findings, released this year, is that by large margins, Americans feel dissatisfied with the course of national events—and by even larger margins, they feel satisfied with and connected to local institutions and city governments. "When you talk with people, across the board they are optimistic about their own communities, and hopeful about their local futures," Abrams told me. The AEI team found that 80 percent of Americans considered their own town and neighborhood to be an "excellent" or "good" place to live, and 70 percent said they trusted people in their neighborhood. Does this mainly reflect self-segregation—people of common background or affinity clustering together? "That's been exaggerated," Abrams said. "America is less monolithic, and more functional at local levels, than people think."

In *Escape From Rome*, Scheidel writes that "a single condition was essential" for the cultural, economic, and scientific creativity of the post-Roman age: "competitive fragmentation of power." Today, some of the positive aspects of fragmentation are appearing all around us.

————————

Five years ago, after writing about a "can do" attitude in local governments in Maine and South Carolina, I got an email from a mayor in the Midwest. He said that he thought the underreported story of the moment was how people frustrated with national-level politics were shifting their enthusiasm and their careers to the state and local levels, where they could make a difference. (That mayor's name was Pete Buttigieg, then in his first term in South Bend, Indiana.) When I spoke with him at the time, he suggested the situation was like people fleeing the world of *Veep*—bleak humor on top of genuine bleakness—for a non-preposterous version of *Parks and Recreation*.

At the national level, "policy work is increasingly being done by people with no training in it, and who don't care about it, because they're drawn into national politics purely as culture warriors," I was told by Philip Zelikow, of the University of Virginia, who worked as a national-security official for both Presidents Bush. "There's a fiction that mass politics is about policy." The reality, he said, is that national-level politics has become an exercise in cultural signaling—"who you like, who you hate, which side you're on"—rather than about actual governance. Meanwhile, the modern reserves of American practical-mindedness are mainly at the local level, "where people have no choice but to solve problems week by week."

Based on my own experience I could give a hundred examples of this attitude from around the country, virtually none of them drawing national attention and many of them involving people creatively expanding the roles of libraries, community colleges, and other institutions to meet local needs. Here is just one, from Indiana: The factory town of Muncie is famed as the site of the *Middletown* sociology studies a century ago. It was the longtime home of the Ball Brothers glass-jar company, since departed. It is still the home of Ball State University, steadily growing. Like other manufacturing cities in the Midwest, Muncie has battled the effects of industrial decline. Among the consequences was a funding crisis for the Muncie Community Schools, which became so severe that two years ago the state took the system into receivership.

Last year, Ball State University became the first-ever public university in the country to assume direct operational responsibility for an entire K–12 public-school system. The experiment has just begun, and its success can't be assured. But getting this far involved innovation and creativity in the political, civic, financial, and educational realms to win support in a diverse community. "I was talking with a state senator about the plan," Geoffrey S. Mearns, who has been president of Ball State since 2017 and is a guiding force behind the plan, told me this year in Muncie. "After listening for 15 minutes, he said, 'You're crazy.

Don't do this. Run away.' After another 15 minutes, he said, 'You're still crazy. But you have to do it.'"

This craziness and commitment keeps a culture alive. A new world is emerging, largely beyond our notice.

Even when the formal ties of the Roman empire had broken, informal links connected its various parts. In the absence of the Roman state, there was still the Latin language as the original lingua franca; there was still a network of roads. Christianity in some form was a shared religion. Today the links include trade, travel, family lineage, and collaborative research—links that, like the internet, were forged in an era of functioning national and global institutions but with a better chance to endure. "With the waning of federal government, you'd see some states really big enough to act as countries, starting of course with California," Anne-Marie Slaughter, the CEO of the think tank New America, told me. "You could imagine Texas working with Mexico, and New England with Canada—and the upper-Midwest states as a bloc, and the Pacific Northwest." She pointed out that states can't sign formal treaties—but then again, the U.S. Senate has not approved a major treaty in years.

Morley Winograd, a former adviser to Al Gore and a co-author of the new book *Healing American Democracy: Going Local*, argues that networked localities have already taken effective control of crucial policy areas. "If recent trends continue," he told me, "there's no reason why community colleges won't be tuition-free across the country, without any federal role. It's happened in 13 states, and we're near a tipping point." After Donald Trump withdrew the United States from the Paris climate accord, more than 400 U.S. mayors, representing most of the U.S. economy, said their communities would still adhere to it. "That is where most of the leverage lies on sustainability—with mayors and governors," Winograd told me. He gave the example of planting trees, which might sound insignificant but, according to a new study by researchers in Switzerland, could be a crucial step toward removing excess carbon dioxide from the atmosphere. "This could spread city by city, state by state, with no federal involvement or limitation," he said. Last year, the Trump administration said it would abandon the targets for cutting automobile emissions and improving fuel efficiency that the Obama administration had said automakers must reach. This year, Ford, BMW, Volkswagen, and Honda announced that they would ignore the shift in federal policy. Instead, they would "recognize California's authority" to set strict emissions and efficiency standards, and would sell cars meeting those standards in all 50 states.

———————

Peter Brown observed that "a society under pressure is not necessarily a depressed or a rigid society." The revival that followed the Roman empire's collapse, whose full effects were visible only in retrospect, was possible because with the weakening of central government, Roman society became "exceptionally open to currents from below."

The world changes as we live in it; we're all part of a pattern that we can glimpse only dimly. Historians in a thousand years will know for sure whether the American empire in this moment was nearing its own late antiquity. Perhaps by then Muncie and South Bend will loom as large in the historical imagination as the monasteries of Cluny and St. Gall do today. The ancient university towns of Palo Alto and New Haven may lie in different countries. In the meantime, we would do well to recognize and, where possible, nurture the "astounding new beginnings" already under way.

THE POSSIBILITY
OF AMERICA

by David W. Blight

[DECEMBER 2019]

In 1869, Frederick Douglass began delivering a speech entitled "Our Composite Nationality" to audiences nationwide. The Civil War remained a savage scar. The Reconstruction Amendments had not yet all been ratified. In the speech, his most sanguine vision of what the future might hold, Douglass looked forward to an America that had become "the perfect national illustration of the unity and dignity of the human family." Douglass was a realist, searing in his perceptions and surgical in his denunciations. "One might well wonder," the historian David W. Blight wrote in a 2019 *Atlantic* essay, "how a man who, before and during the war, had delivered some of the most embittered attacks on American racism and hypocrisy ever heard could dare nurse the optimism evident from the very start of the speech."

David W. Blight is the Sterling Professor of History at Yale University and the author, most recently, of *Frederick Douglass: Prophet of Freedom* (2018), for which he received the Pulitzer Prize.

We are a country of all extremes, ends and opposites; the most
conspicuous example of composite nationality in the world . . .
In races we range all the way from black to white, with inter-
mediate shades which, as in the apocalyptic vision, no man can
name or number.

—Frederick Douglass, 1869

I n the late 1860s, Frederick Douglass, the fugitive slave turned prose poet of American democracy, toured the country spreading his most sanguine vision of a pluralist future of human equality in the recently re-United States. It is a vision worth revisiting at a time when the country seems once again to be a house divided over ethnicity and race, and over how to interpret our foundational creeds.

The Thirteenth Amendment (ending slavery) had been ratified, Congress had approved the Fourteenth Amendment (introducing birthright citizenship and the equal-protection clause), and Douglass was anticipating the ratification of the Fifteenth Amendment (granting black men the right to vote) when he began delivering a speech titled "Our Composite Nationality" in 1869. He kept it in his oratorical repertoire at least through 1870. What the war-weary nation needed, he felt, was a powerful tribute to a cosmopolitan America—not just a repudiation of a divided and oppressive past but a commitment to a future union forged in emancipation and the Civil War. This nation would hold true to universal values and to the recognition that "a smile or a tear has no nationality. Joy and sorrow speak alike in all nations, and they above all the confusion of tongues proclaim the brotherhood of man."

Douglass, like many other former abolitionists, watched with high hopes as Radical Reconstruction gained traction in Washington, D.C., placing the ex–Confederate states under military rule and establishing civil and political rights for the formerly enslaved. The United States, he believed, had launched a new founding in the aftermath of the Civil War, and had begun to shape a new Constitution rooted in the three great amendments spawned by the war's results. Practically overnight, Douglass even became a proponent of U.S. expansion to the Caribbean and elsewhere: Americans could now invent a nation whose egalitarian values were worth exporting to societies that were still either officially pro-slavery or riddled with inequality.

The aspiration that a postwar United States might slough off its own past identity as a pro-slavery nation and become the dream of millions who had been enslaved, as well as many of those who had freed them, was hardly a modest one. Underlying it was a hope that history itself had fundamentally shifted, aligning with a multiethnic, multiracial, multireligious country born of the war's massive blood sacrifice. Somehow the tremendous resistance of the white South and former Confederates, which Douglass himself predicted would take ever more virulent forms, would be blunted. A vision of "composite" nationhood would prevail, separating Church and state, giving allegiance to a single new Constitution, federalizing the Bill of Rights, and spreading liberty more broadly than any civilization had ever attempted.

Was this a utopian vision, or was it grounded in a fledgling reality? That question, a version of which has never gone away, takes on an added dimension in the case of Douglass. One might well wonder how a man who, before and during the war, had delivered some of the most embittered attacks on American racism and hypocrisy ever heard, could dare nurse the optimism evident from the very start of the speech. How could Douglass now believe that his reinvented country was, as he declared, "the most fortunate of nations" and "at the beginning of our ascent"?

Few Americans denounced the tyranny and tragedy at the heart of America's institutions more fiercely than Douglass did in the first quarter century of his public life. In 1845, seven years after his escape to freedom, Douglass's first autobiography was published to great acclaim, and he set off on an extraordinary 19-month trip to the British Isles, where he experienced a degree of equality unimaginable in America. Upon his return, in 1847, he let his profound ambivalence about the concepts of home and country be known. "I have no love for America, as such," he announced in a speech he delivered that year. "I have no patriotism. I have no country." Douglass let his righteous anger flow in metaphors of degradation, chains, and blood. "The institutions of this country do not know me, do not recognize me as a man," he declared, "except as a piece of property." All that attached him to his native land were his family and his deeply felt ties to the "three millions of my fellow-creatures, groaning beneath the iron rod . . . with . . . stripes upon their backs." Such a country, Douglass said, he could not love. "I desire to see its overthrow as speedily as possible, and its Constitution shivered in a thousand fragments."

Six years later, as the crisis over slavery's future began to tear apart the nation's political system, Douglass intensified his attacks on American hypocrisy and wanted to know just *who* could be an American. "The Hungarian, the Italian, the Irishman, the Jew and the Gentile," he said about the huge waves of European immigration, "all find in this goodly land a home." But "my white fellow-countrymen . . . have no other use for us [blacks] whatever, than to coin dollars out of our blood." Demanding his birthright as an American, he felt like only the "veriest stranger and sojourner."

The fact that emancipation, extracted through blood and agony, could so quickly transform Douglass into the author of a hopeful new vision of his country is stunning, a testament to the revolutionary sense of history embraced by this former slave and abolitionist. Yet he had always believed that America had a "mission"—that the United States was a set of ideas despite its "tangled network of contradictions." Now the time had come to reconceive the mission. Douglass's immediate post–Civil War definition of a nation came quite close to the Irish political scientist Benedict Anderson's modern conception of an "imagined community." In his "Composite Nationality" speech, Douglass explained that nationhood "implies a willing surrender and subjection of individual aims and ends, often narrow and selfish, to the broader and better ones that arise out of society as a whole. It is both a sign and a result of civilization." And a nation requires a story that draws its constituent parts into a whole. The postwar United States served as a beacon—"the perfect national illustration of the unity and dignity of the human family."

Americans needed a new articulation of how their country was an idea, Douglass recognized, and he gave it to them. Imagine the audacity, in the late 1860s, to affirm the following for the reinvented United States:

> A Government founded upon justice, and recognizing the equal rights of all men; claiming no higher authority for its existence, or sanction for its laws, than nature, reason and the regularly ascertained will of the people; steadily refusing to put its sword and purse in the service of any religious creed or family.

Few better expressions exist of America's founding principles of popular sovereignty, natural rights, and the separation of Church and state. From his enslaved youth onward, Douglass had loved the principles and hated their flouting in practice. And he had always believed in an Old Testament version of divine vengeance and justice, sure that the country would face a rending and a renewal. Proudly, he now declared such a nation a "standing offense" to "narrow and bigoted people."

In the middle section of his speech, Douglass delivered a striking argument on behalf of Chinese immigration to America, then emerging as an important political issue. In the Burlingame Treaty, negotiated between the U.S. and the empire of China in 1868, the American government acknowledged the "inalienable right" of migration and accepted Chinese immigrants, but it denied them any right to be naturalized as citizens. Douglass predicted a great influx of Chinese fleeing overcrowding and hunger in their native country, and finding work in the mines and expanding railroads in the West. They would surely face violence and prejudice, Douglass warned. In language that seems timely today, he projected himself into the anti-immigrant mind. "Are not the white people the owners of this continent?" he asked. "Is there not such a thing as being more generous than wise? In the effort to promote civilization may we not corrupt and destroy what we have?"

But this rhetorical gesture of empathy for the racists gave way to a full-blown attack. He urged Americans not to fear the alien character of Asian languages or cultures. The Chinese, like all other immigrants, would assimilate to American laws and folkways. They "will cross the mountains, cross the plains, descend our rivers, penetrate to the heart of the country and fix their home with us forever." The Chinese, the "new element in our national composition," would bring talent, skill, and laboring ethics honed over millennia. Douglass invoked the morality of the natural-rights tradition. "There are such things in the world as human rights. They rest upon no conventional foundation, but are eternal, universal and indestructible." Migratory rights, he asserted, are "human rights," and he reminded Americans that "only one-fifth of the population of the globe is white and the other four-fifths are colored."

Just as important, he placed the issue in the context of America's mission. The United States ought to be a home for people "gathered here from all quarters of the globe." All come as "strangers," bringing distinct cultures with them, but American creeds can offer a common ground. Though conflict may ensue, a nation of "strength and elasticity" would emerge through contact and learning. What might sound like a manifesto for multicultural education in the 1990s or a diversity mission statement at any university today actually has a long history.

Douglass made sure to embed his bold vision in first principles. To the argument that it is "natural" for people to collide over their cultural differences and to see one another only through mutual "reproachful epithets," he countered with the notion that "nature has many sides," and is not static. "It is natural to walk," Douglass wrote, "but shall men therefore refuse to ride? It is natural to ride on horseback, shall men therefore refuse steam and rail? Civilization is itself a constant war upon some forces in nature, shall we therefore abandon civilization and go back to savage life?" Douglass called on his fellow citizens to recognize that "man is man the world over . . . The sentiments we exhibit, whether love or hate, confidence or fear, respect or contempt, will always imply a like humanity." But he did not merely ask Americans to all get along. He asked his fellow countrymen to make real freedom out of slavery, out of their sordid history—to see that they had been offered a new beginning for their national project, and to have the courage to execute it.

Swept up in hope, Douglass did not anticipate the rising tide of nativism that lay ahead in the Gilded Age. The U.S. passed a first Chinese-exclusion law, directed at women who were deemed "immoral" or destined for forced labor, in 1875. By 1882, Sinophobia and violence against the Chinese led to the federal Chinese Exclusion Act, banning virtually any immigration by the group—the first such restrictive order against all members of a particular ethnicity in American history. Those who remained in the country lived constrained and dangerous lives; in the late 1880s, Chinese miners were gruesomely massacred in mines across the West. The Chinese also faced the hostility of white workers who now fashioned the ideology of "free labor" into a doctrine that sought to eliminate any foreign competition for jobs, especially in economic hard times. For Douglass, these bleak realities were just the outcomes he had warned against as Reconstruction gathered momentum.

Immigrants from Europe continued to stream into the United States, even as a resurgent white South gained control of its society in the latter days of Reconstruction. As nativism, racism, and nationalism converged in the closing decades of the 19th century, the idea of America as a cosmopolitan nation of immigrants fought for survival. Eugenics acquired intellectual legitimacy; and violence, and eventually Jim Crow laws, consolidated a system of white supremacy.

By the 1890s Douglass, aging and in ill health but still out on the lecture circuit, felt hard-pressed to sustain hope for the transformations at the heart of the "Composite Nationality" speech. He never renounced his faith in natural rights or in the power of the vote. But in the last great speech of his life, "Lessons of the Hour"—an excoriating analysis of the "excuses" and "lie" at the root of lynching—Douglass betrayed a faith "shaken" and nearly gone. Disenfranchisement and murderous violence left him observing a nation mired in lawless horror. Lynchings were "lauded and applauded by honorable men . . . guardians of Southern women" who enabled other men to behave "as buzzards, vultures, and hyenas." A country once endowed with "nobility" was crushed by mob rule. His dream in tatters, Douglass begged his audiences to remember that the Civil War and Reconstruction had "announced the advent of a nation, based upon human brotherhood and the self-evident truths of liberty and equality. Its mission was the redemption of the world from the bondage of ages."

Many civil wars leave legacies of continuing conflict, renewed bloodshed, unstable political systems. Ours did just that, even as it forged a new history and a new Constitution. In 2019, our composite nationality needs yet another rebirth. We could do no better than to immerse ourselves in Douglass's vision from 1869. Nearly 20 years earlier, he had embraced the exercise of human rights as "the deepest and strongest of all the powers of the human soul," proclaiming that "no argument, no researches into mouldy records, no learned disquisitions, are necessary to establish it." But the self-evidence of natural rights, as Douglass the orator knew, does not guarantee their protection and practice. "To assert it, is to call forth a sympathetic response from every human heart, and to send a thrill of joy and gladness round the world." And to keep asserting those rights, he reminds us, will never cease to be necessary.

Practicing them is crucial, too. In an 1871 editorial he took a position worth heeding today. The failure to exercise one's right to vote, he wrote, "is as great a crime as an open violation of the law itself." Only a demonstration of rebirth in our composite nation and of vibrancy in our democracy will again send thrills of joy and emulation around the world about America. Such a rebirth ought not to be the object of our waiting but of our making, as it was for the Americans, black and white, who died to end slavery and make the second republic.

WHAT ART CAN DO

by Lin-Manuel Miranda

[DECEMBER 2019]

How should artists respond during a period of peril and uncertainty? "What artists can do," wrote Lin-Manuel Miranda in a 2019 *Atlantic* essay, "is bring stories to the table that are unshakably true—the sort of stories that, once you've heard them, won't let you return to what you thought before." In other words: They can do what they should be doing anyway. Truth is timeless, and will always speak to our politics. Lin-Manuel Miranda is a composer, lyricist, and actor, and the creator and original star of the musicals *In the Heights* (which won two Tony Awards) and *Hamilton* (which won 11 Tony awards and the Pulitzer Prize for Drama).

All art is political. In tense, fractious times—like our current moment—all art is political. But even during those times when politics and the future of our country itself are not the source of constant worry and anxiety, art is still political. Art lives in the world, and we exist in the world, and we cannot create honest work about the world in which we live without reflecting it. If the work tells the truth, it will live on.

Public Enemy's "911 Is a Joke," George Orwell's *1984*, Rodgers and Hammerstein's whole damn catalog—all are political works that tell the truth.

Yes, Rodgers and Hammerstein. Consider *The Sound of Music*. It isn't just about climbing mountains and fording streams. Look beyond the adorable von Trapp children: It's about the looming existential threat of Nazism. No longer relevant? A GIF of Captain von Trapp tearing up a Nazi flag is something we see 10 times a day on Twitter, because all sorts of Nazis are out there again in 2019. As last spring's searing Broadway revival of *Oklahoma!* revealed, lying underneath Hammerstein's elephant-eye-high corn and chirping birds is a lawless society becoming itself, bending its rules and procedures based on who is considered part of the community (Curly) and who is marginalized (poor Jud . . . seriously, poor Jud). Or consider your parents' favorite, *South Pacific*. At its center, our hero, Nellie Forbush, must confront her own internalized racism when she learns that the new love of her life has biracial children from a previous marriage. Let your parents know if they forgot: Rodgers and Hammerstein musicals form the spine of Broadway's "golden age," and they also deeply engage with the politics of their era.

My first Broadway musical, *In the Heights*, is an example of how time can reveal the politics inherent within a piece of art. When I began writing this musical, as a college project at Wesleyan University, it was an 80-minute collegiate love story with a promising mix of Latin music and hip-hop, but it was pretty sophomoric (which is appropriate; I was a sophomore). After college, I started from scratch with the director Thomas Kail and the playwright Quiara Alegría Hudes, and we shifted the show's focus from the love story to Washington Heights, a neighborhood in Upper Manhattan where everyone is from everywhere. In the 20th century, Washington Heights was often home to the latest wave of immigrants. It was an Irish neighborhood; it was a Russian Jewish neighborhood (Yeshiva University is up there). If you take the Dominican store sign down you'll see a sign for an Irish pub underneath it, and if you take that down you'll find Hebrew. Washington Heights was heavily Dominican when I was growing up, and it remains so, with a vibrant Mexican and Latin American immigrant community as well.

As we wrote about this Upper Manhattan community on the verge of change, we looked to our musical-theater forebears. In *Cabaret*, the upheaval facing the characters in Berlin is the rise of the Nazi Party.

In *Fiddler on the Roof*, the town of Anatevka struggles to hold on to its traditions as the world changes around it, and the threat of pogroms looms. For our musical world, upheaval comes in the form of gentrification. This is obviously different from fascism and pogroms; it's not even in the same moral universe. How you begin to dramatize something as subtle and multifaceted as gentrification poses some tricky questions. We threw our characters into the same dilemma faced by their real-life working-class counterparts: What do we do when we can't afford to live in the place we've lived all our lives, especially when we are the ones who make the neighborhood special and attractive to others? Each of the characters confronts this question differently: One sacrifices the family business to ensure his child's educational future. Another relocates to the less expensive Bronx. Our narrator decides to stay, despite the odds, taking on the responsibility of telling this neighborhood's stories and carrying on its traditions.

We received great reviews. If critics had a common criticism, it was that the show, its contemporary music aside, was somehow old-fashioned or "sentimental." Gentrification, the businesses closing, the literal powerlessness as the characters face a blackout that affects only their neighborhood—these issues, always there in the material, didn't register with most theater critics in 2008. *In the Heights* was considered a hit by Broadway standards. It didn't leap off the Arts page and into the national conversation like *Hamilton* would, but we won some Tonys, recouped our investment, and had a wonderful three-year run at the Richard Rodgers Theatre, where *Hamilton* now lives. We posted our Broadway closing notice at the end of 2010.

What a difference 10 years makes.

Right now, Jon M. Chu is editing his feature-film adaptation of *In the Heights*, which is scheduled to be released in June. We spent a joyous summer shooting the film—on location, in our neighborhood—and issues that were always inherent in the text now stand out in boldfaced type. Gentrification has rendered Lower Manhattan, Harlem, and much of Brooklyn unrecognizable to the previous generations that called those neighborhoods home. The East Village of Jonathan Larson's *Rent* is nonexistent, lettered avenues notwithstanding. And the narrative of immigrants coming to this country and making a better life for themselves—the backdrop of everything that happens in *In the Heights*, across three generations of stories—is somehow a radical narrative now.

Donald Trump came down the escalator to declare his presidential run, and in his first speech he demonized Mexicans: *They're rapists; they're bringing drugs; they're not sending their best people.* We young Latinos had thought of our parents and grandparents as the latest wave making its home in this country, and we thought that we would be the next group to make this place a better place, to prove once again that the American dream wasn't just a figment of some propagandist's imagination. And now we're in a different age when, for some, considering an immigrant a human being is a radical political act.

Consider this rap, written 12 years ago and delivered by Sonny, *In the Heights'* youngest character, in a song called "96,000":

> *Your kids are living without a good edumacation,*
> *Change the station, teach 'em about gentrification*
> *The rent is escalatin'*
> *The rich are penetratin'*
> *We pay our corporations when we should be demonstratin'*
> *What about immigration?*
> *Politicians be hatin'*
> *Racism in this nation's gone from latent to blatant*

It was always political. It was always there. Donald Trump made it even more true.

Trump uses language to destroy empathy. He criminalizes the impulse and imperative to seek asylum, to seek a place to live thousands of miles away because the alternative at home is worse. Through his lens, these seekers are not people; they're "animals" or "bad hombres."

What artists can do is bring stories to the table that are unshakably true—the sort of stories that, once you've heard them, won't let you return to what you thought before. I think about the crisis on the border constantly. I think about the famous photograph of a little girl crying beside a Border Patrol truck. That picture went viral because it seemed to capture the horror of family separations. But it turned out that the girl wasn't being separated from her mother—her mother had simply been ordered to put her daughter down while she was searched by agents. The family was in distress, and the border crisis was real, but people used the details of this particular incident to close themselves off from empathy. "Fake news," they said. A child is crying for her mother, but that's not enough to keep people from pushing empathy away. I believe great art is like bypass surgery. It allows us to go around all of the psychological-distancing mechanisms that turn people cold to the most vulnerable among us.

At the end of the day, our job as artists is to tell the truth as we see it. If telling the truth is an inherently political act, so be it. Times may change and politics may change, but if we do our best to tell the truth as specifically as possible, time will reveal those truths and reverberate beyond the era in which we created them. We keep revisiting Shakespeare's *Macbeth* because ruthless political ambition does not belong to any particular era. We keep listening to Public Enemy because systemic racism continues to rain tragedy on communities of color. We read Orwell's *1984* and shiver at its diagnosis of doublethink, which we see coming out of the White House at this moment. And we listen to Rodgers and Hammerstein's *South Pacific*, as Lieutenant Cable sings about racism, "You've got to be carefully taught." It's all art. It's all political.

Afterword

BETWEEN BRAVADO
AND DESPAIR

by Anne Applebaum

O ur bookshelves are full of works describing the events leading up to disasters. Books like *The Origins of the Second World War* or *The Sleepwalkers: How Europe Went to War in 1914* win prizes and become enduring classics. They also influence political thinking: Invariably, the fatal mistakes of the past become lessons for the present. Following the Russian invasion of Ukraine in 2014, for example, Europeans were arguing about whether the situation most resembled 1914, 1938, or some other date. The "lessons" to be drawn were different, depending on which precedent was selected.

By definition, it is far more difficult to study disasters that have been avoided, let alone to draw lessons from them. Wars and social upheavals that have not taken place do not figure prominently in history books, and the interventions that stopped them do not receive the attention that they should. But this collection is an argument for thinking about precisely that: the plans and reforms that mitigated catastrophe before it happened.

We are today witnessing the spread of a whole host of old and familiar American pathologies, some of them in new forms: nativism and white supremacism; extremism on both the far left and the far right; the spread of conspiracy theories; the entrenching of corruption; the disappearance of jobs; the widening of inequality; the growth of a complex physical- and mental-health crisis created by opioids, food insecurity, and limited health care. In the spring of 2020, all of these things combined to create the perfect storm: an unprecedented medical and economic crisis, sparked by a new virus but made worse by the authoritarian culture built inside the White House. In May and June, outrage over the police killing in Minneapolis of a black man named George Floyd led to protests, riots, and a blizzard of disinformation from extremists of all kinds and brought the nation to a halt. The president's inappropriate use of military force in Washington, D.C., as well as his tweets calling for violence, inflamed the situation. For a long time, we have watched a deepening of political divisions, a phenomenon that we now call "polarization," but which is nothing new, in our country or any other. Our Civil War has imprinted on all of us the memory of how irreconcilable political divisions can lead to debilitating mass violence. Bad decisions and bad leadership at this crucial moment could lead us in that direction once again.

But there have also been moments, in our history and in the history of other nations, when intelligent leadership healed equally profound divisions without resorting to violence. Not enough time these days is spent thinking about the presidency of Theodore Roosevelt, for example. Although his face is carved into the rock of Mount Rushmore, the memory of the first Roosevelt presidency has somewhat faded into clichés involving eyeglasses, jodhpurs, and big sticks. But Roosevelt—a vice president who took over after the shocking assassination of President William McKinley, becoming the 26th president and the youngest one in American history—deserves more attention for the role he played in anticipating, and seeking to prevent, a social crisis. His presidency occurred in the long shadow of the panic of 1893, at a moment when the nation had technically recovered. Although growth had returned, the economic and political fallout had already inspired a "populist" political movement, a loss of trust in institutions, a deep urban-rural divide, and even acts by violent anarchists, such as the man who killed McKinley.

Roosevelt, a Republican, was himself a beneficiary of the Gilded Age, and possessed many of the prejudices of his time and his class. Nevertheless, he understood both that many Americans perceived their society to be fundamentally unfair, and that his job was to fix it. Writing in *The Atlantic* as early as 1891, he took on corruption in government and made the case for a professionalized civil service: "We have to do constant battle with that spirit of mean and vicious cynicism which so many men, respectable enough in their private life, assume as their attitude in public affairs."

Roosevelt was not "anti-capitalist," to use modern terminology, and he was by no means a "socialist." But he did denounce the "unfair money-getting" that had created "a small class of enormously wealthy and economically powerful men, whose chief object is to hold and increase their power." In office, he did not arrest this class or destroy their companies, as his Russian counterparts would do a couple of decades later, but he did regulate them. He broke up their monopolies and changed some of the rules so that the economy would "work for a more substantial equality of opportunity and of reward for equally good service," in his words. Recognizing how fundamental American natural resources are to American national identity, he also took the first steps in the direction of what we would now call environmentalism.

Once again, we are living in the long aftermath of a crash, at a moment of deep distrust in the government and at a time when a new and frighteningly powerful set of monopolies—Google, Facebook, and Amazon—have rapidly reshaped both economics and politics. This is not to suggest that there are exact analogies, let alone a recipe we can follow, cutting and pasting early 20th-century remedies onto the problems of the 21st century. To overcome our current crisis, we should focus not on the specific policies that Roosevelt used, but rather on his instincts—his beliefs, for example, that the American economy has to work for all Americans; that natural resources are finite; that the state exists to create fair rules, and not to favor particular groups or industries; that Americans can still be unified by their mutual faith in the language of our Constitution. Or his understanding that the economy operates according to a set of rules that can be changed: "The citizens of the United States must effectively control the mighty commercial forces which they have called into being." He also understood that violent change was dangerous: "I am not advocating anything revolutionary. I am advocating action to prevent anything very revolutionary."

At other times and in other places, a similar set of attitudes and instincts helped prevent other countries from sliding into crisis. The reforms of the Victorian era in Great Britain, for example, not only increased economic protection for people whose lives had been disrupted by the Industrial Revolution, they extended the political franchise to them as well, allowing Britain to democratize as well as modernize. The Meiji Restoration in Japan, inspired by the realization that Western technology had leapt far ahead of Japanese technology, modernized Japanese politics and economics, too. In response to the outside challenge, Japanese reformers adopted and adapted elements of Western culture, including mass education and scientific research, to Japanese circumstances. They prepared the nation to think differently about a changed world. This was not an easy or obvious choice: The Ottoman empire, in contrast, reacted to its discovery of Western technological superiority in precisely the opposite manner, by limiting its citizens' contacts with the West.

All of these strategies, in the U.S., Great Britain, and Japan, were evolutionary rather than revolutionary. But *evolutionary* does not mean insignificant. These reform programs were deep and profound. They altered the nature of the national elite, changed the class structure, reshaped the business community, upended property structures, rewrote the rules of commerce, reformed education and the arts, and brought new people and new ideas into mainstream politics.

Many were also centralizing, removing power from older elites, from aristocrats or industrialists, and transferring it to the state. The Meiji Restoration reduced the influence of the samurai, for example; the American antitrust laws reduced the power of Standard Oil. The same is even more true of FDR's New Deal, of course, which brought enormous new powers to the government. By contrast, the successful national-reform programs of the 21st century may not be centralizing at all—quite the opposite, perhaps. But again, it is the spirit of these 19th- and 20th-century movements, their comprehensiveness and their ambition, not their specific policy prescriptions, that we should look to as an example.

Their optimism should be a model for us, too. For decades, the majority of Americans have lived in a warm cocoon of self-congratulatory self-confidence, convinced that ours was the best of all possible systems, that we had not only the most freedom but the greatest wealth, the strongest army, the most positive influence around the world. In some ways, this was a useful illusion—it helped us expand opportunities, encouraged us in many positive and generous actions—but it also blinded us to many of our own flaws. The 2016 election and the multiple disasters of the Trump presidency have led many to draw the opposite conclusion: We are a failed democracy, even a failed state.

But our own history, and the history of other states, offers a path between bravado and despair. We can have faith in ourselves, and in our values, without magical thinking. Our self-confidence can be tempered by realism. Theodore Roosevelt himself once described optimism as a "good characteristic," but warned that "if carried to an excess, it becomes foolishness." We have found this middle ground before, between optimism and foolishness. We have found the ability to make deep changes without destroying those elements of our system that are useful and good. And if we did it once, we can do it again.

Acknowledgments

Thank you, first of all, to the writers and editors of *The Atlantic*. During most of the period when this book was coming together, the entire staff was working remotely because of the pandemic—and in those several months somehow managing to publish more than a thousand articles in print and online. The magazine's first editor, James Russell Lowell, also worked remotely, but that involved little more than stuffing manuscripts into the lining of his hat for the walk home.

The American Crisis was conceived by Jeffrey Goldberg, *The Atlantic*'s editor in chief. There have been other *Atlantic* collections over the years; this is the first one devoted so tightly to a moment and reflects the magazine's intensive focus on the condition of the country in a troubled age. The book took shape in the course of conversations that included Jeff; Yoni Appelbaum, the Ideas editor; and Sarah Yager, one of the managing editors. Sarah and Ena Alvarado-Esteller, an assistant editor, took the lead in organizing and overseeing the many strands of the editorial process. Karen Ostergren, the deputy copy chief, copy edited the manuscript. Anna Bross and Helen Tobin led communications for *The Atlantic*. Allison Prevatt handled legal questions.

The *Atlantic* contributors who appear in this volume are listed prominently. It is a privilege to republish what they wrote; and, in the case of Anne Applebaum, to publish a new afterword as well. The editors who worked with these contributors include Don Peck, Adrienne LaFrance, Swati Sharma, Denise Wills, Yoni Appelbaum, Thomas Gebremedhin, Ann Hulbert, Kate Julian, Christopher Orr, Dante Ramos, Rebecca Rosen, Scott Stossel, John Swansburg, and Amy Weiss-Meyer. Yvonne Rolzhausen has headed the magazine's fact-checking staff for two decades (fact-checking note: actually, 21 years). Janice Wolly is the copy chief. Emilie Harkin, Rob Hendin, Sam Rosen, and Gillian

White have been engaged in promotion for the book. The cover of *The American Crisis* is the work of *The Atlantic*'s creative director, Peter Mendelsund, and its design director, Oliver Munday.

We're grateful to our collaborators at Simon & Schuster—president and chief executive officer Jonathan Karp, executive editor Stephanie Frerich, and assistant editor Emily Simonson. They were drawn at once to the idea of this collection, and to the urgency, and have been enthusiastic and immensely capable in their support. Sloan Harris, the co-president of ICM Partners, brought all of us together.

A special thank-you also goes to David Bradley and Laurene Powell Jobs, owners and stewards of *The Atlantic*, for providing a home for great journalism and great journalists.

—*Cullen Murphy*

Index